HARD TIME

CONTEMPORARY ISSUES IN CRIME AND JUSTICE SERIES

Hard Time

Understanding and Reforming the Prison

Second Edition

ROBERT JOHNSON
The American University

Wadsworth Publishing Company
I⟨T⟩P™ An International Thomson Publishing Company

Belmont • Albany • Bonn • Boston • Cincinnati • Detroit • London • Madrid
Melbourne • Mexico City • New York • Paris • San Francisco • Singapore
Tokyo • Toronto • Washington

Criminal Justice Editor: Sabra Horne
Editorial Assistant: Janet Hansen
Production Editor: Jennie Redwitz
Managing Designer: Stephen Rapley
Print Buyer: Karen Hunt
Permissions Editor: Jeanne Bosschart
Copy Editor: Lee Motteler
Composition: Joan Olson/Wadsworth Digital Productions
Cover: Sandra Kelch/Third Space Design
Printer: Quebecor Printing Book Group/Fairfield

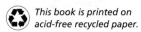
For more information, contact Wadsworth Publishing Company.

Wadsworth Publishing Company
10 Davis Drive
Belmont, California 94002
USA

International Thomson Editores
Campos Eliseos 385, Piso 7
Col. Polanco
11560 México D.F. México

International Thomson Publishing Europe
Berkshire House 168-173
High Holborn
London, WC1V 7AA
England

International Thomson
Publishing GmbH
Königswinterer Strasse 418
53227 Bonn
Germany

Thomas Nelson Australia
102 Dodds Street
South Melbourne 3205
Victoria, Australia

International Thomson Publishing Asia
221 Henderson Road
#05-10 Henderson Building
Singapore 0315

Nelson Canada
1120 Birchmount Road
Scarborough, Ontario
Canada M1K 5G4

International Thomson Publishing Japan
Hirakawacho Kyowa Building, 3F
2-2-1 Hirakawacho
Chiyoda-ku, Tokyo 102, Japan

Library of Congress Cataloging-in-Publication Data

Johnson, Robert
    Hard time: understanding and reforming the prison / Robert Johnson.—2nd ed.
      p. cm.—(Contemporary issues in crime and justice series)
    Includes bibliographical references and index.
    ISBN 0-534-18750-1 (pbk.)
    1. Prisons—United States 2. Prison psychology 3. Prison administration—United States.
I. Title. II. Series.
HV9471.J64 1996   95-2858
365'.7'0973—dc20

For my mother, Kay,
ever my most accepting reader

For my wife, Deirdra,
always my most devoted reader

For my sons, Brian and Patrick,
surely my most avid readers

Contents

Preface

Hard Time, now entering its second edition, is a book about maximum-security prisons for men. The focus of the book flows from two salient facts: (1) the vast majority of prisoners, roughly 95 percent, are men, and (2) the men's maximum-security prison has been and remains the dominant prison type. The maximum-security prison for men has served as the explicit or implicit model—the point of departure if not indeed the template—for virtually all men's prisons and many women's prisons as well. Life in these prisons is depriving and painful. On that score at least, prisons vary in degree, not kind. The inhabitants of prison—every prison—serve hard time. Nothing can change this basic and enduring fact. That hard time can also be constructive time is, in my view, the key to understanding and reforming the prison.

The thesis of this book is simple. Prisoners serve hard time, as they are meant to, but typically learn little of value during their stint behind bars. They adapt to prison in immature and often destructive ways. As a result, they leave prison no better, and sometimes considerably worse, than when they went in. But mature coping is possible in prison, can be facilitated by staff and programs, and can result in the correction or rehabilitation of offenders. Prisons, then, can be decent, humane institutions; imprisonment can be a constructively painful experience. It is my contention that we can ask no more of our prisons, and should settle for no less.

Hard Time is divided into three parts. The history of prisons, reviewed in Part One, covers the earliest forms of incarceration (Chapter One), the first disciplined prisons or penitentiaries (Chapter Two), and the various progeny of the penitentiary that have emerged during this century (Chapter Three). The chapters in Part One are linked by an emphasis on pain as a central feature of prison life. First-person accounts of adaption to the pains of confinement in early prisons are emphasized. In Part Two, patterns of adjustment to the pains of contemporary prisons are examined, again with an emphasis on first-person accounts. Continuities in prison adjustment over time, from early to modern prisons, are noted and examined. The notion of mature coping in and out of prison, developed in Chapter Four, guides the reader through this section. The social adjustments of the prisoners (Chapters Five and Six) and the staff (Chapters Seven and Eight) are then considered in turn. Prospects for mature coping among prisoners, with support from the staff, are emphasized. In Part Three (Chapter Nine), the book concludes with a review of the latest developments in the management of prison environments and the provision of prison programs, culminating in a reform proposal in which mature adaptation to the pains of imprisonment is made a primary objective of correctional work.

Readers of the first edition may want to know how I have gone about revising the book. First, I have brought the book up to date in the obligatory ways, revising statistics and incorporating the latest research on the various issues broached in the text. More importantly, I have tried to clarify some key concepts laid out in the first edition. Coping, criminality, and correction, the core concepts in this book, are more fully developed and more thoroughly woven into the fabric of discussion at various points throughout the book. I have gone to some lengths to define what is meant by a decent, humane prison, and to show how such prisons offer the prospect of mature coping—and hence rehabilitation—to their inmates. Both the historical and contemporary realities of prison life are discussed with a more consistent and thoroughgoing emphasis on first-person accounts offered by inmates and staff. One result, I hope, is a more vivid and authentic view of prisons as human institutions. (I draw on the works of a number of prison poets, for example, which adds a rich dimension to discussions of prison life.) Finally, in closing the book, I make explicit an important point that was only implicit in the first edition: prisons are limited institutions that should be treated as scarce resources, and they should be used maturely in our various campaigns to control crime. For the record, I do not advocate the use of prisons at the levels we see today or with all of the offender populations we see behind bars these days. On the other hand, there is no doubt that prisons are here to stay, and I continue to be committed to the constructive use of prisons where and when this is possible.

Hard Time is meant to serve as a secondary text in courses relating to the criminal justice system, public policy and crime control, and institutional corrections. It may also be used as an ancillary text in sociology and psychology courses that deal with personal adjustment, social control, and punishment. *Hard Time* might even find its way into an occasional course on the philosophy of punishment and rehabilitation, and perhaps also be assigned in courses on the history of prisons and other institutions of social control.

I have had the good fortune to receive critical reviews of this book from a number of distinguished colleagues. Reviewers of the first or second editions, or both, include: Marianna Burt, Towson State University; Leo Carroll, University of Rhode Island; Thomas Carroll, University of Missouri–Kansas City; John Conrad; Francis T. Cullen, University of Cincinnati; Lynne Goodstein, Pennsylvania State University; Paul Leighton, University of San Francisco; Robert Levinson, The American Correctional Association; Lucien Lombardo, Old Dominion University; Norval Morris, University of Chicago; Alexander Pisciotta, Kutztown University; Jeffrey Reiman, The American University; Martin Schwartz, Ohio University; Hans Toch, SUNY–Albany; and Edward Zamble, Queens University. My thanks to them all. Leighton and Toch deserve special mention. Paul Leighton, formerly a doctoral student under my supervision at The American University, provided a most scholarly and insightful review; Hans Toch, my mentor and friend, offered a most authoritative commentary and assessment. I am in the debt of all my reviewers, but especially Leighton and Toch.

It has also been my good fortune to be well and generously served by a host of research assistants and administrative support personnel at The American University. I extend a warm thanks to Tanuda Pittiyatkin, David A. Blansky, Julie Read, and Deborah Beth Daniels, student assistants who were most generous with their time and insights, and I am also grateful to Fannie Norwood and Lynn A. Taylor, my past and present administrative assistants, respectively, each of whom provided invaluable organizational support during the development of this book. Finally, I wish to offer special thanks to my colleagues in the Department of Justice, Law and Society, and to Neil Kerwin, Dean of the School of Public Affairs, who has dedicated himself to the cultivation of a climate of scholarship in our school and the larger university.

Robert Johnson
The American University

Prison time must be hard time, a metaphorical death,
a sustained, twilight condition of death-in-life...
Yet the little death of a prison sentence doesn't quite kill
the prisoner, because prisons, in spite of their ability
to make the inmate's life unbearable, can't kill time...
Life goes on and since it does, miracles occur.

JOHN EDGAR WIDEMAN
Brothers and Keepers

HARD TIME

❖

PART I

The Enduring Pains of Imprisonment

1

The Roots of Imprisonment

I opened an earlier incarnation of this book with an old joke. The joke is by now somewhat worn, but it still makes a point. Bear with me while I retell it, with a little embellishment to compensate readers of the first edition for the redundancy.

A ship exploring unknown waters hits a rock and sinks, leaving but one survivor, who drifts for days on debris from the ship's hull before washing up on a sandy beach. Hungry and tired, he crawls inland for hours, only to fall into a deep sleep as night settles. He awakens hours later with the rising sun and is immediately gripped with fear. His situation is desperate. Far from home, defenseless and alone, he considers what manner of man or beast might await him. Or not await him. What if the island is deserted? Might his fate be to survive treacherous waters only to languish on land? Presently he raises his head and his gaze falls upon a gallows. He stares dumbly at first, then heaves a sigh of relief. "Thank God," he says, "I've reached civilization!"

Variations on this joke have been noted by other students of punishment, notably the redoubtable Lewis Lawes, warden of Sing Sing during the early decades of this century (see Lawes, 1932:305). His rendition features a land-locked pilgrim, ours a beached seafarer. The point, of course, is that either character could just as well have ended his journey at the gates of a prison, for we have been confining criminals almost as long as we have laid claim to being civilized.

Indeed, if we transport our wandering heroes to modern times, they would surely find a prison more readily than a gallows. That prison might contain a gallows, to be sure, though more likely it would house a death chamber equipped with an electric chair or a lethal injection machine. My point is that prisons have taken on a peculiar salience these days. Prisons are a fact of modern life, as solid and imposing as the walls that surround and contain them. Individual prisons may come and go, but the institution of the prison endures. Unlike the Wall of Jericho or, more recently, the Berlin Wall, the prison edifice stands firm. Indeed, prisons are a more central feature of our criminal justice system than at any time in history.

It is hard to think of crime without also thinking of prison. To most citizens, crime means street crime, especially violent street crime. The punishment of choice for crime is the prison, and our image of the prison is largely formed by the Big House of Hollywood fame. Prisons are recurring subjects of songs, books, and movies, and even cartoons and jokes, some featured in such sober publications as *The New Yorker*. (My favorite is a *Far Side* cartoon featuring two prisoners hanging by their wrists from a dungeon wall. Off in the corner, a third prisoner is tied to a rack. No one struggles; everyone is utterly defeated. On the wall is a plaque that reads, in bold letters, "Congratulations, Bob. Torturer of the Month.")[1] For us, prison as a setting of punishment—though not torture, which is why the cartoon makes us laugh rather than cry—comes to mind with the same easy facility that earlier generations thought of corporal or capital punishment. Just as errant English children in centuries past were warned that they would "come to a bad end," meaning the end of the hangman's rope, or threatened with a "lick" from the vicious "cat" (the cat-o'-nine-tails, a nine-tailed whip), we caution our delinquents about the rigors of life behind bars, hoping to scare them straight.

Confining dangerous people is an old if not venerable practice that, though generally carried out on a small scale, dates back at least to Biblical times. Like the death penalty, prison can be considered a civilized punishment. Its use is associated with comparatively developed societies, and it typically represents an instance of restrained (albeit sometimes barely restrained) vengeance. Unlike the death penalty, however, prison can also be a *civilizing* penalty.[2] Prisons can reflect Plato's dictum that the person subject to punishment should emerge "a better man, or failing that, less of a wretch."[3] That is, imprisonment is a punishment from which the offender can learn something of value: how to deal with pain and loss in mature ways. He can at once pay his debt to society and learn to cope more responsibly with the many pressures and constraints found in prison and the free world alike.

Yet the prison has been a source of mostly gratuitous and destructive pain, offering not so much a lesson in civilization as an exercise in abuse and neglect. Most prisons have been anything but civilized, and their effects have been considerably less than civilizing. On the whole, this is not surprising. Confinement is, in essence, a way to expel criminals from the community, to get them out of sight. It is thus little more than a sophisticated version of banishment, which is "society's most primitive form of self-defense" (Sherman &

Hawkins, 1981:55). For prisons to be civilizing institutions, there must be a conscious effort to make decent, humane settings of confinement.

The prison is here to stay, a sober fact that has implications for us all. A minority among us—inmates past, present and yet to come—comprise prison's reluctant alumni. Most of us, perhaps all of us, pay for prisons in one way or another: with tax dollars, spent out to cover prison costs that now run into the billions on an annual basis; with loved ones lost to confinement, some permanently, most for varying periods of time, but all changed by prison, irrevocably; with the violation of our humane values, the silent casualties of the brutal excesses of some prisons. It is common to think of prisons as necessary evils that must be stoically endured, but that is only partially true. Prisons are necessary but they need not be evil. We can and must make our prisons decent, humane institutions of social control.

In symbol and in practice, prisons will *always* be a central feature of crime control in modern societies. Whether we imprison too many criminals or too few, serving sentences too long or too short, under conditions too harsh or too lax, prisons will be with us. And we will use prisons with much the same array of offenders we do today and have done for centuries. In the main, prisons house a motley crew of impulsive, inadequate, pathetic but noxiously intrusive characters. Their crimes, often fueled by drugs or alcohol (or both), run the gamut from lesser property crimes like larceny, drunk driving (DWI), and handling stolen property, to the more serious and threatening property crimes such as burglary and robbery, to the unambiguously violent crimes of rape and homicide.

Today's prisons are unusual in historical terms in that they hold a large and growing population of drug offenders. Contrary to impressions left by movies and the media, these are not, with rare exceptions, mafia kingpins or Columbian warlords but small-time runners, dealers, and addicted users (see Tonry, 1995). Most of them are young black men, and many, including a fair number of first offenders, face long mandatory minimum sentences "that are comparable to the sentences for homicide" (Blumstein, 1994:399). Some of these drug offenders, similar to offenders generally, lead impoverished and disorganized lives, eking out a precarious existence on the fringes of conventional society (see Irwin & Austin, 1994). Many others, however, are more fully integrated into the larger society; as many as two-thirds have a high-school education; others have maintained reasonably stable employment histories. These are not, generally speaking, the down-and-out element of society, but people with some social attachments and hence some prospects for a decent life (see Lynch & Sabol, 1994). For the most part, their crimes are neither violent nor predatory in any meaningful sense of those terms; they are small fish passed off to an angry and frightened public as big catches in a largely futile and highly selective War on Drugs (see Reiman, 1995). It is, in my view, both unjust and unwise—and perhaps racist as well—to imprison such offenders at all, let alone for long sentences, when suitable community options abound (see Tonry, 1995; Clear & Braga, 1994; see generally, Morris and Tonry, 1980).

There is no escaping prisons, whether they are used wisely or unwisely, or in racist or color-blind ways. Nor should we try. Putting the matter of low-level drug offenders and the occasional petty property offenders to one side, it is fair to say that, on balance, prisons are better than the competing alternatives available to control predatory criminals. Many prisoners are violent or repeat offenders, and those who are violent repeat offenders make up a sizable minority. Society must be protected from the predations of these criminals. Incarceration, from which escape is rare, virtually guarantees such protection for the term of the sentence imposed by the court. No viable alternative sanction has a comparable track record of success at this basic mission of social protection (see Garland, 1990). Our sensibilities lead us to conclude that locking up predatory criminals is better than torturing or, except in extreme cases, killing them. Our common sense, backed by research, leads us to conclude that locking up predators is better than releasing them directly to community supervision, even intensive community supervision, where the opportunities to prey on innocent citizens are rife and, for many, seemingly irresistible (see Petersilia & Turner, 1990 & 1993). The societal consensus with respect to predatory criminals is this: Prison comes first, then community sanctions; protect society, punish the offender, then take measured risks in the community, backed by the threat of further incarceration.

If there is no escaping prison, there is also no escaping the fact that we must reform our prisons if they are to be institutions of just punishment. Many of our prisons are fundamentally indecent, inhumane institutions that traffic in abuse or neglect. Perhaps the most obvious and serious problem is violence. Prisoners abuse one another, and sometimes the staff, quite viciously. This violence usually is the work of hard-core convicts who prowl the prison yard, making it a no-man's land for staff and inmate alike (see Chapter Five). Though prisons hold many violent offenders, comparatively few prisoners turn to violence when in prison. Those who do act in defiance of the peaceful social order that is sought by most members of the prison staff, supported by most inmates, and achieved in most sectors of contemporary prisons (see Chapter Six). Brutality on the part of guards also occurs in contemporary prisons. As we shall see in Chapter Seven, this brutality is sometimes disturbingly common. But these abuses, like their counterparts among the inmates, are usually perpetrated by a minority of the staff, and they always represent flagrant disregard of prison policy (see Chapter Eight). Thus the contemporary prison, for all its shortcomings, is often quite civilized: most of its officials and prisoners do what they can, with the resources at their disposal, to keep the pains of prison life to a minimum.

Violence is plain to see and easy to abhor. A less obvious problem is human warehousing. Many prisons today are all play and no work—few jobs, little schooling, limited training, anemic programs. If these prisons sent out brochures—of course, they don't; no prisons do—these "promotional" materials would feature leisure time activities, mostly sports. Men in sweat suits and jogging shoes, some running, others doing calisthenics, would grace the cover of our hypothetical prison brochure. In the background, we would see rows of bleachers with a complement of spectators, some working on their tans, others catching up on the latest prison gossip. But surface appearances to the contrary, these prisons are not country clubs: the guests are involuntary, the conditions generally spartan, and the routine deadly dull. Little can be found in these institutions to lift the human spirit or mend broken lives. Most prisoners spin out empty days—killing time napping in their cells, walking the yard with their buddies, exercising or, most commonly, slouching semicomatose before incessantly blaring TVs, which have become the babysitter of choice in many of our prisons.

The Maryland Penitentiary is a reasonably typical maximum-security state prison for men. The prisoners who choose not to work—fully two-thirds of the roughly one thousand there—have days filled with unstructured time that they devote to recreational pursuits of one sort or another. In the words of one Maryland prisoner:

> They can take showers, use the phones or go outside in the yard. They can run, play softball or football depending on the season, lift weights or engage in the boxing and basketball competitions that are organized in some form all year long. But as often as not you can find them before the TV, which goes all day long. In the unbearably lonely and empty life of an inmate, 'Oprah,' game shows and the soaps provide a powerful distraction and consolation (Bratt, 1993:C2).

Free citizens imagine they would enjoy such a daily regimen. The very idea of an inmate filling his day with sports and television sets the average taxpayer's teeth on edge. Indeed, there is a recent move afoot in a number of state legislatures to cut out television and sports in prison, with the explicit aim of "making hard time harder" (Nossiter, 1994). Few of these reforms have been put into policy or law, and in a sense they are entirely superfluous. Even with these modest amenities, as our Maryland inmate makes clear, prison offers an "unbearably lonely and empty life," punctuated on occasion with violence emanating from fellow inmates or, less often, from staff. In the absence of other reforms, simply making prison conditions more restrictive is apt to promote gratuitous pain and pointless suffering. "I don't see how they can make this place any worse," observed one inmate of a notably spartan and often violent Florida state prison. "I guess they could beat us" (Booth, 1994:A1 &A8). This inmate's comments may prove prophetic. Prisons that offer nothing but restricted confinement tend to have high levels of violence, including violence used by staff as part of last-ditch efforts at social control (see Kauffman, 1988; Irwin & Austin, 1994).

Warehouse prisons, with or without occasional creature comforts, are empty enterprises. Mostly, they squander human potential. The intentions of the officials who manage these prisons are no doubt benign, but the effects are not. Human beings are not meant to be warehoused, with or without the distraction of television or sports. Warehouse prisons offer an existence, not a life. Their inhabitants survive rather than live. Warehouse prisons are our modern-day houses of the dead, to draw on Dostoyevsky, not because of brutality but because of inertia. They provide some comforts but they are not comfortable. They don't instruct or correct. They merely contain. Apathy, that most destructive of sentiments, reigns supreme. In a modern-day gesture reminiscent of Marie Antoinette, we in effect say, "Let them have cake . . . and basketball and TV." Anything to keep the natives quiet. The empty lives such prison regimes offer are themselves a kind of violence, the violence of neglect.

Some critics argue that a decent prison is an oxymoron, a contradiction in terms. In this view, prisons are inherently corrupt and unregenerate institutions. Of course, some prisons are miserable, brutal places that traffic in violence on a daily basis; others feature neglect, as we have noted, offering leisure time pursuits as a substitute for productive activity. Many prisons prove stubbornly resistant to reform. But prisons are not inherently good or bad. Prisons are human institutions, and as such they are as good or bad as we make them. Decent prisons are possible because they are simply prisons that are adequate for human habitation. As human institutions, prisons can be arranged to support human life—to allow inmates to *live as human beings* during the course of their confinement.

In decent prisons, inmates are not treated like so many objects or animals to be stored or caged, neglected or abused. Human life made small unfolds behind the walls of decent prisons, but it is a human life all the same. If a society can be judged by the quality of its prisons, as Churchill maintained, a civilized society must strive to house its criminals in decent prisons. It stands to reason that civilized prisons are likely to prove civilizing as well, to the benefit of us all.

Other critics of the prison question whether offenders deserve decent treatment in a world in which some free and innocent people suffer indecent conditions on a daily basis (c.f., Logan & Gaes, 1993). This is called the less eligibility principle. Criminals, the undeserving, are said to deserve less than any noncriminal member of society. Stated in general terms, this principle is deceptively appealing. Why should *any* criminal live better than *any* law-abiding citizen? Mustn't virtue have its rewards, crime its punishment? Yet in practice, the principle of less eligibility leads us to endorse the untenable proposition that a society can take full and complete control over prisoners and hence be responsible for them, and then can, perhaps even should, *purposely* subject those prisoners to brutal and unjust conditions merely because brutality and injustice exist in the free world. The proposition fails because citizens and prisoners cannot be directly compared in this way. Free citizens have control over their own lives and are, as a result, responsible for them. Society, through its agent, the prison, assumes control over the lives of prisoners with the aim or goal of promoting within them the capacity to lead responsible lives—the capacity to function like citizens. To run indecent prisons for the sake of some abstract notion of equity is barbaric and, if you will, an injustice to criminals and the larger society to which they will one day return, further inured to violence (see Conrad, 1988).

Decent prisons are merely "good enough" institutions—prisons good enough for the job of housing offenders under humane conditions. Many people define humaneness to mean comfort, and hence to infer that a humane prison is a materially plush and comfortable one. Nothing could be further from the truth. Such a prison would be as indecent as a prison marred by violence. Prisoners do not have a right to an easy or comfortable time behind bars. Nor do they have a right to a life of penal leisure, even under physically barren or otherwise uninviting conditions.

Prisoners must serve hard time. This is both just, since criminals deserve to suffer for the harms they have done to others, and inevitable, since prisons are inherently painful. But hard time can also be constructive time: prisoners can learn something worthwhile during their confinement. The most valuable lessons that prisoners can learn are those that enable them to cope maturely with the pains of imprisonment. As I define mature coping, it means: (1) dealing directly with one's problems, using the resources legitimately at one's disposal; (2) refusing to employ deceit or violence other than in self-defense; and (3) building mutual and supportive relationships with others. Inmates who cope maturely come to grips with problems in prison living, and they do so without violating the rights of others to be safe in their person and in their property. More generally, they treat others, staff and inmate alike, as fellow human beings who are possessed of dignity and worth. These inmates are the solid citizens of the prison community.

It goes without saying that mature coping comes hard for the veteran criminals who fill our prisons. Most criminals cope immaturely with life's problems, which is in large measure why they find themselves in prison. Often, they deny problems rather than deal with them directly. When they confront problems— often because those problems are looking them squarely in the face—they do so impulsively, with little thought or reflection. Their thinking, moreover, is distorted and self-defeating. They see themselves as pawns of life and victims of injustice. Accordingly, they live by the preemptive strike, turning the Golden Rule on its head. Their motto: Do unto others before they do unto you. Ultimately, might makes right—because it works, at least in the short run.

All prisoners were outlaws in the free world, and some of them remain outlaws behind bars. Most inmates, it is true, bemoan the primitive dangers of the prison yard; they prefer to live more civilly in relatively sheltered environments, squirreling themselves away in their cells or spending most of their time in one form of recreation or another. Their goal, however, is merely to avoid the more unruly members of the community of criminals who populate prison. They do not cope with their problems; they avoid them. Nor do they build constructive ties to others. They simply want to do their own time in prison as safely and comfortably as possible. We can only suppose that upon release they take up once again the disorganized and essentially purposeless lives that led them to crime and ultimately to prison.

Yet some prisoners, admittedly a minority, learn to cope maturely. They live and work in what I call constructive niches or sanctuaries (see Chapter Six); often, they are supported in their adjustment efforts by concerned correctional officers (see Chapter Eight). These inmates use niches not merely as havens from prison violence, but as arenas for responsible living and personal reform. They honor the obligations of prison citizenship. With appropriate policy reforms (developed in Chapter Nine), other prisoners could be placed in supportive prison environments and encouraged to live as citizens of the prison community. As a natural result of their enhanced self-confidence and emerging commitment to conventional values, they could also be encouraged to develop the educational and vocational skills that are essential to their successful adjustment upon release from prison.

Lessons in mature living learned in prison are of more general value than one might first suppose. Though it may not be obvious, there are parallels, sometimes striking parallels, between the pains of prison and the pains of life in general. These similarities can be exploited for correctional purposes. Prison citizenship can serve as a rehearsal for citizenship in other harsh environments, most notably the low-income, high-crime (and distinctly prisonlike) milieus from which most prisoners are drawn and to which the vast majority of them will return. Paradoxically, then, the pains of imprisonment, properly managed by officials and adapted to maturely by inmates, can be the primary source of the prison's correctional agenda.

Prisoners, all prisoners, retain a right to conditions of confinement that show consideration and respect for their humanity. Prisoners are in varying degrees responsible for their crimes and they deserve to suffer for the harms they have done to others. This means that, first and foremost, offenders must be treated as persons who deserve to suffer the deprivation of freedom inherent in imprisonment, as well as the loss or attenuation of many of the comforts and privileges that attach to freedom in our society. Our modern understanding of this arrangement is that offenders are sent to prison *as* punishment— loss of freedom—not *for* any additional punishment that might be given out behind bars. Earlier prisons were settings of punishment, notably corporal punishment, which was meted out with some regularity. Modern prisons are settings of deprivation.

A decent prison, then, has a bare-bones, spartan quality to it. The regime is one that is short on amenities but long, so far as is possible, on autonomy. For a spartan regime need not entail the elimination of choice. The hallmark of personhood is self-determination, which brings with it the capacity for personal growth and, potentially, self-actualization (Maslow, 1966). Note that self-determination requires that a person deal directly with problems, the first element of mature coping. No just punishment—and hence no decent prison—can abrogate the prisoner's capacity for self-determination. Persons have the moral right to make choices that influence their lives and the moral obligation to bear responsibility for the consequences of those choices. In a sense, prisoners have chosen the punishment of prison as a consequence of their crimes, but prison need not be a human wasteland. To the maximum extent feasible, prisons must promote autonomy even as they limit freedom. Certainly prisoners are not free to leave the prison or even free to move about within the prison at will. They are not free to exploit or abuse others or to commit crimes behind bars. But prisoners should be free to make choices within the prison world that have meaningful implications for the quality and character of the lives they will lead behind bars and, ultimately, upon release.

Self-determination develops best and operates most effectively in a se-cure, stable environment. In a stable world, people can plan and direct their lives in accordance with their choices, producing more or less anticipated consequences for which persons can be readily held accountable. In an inse-cure and unstable world, unpredictable contingencies tend to shape existence. Essentially random events, or events over which one has no reasonable con-trol, overshadow individual choice. Hence, one's choices bear little relation-ship to the consequences one suffers or to the larger contours of one's life. In such a world, impulsive, present-centered behavior comes to dominate indi-vidual adjustment; social relations become less stable, and planning less likely to bear fruit. A sense of irresponsibility reigns, which can produce resigna-tion, or, as in the case of criminals, license. The world is unfair, says the crimi-nal, so I will do anything I can to get what I want. I am an innocent victim, so I am entitled to victimize others in turn. Life is hard, so I will be harder, more unfeeling, more brutal.

Decent prisons must offer an alternative to the predatory world of the street criminal. They must be secure institutions, settings in which individuals are safe from the predations of others and hence free, if they so choose, to live without resort to deception or violence in their dealings with others. Free, in other words, to deal with one another in a mature fashion. Free, if they wish, to arrange their lives in accordance with choices made upon reflection and not under duress. In such a world, prisoners can learn to anticipate and accept the consequences of personal choices.

Human beings are, by nature, social animals. As Allman (1994:20) has suc-cinctly observed, "The key to understanding our evolutionary success, as well as the unique combination of everyday behaviors that set us apart from every other living thing today, is our unique talents as social beings." All human en-vironments have a social component to them. We are reared in families, live in communities, and work and play in groups. Even when we are alone, our minds are populated by thoughts of others and by experiences drawn from the world of people. Though we enter and leave the world alone, most of us—and perhaps at some level, all of us—are possessed of an appetite, a genuine hunger, for relations with others. We must cope with life, and for most people most of the time, that means we must cope with other human beings. Our choices often are about how (and not whether) we will relate to others, even if, as with criminals, those choices often feature destructive relations with others.

A decent prison must feature a secure *social* world in which offenders have open to them the opportunity to develop constructive interpersonal relations with one another, with staff, and with people from the free world.[4] Stated dif-ferently, the social world of a decent prison is built on mature social relations. Such relations are the bedrock upon which our "moral sense" is built (see Wil-son, 1993). Our basic notions of right and wrong, in other words, are premised on our capacity to feel for and relate to other human beings, to take their in-terests seriously and, moreover, to take the needs and concerns of others into account when we fashion our own lives. The goal in a decent prison, then, is for the prisoners to adapt to life behind bars in healthy and responsible ways, and from such adaptations to develop a mature coping strategy for life in the free world as well.

Prisons today are a booming industry; they are filled in record numbers. On June 31, 1994, the most recent date for which complete figures are available, federal and state prison populations reached a record high of over one million inmates—1,012,851 to be exact (see Beck & Bonczar, 1994). This represents a phenomenal increase from 1980, when the prison population, then considered large, stood at 329,821. Another measure of the incredible growth in the use of prison over the last decade is found in incarceration rates. As of June 30, 1994, the overall rate of incarceration in the United States was a record 373 prisoners per 100,000 people in the population, a dramatic increase since 1980, when the rate was 139 per 100,000 (see Beck & Bonczar, 1994:1; Gilliard & Beck, 1994:1). Prison growth patterns have proven persistent and robust. Since 1991, the *rate* at which the prison population has increased—not merely the absolute number of prisoners—has continued to rise each year, from 6.7 percent to 7.4 percent (Gilliard & Beck, 1994:1).

Overall incarceration rates help us track dominant trends, yet they mask important variations in the use of incarceration. One source of variation is by region. Incarceration rates per 100,000 are substantially higher in the South (381) and West (317) than in the Northeast (272) and Midwest (283) (see Gilliard & Beck, 1994:2). Incarceration rates also vary by gender and race. Rates of confinement are much greater for men than for women. For men, figures from June 30, 1994 reveal a confinement rate of 719 per 100,000; for women, the comparable figure is 43 per 100,000. The male incarceration rate is thus more than sixteen times higher than the female rate, though rates of confinement for women are growing at a somewhat higher pace than that for men (see Beck & Bonczar, 1994:2–3; Gilliard & Beck, 1994:4). Overall, men make up 94 percent of the total prison population, while women comprise only 6 percent.

Incarceration rate differences by race are also quite large, and these differences hold for men and women and for prisoners of different age groups. For black males, the 1992 incarceration rate was 2,678 per 100,000, which represents a rise of 141 percent since 1980, and is fully seven times the incarceration rate of white males (372 per 100,000). The figures are lower for women, but the same racial disparities prevail. Thus, the incarceration rate for black women is 143 per 100,000; for white women, the rate is 20 per 100,000. Looking at the intersection of race and age, we see some especially disturbing figures. Figures for 1991, the most recent year for which data are available for age and race, document incarceration rates for black men between the ages of 20 and 35—the prime years of life—that range from 4,775 to 5,577 per 100,000. These rates are between six and nine times the comparable rates for white males (Gilliard & Beck, 1994:9).

The composition of today's prisons differs markedly from the prisons of 1980. Stated simply, our prisons hold more drug offenders and more black offenders than ever before. Drug offenders made up 30.5 percent of the 1992 prison population, which is up from a mere 6.8 percent in 1980. Almost unbelievably, "The increase in drug offenders admitted to prison accounted for nearly 46 percent of the total growth in new court commitments since 1980" (Gilliard & Beck, 1994: 7–8). New court commitments, in turn, make up the bulk of the growth of prison populations. The dramatic growth in persons imprisoned for drug offenses reflects two trends: a rise in the number of offenders arrested for drug violations, a 108 percent increase since 1980; and an increased rate of incarceration for those convicted of drug offenses, from 19 offenders per 100,000 sent to prison in 1980 to fully 104 offenders per 100,000 sent to prison in 1992, a five-fold increase (Gilliard & Beck, 1994:8).

The growing prevalence of drug offenders in our prisons produces the ironic result that persons convicted of serious offenses of violence—murder, sexual assault, robbery and aggravated assault—represent a substantially reduced percentage of the prison population, dropping from 48.2 percent in 1980 to 28.5 percent in 1992. The same holds for serious property offenders, notably burglars. Serious property offenders made up 41.1 percent of the prison population in 1980; in 1992, that figure fell to 31.2 percent. Perhaps the easiest way to appreciate the growth of drug offenders in our prisons is to look at the raw numbers. In 1980, 8,900 prisoners were confined for drug violations; in 1992, that number had grown to 102,000 (Gilliard & Beck, 1994: 10).

The growth in our prison population also reflects particularly dramatic increases in incarceration rates for black men, especially young black men, many of whom, as we have noted, are doing time for drug violations (Gilliard & Beck, 1994:9). For the first time, blacks now make up an absolute majority of our nation's prisons—more than half the prison population—though they represent roughly 13 percent of the general population (Gilliard & Beck, 1994:9). Incarceration rates in America for offenders generally and for black offenders in particular are quite high by international standards, and indeed may be the highest in the world (Lynch, 1993; Maurer, 1992). These figures are for prisons only and do not include people in other settings of punitive confinement or in the community but still under the control of the correctional system. Austin (1995) reports that "In 1993, the most recent year that national data are available, there were 455,000 inmates in jails, 94,000 youths in juvenile facilities, 2.8 million probationers, and 672,000 parolees."

Prisons house a virtual nation of convicts. It is a nation most of us wish to forget, comprised primarily of poor men, and especially poor young black men. A case can be made that we use prison too freely, and in ways that are essentially racist. We will return to these important points in the final chapter of this book, when we place prison reform in a broader social and political context. For now, it sufficient to stress that, whatever the size of our prisons and independent of the types of offenders they contain, it is unconscionable for society to relegate prisoners to a human junk heap, to sentence them to endure pain without any redeeming social benefit or purpose. Men punished in this futile and demeaning way will leave prison no better, and sometimes much worse, than when they went in. Instead, prison policy must be fashioned to promote mature adjustment to the inevitable pains of confinement. The goal is citizen-building; first in decent prisons, later in the free world. This is an altogether appropriate correctional endeavor. For prisons must promote the virtues of citizenship even as they confine and punish our most wayward citizens. They must be instruments of punishment that are in fact both civilized and civilizing.

To place today's prisons in perspective, and to help us develop a realistic agenda for prison reform, we will examine the history of prisons (Chapters One through Three). We will focus on the evolution of prisons as social environments—as places where people live and work. Our aim will be to assess prisons over time in terms of their decency, that is, the extent to which prison regimes permit or encourage self-determination among the inmates and their keepers. We will see, in our examination of contemporary prisons (Chapters Four through Eight), that it is only in the last generation or so that prisons have achieved a social order and management structure that allow staff, potentially if not often in practice, to hold out to prisoners the prospect of developing as human beings during their confinement. We will conclude (Chapter Nine) with a reform agenda that spells out the contours of a decent prison in terms of its organizational structure, social environment, and program opportunities.

PRISON AS A NATURAL
MEANS OF PUNISHMENT

The claim that prisons have been around for centuries, made at the outset of this book, may surprise some readers. Many criminologists regard the prison as a British or American invention of fairly recent vintage. The sense in which the prison is a modern and uniquely American institution will be taken up in the next chapter. The fact is, however, that confining people who hurt or threaten us is an old practice because it is a natural thing to do, perhaps even as natural as striking out and physically hurting our enemies and then banishing them from our midst. Better, it is natural to hurt our enemies physically and then lock them up for good measure—to keep them under control and hence subject to further injury, including execution or banishment.

As a system of punitive control, prison beats hands down the competing alternatives of execution and banishment. There is, after all, a limit to the number of executions a society can carry out; no regime in human history has had sufficient appetite for blood to execute all or even most of its offenders. And banishment, though simple and appealing in principle as a means to rid society of undesirables, is apt to be seen as too easy or too unreliable. The banished person is set free in a new world, a fate that is not always or obviously a punishment. The plain fact is that many offenders have welcomed this sanction (see Stern, 1987:10). Others have returned to the scenes of their original crimes after completion of their sentences, only to take up once again their predatory activities (see McLynn, 1989:76). An added difficulty with banishment is that one must have a place to which prisoners can be exiled, and the availability of such settings is never assured. With prison, at least, there is the assurance of punitive restraint and control of the deviant for the time and purpose set by the relevant authorities.

To be sure, early prisons were self-consciously punitive and controlling; their internal regimes were intentionally inhumane. No warden of an early prison cared about decency. No thought whatsoever was given to allowing self-determination to prisoners. Constructive manifestations of autonomy, security, and relatedness to others were nowhere in evidence. The earliest prisons were haphazardly arranged, inflicting pain without purpose or, put another way, meting out pain for pain's sake.

Incarceration is, as we have noted, a convenient means of holding a person until some other punishment can be carried out. Confinement was often used in this way in the past, most notably to coerce people into paying their fines, or to hold those awaiting banishment or execution. But imprisonment is a punishment in itself, and has always been used as such. The Mamertine Prison, probably the first formal and enduring prison, was built under the sewers of Rome in 64 B.C. and contained dungeons in which "prisoners were confined in what were basically cages" (ACA, 1983:3).[5] It is evident that this institution was built (under a primitive sewer!) for no other purpose than causing prisoners to suffer great discomfort while confined there. Its internal environs have been described as "repulsive and fearful, because of the neglect, the darkness and the stench" (Peck, 1922:279). It is as if the Fathers of Rome saw the threats to public health posed by human waste and by human deviance as equivalent, and opted to expel both from the sight and consciousness of the Roman citizenry. As it turns out, their thinking, though not the organization of their prisons, anticipated the preoccupation with contamination and infection that gave impetus to the modern penitentiary.

Punishments formally expressed in the loss of liberty over time, like contemporary prison sentences of so many years duration, are a modern phenomenon.[6] But the use of prison to produce pain is not new. Nor are the pains of prison subtle or hard to understand, especially in the crude form in which confinement was originally practiced. The person thrown into a cage, and perhaps tied or chained to a wall for good measure, suffers obvious deprivations. (Obvious enough to be the subject of slightly perverse cartoon humor, as noted earlier.) Isolated and immobilized, he is reduced to the status of a child or even an infant who is, to quote Willard Gaylin (1978:19), at once "helpless and unloved." He is forced to enter what Gaylin describes as "the matrix of disaster": a situation of primal and extreme vulnerability, subject to indiscriminate physical and emotional abuse. His fate is in some respects "comparable to death" because we are social beings whose very nature requires relationships with others (Gaylin, 1978:22). Incarceration strains and often sunders vital social bonds. No alternative society or subculture within the prison can fully restore or replace them. Indeed, it is hard to envision inmates in early prisons as anything other than "the living dead," physically alive but forgotten by the world outside the prison walls. Those who built and used the first prisons to achieve this mass burial no doubt had some idea what they were creating.

Early prisons served retributive functions. Imprisonment was part of the suffering intentionally visited upon the offender to pay him back for the harm done to the victim. Confinement may have been only a small part of this retribution because, after all, other punishments, featuring burned or torn or mutilated flesh, were considerably more dramatic and painful. As real and obvious as it is, the pain of confinement in itself can be discounted or minimized; it leaves no visible traces, no bodily testimony in the form of welts or scars. Moreover, the pain of isolation is never spectacular, and early punishments often relied on the spectacle of pain to frighten the masses and hence secure their obedience to the sovereign (Foucault, 1977).

Still, prison could and no doubt did serve as an adjunct to the public punishment of the body, reinforcing and extending its message. Imprisonment is an intimidating, even terrifying, experience, a reason in itself to avoid crime. The prospect of a stint beneath the sewers of Rome could reasonably be expected to deter some criminals. Even more obvious is the role confinement plays in the incapacitation of convicted offenders. Criminals in cells don't commit crimes against the free citizenry. And this effect can be envisioned without the aid of a statistical projection. It is easy to anticipate, since the restraint of confinement is a simple elaboration of wrestling someone into submission. Confinement simply extends the period of submissive immobility.

Imprisonment is thus a punishment that can reasonably be expected to hurt, deter, and incapacitate offenders, as well as to hold them for other punishments. It is also easy and inexpensive to confine people, at least on a small scale and for short periods of time. Building a few cages or simply fencing a common area is no more difficult or costly than constructing a whipping post or a gallows. In each instance, the criminal can be set to work building the agency of his punishment, and each of these instruments of punishment can be used over and over again. Prisoners have to be fed and otherwise maintained and this might sometimes prove costly, but it was not uncommon for prisoners, including those condemned to die, to pay their own keep in money, goods, or labor (McConville, 1981). Prison made revenge simple and sweet, like the various corporal punishments used throughout history, both in and out of prison.

The logic of confining dangerous people is so basic and compelling that one is tempted to see the act of imprisoning as an instinctive response—like fight or flight—to a kind of adversity. In this view the notion of confinement (as distinct from its embodiment in any particular institution) would derive from reactions to recurring experiences in nature, particularly those that posed threats to the survival of the species. The original threat that resulted in confinement was probably contagious disease.

PRISON AS A NATURAL
MEANS OF QUARANTINE

Some type of expulsion from the community, backed by restraint and confinement, would be a natural means of isolating a diseased person from the community and would prevent his returning to infect the healthy. It would be preferable to fighting or attacking the diseased person and thus risking contamination, or to fleeing from him and therefore forfeiting one's property and means of livelihood. Confinement would ensure the absence of the diseased person, who is presumably a source of anxiety, fear, and perhaps even dread, particularly if the disease produced disfiguring symptoms. At the same time, confinement would punish the person for his impurity in a way that is poignantly symbolic: as a pariah, a person physically and, supposedly, morally contaminated, he has placed himself outside the human community and hence is a fit subject of abandonment by his fellows. He would be guarded by other pariahs, drawn from his own or from equally disreputable ranks, and would be eligible for other punishments, such as stoning, which could be inflicted from a distance.

The earliest and most notable connection between disease and confinement has to do with leprosy, which has ancient origins and gave rise to a number of practices of exclusion, among which were leper colonies. It is "the image of the leper," states Foucault, "cut off from all human contact, [that] underlies projects of exclusion." One of the more ambitious "projects of exclusion" is the prison.[7]

Prisons were meant to be painful, and early settings of confinement were suitably miserable. The Roman Mamertine Prison, described earlier, is a telling case in point. Later prisons were little better. Prisoners were variously stored in sulphur pits, mines, stone quarries, and the hulls of ships (ACA, 1983). The famous gaols, predecessors of today's local jails, were at best human warehouses in which men, women, and children—and sometimes animals as well—were confined in public rooms with little or nothing constructive to do (McConville, 1981; Byrne, 1989). These penal institutions were typically filthy, disease-ridden, and marked by chronic violence. Promiscuity and even prostitution were common; and, one imagines, so was rape, as no attempt was made to separate the sexes or to control "the ample supply of cheap alcohol" available in these prisons (Byrne, 1989:25).

Prisoners, seen as polluted creatures beyond the reach of care or compassion, were free to abuse one another at will. And to die, mostly from disease and often at high rates, making a public death within the prison's congregate wards a common spectacle. William Fennor, jailed in 1616 for assault, provides this account of death in an English goal:

> In this place a man shall not look about him but some poor soul or other
> lies groaning and labouring under the burden of some dangerous disease;
> the child weeping over his dying father, the mother over her sick child;
> one friend over another, who can no sooner rise from him, but he is ready
> to stumble over another in as miserable a plight as him he but newly took
> leave of. So that if a man come thither he at first will think himself in
> some churchyard that hath been fattened with some great plague, for they
> lie together like so many graves. (Quoted in Byrne, 1989:49)

Geffray Mynshul portrayed King's Bench prison in 1617 as "a grave to bury men alive." The social environment that developed in this and other funereal prisons, he contended, was a microcosm of suffering or, in Mynshul's words, "a Microcosmoos, a little world of woe, . . . a mappe of misery" (quoted in Byrne,

1989:106). Penal settings such as these, whenever and wherever they emerge, may indeed trace their lineage to the leper colony.

(One can find a limited but telling contemporary parallel to this situation in segregation units reserved for inmates with HIV/AIDS. At Alabama's infamous Thunderdorm, for example, infected inmates are kept at arms length by officials, who wear rubber gloves and want nothing to do with the prisoners. The prisoners, in turn, are admonished to care for the dying among them, since no one in authority will reach out to touch and help them. Thunderdorm is, indeed, a modern-day "mappe of misery," exploring the limited terrain allotted to these inmates with HIV/AIDS, who are treated as modern-day lepers.[8] Reforms in the management of HIV-positive inmates are discussed in Chapter Nine.)

In later centuries, and particularly during the Middle Ages, some prisons took on a more disciplined cast and added reformation of the wayward to their objectives. These settings were less reminiscent of amorphous, static colonies and more like organized societies with a job to do. That job was penance, and the object of penance was spiritual purity. This reflected the influence of the monastery on the prison, and indeed as early as the fourth century there is evidence of cells in monasteries reserved for persons consigned to years of solitary penance (ACA, 1983:3). In McConville's (1981:31) words,

> Monastic prisons isolated the malefactor, partly as duress and punishment, partly in order to reduce moral contagion, but also with the intention of curing the offender's physical and spiritual defects. Such prisoners were kept in silence, subjected to a special diet, and allowed only the distraction of approved books and conversation with their abbot or some designated elder brother.

It was not until the thirteenth century, during the Inquisition, however, that prisons began to feature a regime of solitary reflection (Newman, 1978). Religious "criminals" (heretics) were to plumb their consciences in dungeon cells and repent their sins; 600 years later, at the turn of the nineteenth century, common criminals in penitentiaries were expected to expiate their crimes.[9] The sinner and the criminal were to be cleansed of their impurities. In pursuing their rehabilitation through solitary reflection, they were following a purifying routine of solitude that "has been recommended, both by practice and precept of holy men, in all ages, sometimes to retire from scenes of public concourse, for the purpose of communing with our own hearts, and meditating on heaven" (Hirsch, 1982:1209).

The connection between solitude and purity, seen first in monasteries and later in prisons, may also originate with the problem of contagious disease. One lesson drawn from the management of sick people is simply that the impure can be excluded from society at large but allowed to intermingle freely and further contaminate one another. This is the lesson embodied in the leper colony and related "projects of exclusion." A different lesson may be learned about the preservation of those who are well: isolation can protect health by preventing exposure to disease. And if the sick are isolated (quarantined) from each other, health may be restored. The good (healthy) or reformed (cured) person leads a pure existence, and this is measured in solitude and good thoughts rather than in fellowship and good works. In social isolation there is purity and life; in sociability there is danger of contamination, soiling, illness, and death. Reform, for those deemed worthy, requires the pristine sterility of solitary confinement and the inner purification of reflection and penance. It is in this disciplined silence that the sinner is reclaimed for God, the criminal for society.

The Plague and the Penitentiary

The tradition of reform resulting from strict quarantine, initially a province of the monastery, would be accentuated and disseminated during the Middle Ages, a time when "the problem of disease hung like a sword of Damocles over the head of medieval man" (Rosen, 1967:760). In antiquity, pestilences of leprosy and even plague were an occasional menace but had limited implications for daily life (Rosen, 1967; Gottfried, 1983). By the Middle Ages these diseases were so common as to be routine, and repositories for the sick and dying dotted every landscape. In the thirteenth century, for example, there were enough lepers to fill the 19,000 leper colonies in existence throughout Europe (Rosen, 1967:760). A century later, the Black Death struck, beginning a series of epidemics that would last for upwards of four centuries and make death a voracious guest at the medieval table. The scope and magnitude of death is conveyed in accounts of seventeenth century London, for example, when people died en masse and were interred in common graves. In the words of a contemporary observer,

> Before the jewel of the morning be fully set in silver, a hundred hungry graves stand gaping, and every one of them, as at a breakfast, hath swallowed down ten or eleven lifeless carcasses. Before dinner, in the same gulf are twice so many more devoured; and before the sun takes his rest, those numbers are doubled (Hibbard, 1951:179–80).

Quarantines were a fact of life during the plague (Gottfried, 1983). Initially there were many plague colonies throughout Europe, since the plague was first treated as a variant of leprosy and lepers were traditionally placed in colonies set apart from the healthy (Rosen, 1967:760). Plague victims were also hospitalized in great numbers, but this amounted to much the same thing. The hospitals of this time

> were institutions designed primarily to isolate, rather than cure, the sick—to remove them from the mainstream of society so that they would not infect or offend the healthy. When a sick person entered a hospital, he was treated as if he were dead. His property was disposed of and, in many regions, a quasi-requiem mass was said for his soul; certainly, no one expected to see the poor wretch again . . . [Hospitals] offered little help to the victims of infectious diseases. (Gottfried, 1983:119–20)

But plague presented a more insidious health threat than leprosy or any other known infectious disease. Simple isolation of the sick, whether in a colony or in a hospital, was not enough; a policy of isolating the sick was tantamount to a death sentence for a sizable segment of the populace. Still, raw fear and the convenience of imposing isolation sometimes combined to produce tragic failures of disease control. The municipal authorities in fourteenth-century Milan, for instance, "walled up those houses in which plague victims were discovered, isolating in them the healthy as well as the sick," leaving them all to die (Gottfried, 1983:49). The idea caught on. "So popular did this become," in fact, "that many householders followed suit, in some cases killing members of their own families" (Gottfried, 1983:49). Some authorities blamed lepers, others the Jews, for the pollution that was sweeping over Europe. Massacres followed, particularly in French and German cities, in which many would-be culprits were burned alive (see DiBacco, 1994:15). Panic-inspired policies such as these were gradually supplanted by more rigorous treatment of hospital patients and systematic quarantines in which sick and healthy alike were, insofar as was possible, both kept alive and sequestered from one another.

Imposing a quarantine to stem the plague proved to be no easy matter. One had to move fast, since plague victims typically died in a matter of days and in numbers that are almost incomprehensible. In the three-year period between 1348 and 1351, for example, some 24 million people, fully one-third of Europe's population, died of plague (Gottfried, 1983:77). It is hard to imagine the sense of vulnerability produced by the plague. Disease and death were everywhere. People were, literally, afraid to breathe. On the one hand, some people were warned by doctors against breathing too much "bad" air. Others, following medical advice, spent "their wakeful hours inhaling the stench from human waste" to avoid taking in too much "good" air (DiBacco, 1994:15). Contagion was considered a risk of every possible human encounter. "It was thought that the breath, clothing, bedding, or even stare of an infected individual could pass on the deadly plague" (Gottfried, 1983:113). Moreover, the symptoms of plague in its early stage (sores around the groin or underarm, discreetly hidden by clothing) were sufficiently subtle to render everyone a potential agent of infection.

The challenge, then, was to isolate the healthy not only from the sick but, more importantly, from the *possibly* sick. In a very real sense, *anyone* could be classified as possibly sick. Under these conditions, no one could feel safe around anyone else. One response, naturally enough, was to abandon hope for the future and live each moment as if it were one's last. This was frequently done, and there is a body of literature and art that testifies to the prevalence of unrestrained hedonism during this era.[10] Another course of action was to place entire towns under strict and comprehensive quarantines.

DISCIPLINED PRISONS

Those plague-stricken towns that imposed total quarantines in effect turned themselves into disciplined prisons to ensure the safety of their citizens. A medieval town-as-prison, described vividly by Foucault, predates by centuries the first formal disciplinary prison, yet within its confines we see the essential ingredients of the penitentiary: isolation, regimentation, organized surveillance, custodial maintenance and, no doubt, prayer and penance as well. We behold the natural development of a total institution:

> First, a strict spatial partitioning: the closing of the town and its outlying districts, a prohibition to leave the town on pain of death, the killing of all stray animals; the division of the town into distinct quarters, each governed by an intendant. Each street is placed under the authority of a syndic, who keeps it under surveillance; if he leaves the street, he will be condemned to death. On the appointed day, everyone is ordered to stay indoors: it is forbidden to leave on pain of death. The syndic himself comes to lock the door of each house from the outside; he takes the key with him and hands it over to the intendant of the quarter; the intendant keeps it until the end of the quarantine. Each family will have made its own provisions; but, for bread and wine, small wooden canals are set up between the street and the interior of the houses, thus allowing each person to receive his ration without communicating with the suppliers and other residents; meat, fish and herbs will be hoisted up into the house with pulleys and baskets. If it is absolutely necessary to leave the house, it will be done in turn, avoiding any meeting. Only the intendants, syndics and guards will move about the streets and also, between the infected houses, from one corpse to another, the "crows," who can be left to die: these are "people of little substance who carry the sick, bury the dead, clean and do many vile and abject offices." It is segmented, immobile, frozen space. Each individual is fixed in his place. And, if he moves he does so at the risk of life, contagion or punishment.
>
> Inspection functions ceaselessly. The gaze is alert everywhere: "A considerable body of militia, commanded by good officers and men of substance," guards at the gates, at the town hall and in every quarter to ensure the prompt obedience of the people and the most absolute authority of the magistrates, "as also to observe all disorder, theft and extortion." At each of the town gates there will be an observation post; at the end of each street sentinels. Every day, the intendant visits the quarter in his charge, inquires whether the syndics have carried out their tasks, whether the inhabitants have anything to complain of; they "observe their actions." Every day, too, the syndic goes into the street for which he is responsible; stops before each house; gets all the inhabitants to appear at the windows (those who live overlooking the courtyard will be allocated a window looking onto the street at which no one but they may show themselves); he calls each of them by name; informs himself as to the state of each and every one of them-"in which respect the inhabitants will be compelled to speak the truth under pain of death"; if someone does not appear at the window, the syndic must ask why: "In this way he will find out easily enough whether dead or sick are being concealed." Everyone locked up in his cage, everyone at his window, answering to his name and showing himself when asked-it is the great review of the living and the dead. (Foucault, 1977:195–96)

Now it is clear that most medieval towns did not respond to the plague in this way, though quarantines of a lesser order were quite common (Gottfried, 1983). But some towns did resort to total quarantines, and in doing so foreshadowed the modern prison. Foucault (1977:198) may well be correct when he maintains that "the plague gave rise to disciplinary projects.... Underlying disciplinary projects the image of the plague stands for all forms of confusion and disorder." The first of these disciplinary projects was the prison-town constructed to stem the "confusion and disorder" of the plague. A descendant of this curious town is the American penitentiary, a disciplined and orderly response to the confusion and disorder of life in the New World.

NOTES

1. My colleagues promptly altered my copy of the cartoon, replacing Bob with Rob, which is what my friends call me. Who said academics were a humorless lot?

2. I am indebted to my colleague Jeffrey H. Reiman, William Fraser McDowell Professor of Philosophy at The American University, for the notion that punishment should be both civilized and civilizing.

3. Plato did in fact support the death penalty, but for reasons that are irrelevant today. He saw crime as a kind of disease that contaminated and tortured its host; the serious and incurable criminal would be released from his earthly bondage by execution, a punishment that was presumed to make him less of a wretch. Philippe Aries (1982) tells us that other notions of death prevalent before the twentieth century, particularly those associated with a forgiving God and a congenial afterlife, made a foreseen death a tame and desirable arrangement. Here, too, execution might be conceived as a blessing of sorts, allowing the criminal to come to terms with his Maker. In our secular age, where people are neither believed possessed by criminal demons of one sort or another nor the confident beneficiaries of a guaranteed afterlife, the benefits of death cannot be invoked to defend the death penalty (see Johnson, 1990:151–55). For more on Plato's views on punishment, see Mackenzie (1981).

4. People from the outside world would include those who enter the prison as volunteers, usually associated with community programs, as well as visitors and others from the outside world with whom inmates come in contact over their terms.

5. The name "Mamertine" is of medieval origin. In the classical period, this prison was referred to as the Tullianum (Peck, 1922:278). It was the site of both executions and punitive confinement (Lanciani, 1900:285–86). The date of its origin is in dispute. The 1983 ACA document dates the construction of the prison at 64 B.C., and I have adopted their figure because it is a source easily available to criminologists and penologists. However, the building "in part at least, is as old as any structure in the city" of Rome (Platner, 1904:240), which means that it could have originated as early as 753 B.C. That is unlikely, but the building's "construction is so old," in the words of one historian, "that it points to a time when the arch was not used in Roman architecture" (Peck, 1922:278). There also is some dispute as to the prison's size. The ACA document refers to it as "vast," but other accounts suggest that it may have comprised only a few dungeons (Peck, 1922:279). There is, finally, some dispute as to whether this structure was originally built to serve as a prison or was initially a spring-house or an ancient tomb that was later used as a prison (Platner, 1904:242). In any event, it is the view of Platner (1904:242), an authority on Roman history and topography, that "there is no doubt that this was the Carcer of the republic," which would delimit its point of origin to 527–509 B.C. There

were other, lesser prisons during the republican period as well, including one (the Lautumiae) built in a stone quarry (Peck, 1922:279).

6. The historical conditions that made such sentences possible mark the birth of the prison as a major institution of punishment. These conditions will be explored in the next chapter. For now, it is sufficient to note, in the words of Melossi and Pavarini (1981:3), that

The transition from private vendetta to retributive punishment, that is, the transition from an almost "biological" phenomenon to a juridical category, requires as a necessary precondition the cultural dominance of the concept of equivalents based on exchange value . . . "[F]or it to be possible for the idea to emerge that one could make recompense for an offense with a piece of abstract freedom determined in advance, it was necessary for all concrete forms of social wealth to be reduced to the most abstract and simple form, to human labour measured in time." Thus, under a socioeconomic system such as feudalism—in which the historic development of "human labour measured in time" (read: wage labour) was still incomplete—retributive punishment, determined by an exchange value, was not in a position to find in the privation of time the equivalent of the crime. Instead, the equivalent of the injury produced by the crime was realised in the privation of assets socially valued at that time: life, physical wholeness, money, loss of status.

In this context, Melossi and Pavarini (1981:2) make the claim that "in precapitalist societies prison as a form of punishment did not exist. This can be seen to be the case historically so long as we bear in mind that it was not so much the prison institution that was unknown . . . [as] the penalty of confinement as a deprivation of liberty."

7. In addition to the prison, projects of exclusion include capital punishment and deportation. Each such punishment can be considered a kind of social and/or physical death sentence (see Sherman & Hawkins, 1981:55).

8. The quarantined housing for inmates with HIV/AIDS at Alabama's Thunderdorm (Limestone Prison) amounts to "a new kind of death row, one that houses

every male prisoner in the state who carries the AIDS virus. Hemmed in by double chain-link fences topped by razor ribbon, and forbidden to have contact with other, uninfected prisoners or perform ordinary prison jobs, the 130 residents of the Thunderdorm form one of America's first AIDS colonies" (Whitman, 1990:21). The name *Thunderdorm* is "derived from the so-called Thunderdome, a brutal arena where gladiators fight to the death in a 'Mad Max' film" (Whitman, 1990:21). The number of male prisoners in Alabama's Thunderdorm has grown to nearly two hundred; currently two dorms are set aside for male inmates with HIV/AIDS. Alabama runs a separate segregation unit for female prisoners with HIV/AIDS at the Julia Tutwiler Prison for Women (see Thrush, 1994). Conditions are essentially the same as those for men. In Alabama and Mississippi, inmates who test positive for HIV "are shut out of work-release programs, vocational training, sex-offender treatment, assignments in prison factories, workshops and farms, sports and fitness facilities, even menial jobs in the prison cafeteria and laundry" (Thrush, 1994:85).

In the mid-eighties, at the height of the AIDS scare, segregation of infected inmates was common (Whitman, 1990). Today, only the Mississippi and Alabama prison systems house HIV/AIDS inmates in segregation units. All other prison systems, state and federal, integrate or mainstream these prisoners in varying degrees.

9. Norris (1985:23) reminds us that the first penitentiaries "were in a sense monastic prisons where penance replaced civic punishments." The link between penance and punishment is implied in the term "penitentiary," which comes from "the Latin word for 'penitence' and 'repentence,'" and shares "the same root as the words for punishment, pain, and revenge" (Norris, 1985:75).

10. Chaucer's ribald and occasionally bawdy *Canterbury Tales* is one of the best known testimonials to this lifestyle. So, too, is Boccacio's *Decameron,* which is more explicitly concerned with life in the shadow of the Black Death.

REFERENCES

Allman, W.F. *The Stone Age Present: How Evolution has Shaped Modern Life— From Sex, Violence, and Language to Emotions, Morals, and Communities*. New York: Simon & Schuster, 1994.

American Correctional Association. *The American Prison: From the Beginning . . .* ACA Publishers, 1983.

Aries, P. *The Hour of Our Death*. New York: Vintage, 1982.

Austin, J. "Correctional options: An overview."*Corrections Today* (February 1995) (Article not paginated in journal).

Beck, A. J., and T. P. Bonczar. "State and federal prison population tops one million." *Bureau of Justice Advance Report* (October 27, 1994):1–6.

Blumstein, A. "Prisons." In J. Q. Wilson, and J. Petersilia (eds.). *Crime*. San Francisco: ICS Press, 1994:387–420.

Booth, W. "Without the 'rock,' Florida inmates get the hard place." *The Washington Post* (October 30, 1994): A1 and A8.

Bratt, L. "Menace II the mind: For a generation of black men in prison, television is the dangerous drug of choice." *The Washington Post* (July 11, 1993):C1, C2.

Bureau of Justice Statistics. "The prevalence of imprisonment." *Special Report*. July, 1985.

Byrne, R. *Prisons and Punishments of London*. London: Harrap, 1989.

Clear, T. R., and A. A. Braga. "Community corrections." In J. Q. Wilson and J. Petersilia (eds.). *Crime*. San Francisco: ICS Press, 1994:421–44.

Conrad, J. P. "What do the undeserving deserve?" In R. Johnson and H. Toch (eds.). *The Pains of Imprisonment*. Prospect Heights, IL.: Waveland Press, 1988:313–30.

DiBacco, T. V. "The dark history of the 'black death'." *The Washington Post* (October 4, 1994) Health section:13, 15.

Foucault, M. *Discipline and Punish: The Birth of the Prison*. New York: Pantheon, 1977.

Garland, D. *Punishment and Modern Society: A Study in Social Theory*. Chicago: University of Chicago Press, 1990.

Gaylin, W., "In the beginning." In Gaylin et al. (eds.). *Doing Good: The Limits of Benevolence*. New York: Pantheon, 1978.

Gilliard, D. K. and A. J. Beck, *Prisoners in 1993*. Bulletin, Bureau of Justice Statistics, 1994:1–10.

Gottfried, R. *The Black Death: Natural and Human Disaster in Medieval Europe*. New York: Free Press, 1983.

Hibbard, G. R. (ed.). *Three Elizabethan Pamphlets*. London: George G. Harrap & Co., 1951.

Hirsch, A. J. "From pillory to penitentiary: The rise of criminal incarceration in early Massachusetts." *Michigan Law Review*, 80 (1982).

Irwin, J. I. , and J. AUSTIN. *It's About Time: America's Imprisonment Binge*. Belmont, CA.: Wadsworth, 1994.

Johnson, R. *Death Work: A Study of the Modern Execution Process*. Belmont, CA: Wadsworth, 1990.

Kauffman, K. *Prison Officers and Their World*. Cambridge: Harvard University Press, 1988.

Lanciani, R. A. *The Ruins and Excavations of Ancient Rome*. Boston: Houghton Mifflin, 1900.

Lawes, L. L. *Twenty Thousand Years in Sing Sing*. New York: Ray Long & Richard R. Smith, 1932.

Logan, C. H., and G. G. Gaes. "Meta-Analysis and the rehabilitation of punishment." *Justice Quarterly* 10 (2) 1993:245–63.

Lynch, J. P., and W. J. Sabol. "The use of coercive social control and changes in the race and class composition of U.S. prison populations." Paper presented at the 1994 Annual Meeting of the

American Society of Crimonology, Miami, November 9, 1994.

Lynch, J. P. "A cross-national comparison of length of custodial sentences for serious crimes." *Justice Quarterly* 10 (4) 1993:639–60.

Mackenzie, M. M. *Plato on Punishment.* Berkeley: University of California Press, 1981.

Maslow, A. *Eupsychian Management.* Homewood, IL.:Irwin, 1966.

Mauer, M. "America behind bars." A report of *The Sentencing Project.* February 1992, 20 pages.

McConville, S. *A History of English Prison Administration.* London: Routledge & Kegan Paul, 1981.

McLynn, F. *Crime and Punishment in 18th Century England.* London: Routledge, 1989.

Melossi, D., and M. Pavarini. *The Prison and the Factory: Origins of the Penitentiary System.* Translated by G. Cousin. Totowa, NJ: Barnes & Noble, 1981.

Morris, N. & M. Tonry. *Between Prison and Probation: Intermediate Punishments in a Rational Sentencing System.* New York: Oxford, 1990.

Newman, G. *The Punishment Response.* Philadelphia: Lippincott, 1978.

Norris, R. L. *Prison Reformers and Penitential Publicists in France, England, and the United States, 1774–1847.* Unpublished dissertation: The American University, 1985.

Nossiter, A. "Making hard time harder: States cut jail TV and sports." *The New York Times* (September 17, 1994):1, 11.

Peck, H. T. (ed.). *Harper's Dictionary of Classical Literature and Antiquity.* New York: American Book, 1922.

Petersilia, J., and S. Turner. "Comparing intensive and regular supervision for high-risk probationers: Early results from an experiment in California. *Crime & Delinquency* 36 (1) 1990:87–111.

Petersilia, J., and S. Turner. "Intensive probation and parole." In M. H.

Tonry (ed.). *Crime and Justice: A Review of Research.* Chicago: University of Chicago Press, 1993.

Platner, S. B. *The Topography and Monuments of Ancient Rome.* Norwood, MA: Norwood Press, 1904.

Reiman, J. *The Rich Get Richer and the Poor Get Prison.* New York: Allyn and Bacon, 1995.

Rosen, G. "Public health." *Encyclopedia Americana* Book 22, 1967:759–67.

Sherman, M. E., and G. Hawkins. *Imprisonment in America: Choosing the Future.* Chicago: University of Chicago Press, 1981.

Stern, V. *Bricks of Shame: Britain's Prisons.* New York: Viking Penguin, 1987.

Thrush, G. "AIDS: Words from the front." *Spin* (June 1994):85–86.

Tonry, M. *Malign Neglect: Race, Crime, and Punishment in America.* New York: Oxford University Press, 1995.

Whitman, D. "Inside an AIDS colony." *U.S. News & World Report* (January 29, 1990):20–26.

Wilson, J. Q. *The Moral Sense.* New York: Free Press, 1993.

2

The Penitentiary

PART ONE: THE BIRTH

OF THE MODERN PRISON

The penitentiary employed a regime of disciplined isolation. The purpose was twofold: To protect prisoners from moral contamination, and to restore them to habits of correct living. The penitentiary was a plague-town, if you will, in which the object was both to protect health and improve character. The prisoner was to leave his confinement not only untouched by the confusion and disorder—the criminogenic plague—that had pursued him to the walls of his prison home, but also at peace with himself, his God, and his society. He would keep a lonely and ascetic vigil, and his reward would be to emerge a new, reformed man (Rothman, 1971; Ignatieff, 1978).

The penitentiary was meant to be a grand and even noble experiment in prison reform. Although, for reasons we will examine later in this chapter, this institution proved to be an exercise in organized brutality, the ideal of reform through discipline captured the American imagination. Americans thought of the penitentiary as nothing less than a new punishment for a new world. They embraced it with what the French penal authorities Tocqueville and Beaumont termed a *monomanie* shared by no other nation.[1] In this sense the penitentiary was distinctively American. It reflected many aspects of American character and history, and its emergence and fate tell much about the institution of the prison, then and now.

AMERICAN PRISONS
BEFORE THE PENITENTIARY

Though Americans may claim the penitentiary as their own, it did not exist in the colonial period. Then, criminals were not confined for purposes of personal reform or even, until late in the colonial period, for a sentence of punishment. Walker (1980:47) reminds us that the American colonists "took a pessimistic view of humankind: man was a depraved creature cursed by original sin. There was no hope of 'correcting' or 'rehabilitating' the offender. An inscrutable God controlled the fate of the individual." Accordingly, the penitentiary had no place in the Puritan world.

The Puritan view of crime and punishment was, on the whole, a harsh one. Still, the notion of who was an offender under God's inscrutable control was applied with considerable compassion, at least in the early days of the colonial experience, when towns were small, intimate communities and those who turned to deviance were seen as wayward citizens—fallen neighbors rather than evil criminals. For at least at the outset of the colonial experience, Puritans maintained that criminality, like disease, was treatable *if* it was caught early:

> Criminal tendencies were frequently equated with an infectious and progressive disease. If discovered before the criminals had slid too far and become "harden[ed] . . . in their evil courses," there was hope for them. But if the infection could not be arrested, as demonstrated by repeated offenses, a criminal would be deemed "incorrigible" and dealt with accordingly. (Hirsch, 1982:1222–23)

When a person's transgressions were few or minor, and hence criminality was seen as in its early stages, the Puritans saw punishment as a vehicle of healing and reintegration. Communities were close, intimate; the offender was typically a neighbor, someone you cared about and hoped to save. "The first impulse of all concerned," notes Hirsch (1982:1223–24), "was to heal the wounds as best they could." The pillory and stocks, for example, at least as originally used in Puritan villages, were meant to admonish the offender and to draw him back into the fold. The miscreant was placed on a wooden frame or platform with holes into which his head and hands (and in the stocks, his stocking feet, hence the name stocks) were locked securely. Often, a sign or placard would indicate the offense in question. Passersby were invited to express their contempt for the offender's behavior. The message embodied in this punishment was, in essence, "shame on you; you know better; change your ways while you still can." Exclusionary punishments, like banishment, mutilation, and the death penalty, marked a person as permanently beyond the protection of the community. They were used only as a last resort in the colonies, especially the Massachusetts Colony.[2]

But times change, and with them, the meaning of crime and punishment changes as well. As the population of the Massachusetts Colony grew during the eighteenth century, the various communities making up the colony became less stable; residents were more transient, communities less intimate. The offender was, in fact as well as perception, more often a stranger than a wayward neighbor. As a stranger who made trouble for the good people, he was seen as an evil being; typically, he was seen as "a member of antagonistic subculture" and a villain pure and simple (Hirsch, 1982:1240). In this context, the old ways of public punishment backfired. A reprimand from a neighbor may move one to repent; censure from an authority will likely harden and embitter. The pillory and stocks, which often included whipping, became occasions of alienating humiliation rather than exercises in moral reeducation. Such punishments "destroyed the fear of shame," noted a social commentator in 1784, "and produce[d] a desire of revenge, which serve[d] to stimulate their vicious inclination" (quoted in Hirsch, 1982:1233).

Shameless criminals rather than contrite wayward neighbors came to dominate the ranks of the deviant. It is against this backdrop, in what can be described as the comparatively impersonal communities of eighteenth century colonial America, that incarceration as a formal banishment became more common. At this juncture, it would be fair to say that colonists began to punish offenders with a growing vengeance because God's will demanded it. The underlying notion was that all laws "were ultimately God's laws and to fail to enforce them would compound the ill by offending against Him" (Sherman & Hawkins, 1981:81). Punishment at this point in history was expected to produce few social benefits. Perhaps fittingly, little was expected of the prisons of this day, other than incapacitation.

Ironically, public punishments lingered for a brief time in colonial prisons, the very institutions that had arisen to take the place of now-defunct community punishments. Here, it was presumed, a community of sorts still existed. "Most ironically," states Hirsch (1982:1242), public punishment

> lived on for a short time within the walls of the State Prison itself. By statute, violations of prison discipline were punishable by up to thirty lashes, and a platform was constructed in the prison yard on which offending prisoners were forced to stand, holding signs or wearing dunce caps. Even as public sanctions were discarded by society at large, they were retained by the very institution that was to serve as a substitute. Of course! The penitentiary was one "community" in Massachusetts still intimate enough for the old formulas to remain effective.

As it turned out, these prisons, in Massachusetts and elsewhere in the Colonies, did not house communities in any meaningful sense of the term. Public prison punishment died out quickly, in part because the practice was seen by the convicts not as moral education but as raw abuse. As had occurred in the free world, prisoners subjected to these public punishments were alienated rather than reclaimed by this treatment.

Likewise, efforts to place admonitory placards and signs strategically about the prison compound, drafted from the practices of Puritan villages as a means to instruct and chastise wayward convicts, proved short-lived. Coffey, writing in 1823 about the New York State Prison, describes these signs, most calling prominently for repentance, as utterly ridiculous in the eyes of the prisoners.

> The Inspectors, grasp at every opportunity of shewing a reformation in the convicts, through their immediate means. They state in their report, to the Legislature, that on the 24th of April, 1822, "they placed boards in different parts of the prison yard, on which are sentences of admonition; such as reminding the prisoner of the evil consequences of transgression, and the folly of being self tormentors; which has operated powerfully upon the minds of many" ... When they were affixed in the prison yard, the convicts were perfectly surprised at the imbecility that had suggested them. Some of them most wittily paraphrased several of the inscriptions; many ridiculed and laughed them to scorn; and others openly pitied the impotency of the Inspectors. (Coffey, 1823:194)

Colonial prisons, like most if not all early prisons, were not intimate communities but impersonal institutions marked by brutality and neglect. These prisons served as places of confinement—as jails, perhaps—that offered few comforts. With the exception of brief and misguided efforts at public punishment and moral instruction, these institutions made no pretense at reform or rehabilitation. The grim quality of life within their environs is captured in the very term *jail* or, in its English variant, *gaol* (which has the same pronounciation). As Hirsch has observed, "The Latin root of the word 'jail' (or 'gaol') is 'gaviola,' which means cage or hole." As Hirsch wryly notes, "This probably indicates the earliest form of this familiar institution" (see Hirsch, 1982:1180).

Even the first American prisons, built after the Revolution in the closing decades of the eighteenth century, were not meant to be penitentiaries—places of correction—but were erected as specters of punishment and deterrence.[3] They were forbidding in appearance, and their internal policies of punishment were notoriously harsh. Few believed or even "imagined that life inside the prison might rehabilitate the criminal. . . . A repulsion from the gallows rather than any faith in the penitentiary spurred the late eighteenth century [prison] construction" (Rothman, 1971:54; see also Mazur, 1989). These prisons were, by all accounts, deplorable; their counterparts in England were known by the telling designation *Squalor Carceris*, which could have applied with equal force to the American institutions.[4]

At least one such American prison, Newgate Prison, built in Connecticut in the 1770s, was essentially a large hole in the ground, carved from a rock cavern. Prisoners lived like lepers within this underground world, mingling without supervision or restriction, in conditions that would parallel those of the Mamertine prison (see Durham, 1989). Interestingly, there are similar accounts of life in the Thomaston Prison in Maine. Dating to 1870, well into the era of the penitentiary, they reveal that Thomaston was also little more than a pit dug deep into the ground, the better to bury alive its inhabitants, whose lives in confinement were marked by unsupervised congregation, chronic hunger and hard labor (Moore, 1892). To be sure, Thomaston was an anomaly for late nineteenth-century prisons, most of which bore at least some traces of the penitentiary model, but the larger point is that reforms spread unevenly across social institutions like the prison. Long after the advent of the penitentiary, then, primitive prisons offering unadulterated punishment were still to be found throughout the New Republic.

The first American prison reform group, established in the latter part of the eighteenth century, set for itself the task of "alleviating the miseries of public prisons," which were by all accounts legion (Norris, 1985:82). The most notable of these problems was the prevalence of contagious diseases. "Early prison reformers," Norris (1985:82) reminds us, "had good reason to suspect that gaol fever killed more inmates than the death penalty." One observer characterized the prisons of this day as less healthy than a "pest house in times of plague" (Norris, 1985:82). London's Newgate Prison (not to be confused with Newgate Prison in Connecticut, described above, though conditions were essentially the same in each institution) provides a telling case in point. It was, noted Byrne (1989:25), "a prison whose stench in warm weather forced neighboring shops to close, a prison which no doctor would visit, a 'tomb for the living'" (Byrne, 1989:25). Though repellent and life-threatening—in a word, squalid—Newgate was an altogether unremarkable institution in its day.

Among the earliest prison reforms in both England and America was the separation of prisoners, where possible, into cells or some other form of relatively isolated quarters. (As we noted in Chapter One, before the advent of penitentiary reforms, prisoners lived like lepers, often in groups mixing men, women, children, and even animals.) Separation was accepted as a penological principle because it prevented or at least reduced the spread of disease among the prisoners and those who associated with them, primarily their keepers and the agents of the court. The excesses of *Squalor Carceris* were originally moderated, then, not for humanitarian reasons but because the diseases bred by such confinement "came to be seen as a threat to the well-being of society" (McConville, 1981:86). It took some time before separation was also seen as a means of preventing moral contamination and ultimately as a vehicle for reforming the prisoner (McConville, 1981:98). Only gradually, then, were reformers able to "make our prisons Penitentiary Houses and places of correction" rather than stark and disease-infested human warehouses (ACA, 1983:14).

AN AMERICAN PLAGUE OF DEVIANCE:
AN ENLIGHTENED QUARANTINE

The first American penitentiary, the Walnut Street Jail, was erected in 1790. The construction of penitentiaries was not undertaken on a large scale, however, until the Jacksonian era, between 1820 and 1830 (Rothman, 1971). From the outset, penitentiaries were meant to be experiments in rational, disciplined living that combined punishment and personal reform. They can be seen, in part, as the culmination of a number of penal innovations originating in Europe, particularly in England and Scotland.

The British Influence

The main predecessors of the American penitentiary are the English Bridewell of the mid-sixteenth century and its various offspring, which include the English and Scottish Houses of Correction (often called, simply, "bridewells"), as well as the famous Rasp Huis of Amsterdam, upon which many subsequent European prisons were modeled (McConville, 1981:22–23). In McConville's words,

> Bridewell was an attempt to entrust imprisonment with reformatory and punitive objectives, which were to be secured by a closely regulated regime. This use of prison was a radical departure from existing practice . . . [and] can truly be treated as the first example of modern imprisonment.

There were also several local English prisons that approximated the penitentiary design, culminating in 1789 in Petworth Prison. According to McConville (1981:95), Petworth

> consisted of thirty-two cells on two floors; a separate system . . . chapel of thirty-two pews; two infirmary rooms, and two turnkeys' rooms. There were four airing yards, in each of which one prisoner at a time was exercised for one hour; for the remaining twenty-three hours of each day they were locked up except for attendance at (daily) divine service. Petworth was the first prison in which building and system of discipline were so closely related.

The Edinburgh (1795) and Glasgow (1798) bridewells deserve mention. Each afforded the keepers easy surveillance of their charges. The architecture of the Glasgow bridewell "appears to have been the closest approximation to Bentham's panopticon ever constructed" (Dobash, 1983:11). Its circular formation of cells allowed the keepers, located in a cylindrical observation post in the center or core of the cell block, ready visual access to all prisoners at all times (hence the notion of a "panoptical" or all-seeing architectural plan). There was, finally, England's National Penitentiary at Millbank, which opened in 1816. Its charter, drafted in 1811, described Millbank as "a system of imprisonment not confined to the safe custody of the person, but extending to the reformation and improvement of the mind, and operating by seclusion, employment and religious instruction" (quoted in McConville, 1981:131). Millbank proved to be a curious and ultimately unworkable amalgam of competing administrative systems designed to achieve punishment and correction (McConville, 1981:140). It should be noted that none of these institutional regimes appear to have been carried into practice on a scale commensurate with that of the first American penitentiaries or with the devotion to detail and plan shown in the American institutions.

The Enlightenment and Prison Reform

The emergence of the penitentiary in America naturally reflects widespread social forces at work at the turn of the nineteenth century. In particular, the penitentiary was affected by a number of trends that made the resolution of such social problems as poverty, mental illness, and crime appear to be within easy reach. The most general of these was the spirit of the Enlightenment, per-haps best captured in Locke's assertion, widely endorsed in intellectual circles at the time, that the mind is at birth a *tabula rasa* or "blank slate" upon which Nature, following Laws that can be studied, fashioned a person's character and predilections. This was taken by American reformers to mean that one could understand deviance as a worldly problem, specifically an environmental prob-lem, and do something about it. A penitentiary—a prison that provided a healthy environment and hence reformed criminals—was possible.

To the American and, to a lesser extent, the English prison reformers of this time, the Enlightenment was an invitation to social engineering with criminals (see Rothman, 1971:57). Yet neither Locke nor any of his fellow philosophers envisioned the prison as the setting of enlightened punishments (Norris, 1985:9). This partly reflects the dominance of *Squalor Carceris* during their time. That most unenlightened form of incarceration made the galleys and even the notorious hulks look more promising as avenues of punishment (Norris, 1985). A more fundamental obstacle to an enlightened penitentiary, however, was the possibility that Locke's *tabula rasa* was indeed a blank slate: we may not come into the world with a conscience, the source of the penance integral to the penitentiary.

> Duty, Locke had insisted, was not inscribed on the human heart. It was an obligation learned through the rewards and punishments that a child re-ceived at the hands of authority. People were rational enough to discern the good, Locke believed, but if their moral socialization was faulty, there was no inner voice of conscience to call their ego back from its restless search for pleasure. . . . [Hence] Locke . . . had been dubious about the reclamation of offenders. He doubted that they had a conscience to work upon . . . [and] dismissed them as slaves, whose wrongdoings conferred on society the right to exploit them as it saw fit. (Ignatieff, 1978:71 & 73)

Reformers simply glossed over this gloomy aspect of Enlightenment thinking, which would seem to anticipate modern concerns with anti-social personali-ties and the difficulties one faces in moving such persons to feel for and relate civilly to others. Instead, penitentiary-era reformers simply assumed, as do many reformers even today, that offenders are basically like them, just mis-guided. Hence these reformers assumed without supporting evidence that soli-tude, discipline, and religious instruction would rouse *any* prisoner's conscience and move him to repent.

Social Sources of Prison Reform:
Optimism Amidst Chaos

Fatalism about crime and deviance was dead. This was nowhere more in evi-dence than in America. To the social reformers of early nineteenth-century America, social problems begged for social solutions. Belief in a potentially ra-tional, comprehensible, and, above all, malleable universe fit especially nicely with the mood of an America standing at the threshold of a rich and uncharted world. America, only recently liberated from England, was in its adolescence, and was moved by the energy and idealism of youth. The new world would be rid of such old (and Old World) problems as poverty and crime.[5] In this context, corporal punishment seemed primitive and capital punishment barbaric. The warehouse prison looked little better. These punishments were vestiges of the Old World. In the New World, by contrast, it was self-evident that the criminal was not a preordained sinner; his fate was not sealed by the Almighty. He was, instead, a product of society. And while he deserved punishment for his crimes, he also deserved to be reclaimed by and for the society. The penitentiary, the first prison systematically designed to harness pain in service of the reformation of men, thus embodied a glorious reform dream, providing a new prison for a new world.

Yet the New Republic was a tumultuous place, for with an open future came an unstable present. As the nineteenth century unfolded, America was an increasingly impersonal capitalist nation with growing urban centers of production. Small-town agrarian America, the America of cozy colonies with village artisans and small farms, was on the decline. The old folkways were gradually breaking down, or at least seemed fragile and easily corrupted in this new environment. Crime and other social ills were on the rise (Lane, 1979 & 1980), including the emergence of urban mobs and occasional riots, sometimes associated with public executions.[6] Neither family nor church nor school seemed able to hold the line against the forces of disorder that were sweeping over the young American cities. To the growing middle class, from which much support for the penitentiary was drawn, these various signs of social decay were especially repugnant. This group, Mazur (1990:8) observes, "dreaded vice, craved order, advocated self-control, and valued social privacy." Public punishments were seen by this elite as crass and brutalizing, and as invitations to unruly mob behavior. Private punishments, notably indoor executions (held within prison walls) and the use of the penitentiary, offered the hope of civilized sanctions that might shield offenders from these sources of corruption and move them to repent (see Mazur, 1990).

The New Republic was indeed a different place from its colonial predecessor, and at least in terms of the quality of community life, most of the differences seemed bad. Rothman (1971:70–71) tells us that during this period, biographies of criminals painted "a dismal picture . . . of a society filled with a myriad of temptations" awaiting the person who ventured out into its crowded, corrupt places.

> It was almost as if the town, in a nightmarish image, was made up of a number of households, frail and huddled together, facing the sturdy and wide doors of the tavern, the gaudy opening into a house of prostitution or theater filled with dissipated customers; all the while, thieves and drunkards milled the streets, introducing the unwary youngster to vice and corruption. Every family was under siege, surrounded by enemies ready to take advantage of any misstep. The honest citizen was like a vigilant soldier, well trained to guard against temptation. Should he relax for

a moment, the results would be disastrous. Once, observers believed, neighbors had disciplined neighbors. Now it seemed that rowdies corrupted rowdies.

Moreover, one's neighbors, rowdy or not, were less likely to take responsibility for their fellows, especially their marginal and troublesome fellows. For in a burgeoning capitalist economy, the web of community relations inexorably gave way to impersonal wage relations (Scull, 1977:2425) and greater personal freedoms (Ignatieff, 1978:212). Those unable to cope on their own— orphans, the poor, the mentally ill—were a burden that individuals increasingly passed along to the state, which was fast becoming the new "community" and indeed even the new "parent" in modern society (Kittrie, 1971). Criminals, whose adjustment problems were thought to overlap quite a bit with the dependent classes, also became the province of the state. A panoply of state institutions—orphanages, poor houses, insane asylums and penitentiaries—originated or proliferated at this time, and quickly became the option of first resort for the management of delinquents (Rothman, 1971). Their shared mission was to instill in wayward citizens the discipline and self-control essential to a productive existence in the changing social order that would culminate, within a scant few decades, in the Industrial Revolution (Rusche & Kirchheimer, 1939; Foucault, 1977; Ignatieff, 1978; Dobash, 1983).

A Punishment for the Times

The shift from a local and largely community-based response to deviance to a centralized and institution-based response had many causes and consequences that are beyond the scope of this book. For our purposes, it is essential to note that the reformers and legislators who supported the penitentiary did so with one firm criterion: that the punishment be humane and not replicate the brutal punishments of the past (Norris, 1985). Against a backdrop of social chaos and disorder, punctuated on occasion by such official barbarities as public corporal punishment and execution, the penitentiary appeared to be a more civilized sanction than any other in use at the time.

Painful, certainly. After all, solitary confinement cells, central to the penitentiary regime, had from the very first policy of segregation in the early American prisons been "branded in the public mind as punishment cells, for the protection of society and for the infliction of the hardest endurable conditions" (Sherman & Hawkins, 1981:85). There were no illusions about the fact that confinement was painful. But there was a strong and deeply rooted belief that this type of pain could be uplifting, purifying, redeeming pain. This belief is as old as the Bible, and one can be sure that most Americans of this time read the Bible with care and devotion. Indeed, supporters of the penitentiary displayed an almost religious faith in the reformative powers of enforced solitude. They did not hesitate to confine even minor offenders under conditions of physical isolation or its functional equivalent, silent congregate confinement.

Why was there so much enthusiasm for the penitentiary regime? One reason was its religious appeal, its claim to set the wayward straight with man and

God. "Religion," Norris (1985:11) observes, "played an important role in the emergence of the penitentiary." The great awakening of religious sentiment in the United States and England was, in large measure, the source of a rising tide of humanitarian activity during the early decades of the nineteenth century. This, in turn, contributed greatly to the prison reform movement that gave birth to the penitentiary (Norris, 1985). An even stronger attraction of the penitentiary was its clean, calculated rationality. The penitentiary may have been compatible with the Bible but it was a child of the Enlightenment, a monument to reason and restraint in a world too often beset by needless irrationality and senseless passion. Reason and religion were thought to merge in the operation of the well-ordered penitentiary. By its ubiquitous "authority of rules," the penitentiary made both the prison officials and the prisoners conform to a regime that was rational and moral, where formerly irrationality and corruption had prevailed (Ignatieff, 1978:77). It bears noting that the juxtaposition of reason and religion as bulwarks of the penitentiary seemed quite natural to many of the prison reformers of the day. Thus it was that Benjamin Rush, a prominent figure in the penitentiary movement, "viewed imprisonment as a rational humanitarian punishment that would 'pierce the soul' of the offender" (Norris, 1985:13).

To the enlightened mind, there must also have been a pleasing egalitarianism and a simple elegance to the prison, a sanction that assessed the wages of crime in neatly calibrated units of time. As Foucault (1977:232) has said,

> How could prison not be the penalty par excellence in a society in which liberty is a good that belongs to all in the same way and to which each individual is attached . . . by a "universal and constant" feeling? Its loss has therefore the same value for all; unlike the fine, it is an "egalitarian" punishment. The prison is the clearest, simplest, most equitable of penalties.

Likewise, the notion not only of reform but reform through a scheduled, ordered, disciplined life of work and solitary reflection must have seemed in itself the very apotheosis of the Enlightenment world view. In Bentham's view, drawing explicitly on Lockean psychology, criminals were victims of a stunted social growth that left them like children in need of daily structure and control of the sort only a penitentiary regime could afford (Hirsch, 1982:1203). They represented, in Bentham's words,

> a particular class of human beings, that, to keep them out of harm's way, require for a continued length of time that sort of sharp looking after, that sort of peculiarly close inspection, which all human beings, without exception, stand in need of, up to a certain age. (Quoted in Hirsch, 1982:1203)

Community sanctions were entirely inadequate with these essentially overgrown children, Bentham maintained, because, lacking a disciplined regime, they were "radically incapable of administering that corrective aid which, in the case in question, is so perfectly indispensable" (quoted in Hirsch, 1982:1203).

Of particular concern was the much-despised laziness of the delinquent. Indeed, combatting the "habit of idleness" was central to the penitentiary's rehabilitative agenda. As Hirsh has observed, the answer was a regime built around hard and unremitting labor.

> The challenge of rehabilitation lay in destroying the "habit of idleness" and replacing it with a "habit of industry" more conducive to an honest livelihood. The therapy, at once depriving the deviant of old habits and instilling the new, was hard labor. (Hirsch, 1982:1205)

The penitentiary's reformative regime of discipline, though extreme by today's standards, was arguably not unlike that of other institutions of the day. It was, in Foucault's (1977:233) words, "rather like a disciplined barracks, a strict school, a dark workshop, but not qualitatively different." Offenders, we shall see, had a very different view of the world they inherited at the grace of reformers, but it cannot be denied that, to reformers and even the ordinary citizens of the day, the penitentiary was thought to be eminently rational, fair, and familiar. It seemed to guarantee the proper measure of pain for the times, "the most immediate and civilized form of all penalties" (Foucault, 1977:233).

The penitentiary sought "a just measure of pain" for the delinquents under its care (Ignatieff, 1978). Implicit in the operation of the penitentiary is an appeal to the conscience of a prisoner, whose repentance is sought on the premise that guilt is a more civilized and reliable taskmaster than fear (Ignatieff, 1978:211). But only just punishments evoke guilt. As a result, "the efficacy of punishment" in the penitentiary "depended on its legitimacy" (Ignatieff, 1978:72). To feel guilt, as opposed to fear or even terror, offenders had to believe that they deserved their punishment. Harsher punishment meant more guilt and hence more profound personal reformation, but only if such punishments were administered under "the strictest standards of justice and morality" (Ignatieff, 1978:72). Such deserved punishments offered the prisoners

> no psychological escape into contempt for the punisher, assertions of innocence, or protests against its cruelty. Nothing in the penalty's infliction would divert offenders from contemplating their own guilt. Once convinced of the justice of their sentence and the benevolent intentions of their captors, they could only surrender to the horrors of remorse. (Ignatieff, 1978:72)

The prisoner of the penitentiary, then, was to be bound by "cords of love," a thoroughly modern punishment that would immobilize him "in guilty remorse" (Ignatieff, 1978:74). His guilt, in turn, was meant to bring home to him his personal responsibility for his shameful and degraded state before both God and man; formerly, social class or, more generally, fate were thought to explain a man's standing in the moral universe (see Sennett, 1981)—hence the justice and urgency of the penitentiary prisoner's repentance, which was to make amends for his personal failings (Dobash, 1983). Suffocating cords of love would be fashioned by the chaplain, that ever-present font of religious and moral instruction in the penitentiary, whose sermons and ministrations "would enclose [the prisoners] in the ideological prison" (Ignatieff, 1978:75). Thus, in the ideal penitentiary,

> No rough or brutal hands were laid upon the offenders. The state, as it were, struck off their chains and withdrew, leaving them alone with their conscience. In the silence of their cells, superintended by an authority too systematic to be evaded, too rational to be resisted, prisoners would surrender to the lash of remorse. (Ignatieff, 1978:78)

The disciplined and spiritually pure inner world of the penitentiary seemed to make it an ideal setting for the punishment and reformation of the social misfits of the day. In the most general sense, it quarantined criminals from a world that was too much with them, providing an isolation that was painful but curative; at once a severe punishment but also a haven for the harried soul and a medium for its regeneration.[7] At bottom, the penitentiary sought a humane but harsh rendering of the Enlightenment's search for rational, correctional punishments. It sprang from a "hard faith in human malleability" under proper conditions and "epitomized the liberal utopia of a punishment so rational that offenders would punish themselves in the soundless, silent anguish of their own minds" (Ignatieff, 1978:213).

MODELS OF REFORMATIVE PENITENTIARY QUARANTINE

The Separate System

The American penitentiary initially reflected two models of reformative quarantine. Each called for isolation, silence, obedience, and work, and sought some form of repentance and hence reformation of the offender. The first version was the separate system, originating in Philadelphia at the Walnut Street Jail and sometimes called the Philadelphia or Pennsylvania System. The regime was one of solitary confinement and manual labor, a simple monastic existence in which the prisoners were kept separate from one another as well as from the outside world. Describing this system, Beaumont and Tocqueville (1833/1964:57) observe that its advocates

> have thought that absolute separation of the criminals can alone protect them from mutual pollution, and they have adopted the principle of separation in all its rigor. According to this system, the convict, once thrown into his cell, remains there without interruption, until the expiration of his punishment. He is separated from the whole world; and the penitentiaries, full of malefactors like himself, but every one of them entirely isolated, do not present to him even a society in the prison. If it is true that in establishments of this nature, all evil originates from the intercourse of the prisoners among themselves, we are obliged to acknowledge that nowhere is this vice avoided with greater safety than at Philadelphia, where the

prisoners find themselves utterly unable to communicate with each other; and it is incontestable that this perfect isolation secures the prisoner from all fatal contamination.

Imprisonment was meant to involve a complete and austere system of moral quarantine. The prisoner served time in a manner reminiscent of the monk of antiquity, the heretic of the early Middle Ages, the citizen of the medieval plague-town. The sentence was officially measured in loss of freedom, following the conception of time and wage labor specified by Melossi and Pavarini (Chapter One, Note 6). But the aim of punishment was penance resulting in purity and personal reform. At issue was a fundamental change of character, a conversion. Here the penitentiary was a "place of penance" in the full sense of the word. Even the prisoner's labors, essentially craftwork, were intended to focus his consciousness on the simple things of nature and hence to bring ever to mind the image of his Maker. For the prisoner of the separate system, there was to be no escape from his cell, his thoughts, or his God.

But the separate system, for all its asceticism and simplicity, was expensive. The overhead costs admittedly were low. Solitary confinement required only a skeleton staff to administer the daily requirements of life, since the prisoners never left their cells and hence did not require much supervision (Melossi & Pavarini, 1981). However, solitary confinement required spacious (and therefore expensive) cells (Beaumont & Tocqueville, 1833/1964). Solitary confinement also restricted prison tasks to what could be achieved by the simple artisan, which generated little income for the prison and reflected, in any case, the economic realities of a rapidly passing era. There was, one might say, much industry but little profit (Conley, 1980:257). The penitent artisan was dwarfed in productivity by his contemporary in the factory workshops of the congregate prison. Thus it was not long before the separate system was modified or abandoned in favor of that system, and the solitary artisan joined the prison's congregate factory workforce.

The Congregate System

The alternative penitentiary model is referred to as the silent or congregate system, or simply as the Auburn System, after the first prison of this type. Once again the outside world was kept at bay, the prisoner securely entombed within the penitentiary walls.

> "The prisoner," a [prison] chaplain of this period recalled, "was taught to consider himself dead to all without the prison walls." And the warden himself repeated this analogy when instructing new convicts on their situation. "It is true," he told them in 1826, "that while confined here you can have no intelligence concerning relatives or friends. . . . You are literally buried from the world." (Rothman, 1971:95)

Prisoners of this system slept in solitary cells. They congregated for work and meals, but only their bodies mingled. Silence reigned throughout the prison. "They are united," observed Beaumont and Tocqueville (1833/1964:58), "but no moral connection exists among them. They see without knowing each other. They are in a society without intercourse." There was no communication and hence no contamination. Each man left his cell for the greater part of each day, primarily for work and sometimes also for meals, but he carried his own prison within him. He and his fellows gave a special meaning to the term "prison within a prison." For here "everything passes," in the words of Beaumont and Tocqueville (1833/1964:65),

> in the most profound silence, and nothing is heard in the whole prison but the steps of those who march, or sounds proceeding from the workshops. But when the day is finished, and the prisoners have retired to their cells, the silence within these vast walls, which contain so many prisoners, is like that of death. We have often trod during night those monotonous and dumb galleries, where a lamp is always burning: we felt as if we traversed catacombs; there were a thousand living beings, and yet it was a desert solitude.

Here, too, penance and purity were sought; solitary penance by night, pure labor by day, silence broken only by the sound of machines and tools. Throughout, the prisoner "has time to think of . . . his crime and his misery" (Beaumont & Tocqueville, 1833/1964:66). The congregate system retained the monastic features of the separate system, in its solitary cells and silent labor, but blended them with a more contemporary lifestyle. A monastery at night; by day a quasi-military organization of activities (all scheduled), movement (in unison and in lockstep), eating (backs straight, at attention) and work (long hours, usually at rote factory labor) (Rothman, 1971:105–106). The daily routine at Auburn is succinctly described by Beaumont and Tocqueville (1833/1964:65–66):

> With daybreak, a bell gives the sign of rising; the jailors open the doors. The prisoners range themselves in a line, under the command of their respective jailors, and go first into the yard, where they wash their hands and faces, and from thence into the workshops, where they go directly to work. Their labor is not interrupted until the hour of taking food. There is not a single instant given to recreation. . . . In the evening, at the setting of the sun, labor ceases, and the convicts leave the workshops to retire into their cells. . . . The order of one day is that of the whole year. Thus one hour of the convict follows with overwhelming uniformity the other, from the moment of his entry into the prison to the expiration of his punishment.

Regimentation of a most pervasive nature was thus the cornerstone of congregate prison life.

The Systems Compared

These systems reflected not only competing blueprints for personal change but also competing notions of what constituted rehabilitation. The separate system sought a change of heart, a fundamental conversion of the human spirit. Its product was to be a Christian gentleman of virtue and integrity. The congregate system set for itself a more modest agenda. An alteration of habit, of character-in-action, was deemed sufficient. Virtue for its own and God's sake was the ideal, Auburn advocates would acknowledge. It was hoped that silent laboring days and solitary contemplative nights would encourage communion with God and effect a transformation of at least some of the wayward prisoners' souls. But simple conformity to the prison routine—a life of pure habits if not pure intentions—was enough to get a prisoner by in the congregate system. Such persons could be expected to desist from further crime, observed Elam Lynds, warden of Auburn Penitentiary, and some "even become useful citizens, having learned in prison a useful art, and contracted habits of constant labor" (Beaumont & Tocqueville, 1833/1964:164). This, Lynds argued, was the only reform prison could produce and, moreover, "the only one which society has a right to expect" (Beaumont & Tocqueville, 1833/1964:164).

The merits of these reforms were debated hotly and at great length. Could one make a man virtuous or obedient in a penitentiary? What was the value of such an enterprise to society? Would a virtuous man also be useful in society? Would an obedient man honor the spirit and not just the letter of the law? Much was made of the allegedly destructive effects of solitary confinement, the hallmark of the separate system. Southey and Coleridge, describing a prison run on the solitary system, captured the public image of solitary confinement as an inherently evil enterprise:

> As he went through Coldbath Fields he saw
> A Solitary cell:
> And the Devil was pleased, for it gave him a hint
> For improving his prisons in hell.
>
> (In Byrne, 1989:73)

Charles Dickens, following a visit to Eastern Penitentiary, run on the solitary system, concluded that isolation did more damage to inmates than corporal punishment. Though this claim was never substantiated by research, Clear and Cole note that "the public became aroused by reports that prisoners were going insane because they were unable to endure long-term solitary confinement (1990:78).[8] In the end, however, the details of the penitentiary regime in America, and the practical definition of rehabilitation embodied in that regime, were determined as much by financial matters as by the merits of either penological perspective or by any alleged psychological effects of these penal regimes.

Early penitentiaries had to contend with the chronic deficit under which their predecessors, the warehouse prisons, had been run. These deficits "resulted . . . essentially from two causes: the high cost of supervision and the non-productiveness of institutional labour" (Melossi & Pavarini, 1981:125). Each of the original penitentiary models addressed itself to one of these economic realities: the separate system reduced supervision costs, while the congregate system increased the productivity of inmate labor. Neither system was profitable or even covered its operating costs, but the Auburn system was considerably less expensive.[9] It became the model for the American penitentiary at least in part because it provided an affordable quarantine against the dangers and corruptions of the larger world.

The congregate prison was also more modern than the separate system, and this was certainly part of its appeal. Its use of what Rothman (1971:105–106) has termed a military regime[10] for the greater part of daily life, rather than the purely monastic regime of the separate system, was a more timely model of the good and proper life. The American male of the New Republic could more readily see himself in the good soldier, obedient to law and discipline, than in the pious monk in continuous and solitary communion with his God. (It is worth emphasizing that he probably could see himself in both; the difference would be one of degree.) At the same time, the congregate arrangement presented a more intimidating, and hence deterring, picture of prison life. These observations are implicit in Rothman's contention that the congregate penitentiary was meant to be a compelling utopian venture for an America trying to find an old and familiar order in a new and changing world.

> The functioning of the penitentiary—convicts passing their sentences in physically imposing and highly regimented settings, moving in lockstep from bare and solitary cells to workshops, clothed in common dress, and forced into standard routines—was destined to carry a message to the community. The prison would train the most notable victims of social disorder to discipline, teaching them to resist corruption. And success in this particular task should inspire a general reformation of manners and habits. The institution would become a laboratory for social improvement. By demonstrating how regularity and discipline transformed the most corrupt persons, it would reawaken the public to these virtues. The penitentiary would promote a new respect for order and authority. (Rothman, 1971:107)

Yet the originality and ultimately the strength of the congregate system lay not in its military bearing or even in the contemporary American utopia it may have embodied. Rather, the staying power of this system "lay essentially in the introduction of work structured in the same way as the dominant form of factory work" (Melossi & Pavarini, 1981:129). It is the use of factory work that largely explains why congregate prisons were less expensive to run than their competitors (Conley, 1980:257). The relationship between the prison and factory is, however, more complex than a matter of comparative operating costs. At issue is the interplay between broad economic realities and another utopian vision embodied in the penitentiary, that of the perfect factory.

ECONOMIC SYSTEMS AND PRISON SYSTEMS

Typically, the nature of a society's economic system influences and even determines the nature of its prison system. This was true for the fully developed penitentiary and it was also true for other types of prisons. Connections between economic systems and prison systems can in fact be traced to the very origins of systematic or disciplined confinement.

Links of this sort have not been continuous or inevitable, however. For most of the eighteenth century, for instance, when there was presumably a growing need for a disciplined work force, confinement was superseded by punishments that were "direct and physical," usually followed by incarceration in a primitive gaol and then by transportation to one of the colonies (Dobash, 1983:6). (*Squalor Carceris* was at its height at this time; most bridewells and houses of correction deteriorated dramatically during this period.) These harsh punishments reflected social tensions, most notably an increasing intolerance of crime and deviance as the last remnants of feudalism gave way to a more fully capitalist system. The result was that "the English and Scottish aristocracy and the emerging bourgeoisie became more detached from the common people, who were increasingly seen as insolent, rebellious, tumultuous and dangerous" (Dobash, 1983:6), and hence surely beyond the reach of ameliorative confinement. However, by 1775, as a consequence of the American Revolution, transatlantic transportation was no longer available, and a growing population of unruly poor people had to be managed on British soil. (Transportation of criminals to Australia was still possible, but it had become a costly and unpopular option.) At this point, according to Dobash (1983:7), "the modern penitentiary emerged" in England and Scotland "as one of many institutions created to tighten and extend control over the labouring poor" and impose some semblance of discipline in their otherwise chaotic and unproductive lives.[11]

The penitentiary emerged, then, not only because it was functional; it would have been functional in the sixteenth century as well. The penitentiary came into being as a major institution of punishment at least in part because there were no cheap alternatives. Evidently the English would rather have simply gotten rid of most of their criminals, and indeed did just that until transportation became unworkable. Note that banishment or transportation, the standard substitutes for incarceration, were either unavailable or impractical in America, particularly after the Revolution when the British, too, were forced to deal directly with their criminal population. It was at this point that prisons, and soon thereafter formal penitentiaries, became a major form of punishment in both England and America.

Disciplined Labor: The Penitentiary and the Factory

The penitentiary and the factory share common historical origins. The sixteenth-century English bridewell and subsequent houses of correction were the early models of both institutions. In Dobash's (1983:4–5) words,

> As forerunners of the factory some correction houses reached a considerable level of manufacturing sophistication and the labour power of inmates was harnessed for several materialistic purposes.... With the significant exception of solitary confinement, these houses of correction [also] exhibited the fundamental principles upon which the modern penitentiary would be established in the 19th century.

Both the penitentiary and the factory came into full flower at roughly the same time (mid-nineteenth century), and were marked by a forbidding environment, a rigid routine, and disciplined labor (Rothman, 1971; Ignatieff, 1978). During "the 1820s and 1830s," Rothman (1971:105) reminds us, the factory, like the penitentiary, "was also beginning to use rigorous procedures to bring an unprecedented discipline to workers' lives. . . . Both organizations were among the first to try to take people from casual routines to rigid ones." To a degree they were architectural models for one another, particularly the factory for the prison. A "popular alternative" to the military fortress prison "was to construct the prison along factory lines—a long and low building, symmetrically arranged with closely spaced windows, all very regular and methodical. Whatever it lacked in grandeur it tried to make up in fixity and order" (Rothman, 1971:107).

The penitentiary and the factory did more than develop along parallel lines. In some instances, at least, they responded to the same social realities in mutually reinforcing ways. Thus each institution would, by propagating similar architectural and administrative designs, validate the other as a way to organize human materials for productive activity. And together they would, in effect, encapsulate a considerable contingent of common laborers. For as a practical matter, the fate of many nineteenth-century laborers was to work at some form of disciplined labor, usually in either a free-world factory or in a penitentiary; in the latter case, sometimes in a factorylike building and almost always at factory labor. The alternative was to starve. For the spirit if not the letter of the seventeenth-century Poor Laws remained in force; in the colorful yet heartless language of that system, the policy was that "The Sluggard shall be cloathed in Raggs. He that will not work shall not eat" (Scull, 1977:28). The odds were good that the recalcitrant and hungry laborer would sooner or later turn to crime (to eat!) and then find himself in a penitentiary, where he would be fed but forced to work at the very factory labor he resisted in the first place.

There is also an interesting correspondence between the penitentiary as an emerging reformative agent and the needs of the newly developing capitalist industrial system. This has led Scull (1977:30) to speculate that reforming criminals was essentially a way to expand the factory labor pool. Though there is no evidence to support the view that this was a conscious or salient intention of reformers, it is reasonable to suppose that the correspondence of life in the prison and in the factory would be a source of some encouragement for prison administrators, implying that their reform labors were in step with the times. And the means of reform used in the penitentiary—emphasizing discipline in one's life and one's labor—"mimicked the discipline necessary for the factory system" and was, on its face, a plausible way of "instilling the virtues of bourgeois rationality into those segments of the population least amenable to them" (Scull, 1977:26).

It is telling that at this juncture, as Melossi and Pavarini (1981:144 & 148–49) make clear, the penitentiary inmate, particularly the prisoner of the silent congregate regime, served time in what amounted to a mute factory compound, surely the capitalist's utopian dream of docile labor in the emerging industrial age. Here the propertyless worked meekly in service of those with property, and they did not so much as break step or utter a word of complaint! This industrial view of utopia has roots in a shared vision of prisoners and workers, at least at the birth of these institutions. As Melossi and Pavarini (1981:188) put it, "'for the worker the factory is like a prison' (loss of liberty and subordination); 'for the inmate the prison is like a factory' (work and discipline)." There is, then, "a dual analogy: prisoners must be workers, workers must be prisoners." One source of appeal of the penitentiary is its image as a setting that offers the prospect of transforming lazy and shiftless unemployed offenders into productive industrial workers, in the literal sense of this phrase: "the production of proletarians by the enforced training of prisoners in factory discipline" (Melossi & Pavarini, 1981:144). The regimented life and labor of the separate system builds the disciplined character essential to modern life, including the role of the factory worker; but the silent congregate regime goes a step further, seeming to mold this character quite precisely to the conditions of factory work.[12]

Triumph of the Congregate System

We are presented, then, not only with two types of penitentiary and two notions of personal reform, but also with two visions of the ideal world. The first, the separate system, seeks to shape good and proper men, men of disciplined habits and solid virtue, but men also possessed of a preference for simple labors and solitary pursuits. Its imagery is pastoral and its products would seem more at home in a village shop than in an urban factory. Graduates of the separate system are living paradoxes: they display a modern (disciplined) character wedded to antiquated predilections. The prison that spawns them is costly, dated, and never takes root; it is an uninspiring utopia, at least in the expansionist, forward-looking American context. Only a handful of American penitentiaries were built on this model, and none survived long.[13]

The congregate penitentiary, by contrast, seeks to forge a crude urban creature, a tame proletarian worker, oppressed and angry but hungry and compliant: a man for the times forged by a prison for the times. The penitentiary regime that shapes him is, if not pure, at least mechanically precise. The body functions as a machine; the mind is channelled by habit. The administration of the prison moves with the same cadence. It represents a flowering of bureaucracy, in this instance a fairly simple and primitive bureaucracy, but nevertheless an organizational form that is "capable of attaining the highest degree of efficiency" (Weber, 1947:337) and which, in fact, "compares with other organizations exactly as does the machine with non-mechanical modes of production" (Weber, 1946:214). The prison machine is guided by an administrative machine producing men to live and work in a world of machines. The ambiance or image of this penitentiary is military, as Rothman makes clear. But the underlying reality is better described as a testament to the machine and the modern factory age from whose dominant imagery it draws its ethos. Regimentation, discipline, and precision represent not merely ingredients of penitentiary life but its very essence. The disciplined spirituality of the monastery thus had made a modern home in the New Republic: in the congregate penitentiary, at work in a factory, governed by a bureaucracy, enclosed in a military compound, and free from contamination by the plague of deviance and disorder lurking just beyond the prison walls.

PART TWO: INSIDE THE PENITENTIARY:
THE HUMAN LEGACY

For all the rhetoric that praised penitentiaries as experiments in human reform, they offered at best only a deceptive facade of humanity. For all the social theory that links the emergence of prisons to the forces that shaped the factories of the Industrial Revolution, a factory that takes human beings as its raw material is a unique—and uniquely destructive—enterprise. These broad generalizations about penitentiaries and the larger social forces of the time offer insights, to be sure, but they do not tell us about the penitentiary as it was lived, as the institution it was in reality as opposed to principle or design.

From the point of view of the prisoners, pain, both physical and psychological, was a central feature of the penitentiary regime. Prisoners were treated more like slaves than factory hands, and admittedly some factories in the free world during the era of the penitentiary imposed conditions of virtual slavery on their workers. Life in the penitentiary was anything but uplifting; while some prisoners coped better than others, most adjusted poorly. Life in the penitentiary was, in the main, lonely and depressing, and left little room whatsoever for adult autonomy. There was also the crucible of fear, for penitentiaries from the outset were maintained by the threat and practice of violence. In the terms set out in the first chapter of this book, the penitentiary was a profoundly indecent and inhumane institution.

In some cases, there was not even a pretense at humanity. In Virginia, a bill passed in 1796 required that prisoners

> be clothed in habits of coarse materials, uniform in color and make, and distinguishing them from the good citizens of this commonwealth; and the males shall have their heads and beards close shaven at least once in every week, and all such offenders shall, during the said term, be sustained upon bread, Indian meal, or other inferior food . . . and shall be kept as far as may be consistent with their sex, age, health and ability, to labour of the hardest and most servile kind. (Keve, 1986:54)

As Keve observes, the *intention* was to debase and degrade. Men were meant to feel demeaned by their uniforms; they were meant to be hungry and uncomfortable and tired by their daily life in the prison. The term penitentiary was entirely empty of meaning in this context.

Conditions in America's penitentiaries were grim. It was common for the sick and lame to live on short rations because they were less useful workers than their healthy and more robust counterparts (Brice, 1839:52). Periodically, all prisoners in a given institution would face virtual starvation. In the words of one penitentiary convict,

> In the month of January, 1838, I worked in the stone quarry. There were at this time probably about 30 hungry starving men sent into the kitchen to receive some cold victuals, and I myself saw Robert Wiltsie go into the kitchen with a cane and drive them all out; and then he followed them through under the arch, and as I was going up the hill towards the quarry I looked behind me and saw the poor men running with all their might to save themselves from the weight of his vengeance. And what was their crime? Why they had been sent there by their respective keepers, upon complaining of hunger, to receive a pittance of necessary food! (Brice, 1839:64)

Lawes reports that at Sing Sing, the "Prisoners' diet was barely enough to keep body and soul together. Two eggs a year for each man, the records show. Famished prisoners timidly entered the mess kitchen to beg for more food but were driven away, probably lashed for their temerity." One result was a spate of epidemics that claimed many lives. "Dysentery, scurvy, Asiatic cholera, smallpox—all took their overwhelming tolls" (Lawes, 1932:87).

Daily discomforts were the norm in the early penitentiaries. When prisoners weren't starving, they craved food that was palatable. "When food was more plentiful," Lawes states, "it was plain and unappetizing, and unvarying" (1932:87). The term unvarying was meant literally. A convict at Maine's Thomaston penitentiary reports that "There was no change in the food of the prison from one year's end to another" (Moore, 1892:383). The same meal for years on end! As Moore's account makes clear, to call that meal "plain and unappetizing" is an understatement of considerable proportions.

> For breakfast and supper it was a dipper of rye coffee and a loaf of bread, which was often sour. For dinner, it would be salt fish, cooked with the bones, skin and scales, and some unpeeled potatoes, with a small slice of salt pork, or baked beans, stewed beans, salt junk and potatoes, or stewed pease. This was the bill six days of the week, with cold brown bread for dessert; but the seventh day we were given bone-marrow and gristle soup. (Moore, 1892:383)

Hungry men found few distractions from their discomfort. Clothes fit poorly, as did shoes. Uniforms, often featuring stripes, made men look like dishevelled zebras, an image both ridiculous and embarrassing (see Lawes, 1932). (At least one proposal to make "hard time harder" in today's prisons features a return to striped uniforms. See Nossiter, 1994). Of course, no special effort was made to outfit the prisoners; with the rule of silence, prisoners had great difficulty communicating even roughly appropriate sizes to their keepers. Clothes and shoes were, literally, thrown to—or at—silent convicts who had to take what they got.

> The tailor throws out the clean clothes by guess to the applicants, and the shoemaker does the same, without being permitted to speak a word. Such

as are given them they are obliged to put on and go away in silence, whether they are too large or too small it makes no difference. (Brice, 1839:33)

The scene would be humorous if it didn't portray yet another indignity visited upon the hapless convicts.

Hygiene was virtually absent. Baths were taken in groups, some as large as fifty, and were over in seconds. One Illinois State Penitentiary convict reported that they are called "lightning baths," which well describes their character. Lightning strikes rarely, it turns out, and moves on quickly to the next batch of men (Elgar, 1886:29). Even more rare was recreation time in the prison yard. In the early penitentiaries, there was no yard time whatsoever. By 1880, some prisons offered up to five hours a year, this meager amount "doled out on major holidays" (Moore, 1892:566).

Yet putting grim conditions aside, it is fair to say that penitentiaries, even the best ones, were profoundly and inherently destructive enterprises. Reformers were no doubt sincere when they described penitentiaries as punishments very much in step with the times, but to the prisoners themselves, these settings were profoundly alien and uninviting. "For a moment," said one prisoner, expressing a common sentiment, "I asked myself whether I was upon another planet or still upon the same old mother earth?" (Elgar, 1886:5). Rothman comments on what he terms the "'made on Mars' character of the asylum," a characterization that tells much about the origin and impact of this institution:

> The nineteenth-century asylum, whether in Europe or in the United States, did not replicate an already existing institution within the society. It was not a faithful re-creation of the army or the church monastery or the factory, although bits and pieces of each of these organizations entered its design. The pre-modern jail was the town writ small, a reassemblage within a city gate or tower keep of the tavern, the bawdy house, the artisan shop, and the family household. There was nothing imagined about the jail. But in confronting the asylum, we leave the real for what historian Robin Evans has so aptly called the fabricated. Or in the words of another historian, Robert Castel, the asylum presented the need "to construct from nothing a new social laboratory in which the whole of human existence could be programmed." In effect, the asylum first had to be imagined and then translated into reality. (Rothman, 1990:xxvii)

An anonymous prisoner, writing about his experiences in the Wyoming penitentiary at the turn of the twentieth century, after the institution of the penitentiary was in place for some time, penned his memoirs under the heading, "I felt like I must be entering . . . another world" (see Olson, 1975). This nameless prisoners' writing, though barely literate, reflects a central theme in the prisoners' view of the penitentiary. Almost to a man, inmates found the penitentiary to be an alien experience—another world, one for which little in their lives prepared them to cope.

Central to the alien and generally harmful impact of the penitentiary was the rule of silence, which lay at the heart of the penitentiary regime. Enforced silence may sound innocuous at first blush. Certainly reformers never discussed the burden this rule would impose, but rather thought of it as a vehicle of personal reform, perhaps even a blessed respite from the chaos and confusion of daily life. Convicts took a dimmer view of this undertaking.

As well they might: communication is basic to human nature. Communication allows for projects that reflect and sustain autonomous action. Security requires reassuring communications with others in one's environment. Indeed, it may be impossible to feel secure if one is rendered silent. Communication is certainly at the heart of relatedness to others. All relations require communication of some sort. Thus, much of what expresses our distinctive individual humanity is banned under this rule. Seen in this light, the penitentiary's imposed rule of silence is fundamentally dehumanizing.[14]

This pernicious rule, moreover, was enforced with considerable vigor at many penitentiaries. Witness the words of Captain Lynds, first warden of Sing Sing, a passionate advocate of the silent system.

> It is the duty of convicts to preserve an unbroken silence . . . They are not to exchange a word with each other under any pretense whatever; not to communicate any intelligence to each other in writing. They are not to exchange looks, wink, laugh, or motion to each other. They must not sing, whistle, dance, run, jump, or do anything which has a tendency in the least degree to disturb the harmony or contravene to disturb the rules and regulations of the prison. (Quoted in Lawes, 1932:72)

Lawes, warden of Sing Sing in the 1920s and 30s, described Lynds's commitment to the rule of silence as a species of hysteria (1932:72). That is, perhaps, a generous assessment. From our vantage point, something on the order of a lunatic level of control is sought in this rule. It is as if the very humanity of the prisoners was itself deeply offensive and hence had to be suppressed at each and every turn by the keepers, lest they be sullied by human contact with their charges.

Convict accounts provide a glimpse of the human experience offered by the stultifying penitentiary regime. The view is a revealing and disturbing one. Take, for example, the ubiquitous lockstep. Here men are made to move in unison, like parts of a vast machine. Two accounts follow, one from a penitentiary at the midpoint of the nineteenth century, the other in the first decade of the twentieth century.

> The bell taps, and the guard calls, "Time, step"; at the word "time" each prisoner sways his body to the right, raises his left foot, and brings it down with a sharp stamp. This is done with the greatest precision, the whole line swaying and stamping at once, so the sound is as of one mighty stamp. It fairly makes the ground shake . . . At the word "step" each man swings out his left foot, and away we go, very slow, with that steady, measured sway, sway, tramp, tramp, that once seen and heard is never forgotten. (Anonymous, 1871:46).

> The long line of prisoners, in stripes and lockstep, resembles an undulating snake, wriggling from side to side, its black-and-gray body moving forward,

yet apparently remaining in the same spot. A thousand feet strike the stone floor in regular tempo, with alternate rising and falling accent, as each division, flanked by officers, approaches and passes my cell. . . . Head bent, right arm extended, with hand touching the shoulder of the man in front, all uniformly clad in horizontal black and gray, the men seem will-less cogs in a machine, oscillating to the shouted command of the tall guards on the flanks, stern and alert. (Berkman, 1970:99–100)

The mindless marching process can become habitual, to the point where people find themselves locksteping on their own, to their considerable embarrassment.

You will often see one man come up behind another in crossing the yard; as soon as he is within reaching distance, up goes his hand, and that without thinking. I have seen him take it down and look all round sheepishly to see if any one had noticed him. . . . I expect when I go from here the first man I overtake, or come up behind, on the street, I shall slap on the shoulder and take up the lock-step. (Anonymous, 1871:47)

So too can simple, docile obedience become a matter of habit. One prisoner, a newcomer, offers telling observations about the control of prisoners in the mess hall. The prisoners far outnumber the guards, but guards need not lift a finger to keep them in line; the penitentiary routine is their master.

Dinner over, we remained seated, waiting the return of the guards from theirs. As I looked over the sea of heads, I involuntarily searched for the restraining power that held this vast assemblage of assorted desperadoes in check. Only three free men were present, the deputy warden, and a guard seated in a high chair at each end of the hall; and they without arms or means of defense, other than a small walking-stick, which they usually carry. Some of the more timid carry clubs. I could not help being astonished. I was prepared to see numerous guards heavily armed; here were four hundred of what the community called the worst of men, all guarded and held in perfect subjection by three unarmed citizens. (Anonymous, 1871:52–53)

The capacity for social control in this world—that is, control that emanates from the power of routine to suppress or suspend the humanity of the prisoners—could be remarkable, even to those held in thrall by the penitentiary regime.

But such control was by no means uniform. Accounts of trouble and disorder in the penitentiaries are fairly common. Coffey, writing in 1823, gives a laundry list of penitentiaries and their lapses in social control:

The convicts of the Philadelphia prison, the mother of the Penitentiary establishment in America, have rushed, frequently, upon their officers; have broken the walls, and sawed off the gratings of the windows, in order to escape; and are continually in tumult. In New Jersey, I believe the prison was once actually wrested from its officers, by a few desperate convicts, and its doors thrown open, for the escape of the rest. In Maryland and

Virginia, the convicts have been, frequently, detected in their attempts, and many, I am credibly informed, have escaped. And in Connecticut, New-Hampshire and Massachusetts, it requires the greatest vigilance, to keep them in peace and security. (Coffey, 1823:24)[15]

Considerably more common are reports of corruption of the penitentiary routine. The Maryland Penitentiary, for example, was unable to maintain the basic rule of silence. In a revealing general commentary, Gettleman (1961:278) observes that "The Baltimore prison, *like many others of the day*, was a disorderly, unexemplary institution, and its reputation had reached a low ebb by the middle 1820s" (emphasis added). A full decade later, things at this penitentiary were, if anything, even worse:

The directors of the Baltimore prison sadly noted, in 1837, that "in respect to the great moral objects of a penitentiary" the history of the Maryland Penitentiary "is similar to that of most of the others in the country; it has fallen far short, hitherto, of the sanguine hopes and expectations . . . of its founders and supporters and friends of humanity in general." (Gettleman, 1961:277)

The power of observation in the hands of officials enabled them to impose strict discipline in public places like workshops, mess halls, chapels, and during lockstep marches from one place within the prison to another. Talking in such contexts, when it occurred at all, was generally limited in nature and carefully disguised. Still, one could at least gain a primitive sense of the biographies of one's fellows. The following is an account of surreptitious talk carried out in a penitentiary workshop in Southern Indiana State Prison.

Each man who passed me, without ever turning his head or appearing to notice me at all, saluted me with a whispered "where from?" and as he returned, "how long?" very soon he would manage to pass again with, "what for?" and going back, "think you will have to stay it?" Then came, "married or single? live in this state? how old?" and a hundred kindred questions, partly in whispers, and partly in pantomime. I think I was thus interviewed by every man in the shop before night. (Anonymous, 1871:42–43)

Cells allow a degree of privacy. When more than one man is placed in a cell, which happened frequently due to overcrowding, prisoners could, at least on occasion, talk more or less openly among themselves (see Anonymous, 1871:1865–69). Tiers and sometimes entire cell blocks would sometimes be poorly supervised. Communication and interaction would then be possible. In these cracks in the penitentiary routine, a rudimentary prison culture would emerge. Generally, the culture would be a destructive one, in which the worst criminals set the tone for the others. A poem by a penitentiary prisoner, written in 1823, captures the raw elements of this culture:

Here dissipation, vice and folly stare;
Here the base heart is fearlessly laid bare;

Here the weak head is open'd to your sight;
Here ignorance, falsehood, misery and spite
Stalk in your view.[16]

If control was not uniform, neither was it in any sense voluntary. Control did not emanate from the good will of the keepers or the kept, promises of penance and reformation notwithstanding. From the outset, the contrast between the penitentiary's generally well-ordered exterior and the brute force within that made this possible was quite stark, especially in the case of the congregate system. This disparity is well illustrated by Kingston Penitentiary, a Canadian prison described by Charles Dickens as "an admirable jail, well and wisely governed and excellently regulated in every respect" (ACA, 1983:47). But life there was, beneath the surface, a testimony to repression and violence.

> The guards had to "preserve unbroken silence" between inmates, who "must not exchange a word with one another under any pretence whatever and must not exchange looks, wink, laugh, nod or gesticulate to each other." The convicts were to yield "perfect obedience and submission to their keepers" and were, at all times to "labour diligently." Corporal punishment was inflicted for the willful violation of any of these duties. It is reported that a 10-year-old inmate, Peter Charbonneau, who was committed in 1845 [one year after Dickens's visit), was lashed repeatedly for such violations. "Charbonneau's offences were of the most trifling description such as were to be expected of a child of 10 or 11, like staring, winking, and laughing, and for these, he was stripped to the shirt and publicly lashed 57 times in 8 1/2 months." (ACA, 1983:47)

It was impossible to maintain the rigid discipline sought in congregate penitentiaries without resorting to violent corporal punishment, even at Auburn, the acknowledged model institution.[17] At Auburn and elsewhere, getting recalcitrant men to labor in silence proved to be no easy matter. "The problem of enforcement in the congregate system," observed Rothman (1971:101), "raised the dilemma of whether obedience was worth any price." Many prison officials seemed to think it was. "Sing Sing officials in the 1830s were prepared to use every possible form of correction to enforce order. . . . Guards relied freely upon the whip, unhesitatingly using it for the smallest infraction, and their superiors defended this behavior vigorously" (Rothman, 1971:101).

Some notion of what a regular practice of flogging entails is provided by Brice, himself a penitentiary convict:

> Reader, if you could but once witness a state prison flogging. The victim is stripped naked and beaten with a cruel instrument of torture called a cat, from his neck to his heels, until as raw as a piece of beef. I have seen men flogged until their shirt adhered to the flesh; yes, I have seen the backs of some in such a situation that they smelled of putrefaction. The cat consists of a piece of hickory wood about three feet long for a handle, at one end of which is fastened generally about seven small lashes, which are

twisted so hard that they cut and sink into the flesh nearly equal to wire. I have heard those who were suffering under that instrument scream murder so loud that they might be heard a great distance. (Brice, 1839:69)

Sing Sing officials were by no means alone in their commitment to violent punishments, the persistent screams of prisoners notwithstanding. Many other institutions made regular recourse to corporal punishment to maintain discipline.

The whip was commonplace in Auburn and in Charlestown, in Columbus and in Wethersfield. Pennsylvania had recourse to the iron gag, Maine to the ball and chain, Connecticut to the cold shower. And officials wholeheartedly defended these punishments. (Rothman, 1971:102)

Bizarre as it may seem, at least one prison enforced a policy in which violent prisoners whipped one another into submission. Describing one such case, Thompson (1847/1969:358–59) reports:

It is a rule, that if two prisoners fight or quarrel, they will certainly be punished. . . . The prisoners were stripped of coat and shirt—their left hands tied together—a raw hide given to each—and the command, "Now take satisfaction out of each other!" It was cut and slash, over the eyes, the head, or the back, where they thought they could get the most "satisfaction," till one cried "enough," and they were parted.

Thompson went on to wonder what type of men would, in his words,

feast themselves, in seeing their own species act the part of wild beasts, and witness with ecstatic delight, scenes which would make an angel weep and put humanity to blush. (Thompson, 1847/1969:358–59)

Other convicts posed similar questions in their memoirs, though perhaps less eloquently. For it is certainly the view of many inmates that brutal officials are at the root of the abuses so rampant in the penitentiary. Various inmate accounts describe guards as drunken, vulgar, sadistic brutes who abuse convicts at will. In these accounts, guards comprise

the worst men that society could produce; not possessed of common morality; drunkards, swearers, &c. &c.[sic] They were actually monitors of crime for the instruction of the convicts. I have heard them indulge themselves in the most obscene and wicked conversations, with vulgar, profligate and abandoned convicts, to the manifest corruption of many within their hearing. I have heard their profanity, their cursing and their swearing, and have wondered at its known toleration by the Inspectors. And I have not unfrequently, seen them staggering, from intoxication about their shops, abusing every convict whom they casually met, and venting their vulgarity without blushing or reserve. (Coffey, 1823:22)

At the hands of these vile men, "Scarcely a night passes," laments one convict, "but some poor prisoner is dragged from his hard bed and scourged on some lame pretext, merely to gratify the passion of some brutal guard" (Anonymous, 1871:99).

Even granting the veracity of these accounts, the problem of corporal punishment in the penitentiary was not fundamentally one of bad men or bad faith, though both were in evidence on some occasions. (Elam Lynds, Auburn's first warden, was most certainly a mean man who broke faith with penitentiary prisoners. Others like him filled lesser roles in Auburn and elsewhere.) Rather, the threat of violence would seem to be implicit in the act of imprisonment itself. Indeed, violence would seem to be a convenient adjunct to any institution meant to corral and control persons defined as impure and hence worthy candidates for pain. The combination of imprisonment and corporal punishment, in turn, sets the stage for regimes of torture (see Newman, 1983:91), and in fact many penitentiaries more closely resembled houses of torture than houses of correction, whatever the intentions of the reformers or administrators.

The seemingly natural potential for violence in prison, and ultimately for regimes of torture, is accentuated when rules for the use of corporal punishment are vague or nonexistent. Ironically, this was the case in quite a few of the early American penitentiaries, which seemed to have rules for everything but the administration of corporal punishment (see, Moore, 1892:562–63). There were, for example, no written regulations regarding the use of the whip at Auburn or Sing Sing, and even the "inferior agents" (the guards) were authorized to impose this punishment at Sing Sing on a regular basis and at Auburn "in all cases of urgent and absolute necessity" (Beaumont & Tocqueville, 1833/1964:75–76). The prevailing view among the inspectors of the penitentiaries, not to say the wardens themselves, was that "the danger of abuse, is an evil much less than the relaxation of discipline produced by want of authority" (Beaumont & Tocqueville, 1833/1964:206).

To be sure, violent punishments were not the norm in all institutions. In Wethersfield, for example, where the use of corporal punishment was considerably less frequent than at other congregate penitentiaries, written regulations constrained the use of violence. "The regulations of the prison are in writing. The subaltern officers can in no case exercise the right of punishing, with which the superintendent alone is invested, and which he uses with so much moderation" (Beaumont & Tocqueville, 1833/1964:76). Yet moderate authority and restrained punishment were exceptions, and rare exceptions at that, rather than the rule. Violent punishments seemed to flow naturally and with little restraint from the harsh and rigid discipline that marked the penitentiary, particularly since that discipline was explicitly undertaken for the laudable purpose of personal reform. As Rothman (1971:102) explains,

> Penal institutions' widespread and unembarrassed reliance on harsh disciplinary measures [reflects a] close fit between the punitive measures and the reform perspective. . . . Confident that the deviant would learn the lessons of discipline in a properly arranged environment, everyone agreed that prison life had to be strict and unrelenting. And with regularity a

prerequisite for success, practically any method that enforced discipline became appropriate.

As a result, Rothman (1971:260) continues, "It would not be a simple matter to distinguish between the corrections of a sadistic keeper intent on terrorizing his charges and the punishment of a benevolent superintendent trying, in the fashion of the day, to rehabilitate them."

Industrial Violence: Work as Corporal Punishment

So, too, could one confuse the conditions of daily work in the penitentiary with a regime of violence, such as would support work on a slave plantation instead of a factory for the reclamation of men. Who can doubt the implicitly violent conditions of work in factories such Indiana State Prison's trip hammer shop in the 1870s, known to its involuntary laborers as a hell on earth?

> Crossing the yard, we entered a long, low shop, where the din of hammers and the glow of fires both deafened and blinded me. This was the trip-hammer shop, denominated by the men as "hell." And standing in the door, as we stood, and looking down its dusty length, the lurid fires gleaming on their raised platforms, the hot, gaseous air, the horrible din, the half-naked, sweating, swarthy, smoke-begrimed workers passing to and fro with slow and measured steps, or swinging the molten iron from furnace to hammer, turning and fashioning it beneath its powerful strokes, the red sparks sprinkling hot cinders around, one could easily imagine that he stood upon the brink of the "horrible pit," watching the angels of darkness as they fashioned by fire the souls of the dead damned. (Anonymous, 1871:34)

Prisoners worked in silence, and could not, under threat of corporal punishment, raise their eyes from their work without permission. Shops such as this one were quite common in American penitentiaries.

The penitentiaries were caught up in what Shayt (1989:933) has called "the nation's industrial fervor." Unlike the case in European penitentiaries, where the essentially labor-wasting treadmill came to be a salient feature of confinement, most American prisons were subdivided into various shops producing "not only shoes, clothing, and light hardware, but furniture, rifles, steam engines, boilers, silk, and clocks" (Shayt, 1989:933). Said Joseph Hook in 1837,

> I consider the Maryland Penitentiary nothing more than a great state manufactory. The punishment there inflicted has, in my opinion, produced no salutary effect upon the morals of the prisoners. (Quoted by Gettleman, 1961:286)

Prison critics like Hook observed that concern for production outstripped concern for retribution, which would have been ideally served by the humiliating treadmill; or for penance, which would have been better sought in solitary reflection upon the Bible.

Prisoners were not only denied any moral education in such manufactories; conditions of work frequently could be brutal. Often, prisoners were leased to capitalists and treated like slaves, or, to quote a prisoner of the day, "beasts of burden" (Anonymous,1871:282). The very routine of work was often dehumanizing. One can see parallels between the dehumanizing lock-step that conveyed prisoners to and from work and the routine that prevailed during the prisoners' labors:

> I know men here who for years have stood in the same spot, and done the same work over and over, and over again, until the very sameness of life is wearing the souls out of them. Each morning they take their stand, and, as the machinery begins to move, from mere force of habit so do they, and with no more concern than the pulleys and saws that are buzzing around them. They do their work, but they manifest no interest in what they are doing; they are human mills, automatically grinding out the uncertain grist of life; each day is a grain from their hour-glass of time; each year a toll from their three score and ten—a cog from their wheel of life, which they thank God is gone; a revolution that is only the winding up of a weary, wretched existence. (Anonymous, 1871:67)

Such work is entirely without rehabilitative value. Here the worker is al-most literally a cog in a mechanical production process, and he never sees or understands the whole; hence he learns no trade (Anonymous, 1871:68–69). The worker's ignorance is almost certainly an intended result. For it was be-lieved by officials that convicts get proficient at piecework and produce more for the contractor than would be the case if they were shifted about to do all aspects of the trade (Anonymous, 1871:73). It was considered equally undesir-able to provide books, other than Bibles, since books provided pointless dis-tractions from a regime of work (Anonymous, 1871:282). Hence, as an in-tended result of the organization of work, prisoners left these institutions with no marketable skill. Predictably, they would get discouraged and return to their old ways (Anonymous, 1871:73).

In the penitentiary, then, the lash of the whip, administered to maintain discipline or to promote productive labor, took precedence over the lash of the conscience. Discipline stemmed from violence, and the dominant ethos of the institution was dehumanization, the violation of the human spirit.

The Penitentiary in Perspective

By the end of the nineteenth century, the penitentiary had deteriorated from a productive (if oppressive) factory with at least a rhetorical commitment to the reform of men to a custodial warehouse for social refuse. The problem stems, in part, from a disjuncture between the purposes of the penitentiary and the kinds of people it confined. From the outset, the penitentiary was de-signed "not for the hardened professional but the good boy gone bad, the amateur in the trade" (Rothman, 1971:247). Such offenders might well read the Bible, reflect upon their errors, labor obediently, and repent. Amenable offenders of this sort were, however, always in the minority; the courts always sent incorrigible offenders to the penitentiary and used less restrictive op-tions (like assignment to apprenticeships or placement in almshouses) for the less serious offenders. Gradually, these more amenable offenders became candidates for the newly emerging Progressive programs such as probation (see Chapter Three), and were nowhere to be found within penitentiary walls. As a result, the penitentiary was filled—and after the Civil War period, crowded—with recidivists and other serious offenders.

And increasingly, the penitentiary's hardened criminals were drawn from immigrant stock. Prisoners came to be seen more as pariahs who should be banished from society and less as wayward fellow citizens who were candidates for reform (Rothman, 1971). They faced long sentences, ostensibly because time was needed to establish firmly the good habits upon which rehabilitation was presumed to depend. But by this time prison officials and the larger society had lost faith in the reformative powers of discipline; custody rather than rehabilitation was the order of the day (Rothman, 1971).

Prisons opened at the turn of the century reflected this trend. They were "industrial prisons" in which inmates labored to defray operating costs and to fill idle time; little attention was given to the notion of personal reform (Conley, 1980). In effect, these "fallen penitentiaries" were settings of purposeless, gratuitous pain. They simply carried on the custodial warehousing agenda of the earliest prisons in a disciplined and regimented fashion.

If anything, prison factories became more oppressive in the industrial prison era. Even the rhetoric of penance had been given short shrift. Prisons ran on the Auburn plan, replete with rules of silence, solely because it was productive to do so. "Prison officials had come to view their charges as a mere commodity, an adequate supply of which was essential to the continuing quest for profits (Hougen, 1977:308). Work was often sabotaged; sometimes shop officers and even the warden carried a gun to maintain order (Moore, 1892:578). Brutal punishments, including what amounts to medical torture to keep workers on the job, became the norm.[18]

The decline of the penitentiary as a productive milieu was hastened by the closing of markets for prison-made goods. Prison industry at its best had never been especially productive, but now the penitentiary regime of work and worship was utterly pointless. With the larger mission of discipline reduced from the noble goal of reform-through-hard-work-and-honest-living to the more mundane aim of storage and control, the officials' enthusiasm and commitment to the penitentiary waned. Prisoners settled into the routine combining make-work and idleness that remains a salient feature of most modern prisons (see Hawkins, 1976 & 1983). Lapses in discipline became more common, and the fixed patterns of inmate life that characterized the original penitentiary gradually gave way to a subcultural world in which the inmates, as a group, became a force to be reckoned with. Simply issuing orders, even when backed by corporal punishment, was no longer enough to maintain order. Social control required collusion with the tougher convicts, who became *sub rosa* agents of the officials. Control also required violence, by both these convicts and the staff, far in excess of that associated with corporal punishment. This period was probably the most corrupt and brutal in American prison history, and marked the demise of the penitentiary as an instrument of reform (Rothman, 1983:636).

THE CUSTODIAL CHALLENGE

The penitentiary was always, in practice, a custodial institution. It demanded absolute obedience from criminals who "had never learned to respect limits," follow rules, or put in an honest day's work (Rothman, 1971:103) and who, moreover, were the "filthy element" of society (Newman, 1978:187). The obedient inmate was to labor diligently and hence be a productive citizen of the prison if not of the larger society. He would be pure, or at least maintain the appearance of purity through his adherence to a mechanically precise mode of life. He would be a man of character, even if the substance of this character were an artifact of an externally imposed discipline. One might hope and even pray for a more lasting reformation of the prisoner, but one demanded compliance with the custodial regime.

A preoccupation with custody in the form of a disciplined regime marked by obedience and order, backed by violence, and maintaining only a pretense at reform, served as the foundation of the typical prison well into the twentieth century. In many prisons something bordering on an obsession with custody was only grudgingly modified over the last few decades. Rothman (1971:240) was surely right when he maintained that "the promise of reform had built up the asylums; the functionalism of custody perpetuated them."

It is a tragic irony that the penitentiary's promise of reform was, from the very outset, a hollow one. For the penitentiary, by its very nature, isolated offenders from the society to which they would one day have to return, and in that isolation made them into strangers in their own land, beyond the reach and care—and ultimately, the comprehension—of the free world. They were walled up and walled off from the world as we know it, entombed in a society of the dead. In these curious prison catacombs, "the rehabilitative focus shrank from the offender and his place in the community to the offender alone. His orientation was the only factor that the process sought to correct" (Hirsch, 1982:1268).

The communal wisdom of the Puritans, then, was completely abandoned. This sad fact was not lost on some early reformers, who openly bemoaned the fact that

> Convicts are discharged who have no friends, acquaintances or money; or who, by being known as convicts, are avoided as infections and driven by necessity to commit new crimes. They are willing to labour, but can get no employment; and cannot consent to starve, even at the hazard of renewed imprisonment. (Quoted in Hirsch, 1982:1268)

In this way the original penitentiaries, and virtually all prisons that followed in their wake, helped create and sustain what amounts to a criminal underclass, set apart from the larger community. The "ultimate irony," in Hirsch's words, is that the penitentiary "built a wall, instead of a bridge, between offenders and society" (Hirsch, 1982:1269). Offenders might well repent behind prison walls, Hirsch stresses, but society could not know and hence could not forgive and then accept reformed offenders back in their midst. As a result, "the concept of criminal incarceration was flawed from the start" (Hirsch, 1982:1269).

A telling illustration of the isolation of offenders from society was revealed in the growing stereotypes of offenders that sprang up in the wake of the emergence of the penitentiary. Visitors to these facilities would gawk and exclaim, and even bolt and run, when exposed to these now alien creatures. Coffey, himself a prison inmate, provides anecdotes on this score:

> I have heard children, while passing through the prison as visitors, with the utmost astonishment exclaim, as they narrowly eyed the convicts, "Why, dear me, they all look like men!" I have heard middle aged persons wondering that they were not chained; and I once remember to have seen an elderly gentlewoman, run, precipitately, out of one of the prison shops, because one of the convicts had merely moved from his seat. (Coffey, 1823:52–53)

With public punishments, at least, the offenders were recognizably human and remained members, however marginal, of the larger community.

In the isolated and isolating world of the penitentiary, custody readily becomes an end in itself, a substitution of order for meaning and purpose and of repression for human relationships. Custody is thus a basic and profound part of the heritage of the prison, with or without a professed agenda of reform. This is reflected in the prison's ancient origins as a project of exclusion and containment, and in its more modern disciplinary role. Thus, a custodial reality forms the backdrop against which both adaptation to the modern prison and its reform must be understood.

One challenge for contemporary penologists is to mitigate the pains of custodial confinement and hence to ameliorate pointless suffering. A more basic challenge is to fashion ways of living in prison that offer meaningful human relationships behind its massive walls, as well as sturdy bridges to the larger society of which we are all, ultimately, a part.

NOTES

1. Our passion for prison is still with us. Sherman and Hawkins (1981:86) tell us that "except for their ambivalent and intermittent support of capital punishment, Americans have always given imprisonment a monopoly over other forms of serious punishment. It has always been the currency of criminal justice." They are distinguishing between colonial America, where criminal justice reflected English law and featured corporal punishment, and America after the Revolution, when imprisonment became the favored punishment.

2. As Hirsch (1982:1228) has observed,

There remained one last set of punishments designed, not to reintegrate the offender into the community, but to cast him out of it once and for all. Banishment served as the ordinary mechanism whereby Massachusetts communities rid themselves of undesirables. Less common, but equally effective, were branding and mutilation, punishments that fixed upon the offenders an indelible "mark of infamy," to warn community members to keep their distance. Recourse to the gallows also took the offender out of the community, though this most final of all punishments was applied only in extraordinary cases.

3. The first of these was Connecticut's "mine prison," whose dank and desolate environs harken back to the early Roman prisons (most notably the Mamertine prison, which was discussed in Chapter

One, and the Lautumiae prison, mentioned in Note 5 of that chapter) (ACA, 1983:26–27).

4. These institutions reflected the thinking of the "classical" criminological scholars, notably Beccaria and Bentham. According to John Conrad, they saw prisons "as a means of rationalizing the processes of punishment"; for them, "the sentence of imprisonment implied a system of punishment rather than the exercise of vengeance by the state" (personal communication). The object of this system of prison punishment was "maximum general deterrence" (McConville, 1981:xi). Deplorable prison conditions were thought to be humane in the sense that they sacrificed only a few lives but saved many others by deterring would-be criminals (McConville, 1981:62).

5. As Melossi & Pavarini (1981:117–18) have noted:

The euphoria born of the knowledge that one was "living in a different world," the polemical willingness to highlight the new, and the immeasurable horizons still open to the young country, sharpened the critical faculty of American culture in its analysis of its own social reality. In this light, both the struggle against pauperism and the desire to defeat criminality were, on the one hand, seen as rightful movements in opposition to legacies from the old colonial period, that is, they opposed the reality linked to the Old World; on the other hand, these problems were seen as being, in any event, capable of resolution within the new economic context. . . . The optimism of an imminently bright future full of wealth and prosperity for all suffered no exceptions; this ideal tension thus cemented political commitment to the struggle against distress and poverty [and deviance generally] fought in the unwavering certainty of sure victory.

6. Once again, similar forces were at work in England, which was undergoing "a period of tumultuous economic and social change" during the period when penitentiaries were introduced (Ignatieff, 1978:211).

7. In Rothman's (1971:82–83) words,

The promise of institutionalization depended upon the isolation of the prisoner and the establishment of a disciplined routine. Convinced that deviancy was primarily the result of the corruptions pervading the community, and that organizations like the family and the church were not counterbalancing them, they believed that a setting which removed the offender from all temptations and substituted a steady and regular regimen would reform him. Since the convict was not inherently depraved, but the victim of an upbringing that had failed to provide protection against the vices at loose in society, a well-ordered institution could successfully reeducate and rehabilitate him. The penitentiary, free of corruptions and dedicated to the proper training of the inmate, would inculcate the discipline that negligent parents, evil companions, taverns, houses of prostitution, theaters, and gambling halls had destroyed. Just as the criminal's environment had led him into crime, the institutional environment would lead him out of it.

8. The use of solitary confinement is sharply limited in today's prisons because such confinement is seen as a species of cruel and unusual punishment. A notable exception, however, may be such "super-maximum" security prisons as California's Pelican Bay prison, which provide a rough parallel with penitentiaries run on the separate system. Prisoners of Pelican Bay, for example, are "completely isolated from the natural environment" and live within a prison world that is "tightly regulated" by the staff. They can speak and interact with others, but on a very limited basis. Evidence of "extreme psychological damage" has been produced by some researchers. Prisons like Pelican Bay are reserved for disruptive prisoners, and make no pretense whatsoever at reform. These prisons are few in number, but their popularity with prison officials may be on the rise. The constitutionality and humaneness of such prisons are very much in doubt (see Haney, 1993:3).

9. It is widely believed that early penitentiaries of the Auburn style were self-supporting and even turned a profit. Certainly the early financial reports of the wardens would indicate they were cost-effective undertakings, but the accuracy of these reports has been questioned (Conley, 1980; Melossi & Pavarini, 1981). As Conley (1980:262) has observed, "prison administrators were under intense pressure to show a profit in their annual reports." It is perhaps unsurprising that

they "consistently used shoddy accounting practices," which inflated the value of prison production (Conley, 1980:262). Significantly, appropriations of an "emergency" nature were routinely sought to keep the prisons in operation (Conley, 1980:262)

10. Alexander Pisciotta reminds me that this regime was military only in the most rudimentary sense; it is more accurate to say that the congregate penitentiary had a military image or ambiance. Later prisons, such as Elmira Reformatory, had quite explicit "military regimens replete with uniforms, bands" and other military accoutrements (Pisciotta, personal communication).

11. Elaborating on this point, Dobash (1983:7) has observed that

The generalized programmes associated with early mercantilism and the repressive measures of the 18th century were considered to be inadequate and ineffective. With the increasing consolidation of an industrial capitalist order based on factory production, a stronger work and social discipline was required for establishing virtues of sobriety, modesty and exacting habits of mind and body.

12. This line of thinking has recently been criticized as overly functionalist in its orientation. As Ignatieff (1991:177) has observed,

If prisons and factories came to resemble each other in their rituals of time and discipline . . . it was not because the state acted in response to the labor discipline strategies initiated by employers but because both public order authorities and employers shared the same universe of assumptions about the regulation of the body and the ordering of institutional time.

There is little doubt that a shared universe of assumptions is at play here, and that prisons did not develop their regimes at the bidding of prospective factory employers. But those very shared assumptions noted by Ignatieff and others may have made the work environment of the penitentiary a kind of model-in-miniature of the societal ideal to early reformers, who would be heartened by the notion that their reform labors might promote useful workers for the larger economy. The assumption that reformers saw themselves

as under some mandate to produce docile workers for employers who hungrily awaited them offers an overstated and almost conspiratorial view of the origins of the penitentiary. However, it is generally the case that during periods of economic growth, prison programs that seem to promise rehabilitated inmates capable of productive work are given much support by society in general, including prison officials and prospective employers. In the case of the early penitentiary, such forces may have been at work, with the result that one source of support in the society for the penitentiary, among many, was its apparent "production" of useful workers.

The role of the Auburn-style or silent congregate penitentiary as a model of an ideal society of disciplined workers and disciplined factory work environments is perhaps most clear in cases where this prison preceded the development of industrialization in the free world, in Oklahoma and perhaps most other Western states. In Oklahoma, the prison was explicitly seen by state officials "as a model for industrial growth" and a harbinger "of a new economic order" (Conley, 1980:259).

13. The separate system did, however, have considerable impact on penitentiary design in England and throughout continental Europe. There are a number of plausible explanations for this phenomenon. One would be that, in contrast to the Americans' open frontier with its emphasis on collective endeavor and its pressing demand for labor, the English and their European contemporaries were facing narrower social horizons and were possessed of a more inward-looking psychology. This social situation is compatible with the adoption of a separate penitentiary system over a silent congregate one. There may also have been among the British and Europeans a more literal commitment to the goal of penitence as the raison d'etre of the penitentiary (Dobash, 1983). Or, to put this point somewhat differently, they were less willing to tinker with the system and evolve pragmatic versions of isolation like those embodied in the silent system. Perhaps the Europeans simply had a deeper appreciation of the peculiar terrors of solitary confinement, which after all had marked many

instances of political punishment at the hands of monarchs and other powerful central authorities, and thus they were satisfied that such a regime could both deter and reform its subjects (Dobash, 1983:12–13; Norris, 1985). Be this as it may, the separate penitentiary system did not last long on British or European soil (McConville, 1981; Norris, 1985). As had been the case in America, this system proved uneconomical, out of step with the times, and injurious to the physical and mental health of the prisoners (Dobash, 1983:15–17; Norris, 1985). It was gradually replaced by a (nominally silent) congregate laboring system, with inmates deployed on various public works undertaken both outside and inside the prison (Dobash, 1983:16; Norris, 1985).

14. This same rule might well have profoundly different implications in a different environment, such as a monastery. But monks elect to enter monasteries, and hence their submission to rules of silence is voluntary. They are not rendered silent; they choose to be silent. They willingly forgo relations with others to achieve a fuller relatedness to God. Indeed, they find silence essential to their ends. They aspire to silence so that they can leave behind the world of men and women— the human world—and find peace of spirit in the world of God.

15. See also Hirsch, 1982:1255, and Moore, 1892:605.

16. The poet is named Rickman and is otherwise unidentified. The poem is quoted on the title page of Coffey, 1823.

17. Discipline was not considered to be a problem requiring corporal punishment at the Pennsylvania prison and its offspring; more solitary confinement in a "dark cell" proved to be a potent deterrent to misbehavior (Beaumont & Tocqueville, 1833/1964:72). As I have noted, however, the separate system did not take hold in America, so patterns of discipline at these institutions had little bearing on discipline in most American penitentiaries.

18. Hougen, for example, describes the alakazan degree, a common punishment at the Kansas State Penitentiary in the late 1800s.

". . . the "alakazan degree" consisted of shackling the victim's wrists and ankles, then drawing them together behind his back. Arnold's description is horrifying: "His feet are drawn upward and backward until his whole body is stretched taut in the shape of a blow. The intense agony inflicted by this method of torture is indescribable; every muscle of the body quivers and throbs with pain." In this excruciatingly painful position, the victim was locked inside a coffin-like box, known as the "crib," and left to moan out his misery to the walls of an empty cell. (Hougen, 1977:312)*

Olson reports on medical tortures in the Wyoming Penitentiary at the turn of this century:

one sunday when the church services were about over we could hear an unearthly yelling and moaning in the cell house. the screaming sounded as though the man was being subjected to some form of most horrible physical torture. the sounds continued as we marched out over the draw bridge. from this vantage point we could see directly an interesting scene. there was one convict who had been pestering the prison doctor with complaints of an ingrowing toenail which he claimed bothered him to such an extent that he couldn't work. He was tying brooms and the doctor said he was just stalling in order to escape work. he was put in the dungeon but that had no effect. every morning when the doctor came he would be the first one on the list. the doctor would ask him the nature of his ailment and the man would complain of the sore toe. it had finally gotten on the doctor's nerves so that he decided to fix the fellow up. the doctor had given orders to have him kept in the cell during church and as soon as we were all in the chapel they brought him down stairs and under the doctors instructions was lain on his back upon a small table which stood in front of the kitchen door. this table was used to set pans on during meal time. the entire kitchen force was then called out and ordered to hold the man down. this was done to the satisfaction of all concerned. especially the doctor. the doctor of medicine then proceeded to take out a pair of pliers and a pocket knife. with the aid of these instruments he then proceeded to split the offending toe nail down through the center. and pull out the pieces. this naturally explained the yelling. i don't remember of hearing anyone complain of bad toe nails after that. (Olson, 1975:162–63)

REFERENCES

American Correctional Association. *The American Prison: From the Beginning . . .* ACA Publishers, 1983.

Anonymous. *An Illustrated History and Description of State Prison Life, By One Who Has Been There. Written by a Convict in a Convict's Cell.* Globe Publishing, 1871.

Beaumont, G. D., and A. D. Tocqueville. *On the Penitentiary System in the United States and Its Application in France.* Carbondale: Southern Illinois University Press, 1833/1964.

Berkman, A. *Prison Memoirs of an Anarchist.* New York: Schocken Books, 1970 (Originally published in 1912 by Mother Earth Publishing).

Brice, J. R., Esq. *Secrets of the Mount-Pleasant State Prison, Revealed and Exposed: An Account of the Unjust Proceedings Against James R. Brice, Esq., By Which He Was Convicted of the Crime of Perjury, accompanied by affidavits to prove his innocency: Also an account of the Inhuman Treatment of Prisoners by some of the keepers; and an authentic statement of the officers and salaries, with other curious matters before unknown to the public.* Albany, NY: Printed for the author), 1839.

Clear, T. R., and G. F. Cole. *American Corrections.* Pacific Grove, CA: Wadsworth, 1990.

Coffey, W. A. *Inside Out: Or, An Interior View of the New York State Prison; Together with Bibliographic Sketches of the Lives of Several of the Convicts.* (New York: Printed for the author, 1823.

Conley, J. A. "Prisons, production, and profit: Reconsidering the importance of prison industries." *Journal of Social History* 14 (Winter 1980):257–75.

Dobash, R. P. "Labour and discipline in Scottish and English prisons: Moral correction, punishment and useful toil." *Sociology* 17 91(1) 1983:1–25.

Durham, A. M. III. "Newgate of Connecticut: Origins and early days of an early American prison." *Justice Quarterly* 6 (1) 1989:89–116.

Elgar, T. (Convict No. 6179). *Convict Life; or, Penitentiary Citizenship in the Illinois State Pen.* Rochester, NY; 1886.

Focault, M. *Discipline and Punishment: The Birth of the Prison.* New York: Pantheon, 1977.

Gettleman, M. E. "The Maryland penitentiary in the age of Tocqueville, 1828–1842." *Maryland Historical Magazine* 56 (1961).

Haney, C. "Infamous punishment: The psychological consequences of isolation." *National Prison Project Journal* 8 (2) 1993:3–7.

Hawkins, G. "Prison labor and prison industries." In N. Morris and M. Tonry (eds.). *Crime and Justice Annual.* Chicago: University of Chicago Press, 1983:85–127.

Hirsch, A. J. "From pillory to penitentiary: The rise of criminal incarceration in early Massachusetts." *Michigan Law Review* 80 (1982).

Hougen, H. R. "The impact of politics and prison industry on the general management of the Kansas State Penitentiary, 1883–1990," *Kansas Historical Quarterly* 43 (1977):297–318.

Ignatieff, M. *A Just Measure of Pain: The Penitentiary in the Industrial Revolution, 1750–1850.* New York: Pantheon, 1978.

Ignatieff, M. "State, civil society, and total institutions: A critique of recent histories of punishment." In S. Cohen and A. Scull (eds.). *Social Control and the State.* Oxford University Press, 1983.

Keve, P. W. *The History of Corrections in Virginia.* Charlottesville, VA: University Press of Virginia, 1986.

Kittrie, N. M. *The Right to Be Different.* Baltimore: The Johns Hopkins Press, 1971.

Lane, R. *Violent Death in the City: Suicide, Accident, and Murder in Nineteenth-Century Philadelphia.* Cambridge: Harvard University Press, 1979.

Lane, R. "Urban police and crime in nineteenth-century America." In N.

Morris and M. Tonry (eds.). *Crime and Justice: An Annual Review of Research*. Chicago: University of Chicago Press, 1980.

Mazur, L. P. *Rites of Execution: Capital Punishment and the Transformation of American Culture, 1776–1865*. New York: Oxford University Press, 1989.

McConville, S. *A History of English Prison Administration*. London: Routledge & Kegan Paul, 1981.

Melossi, D., and M. Pavarini. *The Prison and the Factory: Origins of the Penitentiary System*. Translated by G. Cousin. Totowa, NJ: Barnes & Noble, 1981.

Moore, L. W. *His Own Story of His Eventful Life*. Freeport, NY: Books for Libraries Press, 1892.

Newman, G. *Just and Painful: A Case for Corporal Punishment of Criminals*. New York: MacMillan, 1983.

Norris, R. L. *Prison Reformers and Penitential Publicists in France, England, and the United States, 1774–1847*. Unpublished dissertation: The American University, 1985.

Nossiter, A. "Making hard time harder: States cut jail TV and sports." *The New York Times* (September 17, 1994):1, 11.

Olson. "'I felt like I must be entering . . . another world.' The anonymous memoirs of an early inmate of the Wyoming penitentiary." *Annals of Wyoming* 47 (1975):153–90.

Rothman, D. J. *The Discovery of the Asylum: Social Order and Disorder in the New Republic*. Boston: Little, Brown, 1971 and 1990.

Rothman, D. "Sentencing reforms in historical perspective." *Crime & Delinquency* 29 (4) 1983:631–47.

Rusche, G., and O. Kirchheimer. *Punishment and Social Structure*. New York: Columbia University Press, 1939.

Scull, A. T. *Decarceration: Community Treatment and the Deviant—A Radical View*. Englewood Cliffs, NJ: Prentice-Hall, 1977.

Sennett, R. *Authority*. New York: Vintage Books, 1981.

Shayt, D. H "Stairway to redemption: American's encounter with the British prison treadmill." *Technology and Culture* 30 (4) 1989:908–38.

Sherman, M. E., and G. Hawkins. *Imprisonment in America: Choosing the Future*. Chicago: University of Chicago Press, 1981.

Thompson, G. *Prison Life and Reflections*. New York: Negro Universities Press, 1847/1969.

Walker, S. *Popular Justice: A History of American Criminal Justice*. New York: Oxford University Press, 1980.

3

Modern Prisons

The Twentieth-Century Experience

Understanding and reforming prisons has been neither easy nor notably successful. Part of the difficulty is that there is a distinctly utopian bias to the work of many prison reformers. The prison has often been cast in terms of one Grand Scheme or another, not assessed as an entity in its own right that must be appreciated on its own terms. Prisons are nothing if not painful, yet the implications of this stark fact have never been fully appreciated by reformers.

There has been a routine tendency to assume that the disciplined isolation that prisoners find to be so painful is really an asset. Many reformers would have it that the prison exists as a separate and pure world, free from the corruptions and constraints of society, and unencumbered by any special liabilities of its own. Here, in this neutral environment—this pallid but pure community—the offender would not so much suffer fruitlessly as be reborn or reconstituted. Upon release, he would emerge as a reformed sinner ready to resist the temptations of free society, as a docile laborer ripe for conscription in the work force or, more recently, as a man primed by one correctional program or another to embrace middle-class values.

Thoroughgoing utopianism of this sort has been less common in this century than in the last. Stateville Prison from the 1930s to the early 1960s was, however, one notable instance. Though the prisoners, almost to a man, found

Stateville to be an oppressively rigid environment, its very regularity and discipline were thought by officials to set Stateville apart from the mundane considerations of life in free society. "Stateville was Joseph Ragen's answer to Walden Two," we learn from a thoughtful commentator on that well-known prison (Jacobs, 1977:31). One would not normally think of a prison, any prison, in the same breadth as a pastoral community of idealists, yet it true, as Jacobs notes, that at Stateville, as at Walden Two,

> Every person and every object had its place. From the award-winning gardens to the clocklike regularity of the movement of prisoners in precise formations from assignment to assignment, the prison reflected its warden's zeal for order and harmony. Indeed, Ragen and the organization's elite looked on the prison as morally superior to the outside society with its petty politics and debilitating corruption. (Jacobs, 1977:31).[1]

Here, as in the penitentiary, a regime of discipline was meant to reform the prisoners. And here, as in the penitentiary, it is as if the prison and the prisoner were, like Rorschach's famous inkblot figures, infinitely adaptable to the ideals of reformers. Reduced to mere props, the prisoners were depersonalized and viewed as being both congenially oblivious to pain and ever open to the prospect of change.

The converse of this utopianism is the tendency of critics to see prison as a malevolent monstrosity that brutalizes all it touches, in which pain is not minimized or denied, but exaggerated to the point where no prisoner could survive it without compromising his humanity. We are led to believe that subterranean beatings of hapless prisoners by brutal guards are the norm, and that at best a mere gloss of humanity covers and distorts the surface of prison life.[2] In this scenario, which is more commonly adopted by those who wish to abolish rather than merely to reform the prison, only contact with the community can cure the prison's ills. The paradox is that the prison is capable of the extremes envisioned by reformers and critics—prisons can offer both human community and dehumanizing violence—but the dominant reality falls between them, on an ecological continuum that we will examine later in this book.

Those who wish to avoid imposing their own ideals on the prison—ideals that may well blind them to the nature of prison life—must operate inductively, from the ground up. They must develop an agenda for prison reform based on what the prison really does to the various people, staff as well as inmates, who inhabit it. This is genuine humanism. It does not impute motives or values but finds them in the experiences of the people under study. From this point of view there is a constant theme in prison history: prisons have offered painful experiences, and been hard places in which to live and work with dignity. Let us then begin the task of understanding and reforming today's prisons by acknowledging that the prisons we inherit are settings of pain. We must define our correctional goals in light of this enduring reality.

THE PAINFUL FACTS OF PRISON LIFE

Utopian reform ventures are less likely to be mounted if one refuses to disguise the fact that prison hurts. As Hans Toch and I have noted, "One of the striking things about prisons is that we make no bones about the fact that we intend them to be uncomfortable" (Johnson & Toch, 1988:13). Prisons are meant to punish and deter, two goals that require pain or discomfort. The Supreme Court has recently reminded us that

> to the extent that [prison] conditions are restrictive and even harsh, they are part of the penalty that criminal offenders must pay for their offenses against society ... the Constitution does not mandate comfortable prisons. ... [Indeed] prisons ... cannot be free of discomfort. (*Rhodes v. Chapman,* 101 S. Ct. 2392 & 2400, 1981)

The Court has little to worry about. Prisons have always been painful and, by their very nature, always will be painful. In the modern prison, from the nineteenth-century penitentiary to today's maximum-security prison, administrators have been deceptive on this score, preaching treatment but practicing punishment. This was evident with the penitentiary, which promised a rejuvenating solitude but delivered only isolation and pain. This theme recurred at the turn of the twentieth century, and was a salient feature of the prison until the mid-1960s. Throughout this period, "progressive penology" marked by individual treatment of prisoners replaced the uniform isolation and discipline of the penitentiary (Rothman, 1980; see also Barnes & Teeters, 1952). Once again, however, a seemingly benign and even generous policy proved in practice to rely on a formidable regime of pain.

The Elmira Reformatory

New York's famous Elmira Reformatory, for example, is often described as the original model from which progressive penology evolved. Opened in 1876, and superintended by Zebulon B. Brockway for some three decades, Elmira was praised as a humanitarian "hospital" or "college on the hill." Elmira offered a host of educational and vocational programs and promised early release to those who reformed themselves (it was ostensibly organized to facilitate personal reform). The prisoners were classified for purposes of treatment; treatment, in turn, was individualized. A formal military discipline prevailed, replete with marching inmates shouldering wooden replicas of weapons. Incarceration at Elmira was billed as an unambiguously constructive experience. The place sported the trappings, if not the substance, of the newly emerging social sciences. Science was assumed to render cures. Pain was not acknowledged as one of Elmira's ingredients.

But the origins of this institution are more complex, and its social reality and legacy more troubling. Scientific penology may have influenced Elmira's formal operations, but its roots can be traced to the fusion of evangelicalism and temperance that are so characteristic of late-nineteenth-century America

(Jenkins, 1984). These social movements were associated with a number of restrictive and even coercive social policies undertaken in the service of moral purification. Elmira was an institutional manifestation of such policies as they applied to crime and its correction.

The social forces that shaped Elmira, moreover, operated directly in its founder's life. Zebulon Brockway was a born-again Christian; "after his conversion, [he] found a new sense of mission in promoting the moral welfare and reform of his prisoners" (Jenkins, 1984:560). This mission culminated in Brockway's "scientific cultural system of regeneration" of criminals at Elmira (Jenkins, 1984:560). But by regeneration Brockway meant spiritual rebirth, not social reform or personal rehabilitation as these terms have meaning today. Brockway had not broken with the penitentiary to develop a new and liberating reformatory. Instead, he had produced a kind of scientific penitentiary.

Thus it is that at Elmira, "the pragmatic implications of [correctional] professionalism were not particularly divergent from the proposals of the nineteenth century [penitentiary]" (Dobash, 1983:18). The underlying reason was that "the need to internalize discipline [within the labor force] far more thoroughly than in the Jacksonian Era" called for a scientific penitentiary capable of differentiated classification and treatment of deviants (Jenkins, 1984:555). The temperance movement and its institutions, most notably the first reformatories for inebriates, responded to similar social realities. These institutions have been described "as part of a wider cooptation of the skilled working class in an age of nascent imperialism . . . [serving] to divide skilled and unskilled workers, while raising standards of self-discipline and motivation among abstainers" (Jenkins, 1984:563). As demonstrated so vividly in the original penitentiaries, however, such global and seemingly benevolent social and economic imperatives produce institutions marked more by harsh conditions and even brutality than by discipline and order. This occurs with distressing regularity because right-minded (not to say righteous) administrators come to feel that almost anything can be justified to reach the laudable ends they have set out to achieve. When their regimes fail, in no small part because these regimes are designed in ignorance of the needs and concerns of their inhabitants, the whip comes readily to hand. Elmira, like many of the twentieth-century penal institutions it helped to inspire, proved to be no exception to this hard rule.

The rhetoric of individual treatment featured so prominently at Elmira, then, merely "changed the form but not the substance of control—Elmira was, in the final analysis, a prison" (Pisciotta, 1983:620). And an exceedingly brutal one at that. Pisciotta (1983:620) tells us that "Brockway presented his charges with a choice: absolute, unerring conformity or swift, severe punishment." His particular methods of punishment, moreover, would have made a penitentiary warden blanch. An Elmira inmate, guilty of no more than failing to complete a work assignment, reported the following experience to the New York State Board of Charities in 1894:

> I knew I was in for a beating and as I knew the terrible treatment received by others, I had a terror of what was coming. I refused to leave my cell.

They stuck into the cell an iron rod with a two-foot hook on the end, heated red hot, and poked me with it. I tried to defend myself with the bed, but my clothing took fire, and the iron burned my breast. My breast is deeply scarred to-day [sic] from the burn. They also had a shortened hot poker, which burned my hands. I have those scars too. I finally succumbed, was handcuffed and taken to the bathroom. I asked Brockway if I had not been punished enough. He laughed at me, and said, "Oh yes, we have just fixed you up a little though," with that a hook was fastened to my shackles, and I was hoisted off the floor. I got half a dozen blows with the paddle right across the kidneys. The pain was so agonizing that I fainted. They revived me, and when I begged for mercy, Brockway struck me on the head with a strap, knocked me insensible. The next thing I knew I was lying on a cot in the dungeon, shackled to an iron bar . . . I stayed in the dungeon that night and the next day shackled, and received only bread and water. The next day I was again hoisted and beaten, returned to the dungeon, and after one day's rest, beaten again. Then I was put in the cell in Murderer's Row, where I remained for twenty-one days on bread and water. (Pisciotta, 1983:621)

Upon hearing this and other testimony from inmates as well as staff, the board concluded that "the charges and allegations against the General Superintendent Z. B. Brockway, of 'cruel, brutal, excessive and unusual punishment of the inmates' are proven and most amply sustained by the evidence" (Pisciotta, 1983:620).

Early on, routine use of force became the norm at Elmira, and remained so well into the twentieth century. Lewis E. Lawes, famous as a pioneering warden at Sing Sing, began his career as an officer at Elmira. He describes a culture of violence that was pervasive at turn-of-the-century Elmira:

Where force is the order of the day, men will resort to it frequently as the easiest way out. Strict disciplinary measures at the Reformatory at times led to physical encounters between officers and their men. I succumbed to the urge on several occasions. Once during the drilling of the 'Awkward Squad' a prisoner was cautioned by his squad leader, another prisoner, about his appearance. It led to a fist fight. I stopped them and in order to properly impress the offender, I landed him one on the chin and knocked him out. We worked on him and he was as good as ever in a few moments. The fellow didn't resent my act. He took it for granted. (Lawes, 1932:39)

Elmira was famous for its apparent discipline and order, both in Brockway's time and for some time thereafter. Based on patterns of abuse brought to light during and after Brockway's tenure, it is safe to conclude that "the orderly demeanor of the inmates observed by visitors and attributed to the effectiveness of the Elmira system was largely a result of fear" (Pisciotta, 1983:622–23).

The Big House

Descriptions of maximum-security prisons during this century routinely belie the claim that they provide humane treatment, individual or otherwise. These institutions, like the prisons that preceded the penitentiary, are essentially human warehouses. Thus, for at least the first three decades of this century, penitentiary-like discipline (and sometimes hard labor) was maintained in prisons for the sake of custody alone. According to the authoritative *Survey of Release Procedures,*

> [I]mprisonment in 1900–1935 was substantially what it had been one hundred years earlier: custody, punishment, and hard labor. By end of the period in many prisons it reverted to just custody and punishment. (Quoted in Barnes & Teeters, 1952:556)

These prisons were colloquially known as "Big Houses," a term that is also used by many criminologists to differentiate them from other prison types (Irwin, 1980). The quintessential Big House, at least in the eyes of the public, was Alcatraz, though Alcatraz was unique in its day in that its regime was marked by exceptionally tight security. Confinement to Alcatraz, moreover, was reserved solely for the most predatory inmates. (Today's successors to Alcatraz are referred to as "super-max" facilities; we will touch briefly on this subject in the final chapter of this book.) It is a matter of historical record that Big Houses like Alcatraz, Sing Sing, and Stateville, to name a few better-known institutions, offered virtually no remedial programs to their inmates, and on the whole "were places of pervasive brutality" (Rothman, 1980:152). As in the penitentiaries that the Big Houses seemed to mimic, with but a passing nod to the ideals of progressive penology, pain was at the heart of the confinement experience.

If one were to think of prisons as having lines of descent, one would say that the Big House was the primary descendant and heir apparent of the penitentiary. The penitentiary drew its meaning and purpose from two concepts: penance and work. With the demise of penance, the industrial prison emerged. With the demise of prison labor, the Big House came into full flower. A disciplined and often silent routine prevailed in the Big House, but for no purpose other than to maintain order.

To be sure, the Big House's lineage was not uniform. Some southern states bypassed the penitentiary entirely. The first prisons in Texas, for example, were essentially extensions of the slave plantation. These plantation prisons were the agrarian equivalent of the industrial prison. The object was disciplined labor of the most servile, back-breaking sort; penance was never given a second thought. From these plantation prisons, the Big Houses of the South emerged.

In the plantation prison, as in the penitentiary, brutal punishments were common. Conditions were primitive. Mortality rates were high.

> Several legislative investigations of the prison took place in the late 1870s, and numerous accounts surfaced in the media of inmates being bitten by

guard dogs, whipped, and even killed by guards. Medical care and sanitation were virtually nonexistent in the camps, and inmates died with alarming regularity. (Crouch & Marquart, 1989:14)

Given the logistics of fieldwork, inmates fled their captors on a regular basis. "In 1876 alone," state Crouch & Marquart (1989:14), "there were 382 escapes in a prisoner population of only 2,367." In the main, the inmates fled a regime of terror that was the functional equivalent of the penitentiary regime, with the notable absence of any pretense at reform.

Of course, the Big House was more than a gutted penitentiary or a tamed slave plantation. Humanitarian reforms helped to shape its inner world, but these had to do with reducing deprivations rather than establishing a larger correctional agenda or purpose. Thus, whereas the penitentiary offered a life essentially devoid of comfort or even distraction, the Big House routine was the culmination of a series of humanitarian milestones that made prison life more bearable.

The first such advance, from the prisoners' point of view, was the introduction of tobacco. First permitted in Sing Sing in 1846, the effect was immediate and dramatic. A prison report of 1847 notes that

> the fact of [tobacco's] introduction upon the discipline [of the men] was almost immediately manifest. It has diffused a measure of contentment over a large class of our inmates who had previously been a source of constant uneasiness and anxiety to the prison authorities and has, I am satisfied, contributed largely to the unusual respect given by convicts to the regulations and government of the prison. (Quoted in Lawes, 1932:80)

This calming effect was noted in other prisons as well. A convict in the Illinois State Penitentiary, writing in 1886, called tobacco "the Soothing Syrup of a penal institution." He noted, insightfully, that

> Detestable and injurious as the habit of chewing tobacco may be, so firm a hold has it upon a man when once he has acquired it, that he would rather forego his Good Time almost, than be deprived of indulging it (Elgar, 1886:12).

It is interesting to note that in today's prisons, the privilege of smoking is becoming a thing of the past. We no longer view addictions as providing solace, or at least sufficient solace to offset concerns for the health and welfare for others in the prison involuntarily exposed to secondhand smoke and likely to seek redress.

The second reform milestone was the abolition of corporal punishment. In Sing Sing, this occurred in 1871. Prior to that time, upwards of 60 percent of the prisoners would be subjected to the whip on an annual basis (Lawes, 1932). Other prisons retained the practice of corporal punishment, but among prisons outside the South, whippings and other physical sanctions became an underground, unauthorized activity by the turn of the century. Tragically, regimes of corporal punishment, official and unofficial, remained in place in southern prisons for much of this century (see, for example, Crouch & Marquart, 1989).

The emergence of significant internal freedoms comprise the third and final reform milestone that paved the way for the Big House. These freedoms came in the wake of the lockstep march, which was abolished in Sing Sing in 1900 (Lawes, 1932). The daily humiliations of constrained movement implied in this shameful march soon gave way to relative freedom of movement in the yard, first on Sundays (beginning in Sing Sing in 1912) and then, gradually over the early decades of the twentieth century, each day of the week.

The first "free Sunday" in Sing Sing occurred in or around 1912. Lawes's account is unclear on the exact date. What is clear is that the event was a momentous one. By all accounts, that Sunday offered a profound departure from the suffocating world of the penitentiary, and one that held out a rudimentary promise of community in the prison world of the Big House.

> Men roamed around the prison courtyard timidly, as if fearful of their steps, like children just learning to walk. Administrators and officials had expressed dire forebodings. The prisoners had no responsibility, no honor. The prison would be terrorized. Prisoners and their guards eyed one another furtively, hardly knowing what to expect of each other. Men breathed deeply of the free outdoors. Authority and subjects moved closer together understandingly. (Lawes, 1932:104)

It is certainly true that inmate and officer moved closer to one another on that first free Sunday, as Lawes claims, but the baseline for this observation was the virtual caste system of the penitentiary or slave plantation regime. Staff and prisoners of the Big House remained segregated into separate and unequal worlds by a regime that remained, at its core, an oppressive one. Even in the face of reforms, Lawes (1932:23–24) reminds us,

> In those days, stolidity was the order of the day in all prisons. The official force went about their duties with humdrum monotony. The prisoners did their tasks with dull indifference. The result was an oppressiveness that hung low and dense over the entire prison.

Oppression, in turn, created a climate of mutual distrust and even hatred.

> Hate, distrust and malice seemed to exude from every eye. Prisoners were allowed very little recreation outside their cells. Only a few moments of marching in the courtyard. Just aimless treading across a barren waste of ground surrounded by high walls. Men talked in whispers, if they talked at all, and their every movement was under the watchful eye of keepers, who held their clubs ready for instant use. (Lawes, 1932:23–24)

At the same time privileges of the yard were allowed, the silent system remained in place with respect to most prison activities. This made the Big House, like the penitentiary, a "city of silent men," gesturing to one another to communicate:

The sign language prevailed. During mess the prisoner used his fingers. If a second helping of bread was wanted he would raise one finger; an extra tin of soup, two fingers; another plate of potatoes, three fingers. In the shop, for an interview with the keeper in charge, two fingers; for permission to leave his task for a few moments, one finger. (Lawes, 1932:33)

As in the penitentiary, order in the Big House was the result of the threat and use of force, including, in the early decades of this century, clubs and guns:

Obedience to prison rules was forced into the hearts and minds of prisoners by ever-present clubs and guns. All officers were required to carry revolvers while on duty within the prison, a regulation long since discarded. (Lawes, 1932:33–34)

Lawes, as a young officer, recalls being admonished to use force freely to maintain control.

"Don't hesitate to use your club," I was told time and time again by older guards. "And when you bring it down, strike hard, otherwise you might get the worst of it." I looked for trouble. I found it soon. (Lawes, 1932:24)

Silence was both a cause and a consequence of order in the Big House, and a profound symbol of the authority of the keepers. "It was the hush of repression" (Lawes, 1932:33–34).

Though more comfortable than their predecessors in the penitentiary, prisoners of the Big House led spartan lives. Cells were cramped and barren; possessions were limited to bare essentials:

My cell measured six by eight feet wide and seven feet high and was on the whole a most cramped and discouraging place. An old deal table, a wooden chair, an aluminum washbasin, a venerable wooden slop bucket; these, besides the narrow bed, were the familiar objects upon which my unwilling eyes were obliged to look each morning. . . . (Nelson, 1936:3–4)

Food was generally in good supply but was utterly uninspiring. It was, in the eyes of the prisoners, fuel for reluctant bodies and nothing more:

At last I would have to get up. Breakfast. Mush and milk. Beans. Whatever it happened to be. It was never any good. How could it be? It was merely fuel. A life-preserving commodity. It was naturally not good nor appetizing food. (Nelson, 1936:10–11)

If the dominant theme of the penitentiary was terror, the dominant theme of the Big House was boredom bred by an endlessly monotonous routine. "Every minute of the day," said one prisoner, "all the year round, the most dominant tone is one of monotony" (Nelson, 1936:15). Nothing one does matters because everything occurs as a matter of routine.

The prisoner did not need to worry about food, clothes, or shelter; he had no rent to pay, no expenses except for smoking supplies and occasional groceries. All these items were supplied him by the State (in however insufficient or unsatisfying quantities). Neither did he have to worry about a job or about planning his day's work; all this was a matter of ordinary prison routine. He was given a daily task to do, and after a time performed it almost automatically. (Nelson, 1936:226)

In the virtually complete absence of responsibility, one literally responds less to the external world. One does less, thinks less, feels less. The prisoner suffers a kind of existential paralysis marked by

> loss of initiative, loss of physical and mental alertness. Never being called upon to exercise these qualities of mind or behavior, his sense of responsibility, his faculty of mental alertness, his powers of initiative became so feeble from disuse that they were often atrophied to the vanishing point. (Nelson, 1936:226–27)

With the demise of penitentiary discipline, taking with it comprehensive regimes of industrial labor, prisoners of the Big House had little to do but pass time. Routines were strict, but empty.

> The prisoner had so much time in which to do things that he never got anything done. This created a habit of indolence, of laissez-faire. The common attitude was, "Swim with the stream!" "There's plenty of time!" "There's no hurry!" "Take it easy!" So that most of his activity eventually consisted in wasting, killing, consuming, frittering away the over-powering leisure. (Nelson, 1936:227)

The emptiness of the regime spread out to all features of the prison world, including the yard where people became more and more listless and came to do less and less.

> Yard time. Recreation. . . . We go from the stuffy shop to the colorless yard. In it is no blade of grass, no tree, no bit of freshness or brilliance. Gray walls, dusty gravel, dirt and asphalt hardness. We walk about, or during our first few months or years manage to throw a ball back and forth and in some degree exercise our bodies. The longer we stay here, the less we do. At last we merely walk at a funeral pace, or lean against a wall and talk. (Nelson, 1936:15–16)

Even yard talk, free of the restrictions imposed by one's keepers, became an empty ritual, with cons speaking at each other rather than to each other:

> We do not converse; we deliver monologues in which we get rid of the stored-up bubblings. We try to live through words and self-dramatization. Our essential need is for actual tangible living, which we cannot have; so we try to live by pretending to live in tall stories based on how we'd like to live, or we long to live. . . . (Nelson, 1936:16)

Numbed by repetitive, pointless work, bored by empty companionship, the cell looks like an oasis. But it, too, harbors yet more boredom, and indeed completes for the prisoner a suffocating circle of monotony from which there is no escape:

Four-thirty. Yard time is over. We march to our cells, taking with us the evening meal. The shop has been so enervating, so weakening, so downright devitalizing, that we are glad to go to our cells. We think, "Well, here's another day done. Another day nearer home. God, but it's good to get back to the cell!" In our hearts, however, we know that the cell is even worse than the shop; and that in the morning we'll be saying, "God, but it's good to get out of that damned cell!" (Nelson, 1936:15–16)

For the prisoner of the Big House, the prison world is rife with signs of his failure and inadequacy.

Perhaps the most important factor in the prisoner's general loss of morale, however, was the sense of failure, the sense of inferiority he felt simply because of his being in prison. (Nelson, 1936:228)

As if to acknowledge defeat, he drifts inexorably into a stupor that is the hallmark of this penal institution. Officials run the place. They can speak. What they say matters. Prisoners simply exist as mute figures, persons locked in a stupor that starts first in the solitary moments in the cell, when they are most fully captive to suppressed human passions, and then spreads out gradually, "until finally it takes full possession of the man, so that he spends most of his waking moments in a species of hypnosis, nearly or utterly incapable of reacting to the normal emergencies of life" (Nelson, 1936:197).

In the extreme, we see a world of captive men, alive yet dead, shuffling where they once marched, heading nowhere, slowly.

All about me was living death: anemic bodies, starved souls, hatred and misery: a world of wants and wishes, hungers and lusts; a world of suffering men. (Nelson, 1936:4)

It is, one supposes, this dreadful image of living death that marked the Big House in the eyes of a new generation of prison reformers as a human wasteland, in urgent need of reform. The legacy of those reforms can be seen in the correctional institution.

The Correctional Institution

With the passing of the Big House and the emergence (circa 1940) of what has been termed the "correctional institution," harsh discipline and brutality by officials became less salient features of prison life. The daily regime of prison life became more relaxed and even accommodating. Corrections programs, though few in number, sometimes offered opportunities for personal growth. Certainly prison stupor became a thing of the past in the correctional institution. Correctional institutions are an improvement over Big Houses, but the benefits of these institutions are easily exaggerated. To my mind, the differences between Big Houses and correctional institutions are matters of degree rather than kind. In general, correctional institutions did not correct. Nor did correctional institutions abolish the pains of imprisonment. These prisons were, at bottom, simply more tolerable warehouses than the Big Houses they supplanted, less a departure than a toned-down imitation. Often, correctional institutions occupied the same physical plants as the Big Houses (Barnes & Teeters, 1952). Indeed, one might classify most of these prisons as Big Houses gone soft.

In comparison with the Big House, correctional institutions were marked by a less intrusive discipline; more yard and recreational privileges; more liberal mail and visitation policies; more amenities, including an occasional movie or concert; and more educational, vocational, and therapeutic programs, though these sometimes were present more on paper than in reality and generally seemed to be thrown in as window dressing (see Barnes & Teeters, 1952; and Irwin, 1980). These changes made life in prison less oppressive. Even so, prisoners spent most of their time in their cells or engaged in some type of menial work. They soon discovered that free time could be "dead" time; though in no sense the living dead Nelson described in the Big House, men in correctional institutions often milled about the yard with nothing constructive to do. Boredom prevailed, though again it was not the crushing boredom born of regimentation as in the Big House.

Gradually, and at first almost imperceptibly, considerable resentment developed among prisoners of correctional institutions. The underlying problem was with expectations, which ran high when correctional institutions were first put in place. Officials had promised programs and rehabilitation, but had not delivered them. The difficulty was that officials, however well intended they might have been, simply did not know how to conduct a correctional enterprise. Nor did they have the resources or staff to make a serious attempt at that task. The correctional institution promised to transform people, in a manner not at all unlike that ostensibly sought at Elmira; but mostly these institutions simply left prisoners more or less on their own (see Irwin, 1980; Rothman, 1980).

This benign neglect was certainly better than the overt and systematic official violence that prevailed at such reform-oriented institutions as Elmira or in the baldly custodial Big Houses. But correctional institutions had a harsh side to them. There was, as just noted, the matter of frustrated expectations regarding correctional programs. Living conditions could also be quite grim. It is significant that the President's Crime Commission report, written in the 1960s when psychological treatment of prisoners in those correctional institutions was supposed to be the norm, found these prisons "at best barren and futile, at worst unspeakably brutal and degrading" (cited in Morris & Hawkins, 1970: 111). Thus the pains of prison endured in the correctional institution, to triumph once again over the rhetoric of reform. As Hawkins (1976:48–49) has noted,

> despite the theoretical emphasis on reform and the widespread use of the terminology of rehabilitation, the actual experience of imprisonment for most persons imprisoned in this country in this century has been simply punitive. . . . The truth is that only a small minority of offenders have ever done their time in a "pastel prison."

For many confined to correctional institutions, the regime included a compulsory round of vocational and educational programs as well as some type of psychological treatment, usually group therapy. The vocational and educational programs sometimes received high marks from the convicts; the therapy programs, on the other hand, were generally seen as sorely out of touch with the prison community onto which they were clumsily grafted. Often the group therapy was run by untrained guards, and the size of groups could range into the hundreds (Irwin, 1980:45). The situation could be laughable, and indeed accounts of ex-offenders are apt to poke fun at self-important therapists who run treatment groups that are utterly out of touch with life as prisoners know it (see, for example, Braly, 1967).

In the 1950s, Trenton State Prison in New Jersey was a fairly typical correctional institution, merging the disciplined and oppressive climate of the Big House with a thin mix of educational, vocational, and treatment programs. Sykes's classic study, *Society of Captives*, describes Trenton State Prison. Significantly, Sykes depicts the dominant reality at Trenton as one of pain. "The inmates are agreed," he emphasizes, "that life in the maximum security prison is depriving or frustrating in the extreme" (Sykes, 1966:63). To survive, the prisoner turned not to programs or officials but to peers. In essence, Sykes concludes that the prisoner must "reject his rejecters" and embrace a convict culture of manliness if he is to survive psychologically. Often, he must reject his weaker fellows as well, since his strength is demonstrated by lording it over the weak. At best, the prisoner "does his own time" and leaves others to their predations, turning a deaf ear to the cries of victims. Treatment and the prospect of mature interpersonal relations are at best a footnote to the Darwinian ebb and flow of daily life in the prison yard of this correctional institution.

Life in Trenton State Prison, though tough and spartan, was altogether unremarkable. The plain fact is that our prisons—all our prisons—are built for punishment and hence are meant to be painful (Barnes & Teeters, 1952). The theme of punishment is nowhere more evident than in the massive walls that keep prisoners both out of sight and out of circulation. As Rothman (1980:157–58) makes clear about the Big House and the correctional institution,

> The image that captures the essence of the American prison is not one of inmates exercising in the yard or attending classes or taking psychometric tests, but of the physical presence of the walls. And the walls were incredible, rising twenty to thirty feet above the ground and going down another five to twenty feet below the ground, with anywhere from five to fifteen towers jutting out above them. The occasional legislator who questioned the enormous expense of erecting these structures was told in no uncertain terms that thirty feet was better than twenty-five feet for preventing inmates from scaling the walls, and that every extra foot below the ground was a necessary safeguard against their tunneling out. In the end, reformers, with their grand hopes of transforming the institution, were up against the wall.

The prison's walls are often grey, as is the interior of most prisons. In fact, the notion of "prison grey" as a distinct color pervades descriptions of penal

institutions. According to Washington, an inmate, prison grey symbolizes monotony and control.

Everything is a shade of grey. That's the color of prison.

The sky is grey. The walls are sand-grey. The yard is grey-black asphalt, and
the inmates' uniforms, which appear green, are really a shade of grey.

Grey as a color is neutral; as a controlling force it is repressive; and debili-
tating as a life influence.

Grey controls all. It gets into the mood, the spirit, and even the food has a
grey-bland taste.

It is no accident that grey is chosen color. An integral part of any con-
troller's plan is the color scheme.

In prison, grey dominates. (Washington, 1981:5)

Some of our contemporary maximum-security prisons are built without imposing grey walls, though these institutions usually feature barbed wire, and
this wire, ironically, is often a shade of grey. Almost all prisons feature an interior environment that is a dull grey or some related drab color. Colorful prisons—the so-called pastel prisons mentioned by Hawkins—are few in number.
And even here, the social climate within remains one of punitive isolation and
containment, grey in spirit if not in physical reality.

The Violent Prison

Most of today's prisons are formally known as correctional institutions, but
this designation is more misleading than ever. As far as I and most other criminologists are concerned, the correctional institution as a type has largely passed
from the prison scene. From the mid-1960s to the present, a new prison type
has emerged. It is defined by the climate of violence and predation on the part
of the prisoners that often marks its yards and other public areas. Known simply as the "violent prison" (see Irwin, 1980), it has been aptly described as a
"human warehouse with a junglelike underground" (Toch, 1988:41).

To be sure, our violent prisons are not monolithic milieus. Inmates are allowed a wide range of possessions in their cells. There are also many freedoms
allowed to prisoners; in particular, internal freedom of movement is readily
available in many contemporary prisons.[3] Resources and mobility combine
to create a remarkable ecological diversity; these prisons have a range of internal environments marked by differing social climates. Indeed, an underlife
of niches and sanctuaries develops to shelter men from the violence of their
peers. The ecology of today's prisons is strikingly parallel to that of our dangerous and yet highly differentiated urban slums. Still, drawing attention to
the distinctive prevalence of inmate violence in contemporary prisons reminds us that these prisons are different from their immediate predecessors in
this century. The evolution of the twentieth-century prison, from a stable if
oppressive Big House, through a brief flirtation with corrections, to what
now often amounts to a contained but turbulent ghetto, tells much about the
character of life and adjustment in the contemporary prison. This evolution

will be discussed at length in Chapter Five. It highlights the enduring reality of prison's pains, as well as the distinctive configuration those pains assume in today's maximum-security penal institutions.

THE CIVILIZATION OF PUNISHMENT

Pain, though it is as permanent and obdurate as the fortress walls that enclose most prisons, is not countenanced in the language of the justice system. Talk of pain seems crude, uncivilized. Instead, the justice system takes refuge in the deceptive claims of rehabilitation or in the neutral tongue of bureaucracy. No pain is meted out: "measures" and "interventions" and "treatments" are undertaken. The high drama of inflicting pain by imprisoning criminals (because we are angry and the offender deserves to suffer) is reduced to the "delivery of a commodity." Nils Christie's observations (1981:16 & 19) on this matter are blunt and to the point:

> the basic law should be called a "pain-law". . . . The penal law professors do most definitely not like to be designated "pain-law" professors. The judges do not like to sentence people to pain. Their preference is to sentence them to various "measures." The receiving institutions do not like to be regarded, or to regard themselves, as "pain-inflicting" institutions. Still, such a terminology would actually present a very precise message: punishment as administered by the penal law system is the conscious inflicting of pain. Those who are punished are supposed to suffer. If they by and large enjoyed it, we would change the method. It is intended within penal institutions that those at the receiving end shall get something that makes them unhappy, something that hurts. . . .
>
> Pain delivery is the concept for what in our time has developed into a calm, efficient, hygienic operation. Seen from the perspective of those delivering the service, it is not first and foremost drama, tragedy, intense sufferings. Infliction of pain is in dissonance with some major ideals, but can be carried out in an innocent, somnambulistic insulation from the value conflict. The pains of punishments are left to the receivers. Through the choice of words, working routines, division of labour and repetition, the whole thing has become the delivery of a commodity.

At first blush, the failure of the justice system to acknowledge the use of pain would appear to be a clearcut case of hypocrisy. Pain that is denied in policy or hidden behind prison walls remains pain nonetheless. As Christie reminds us, it is simply "left to the receivers" to bear while the rest of us go about our daily lives. However, the deeper reality may be that we fail to emphasize pain not because we are lying to ourselves but because we are increasingly ambivalent about it. I made this point in the first edition of this book, and it has been reiterated by Clear 1994:4–5. Clear, however, uses the word harm rather than pain or suffering at the center of his analysis, as when he observes, "Professionals in the field of corrections are loath to admit that they are bureaucrats whose jobs it is to implement judicially decreed harms" (Clear, 1994:5). There is much value in Clear's book, but it is, in my view, misleading to say that we as a society seek to harm or damage offenders when we punish them. Pain and suffering need not produce damage, and indeed can be a source of moral education (see Chapter One). Moreover, the general thrust of modern prison practice is to minimize pain and suffering, and certainly to avoid inflicting damage on offenders. Pain has become, in other words, a necessary evil we aim to minimize, not a policy of choice.

Pain is an inevitable and, within limits, a just feature of imprisonment, but we no longer freely inflict pain in order to make prisons work. We recognize that pain can create more prison management problems than it solves. When pain becomes excessive, prisons become hard to operate. Now it is always possible, in principle, to escalate pain and break the will of the prisoners; to resort, in other words, to outright brutality and run the prison on raw fear. This method may have been more useful in the past—occasionally in the not-so-distant past, especially in southern plantation prisons—but it must have exacted a great cost from inmate and keeper alike. Our historical review offers testimony to the abysmal quality of life (and by implication, work) in the first prisons and in the penitentiaries. Rule by terror—both living under terror and being agents of terror—would seem to have even more obvious drawbacks today. Such a regime is flagrantly illegal and likely to be successfully litigated, those violent southern prisons being good cases in point (see Johnson, 1975). It is also sorely out of step with the times and utterly indefensible in terms of our current values.

More often than intentionally promoting pain, genuine efforts are made by prison officials and others in the justice system to reduce suffering and to keep the pains of imprisonment within tolerable limits.

> In the past, prison administrators sometimes saw themselves as in the punishment business, but no corrections official today defends such a goal. To create pain is not what administrators do intentionally. . . . The goal of wardens and other officials is to deploy their staff and resources to service inmates to the extent budgetary constraints permit. The bottom line is storage. Whatever the prison does, it must retain and restrain inmates. Other bottom-line goals are maintenance . . . and security. . . . Beyond these aims are program-related concerns such as education and training. . . . Pain and stress are the undesired ingredients of prison life the official must live with. As constraints (such as crowding) increase the harshness of imprisonment, ameliorating stress becomes a new and salient goal. Unsurprisingly, many officials come to join prisoners, civil rights groups, and federal judges in the shared desire to modulate the impact of runaway retributive aims. (Johnson & Toch, 1988:14–15)

The contemporary prison, then, is not only a "pain-delivering" institution but also a "pain-limiting" institution. As such, it reflects a larger historical trend away from inflicting excessive pain on criminals, a trend that may be at the very heart of what we mean by civilization. As John Stuart Mill (1977:136) observed, "One of the effects of civilization (not to say one of the ingredients in it) is, that the spectacle, and even the very idea of pain, is more and more kept out of the sight of those classes who enjoy in their fullness the benefits of civilization."

Civilization means a growth in knowledge, which in turn "brings increased power to prevent or reduce pain" (Reiman, 1985:135). Civilization also means an increase in our ability to communicate with others outside our immediate environment, and this "extends the circle of people with whom we empathize" (Reiman, 1985:135). As a result, "progress in civilization is characterized by a lower tolerance for one's own pain and that suffered by others" (Reiman, 1985:135). This means that "the spectacle, and even the very idea of pain" that so troubled John Stuart Mill must be hidden from more and more people. Ultimately, it must seem to disappear from punishment itself. By this growing unwillingness to administer pain do we measure our civilization and, "by our example, continue the work of civilizing" (Reiman, 1985:136).

The Amelioration of Pain: Three Stages

The civilization of punishment, if you will, has passed through three stages. First, punishment was removed from the public view, hidden within prisons. This permitted certain types of abuses, but it eliminated the spectacle of public corporal punishment and the orgies of violence sometimes associated with it. Public floggings and executions, in particular, had a nasty tendency to degenerate into carnivals or mob scenes, neither of which were notably civilized (Foucault, 1977; Newman, 1978). It is one thing to run penitentiaries, however violent or even torturous they may be; it is another to parade torturous practices in the public square, for all to see.

Next, physical pain (that is to say, tangible, visible pain) was eliminated as a permissable part of punishment. Prisoners can no longer be subjected to corporal punishment. Even such infamous settings as Alcatraz and Marion, aptly described by Ward (1994:92) as "standard setters for maximum custody and maximum punishment" from the 1930s through to the 1990s, "have accomplished their missions without employing regimes that involve physical punishment." To the extent that convicts in modern prisons are subjected to physical punishment by guards, it is *always* a violation of official policy. Today, this prohibition of painful assaults on the body applies even to capital punishment. As Foucault (1977:11) has observed,

> Physical pain, the pain of the body itself, is no longer the constituent element of the penalty. . . . If it is still necessary for the law to reach and manipulate the body of the convict, it will be at a distance, in the proper way, according to strict rules. . . . Today a doctor must watch over those condemned to death, right up to the last moment—thus juxtaposing himself as the agent of welfare, as the alleviator of pain, with the official whose task it is to end life. . . . [Thus] the modern rituals of execution attest to . . . the disappearance of the spectacle [of punishment] and the elimination of pain.

Death by lethal injection is the purest case of an execution ostensibly free of both drama and physical pain.[4] The condemned lies on a hospital gurney and is anesthetized before his life is taken, which is indeed a far cry from being drawn and quartered. The more general point, however, is that each of the modern methods of execution—the electric chair, the gas chamber, and lethal injection—was developed with the explicit goal of reducing both the spectacle and the physical pain of capital punishment.[5]

Finally, our notion of what is permissible psychological pain has been progressively circumscribed. The seminal discussion of the psychological pains of imprisonment is provided by Sykes in his book, *Society of Captives*, discussed earlier. Sykes argues that imprisonment, by its very nature, deprives liberty, limits goods and services, deprives or at least sharply reduces access to heterosexual relations, and limits both autonomy and security. These deprivations are inherent in imprisonment, whether in a penitentiary or in any other prison. Of course, in early prisons and in penitentiaries there were physical punishments as well. For today's prisons, the pains of confinement are *limited* to these psychological deprivations, except where failures of policy allow physical brutality to flourish in the form of extralegal, illegitimate punishments.

The first deprivation of imprisonment is the loss of liberty. For the prisoner, states Sykes, "loss of liberty is a double one—first, by confinement to the institution and second, by confinement within the institution" (Sykes, 1966:65). The significance of this loss goes beyond limitations of movement, however frustrating these may be. A deeper loss is found in "the involuntary seclusion of the outlaw" from the larger society, and all that entails in terms of lost contact with loved ones and one's former way of life (Sykes, 1966:65). Deeper still is the pain of moral rejection implied in confinement. For confinement represents, and has always represented, a statement by society that the prisoner is no longer a person to be trusted or respected to move freely among his fellow citizens (Sykes, 1966:65).

The second deprivation is that of goods and services. Prisons consign inmates to conditions of relative poverty. In the early prisons and in the penitentiaries, there was abject poverty and, sometimes, life-threatening shortages of medicine and food. In the Big House, a spartan regime provided adequate food and shelter but few amenities. Today's prisons, as we have noted, are more accommodating; amenities are more common, and recreation is seen as a daily right rather than, as in the Big House, an occasional privilege. There was, of course, no recreation whatsoever in the penitentiaries.

One can imagine a prison that deprived only liberty and left prisoners to idle away their time in luxurious conditions, and indeed many prison critics claim that "country club prisons" offer just such regimes. But this has never been the fate of regular criminals, and only rarely the fate of individual prisoners with unique political or economic circumstances. For the typical criminal, loss of liberty means loss of access to a range of goods and services one might have been able to earn or otherwise acquire were one free.

Many offenders have led miserable lives outside, and as a result, they may find the objective material conditions of prison to be as good as, or even better than, those they faced in the free world. This observation may well hold for prisons of all types, from the Mamertine Prison onward. Still, prisoners are apt to *believe* they could do better in the free world, and hence conclude that prison conditions are "painfully depriving" (Sykes, 1966:67–68). Prison conditions are thus likely to be seen as symbolically inadequate even if they are sufficient for a decent material existence. As Sykes (1966:68) has cogently observed,

> A standard of living can be hopelessly inadequate, from the individual's viewpoint, because it bores him to death or fails to provide those subtle symbolic overtones which we invest in the world of possessions. And this is the core of the prisoner's problem in the area of goods and services. He wants—or needs, if you will—not just the so-called necessities of life but also the amenities: cigarettes and liquor as well as calories, interesting foods as well as sheer bulk, individual clothing as well as adequate clothing, individual furnishings for his living quarters as well as shelter, privacy as well as space.

Hence it is that, even in a prison world seen by outsiders as perfectly adequate, the prisoners are apt to feel aggrieved and to see "its present material impoverishment as a painful loss" (Sykes, 1966:68).

The pain of this material loss, moreover, runs deeper than daily discomfort. For citizens of the nineteenth and twentieth centuries, at least, material goods are taken to be an index of one's worth as a human being. To be poor is to be a failure as a human being. Thus it is that

> impoverishment remains as one of the most bitter attacks on the individual's self-image that our society has to offer and the prisoner cannot ignore the implication of his straitened circumstances. Whatever the discomforts and irritations of the prisoner's Spartan existence may be, he must carry the additional burden of social definitions which equate his material deprivation with personal inadequacy. (Sykes, 1966:70)

Sexual deprivation is the third pain of imprisonment. "If the inmate, then, is rejected and impoverished by the facts of his imprisonment," states Sykes (1966:70), "he is also figuratively castrated by his involuntary celibacy." Until quite recently, with the spread of home furloughs and conjugal visits, heterosexual celibacy among prisoners was complete and the deprivation of heterosexual contact was essentially total.

Sykes notes that the pains of heterosexual frustration go beyond physical discomfort and entail psychological pains that call into doubt the male identity of the lonely convict. Two salient problems emerge. One is pressures toward homosexual satisfaction of one's sexual needs, which provoke anxiety in many prisoners. The other is the tendency for male personality traits such as toughness to become exaggerated in the absence of the moderating effect of women, thus distorting in psychologically painful ways the image of manliness promoted within the prison.

Relatively few prisoners have written about the sexual deprivations of prison life, but those who have done so provide accounts that bear out Sykes's claims. If anything, prisoners who discuss sexual deprivation see this deprivation as uniquely cruel, as perhaps the essential and irreducible pain of confinement. As Nelson, a prisoner of a Big House in the 1920s and 30s observed:

> The imprisoned man is essentially the man isolated from the woman. It is in this respect that he differs most sharply from the man in the free world. If the imprisoned man endures hardships in the way of poverty, mal-nourishment, paucity of entertainment, recreation, and the like, so also does the average man in the free world. But the free man, regardless of his financial, personal, social and other limitations, can and does—legally or illegally—have access to the woman. The imprisoned man is completely and utterly cut off from her. . . . (Nelson, 1936:141–42)

The prisoner thus deprived suffers nothing less than sexual starvation. Sexual starvation is unique in that it, unlike starvation for food, which ends in death, can persist for great periods of time:

> For of all the possible forms of starvation, surely none is more demoralizing than sexual starvation. If one becomes sufficiently hungry or thirsty, one naturally suffers a great deal; but usually only for a comparatively brief time. Relief is always in sight—even if it come in the desperate form of death. But to be starved for month after weary month, year after endless year, in a place where "every day is like a year, a year whose days are long," for sexual satisfaction which, in the case of a lifer, may never come, this is the secret quintessence of human misery. (Nelson, 1936:143)

The fantasies of sexually starved prisoners, to borrow Nelson's metaphor, tend to be overtly erotic. Contemporary prisoners have reported ongoing love affairs with centerfolds displayed prominently on cell walls. George Mosby, Jr., a prison poet, writes lovingly "of an old con" with just such a love object:

> he has grown in love
> with the nude brown centerfold
> on the wall above his bunk
>
> her breasts are too big for her thin body
> and the page has worn sheer
> where he touches her
> before he sleeps to dream each night
> imagining the fragrance of her womb
>
> he knows her eyes
> as a man knows the eyes of a woman
> he's spent a life-time with: they're branded
> in his mind.
>
> he licks his lips sometimes
> as if imagining her kisses
> her tongue wet and slippery as spinach
> in his mouth
>
> (dazed as stone) he sits
> and whips himself with thoughts of her

whispering to her: in twenty years
no-one has ever heard him promise her anything
other than all the love he can muster
and all the man he can be

(In Bruchac, 1984:237)

Other convicts describe imaginative dummies constructed to highlight anatomically appealing features of the female form. It is also probably true that sexual hunger pushes some men into homosexual encounters about which they are anxious or uncomfortable. The larger point though, made in the abstract by Sykes and drawn from real life in Nelson's case, is that sexual hunger is not only a physical yearning but a cry for the companionship of women. "By sexual hunger I mean a hunger not only for sexual intercourse, but a hunger for the voice, the touch, the laugh, the tears of Woman; a hunger for Woman Herself" (Nelson, 1936:143).

In the main, prisoners today probably suffer less sexual hunger than their counterparts from earlier years. Furloughs and conjugal visits, increasingly available since the mid-1970s, allow some access to women. Visiting rooms are settings that are fairly regularly exploited for *sub rosa* heterosexual trysts (see Fishman, 1990). Homosexual outlets, too, are more readily available, partly because prisoners can move about fairly freely in today's prisons and because the stigma associated with such conduct has been sharply reduced in society and in the prison. Thus a contemporary prisoner at Lompoc, a federal prison, told one researcher that "most dudes with homosexuals are married [to them]" (Fleisher, 1989:162). Such marriages may involve formal ceremonies of sorts; when separation or divorce occurs, personal crises may ensue (Fleisher, 1989:163). Fleisher describes a flamboyantly homosexual prisoner at Lompoc who would make the nightly rounds of the cell blocks looking for sex partners. No official of Lompoc prison attempted to thwart him in these endeavors. Nor is there any concerted effort to curb the sexual appetites of the estimated 10 percent of his fellow inmates who were "actively engaged in sex" during the period of Fleisher's study (1989:157). Still, for most prisoners today, homosexual outlets are unavailable, and others who seek such relationships may be unable to secure satisfying homosexual arrangements. Furloughs and conjugal visits must be earned; not all prisoners are eligible, and those who are must often wait years for the privilege. Writing of prison life in the 1970s, and having had the benefit of a furlough, McCall (1995:200) could observe with obvious feeling that "Sometimes sexual tension got so heavy in my chest that I felt I might just explode, blow up in a puff of smoke." McCall was not alone in this reaction. "You're in a place," he notes, "where everybody's got the same problem; everybody feel like Superman with a helluva hump on his back" (McCall 1995:191). The pains of sexual deprivation thus remain substantial.

Loss of autonomy is the fourth deprivation suffered by prisoners. In all prisons, the inmate is under the control of officials and hence is in varying degrees nonautonomous. The threat of brutal punishments reigned in early prisons; autonomy was not even a consideration of the dealings of keepers and the kept, though poor surveillance in the early prisons allowed subterranean areas of human freedoms. In the penitentiary and in the Big House, the prisoner "is subjected to a vast body of rules and commands which are designed to control his behavior in minute detail" (Sykes, 1966:73). Rules are, moreover, nonnegotiable and beyond dispute. Staff need not give reasons; inmates need only obey. In essence, prisoners have been forcibly returned to the helpless, dependent status of children. "Of the many threats which may confront the individual," observes Sykes (1966:76), "either in or out of prison, there are few better calculated to arouse acute anxieties than the attempt to reimpose the subservience of youth." It is perhaps ironic that Nelson, himself an inmate, describes prisoners' attitudes toward rules as similar to children's, with no sense of their larger purpose and only a self-centered resentment of the restrictions the rules entail. "There is," he states,

> simply no respect for laws and rules as necessary adjuncts to civilization and social organization. The prisoner feels that the rules have been made merely in order to prevent him from doing the things he wants to do, and thus he resents them very strongly and breaks them when he can. (Nelson, 1936:125)

In what turns out to be a prophetic observation, Nelson argues that the word of the guard on matters of rule violations is always taken over that of the convict, and that this must be so if the system of discipline is to endure.

> The word of a prison guard naturally outweighs that of a convict—and this gives the guard power which he quickly learns to employ against the prisoners who displease him. They know that whatever the guard says, when reporting them for violating rules, will be believed by the warden. It must be believed, otherwise the whole system of discipline within the prison is shattered. (Nelson, 1936:125–26)

Some thirty years later the word of the guard would be given less weight, as due process and other concerns reduced their authority in the 1960s and 70s. Rules would become less rigid; enforcement would become lax. Explanations would be expected, indeed demanded, by restive convicts. Eventually, explanations from officers would become a matter of course in the enforcement of rules. One result of this change in the meaning of rules in prison was, at least for a time, the virtual collapse of discipline, with a resulting surge in inmate violence (see Chapter Five). Rules still exist, of course, and they irk and restrain most prisoners. But some respect for the prisoner's autonomy is afforded in today's rule enforcement context, which makes this pain of imprisonment less potent than in times past.

Loss of security is described by Sykes as the fifth and final deprivation of imprisonment. In early prisons, from the Mamertine through penitentiaries and industrial prisons, the main source of insecurity was the officers, who wielded nearly total power over the prisoners. Officials were feared figures in plantation prisons and in the Big House, to be sure, as they are in some contemporary prisons, where abuses by staff can become rampant. But whenever freedom of movement emerged in prison, one's fellow convicts came to represent potent threats to personal security.

This occurred in some early prisons, where poor supervision and congregate confinement allowed the community of lepers, if you will, to prey on one another. This occurred in some penitentiaries, when regimes of solitude and silence broke down, allowing convicts to corrupt and debase one another. Prisoners became a progressively more potent threat to one another in the Big House, where sufficient free time and loosely supervised recreation in the yard allowed a full-blown prisoner society to evolve. In such a setting, states Sykes,

> the individual prisoner is thrown into prolonged intimacy with other men who in many cases have a long history of violent, aggressive behavior. It is a situation which can prove to be anxiety-provoking even for the hardened recidivist and it is in this light that we can understand the comment of an inmate of the New Jersey State Prison who said, "The worst thing about prison is you have to live with other prisoners." (Sykes, 1966:77)

By today's standards, Big Houses were well controlled and the prison society operated within sharp constraints. Still, "outlaws" emerged among the prisoners, and could wreak havoc among their fellows. "There are," states Sykes (1966:77),

> a sufficient number of outlaws within this group of outlaws to deprive the average prisoner of that sense of security which comes from living among men who can be reasonably expected to abide by the rules of society. While it is true that every prisoner does not live in the constant fear of being robbed or beaten, the constant companionship of thieves, rapists, murderers, and aggressive homosexuals is far from reassuring.

Accordingly, the prisoner of the Big House can never feel completely safe in the prison. His physical security and psychological integrity are always potentially at risk:

> His expectations concerning the conforming behavior of others destroyed, unable and unwilling to rely on the officials for protection, uncertain of whether or not today's joke will be tomorrow's bitter insult, the prison inmate can never feel safe. And at a deeper level lies the anxiety about his reactions to this unstable world, for then his manhood will be evaluated in the public view. (Sykes, 1966:78)

With the demise of the discipline of the Big House, which will be discussed at length in Chapter Five, there was a period of a some fifteen years—from roughly the mid-1960s until the early 1980s—when prisoner violence was at a high point in many if not most prisons in the nation. Conrad (1988:320) could look back on the "repressive but reasonably safe" Big House with nostalgia, arguing persuasively that the loss of security was greater for convicts during this period than at any time in recent prison history. Conrad was, in my opinion, correct in this assertion. Meanwhile, however, internal reforms have reduced violence considerably in contemporary prisons, to the point where even this deprivation may be reduced relative to prisons of earlier eras. This matter will be discussed at some length in the final chapter of this book, where we take up the matter of prison reform.

It is Sykes's view that the various psychological deprivations of modern prisons represent harms that are equivalent to the physical maltreatment found in prisons of earlier days, notably the penitentiaries. He states,

> These deprivations or frustrations of the modern prison may indeed be the acceptable or unavoidable implications of imprisonment, but we must recognize the fact that they can be just as painful as the physical maltreatment which they have replaced. . . . Such attacks on the psychological level are less easily seen than a sadistic beating, a pair of shackles in the floor, or the caged man on a treadmill, but the destruction of the psyche is no less fearful than bodily affliction. . . . (Sykes, 1966:64)

The destruction of the human personality, which lies at the heart of dehumanization,[6] is indeed a fearful thing, but Sykes overstates the relative magnitude of this harm. Corporal punishments were themselves assaults on the psyche or person as well as on the body of the prisoner. Harms flowing from such terrifying physical abuse would entail psychological as well as physical mutilations. Such practices are both physically brutal and profoundly degrading to the prisoners as persons. To be spared physical abuse is to be spared a great deal of human suffering.

Today's psychological pains of imprisonment are formidable in themselves, to be sure, but they are, I contend, considerably less substantial and hurtful than the pains of life in earlier prisons.[7] The utter indifference and brutality of the ancient prisons, typified in *Squalor Carceris* and the officially orchestrated terror so integral to the running of the penitentiary, are things of the past. In contrast, the comparatively mild emotion of shame occasioned by psychological assaults on the self, present in the penitentiary but subservient to fear, has become the primary source of coercive control in modern "total institutions" such as the prison (Goffman, 1961). Significantly, these institutions now provide something approximating a total world for the inmate, not in the sense that he feels utterly vulnerable and must obey out of raw fear (as in all premodern prisons), but because he is dependent upon the institution for basic resources, feels personally shamed and inadequate under those conditions, and hence can be manipulated or persuaded to follow the dictates of an authority that at once both sustains and demeans him.

The link between dependency and shame, which can be exploited for the sake of punishment, is a modern one. In Sennett's (1981:46) words,

> In aristocratic or other traditional societies, weakness was not per se a shameful fact. One inherited one's weakness in society; it was not of one's own making. The master inherited his strengths; they too were impersonal. Thus in documents of the old regime we often find the plainest speaking of servants to their masters. Man and position were distinct . . . it is not under these conditions humiliating to be dependent.

Nor was it shameful to be dependent according to the philosophy of the Enlightenment. One inherited one's environment, which in turn shaped one's character. Once again, "man and position were distinct"; dependency did not connote shame or subjugation.

This equilibrium gradually shifted during the nineteenth century in response to the rampant uncertainty of social relations under industrial capitalism. Dependency came to be seen as a failing, and hence as a cause for shame. As Sennett (1981:46) has observed,

> The market made positions of dependence unstable. You could rise, you could fall. The most powerful impact ideologically of this instability was that people began to feel personally responsible for their place in the world; they viewed their success or failure in struggling for existence as a matter of personal strength or weakness. . . . Shame about being dependent is the legacy of the 19th century industrial society to our own.

Increasingly, persons in authority were able to punish and control their subordinates by inflicting shame. The result is that "shame has taken the place of violence as a routine form of punishment in Western societies. The reason is simple and perverse. The shame an autonomous person can arouse in subordinates is an implicit control" (Sennett, 1981:95).[8]

The various degradations of life in total institutions like the prison are prime examples of this phenomenon. Gradually the prison, like the larger society, came to rely more on shame and less on violence as a means of social control. Penitentiary inmates were meant to suffer shame in the form of the "lash of remorse" as we noted in Chapter Two, though the daily regime of the penitentiary was not expressly organized to promote and accentuate shame as a means of social control (as distinct from repentance). Over time, shaven heads and ill-fitting uniforms were intentionally inflicted to express the prisoner's dependent and shameful state and to use those disabilities to gain control over his behavior. Bereft of a personal identity—or at least denied respect for what identity he maintained—the confined man increasingly was expected to adopt the *social role* of the inmate and to fall into the prison routine. Brutality became increasingly superfluous and even counterproductive as a source of daily control of prison life. Surveillance, the gaze of authority that lay at the heart of the disciplinary regime, as vividly revealed in the panoptical version of the penitentiary (Foucault, 1977), gradually became the backbone of prison discipline. Where surveillance failed, cooptation of rebellious inmates neutralized discontent. Compliance rather than overt coercion became the preferred mechanism of control.

Yet even in regard to the infliction of the comparatively tame emotion of shame, prisons have become less total, prisoners less dependent on their keepers. In Goffman's (1961:43–48) terms, today's prisoners suffer fewer "mortifications, debasements, and profanations of self." They have more autonomy than their predecessors of only a generation ago; they have more control over their appearance and over the routine that makes up their prison day. They have more possessions and more freedoms, big and small. They are less closely watched. The ambiance of their prisons more closely resembles the modern urban slum street corner than the nineteenth-century penitentiary or the twentieth-century Big House (Carroll, 1988:182). Shame remains a salient feature of prison life, as it does in the slums, but these days shame is apt to evoke defensiveness and anger, even rage, rather than docility (Carmichael & Hamilton, 1967; Grier & Cobbs, 1968). Order is more likely to be negotiated by the prisoners and the staff, though prisoners must bargain from a position of weakness. The notion that staff and inmates can share a constructive agenda—that they might work together in service of a prison community that promotes mature coping and responsible citizenship—looms as a distinct possibility for perhaps the first time in prison history.

CIVILIZED PRISONS: PAIN DELIMITED

We live in a time of tame punishments relative to practices in times past. Our present-day conception of "bloodthirsty" punishment does not call for blood or even for physical pain: our worst murderers face bloodless and, we hope, physically painless executions (see Johnson, 1990). Nor does our notion of harsh punishment encompass the use of calculated psychological abuse of those we confine. Our worst version of prison punishment is captured in the (modern) proverbial notion of "locking the door and throwing away the key." We relegate serious criminals to years of neglect, which is, to be sure, a terrible thing in itself, but it is significant that we do not expect criminals to experience overt physical or psychological abuse as a planned feature of their confinement. It is for these reasons that prisons of only a century ago seem flagrantly inhumane, even barbaric, by contemporary standards.

No one today would seriously consider years of solitary confinement or silent congregate labor as anything other than torture.[9] Nor is brutal corporal punishment, once standard fare in prison, practiced in any contemporary penal institution. In fact, it is widely believed today by prison officials that "no aim of prison—including retributive punishment—is served by arbitrary, gratuitous, ill-distributed distress" (Johnson & Toch, 1988:15). Abuses do occur in today's prisons, and they sometimes take the form of lengthy solitary confinement and staff brutality (the latter practice being a variant of corporal punishment).[10] But such treatment is no longer the norm. It is fair to say that, with a limited array of psychological stresses as the most horrible punishment we are willing to inflict upon our criminals, we are becoming both more civilized and more potentially civilizing in our punishments.

Prisons are still in the pain business, but with well-defined limits. Prisoners may well deserve to suffer for the harm they have done to others, but prison officials are not eager to punish them. They supervise the administration of painful experiences but do not consciously or systematically inflict pain to make prisoners suffer. Indeed, some of the worst pains of today's prisons are the product of the officials' inability to control the more violent prisoners;

prison's slum communities, like their counterparts in the free world, are notoriously hard to police. Prisons can be brutal and degrading but this, with rare
exceptions, is neither intended nor passively countenanced. Certainly brutality
is no longer defended by officials as a necessary component of prison discipline! The brutal prison in today's world reflects a failure of policy, a triumph
of convenience over conscience, and a challenge to responsible prison administrators.

NOTES

1. A less pure and somewhat paradoxical
case of modern correctional utopianism
was provided by some political prisoners
during the 1960s and 1970s, most notably
George Jackson (see Dorin & Johnson,
1979). Prisoners like Jackson acted as
though they held the misguided view that
the rigors of prison made it an ideal milieu
for political recruitment and foment.

2. Hamm and his associates, for example,
maintain that today's prisons are systematically abusive, making them indistinguish-
able from earlier prisons (see Hamm et.
al., 1994). This study is, in my view, short
on method and long on ideology. It ex-
hibits at least two salient flaws. First, the
complex notion of humaneness is used as a
foil, as though humaneness were limited
to matters of discipline and did not encompass the general habitability of prisons.
The prison literature is reviewed selectively and with no sense of history. There
are, if you will, no shades of grey in the
prison world: guards are hacks who prey
on innocent inmate victims; prisons are
settings of brutality featuring daily violence and abuse. Things are today as they
always have been in prison, which is to
say, uniformly awful and degrading. Anyone who argues or presents evidence to
the contrary is uninformed and painfully
naive. All of this makes good rhetoric but
poor social science. Second, the empirical
survey of prison discipline practices that
forms the heart of the study is profoundly
flawed. The sample of respondents returning prison discipline questionnaires is tiny
(10 percent), self-selected (drawn primarily
from prisoners who were members of
prisoners' rights or advocacy groups), and
disproportionately made up of long-term

maximum security inmates; no effort is
made to establish that this group is representative of long-termers in general, let
alone prisoners in general. Responses to
this questionnaire paint a picture of the
prison much like that provided by Jack
Abbott (see Chapter Five), a deeply alienated man who has a penchant for exagger-
ating prison abuses and minimizing his
own role in degenerating encounters with
prison staff and officials. Taking the posture of the innocent and aggrieved victim,
Abbott offered what is essentially a caricature of the contemporary prison. The
respondents in this study appear to do the
same. The result is that we are asked to
reject a "myth" of humane imprisonment
and accept in its place the view that
today's prisons are settings of undiluted
abuse and inhumanity where the victims
are the morally upright (jailhouse lawyers
and "those who exhibit personal
integrity") and the spiritually downtrod-
den (prisoners with mental handicaps), and
the victimizers—the hacks—are essentially
felons in uniform.

3. This is decidedly not the case in the so-
called super-max facilities used with the
most recalcitrant prisoners in the federal
system and in some state prison systems.
These prisons are a small part of any
prison system and do not, as a
consequence, receive much attention in
the book. They are briefly addressed in
Chapter Nine.

4. I say ostensibly because, in point of
fact, anesthesiologists "can find no scientific support for believing the methods
being used [for lethal injection] are effective for quick and painless execution"
(Capron, 1984:A23). Descriptions of other

methods of execution suggest that, at least on some occasions, condemned prisoners experience pain, even if for only brief periods of time (see, for example, Denno, 1994). There is, of course, no way of knowing for sure, since no one has survived an execution to tell about it, except following equipment failure, which of course changes fundamentally the experience of execution (see, for example, Miller & Bowman, 1988).

5. Accounts by prison officials assigned to carry out executions during this century attest to this observation. See, for example, former San Quentin warden Duffy's (1962) impassioned plea for the humanity of using the gas chamber instead of hanging. More generally, see my discussion of the taming of the execution process over the course of Western history (Johnson, 1990).

6. I discuss this matter in some detail in Johnson, 1990, Chapter Eight.

7. This point is obvious to some, and I believe it is correct, but the issue is not as decisively resolved as one would at first suppose. Certainly today's prisons are less objectively painful and depriving than prisons past, and this is an important index of progress. Data on subjective pain—the experience of suffering in prison—would provide another measure of progress. Are modern prisons less subjectively painful than their counterparts in early times, as measured by the suffering of the respective inhabitants? Regrettably, we have no way of knowing whether the *relative suffering* experienced by prisoners today is less than that of their counterparts in earlier times, because we have no way of quantifying perceptions of the pains of imprisonment while at the same time holding constant the level of pain seen as normal or acceptable in life at different stages of history. How painful was a medieval dungeon relative to daily life in the Middle Ages? How painful was Trenton State Prison relative to life in America in the 1950s? How painful are today's prisons relative to daily life in our now violence-infested, drug-suffused slums? The data one would need to pose the question of relative suffering today, let alone for times past, are quite complex. I am aware of no studies

that have broached this area of inquiry, though some promising leads may be found in the emerging field of panetics (see Siu, 1988).

8. The retreat from physical pain as a major part of punishment is the result of a complex historical process. It is not the product of a failure of memory or nerve, as Newman (1983:3 & 25) has suggested in his treatise urging us to return to the primordial (not to say manly) practice of corporal punishment.

9. Death row confinement typically takes the form of extended solitary confinement unbroken by any substantial labor or recreation. I have argued that this is indeed a contemporary instance of torture (Johnson, 1989 & 1990). Super-max prisons, many of which impose extended periods of solitary confinement, are periodically identified by groups like Amnesty International as settings of torture.

10. These abuses are cataloged in Bowker (1980) and in Braswell, Montgomery and Lombardo (1994).

REFERENCES

Barnes, H. E., and N. K. Teeters. *New Horizons in Criminology*. New York: Prentice-Hall, 1952.

Bowker, L. *Prison Victimization*. New York: Elsevier, 1980.

Braly, M. *On The Yard*. Boston: Little, Brown, 1967.

Braswell, M. C., R. H. Montgomery and L. X. Lombardo (eds.). *Prison Violence in America*. Cincinnati, OH: Anderson, 1994.

Bruchac, J. *The Light From Another Country: Poetry From American Prisons*. Greenfield Center, NY: Greenfield Review Press, 1984.

Capron, A. M. "Should doctors help execute prisoners?" *The Washington Post* (December 6, 1984):A23.

Carmichael, S., and C. Hamilton. *Black Power*. New York: Random House, 1967.

Carroll, L. "Race, ethnicity, and the social order of the prison." In R. Johnson and H. Toch (eds.) *The Pains of Imprisonment*. Prospect Heights, IL: Waveland Press, 1988:181–203.

Christie, N. *Limits to Pain*. Oxford: Martin Robertson, 1981.

Clear, T. R. *Harm in American Penology: Offenders, Victims, and Their Communities*. Albany: State University of New York Press, 1994.

Conrad, J. P. "What do the undeserving deserve?" In R. Johnson and H. Toch (eds.). *The Pains of Imprisonment*. Prospect Heights, IL: Waveland Press, 1988:313–30.

Crouch, B. M., and J. W. Marquart. *An Appeal to Justice*. Austin: University of Texas Press, 1989.

Denno, D. W. "Is electrocution an unconstitutional method of execution? The engineering of death over the century." *William and Mary Law Review* 35 (2) 1994:551–692.

Dobash, R. P. "Labour and discipline in Scottish and English prisons: Moral correction, punishment and useful toil." *Sociology* 17 (1) 1983:1–25.

Dorin, D., and R. Johnson. "The premature dragon: George Jackson as a model for the new militant inmate." *Contemporary Crises* 3 (1979):295–315.

Duffy, C. T., with A. Hirshbert. *88 Men and 2 Women*. New York: Doubleday, 1962.

Elgar, T. (Convict No. 6179). *Convict Life; or, Penitentiary Citizenship in the Illinois State Pen*. Rochester, NY: 1886.

Fishman, L. T. *Women at the Wall: A Study of Prisoners' Wives Doing Time on the Outside*. Albany, NY: State University of New York Press, 1990.

Fleisher, M. S. *Warehousing Violence*. Newbury Park, CA: Sage, 1989.

Foucault, M. *Discipline and Punish: The Birth of the Prison*. New York: Pantheon, 1977.

Goffman, E. *Asylums*. New York: Anchor Books, 1961.

Grier, W., and P. Cobbs. *Black Rage*. New York: Basic Books, 1968.

Hamm, M. S., T. Coupez, F. E. Hoze, and C. Weinstein. "The myth of humane imprisonment: A critical analysis of severe discipline in U.S. maximum security prisons, 1945–1990." In M. C. Braswell, R. H. Montgomery, and L. X. Lombardo (eds.). *Prison Violence in America*. Cincinnati, OH: Anderson, 1994:167–200.

Hawkins, G. *The Prison: Policy and Practice*. Chicago: University of Chicago Press, 1976.

Irwin, J. *Prisons in Turmoil*. Boston: Little, Brown, 1980.

Jacobs, J. B. *Stateville: The Penitentiary in Mass Society*. Chicago: University of Chicago Press, 1977.

Jenkins, P. "Temperance and the origins of the new penology." *Journal of Criminal Justice* 12 (6) 1984:551–65.

Johnson, Hon. F. M. "Memorandum of opinion." In *Pugh v. Locke*, January 13, 1975.

Johnson, R. *Condemned to Die: Life Under Sentence of Death*. Prospect Heights, IL: Waveland Press, 1989.

Johnson, R. *Death Work: A Study of the Modern Execution Process*. Belmont Grove, CA: Wadsworth, 1990.

Johnson, R., and H. Toch. "Introduction." In R. Johnson, and H. Toch (eds.). *The Pains of Imprisonment*. Prospect Heights, IL: Waveland, 1988:13–21.

Lawes, L. L. *Twenty Thousand Years in Sing Sing*. New York: Ray Long & Richard R. Smith, 1932.

McCall, N. *Makes Me Wanna Holler: A Young Black Man in America*. New York: Vintage, 1995.

Mill, J. S. "Civilization: Essay on politics and society." *Collected Work of John Stuart Mill*. Vol. 18. Toronto: University of Toronto Press, 1977:119–47.

Miller, A. S., and J. H. Bowman. *Death by Installments: The Ordeal of Willie Francis*. New York: Greenwood Press, 1988.

Morris, N., and G. Hawkins. *The Honest Politician's Guide to Crime Control*. Chicago: University of Chicago Press, 1970.

Nelson, V. F. *Prison Days and Nights*. Garden City, NY: Garden City Publishing, 1936.

Newman, G. *The Punishment Response*. Philadelphia: Lippincott, 1978.

Newman, G. *Just and Painful: A Case for the Corporal Punishment of Criminals*. London: Collier Macmillan, 1983.

Pisciotta, A. W. "Scientific reform: The 'new penology' at Elmira, 1876–1900." *Crime & Delinquency* 29 (4) 1983:613–630.

Reiman, J. H. "Civilization and the death penalty: Answering van den Haag." *Philosophy and Public Affairs* 14 (2) 1985:115–48.

Rhodes v. Chapman, 101 S. Ct. 2392 and 2400, 1981.

Rothman, D. *Conscience and Convenience: The Asylum and Its Alternatives in Progressive America*. Boston: Little, Brown, 1980.

Sennett, R. *Authority*. New York: Vintage Books, 1981.

Siu R. G. H. "Panetics: The study of the infliction of suffering." *Journal of Humanistic Psychology* 28 (3) 1988:6–22.

Sykes, G. M. *The Society of Captives: A Study of a Maximum Security Prison*. New York: Atheneum, 1966.

Toch, H. "Study and reducing stress." In R. Johnson, and H. Toch (eds.). *The Pains of Imprisonment*. Prospect Heights, IL: Waveland Press, 1988:25–44.

Ward, D. A. "Alcatraz and Marion: confinement in super maximum security." In J. R. Roberts (ed.). *Escaping Prison Myths: Selected Topics in the History of Federal Corrections*. Washington, D.C.: The American University Press, 1994:81–93.

Washington, J. *A Bright Spot in the Yard: Notes and Stories from a Prison Journal*. Trumansburg, NY: The Crossing Press, 1981.

❖

PART II

Living and Working in Prison

4

Mature Coping

The Challenge of Adjustment

Prisons today are less overtly and intentionally painful than their predecessors. Neither physical pain nor mental or emotional abuse are planned features of modern imprisonment. The pains experienced in contemporary prisons, for all intents and purposes, originate in psychological stresses. And though these stresses can be quite substantial, today's prisons offer more opportunities for constructive adaptation than did earlier prisons. Still, although contemporary prisons may be comparatively civilized and potentially civilizing, adjustment to prison is always a challenge. We must understand this challenge in the larger context of the offender's adjustment to life, and work to facilitate mature adjustment both in prison and out.

The pains of life in contemporary prisons are real. There is no point in denying them. Nor does it make sense to see pain merely as an obstacle to correctional work, for it is an obstacle that can never be circumvented. Pain is an enduring feature of the correctional enterprise. We must accept this hard reality, and quite explicitly attempt to promote growth through adversity. This is a genuine correctional agenda. For men who cope maturely with prison, I will argue, are men who have grown as human beings and been rehabilitated in the process.

"Imprisonment," as I have observed elsewhere, "is a disheartening and threatening experience for most men" (Johnson, 1976:1). Typically,

> The man in prison finds his career disrupted, his relationships suspended, his aspirations and dreams gone sour. Few prisoners have experienced

comparable stress in the free world, or have developed coping strategies or perspectives that shield them from prison problems. Although prisoners differ from each other, and may feel the pressures of confinement somewhat differently, they concur on the extraordinarily stressful nature of life in maximum security penal institutions (Johnson, 1976:1–2).

Moreover, for many inmates the stresses of imprisonment are aggravated because they cope with prison in immature and ultimately destructive ways. All too often, this is compounded by the immature actions of the staff. Tough, rebellious inmates and callous, insensitive guards may well be the public models of deportment commonly seen on prison yards (as we shall see in Chapters Five and Seven, respectively), but they are not models for mature problem solving. The hard stoicism of the man who can "take it" and "dish it out" without flinching is particularly destructive in today's overcrowded prisons, where close and often abrasive contact calls for tact, diplomacy, and the ability to transcend stereotypical roles and relationships (Lombardo, 1988; Johnson, 1993). Chronic tension and violence are testimonials to failures of adjustment under these conditions (Smith, 1988; Bonta & Gendreau, 1990).

Of course, living in prison has never been easy, and it never will be. This holds true whether prisons are crowded or sparely populated and whether prisoners are veterans or novices. And simply to survive is not enough. Prisoners must cope maturely with the demands of prison life; if they do not, the prison experience will simply add to their catalog of failure and defeat. Mature coping, in fact, does more than prevent one's prison life from becoming yet another series of personal setbacks. It is at the core of what we mean by correction or rehabilitation, and thus creates the possibility of a more constructive life after release from prison (Johnson & Toch, 1988:19–20; Toch, 1988:36–39).

Let me now examine the three major attributes of mature coping, show that much of what passes for adjustment among persistent felons falls short of this goal, and explain why men who respond maturely to prison stress are likely to become reformed citizens. In doing so, I will introduce a number of themes that will be developed in subsequent chapters.

MATURE COPING

In Chapter One, we defined human nature as featuring self-determination or autonomy, which develops most fully in secure social environments that permit and indeed encourage human relationships. Mature coping means, in essence, dealing with life's problems like a responsive and responsible human being, one who seeks autonomy without violating the rights of others, security without resort to deception or violence, and relatedness to others as the finest and fullest expression of human identity. It is of course true that most inmates have not been fully or even largely habilitated—equipped or trained— to behave in these ways, and thus to speak of their need for *re*habilitation is, in a sense, to put the cart before the horse (see Hawkins and Alpert, 1989:184).

But like all people, prisoners have some natural inclinations toward autonomy, security, and relatedness to others, and the experience of prison can build on those inclinations. The result, in my view, can be said to comprise their personal rehabilitation or correction.

Dealing with Problems and Achieving Autonomy

Mature coping means, first, dealing with problems: meeting problems head-on, using all resources legitimately at one's disposal. This aspect of mature coping involves "assertiveness" (Howard & Scott, 1965), a sense of "personal efficacy" (White, 1959; Bandura, 1977), and an "internal locus of control" with respect to one's immediate environment (Rotter, 1966). It is certainly true that "persons who expect to exert control"—who are confident enough to behave assertively and believe that self-directed efforts will pay off—"can find ways to do so even when opportunities for control are severely limited" (Goodstein et al., 1984:352; see also MacKenzie, Goodstein, & Blouin, 1987:65).[1] They follow the sage advice of Gwendolyn Brooks: "When handed a lemon, make lemonade" (cited in McCall, 1995:177). Such persons are, in other words, more autonomous than their passive counterparts.

Autonomy is, in general, a profoundly rewarding experience. "Both people and animals are happier, healthier, more active, solve problems better, and feel less stress when they are given choice and control" (Toch & Adams, 1989:272). There is some specific evidence that prisoners with a sense of control over their lives adjust better to prison and to life on the outside. Such persons are more goal-directed in their adjustment, experience less conflict with authorities, and violate fewer prison rules; they experience less emotional distress and fewer symptoms of physical illness in their daily prison lives (Goodstein and Wright, 1989:24–45).[2] There is preliminary evidence suggesting that these prisoners may recidivate—return to crime on release—at lower levels than other inmates (Zamble, 1990:143). This finding is important, because the issue is not exclusively what works in the matter of adjustment, but what facilitates adjustment within the constraints of legitimate society. Some predators, we know, "assert" themselves in service of internally orchestrated adjustment goals and skillfully elude the authorities, but they do not cope maturely.

In effect, mature coping is doing the best you can with what is rightfully yours. But persistent and serious criminals, who regularly become prison inmates, don't settle for what is rightfully theirs. They have been described, aptly, as "hasty hedonists" and "jungle cats" who live by a preemptive version of the Golden Rule: "do unto others as they would do unto you . . . only do it first" (Nettler, 1984:209; Schwendinger & Schwendinger, 1967:98). The flamboyant posturing often characteristic of this lifestyle is captured in the following statement by a man who is currently serving time for a murder he committed while making a drug deal to support himself "in the life."

> Straight people don't understand. I mean, they think dudes is after the things straight people got. It ain't that at all. People in the life ain't looking for no home and grass in the yard. . . . We the show people. The glamour

people. Come on the set with the finest car, the finest women, the finest vines. Hear people talking about you. Hear the bar get quiet when you walk in the door. Throw down a yard and tell everybody drink up. See. It's rep. It's glamour. That's what it's about. What else a dude gon do in this . . . world. You make something out of nothing. (Wideman, 1984:131)

Men like this can be masters at making something out of nothing. They are possessed of "delinquent egos" (Aichhorn, 1955) that help them to "make hay in the few moments the sun is shining" on their slum street corners and associated hot spots (Toch, 1971:390), and they are ready to do so at the expense of others. The high point of such a life is apt to be found in acts of impulsivity, where the thrill of living on the raw edge of emotion gives meaning, however passing, to a life devoid of lasting achievement. At times, crime has not only adventurous but almost sensuous connotations (see Katz, 1988). In the words of one such man,

> If I could keep only one memory or moment in my life and that was it—all the rest would be erased—I think the one moment that I would keep is the shootout with the police in Glendale. The experience of shooting it out with that cop was absolutely, totally, the most beautiful experience in my life. I'm not crazy. *It was beautiful!* . . . The truth is, I've always liked living on the edge of madness, being the one out there—the one that they are trying to catch—the lone warrior who does his own thing, who answers only to himself. (Earley, 1992:382–83)

This impulsive and often predatory hedonism is adaptive in the short run.[3] Jungle cats survive and even prosper in prisons and ghettos, settings where persons with "middle class egos"—that "sell immediacy short" and are "other directed"—would be "pounced upon and consumed" (Toch, 1971:390).

But many, perhaps even most, chronic felons are by no means masters of the criminal arts or even adept hedonists. Crime for them is not a lifestyle to which they aspired as a result of planning and choice; rather, it is a way of life they selected by default. Many are bumbling, ineffectual people of limited intelligence (Herrnstein, 1994); some—no one knows how many—appear to be saddled with a host of biomedical deficits that, often in conjunction with low IQ, limit their ability to cope with life in conventional ways (see Brennan, Mednick & Volavka, 1994). These offenders are inept at virtually everything they do, including crime. Zamble, Porporino, and Kalotay (1984:64) underscore this point:[4]

> most of our subjects had a great deal of trouble coping with life outside of prison. . . . In general, they had an inadequate repertoire of possible coping responses, especially those involving higher-level strategies. . . . [O]ne might have predicted that some sort of major maladaptive consequences were almost inevitable for many of them: if they had not been imprisoned, some other calamitous events would have occurred.

Most offenders, whether due to personal or social deficits, or both, are not "able to analyze situations rationally or to make choices that facilitate their desires" (Zamble, 1990:138). For most offenders, then, "coping difficulties are a central cause of the maintenance and repetition of criminal acts, if not their origin" (Zamble & Porporino, 1990:56). The problems they confront in life are fairly typical, centering on interpersonal and financial difficulties, but their coping efforts are unsystematic, unsustained and, at best, ineffectual. Too often, their coping efforts *aggravate* the very problems they are intended to solve, making matters worse rather than better.

> Rarely did [their coping efforts] include any consistent attempts at developing some deliberate, persistent, or systematic approach to a situation, a conscious strategy of self-control or other cognitive technique, or any sort of planning and organization. . . . Roughly 70% did things that would be likely to exacerbate at least one of the three situations that inmates identified as their most serious problems, even when the risks were rated conservatively. We repeatedly heard how subjects had reacted to pressure from an employer by sabotaging the job, how they responded to difficulties with their wives by philandering, or how they dealt with the anxiety of money problems by spending all available funds on drugs. (Zamble & Porporino, 1990:57–58)

These offenders are better characterized as troubled and troublesome men than devil-may-care rogues. They lead lives of pain, and inflict pain on others in response to their own inadequacy. Their relations with women, in particular, can be destructive and controlling in the extreme. As one convict observed, absolutely without remorse or shame, women are ready candidates for abuse. "I cracked her a good one," he related in an interview with Earley (1992:416–17),

> because she had it coming. Now, I don't believe in beating up women, but if my old lady is talking to some man, she's gonna get knocked to the floor every time because I know old ladies are good for three things: giving pussy, cooking, and taking care of kids, and if I see her talking to another man, I know she ain't cooking, I know she ain't taking care of his kids, so she and him must be talking about pussy.

There is joy in crime for men such as this, including the crime of wife-beating, but that joy tends to be short-lived. Their lives are deeply unsatisfying.

For persons who have low self-esteem, limited cognitive and interpersonal skills, and few conventional opportunities for success, crime can be quite attractive. As Halleck (1967:72) has observed, "if favorable opportunities for altering the internal or external environment are not available, criminal action looms as a seductive antidote to an unbearable feeling of helplessness." Robbie Wideman expressed this helplessness quite eloquently, if a bit melodramatically, when he observed, "We see what's going down. We supposed to die. Take our little welfare checks and be quiet and die" (Wideman, 1984:132). In contrast to the menial occupation and anonymous existence of the unskilled laborer, a life that looks like death to the average felon, crime offers a "moment of autonomy," high excitement, and a chance for camaraderie with peers (Halleck, 1967:77). (The increasing use of guns these days no doubt adds a special intensity to the moments of autonomy offered by crime, offering an "adrenaline rush" to armed felons who believe they are invincible. See McCall, 1995:68 and 72.) There is also an element of hope for the future, born of the sense that one is attacking one's problems directly by taking what one cannot properly lay claim to (Halleck, 1967:76–83). Fittingly, criminals see themselves as rebels serving the cause of their own self-aggrandizement.

Some criminals commit crimes sporadically and without any discernible pattern. Others adopt crime as way of life. For this latter group, known as chronic or lifestyle criminals,

> Crime can be understood as a lifestyle characterized by a global sense of irresponsibility, self-indulgent interests, an intrusive approach to interpersonal relationships, and chronic violation of societal rules, laws, and mores (Walters, 1990:71).

Lifestyle criminals exempt themselves from the constraints of law-abiding lives; neither laws nor conventional jobs are suitable for them. Only crime, "with its accompanying irresponsibility and self-indulgence" (Walters, 1990:106), meets their needs. Prison doesn't deter them because they know they can survive prison (Walters, 1990:107). Conventional adjustments, on the other hand, have little going for them. They offer both the meager rewards of a middle-class life, which is seen as "exceedingly boring and something to avoid at all cost" (Walters, 1990:109). They are also discouraged by the threat of failure at conventional living; for them, fear of failure can be great, as they have been repeatedly bruised by failures in living throughout their lives. A conventional life is thus seen as a high-cost, low-reward proposition. Naturally, these men do what comes easily, what they enjoy, and what they do best: crime.

The difficulty is that crime offers only illusory benefits. Appearances to the contrary, crime is bad business practice and a miserable way to make a living. The plain fact is that "street crime . . . doesn't pay. It's quite irrational by sound business standards. . . . [T]he criminal stands a 78% chance of winding up in jail before attaining even [the] minimal goal" of a poverty-level income (Mueller, 1985:18). It is, of course, hard to come by reliable estimates of earnings from crime, at least in part because criminals routinely overestimate their take from crime. Even so, there is absolutely no evidence for the common belief that many street criminals get rich as a result of their criminal exploits. As a general rule, earnings from crime are at best modest and "below the earnings these criminals could make at work" (Freeman, 1994:190). The proficient predators—the cream of the criminal crop, notably more sophisticated drug dealers and organized car thieves—may do somewhat better in material terms, but even they pay a high price for what amounts to short-term pleasures and conquests.

The rewards of crime, meager and evanescent as they are, do little to mollify the anger that propels criminals to destructive (and self-destructive) behavior. Like their less adroit brethren, even the best street criminals are possessed of a deeply rooted hostility that seems almost to feed upon itself, touching everyone and everything in its path. As Nettler (1984:313) has said,

> If our nurturing is defective—unappreciative, inconsistent, lax, harsh, and careless—we grow up hostile, and the hostility seems as much turned inward as turned outward. The nurturing environments that produce this denigration of self and others are the same ones that breed criminality.

Lives formed in cold and rejecting criminogenic environments are predictably turbulent and unrewarding. Virtually all chronic felons experience degenerating relations with friends and family (who may too often double as victims), failed work careers and downward social mobility (which add to pressures to prey on others), and a haunting sense that theirs is a pointless, dead-end existence (see Wideman, 1984).

Chronic felons often complicate already badly managed lives by denying rather than facing and resolving their problems. They may successfully resist efforts by loved ones to discipline and control them, displaying "a maddening disregard for the inevitable consequences" of their destructive actions (Wideman, 1984:66). They are deeply immersed in the street life, a life in which one lives from moment to moment, anesthetized by drugs and insulated from concerns about the future. "[T]he average pattern" among felons while in the free world, for example, has been described by Zamble, Porporino, and Kalotay (1984:58) as

> one of casual unplanned days, with greater dependence on friends than family or work, and little focus or goals. . . . [T]his way of spending time was also accompanied by a constant high level of alcohol and drug use. Many subjects must have gone through their days in a haze, and it is not surprising that there was little planning and few efforts at changing anything.

The various elements of this lifestyle "all act to channel the effects of inadequate coping ability into violent and antisocial actions" (Zamble, Porporino & Kalotay, 1984:128). They make it easy to deny one's own problems as well as the damage done to others by one's self-serving forays.

Denial is a coping strategy that, when used to excess, always backfires. Problems denied simply do not disappear. Chronic offenders know this—or should know this—but they ignore its implications for their lives and go about business as usual. They act as if they are invulnerable.

> In much the same way as a young child contemplates his invulnerability while donning a superman costume, the lifestyle criminal is unrealistic in how he appraises himself, his attributes, and his chances of avoiding the consequences of his antisocial actions (Walters, 1990:88).

The very nature of antisocial actions may be distorted in the minds of felons. Criminals regularly minimize the seriousness of their crimes and the degree to which they are culpable for their crimes.[5] They may, for example, convince themselves that their crimes, even crimes of violence, are mere games.

> Ain't nobody gon get killed. You just into cowboy and Indin shit like in the movies. You the gangsters but you the good guys too. No problem. . . .

That's the way we was. Stone gangsters. Robbing people. Waving guns in people's face. Serious shit. But it was like playing too. A game. A big game and we was just big kids having fun. Guns wasn't real. Bullets wasn't real. Wasn't planning on hurting nobody. Pow. Pow. You know. Fall over. I got you. No, you didn't. You missed. Pow. Pow. I got you. You lying. I got you first. Cowboy and Indin shit like the old days. . . . (Wideman, 1985:145)

Chronic offenders tend to let situations deteriorate until they become unmanageable, often ignoring repeated warnings that their criminal exploits are leading to disaster, or that relationships or jobs are in trouble. When failure inevitably materializes—when, for example, criminal games result in apprehension and confinement—they react with bitter fatalism, as if the cards were always stacked against them (see Walters, 1990; Yochelson & Samenow, 1976). Alternatively, impulses reign; the chronic offenders strike out blindly at the immediate cause of frustration (such as the boss who fires them or the police officer who arrests them) and do not analyze the deeper sources of their problems (see Walters, 1990; Yochelson & Samenow, 1976). Tragically, crime victims often bear the brunt of their impotent anger.

Chronic felons combine poor self-control with limited insight into the dynamics of their adjustment. They are, in Walter's (1990:88–89) observations, "lazy" in thought and behavior and, moreover, "overly accepting" of their own half-baked ideas about life and adjustment. Unsurprisingly, they act as pawns of what they take to be an arbitrary fate, juxtaposing passivity and impulsivity where informed and modulated action are called for. This immature behavior is promoted, even extolled, in prison culture. Ironically, what is touted on the prison yard as manliness or toughness amounts to nothing more than a posture of psychological denial that is leavened, to personal taste, with short-run hedonism and resentment of authority. Behind bars, such a stance may have a romantic side. As we shall see in Chapter Five, it pits innocent and aggrieved cons against gratuitously emasculating hacks. But adopting a manliness of this sort virtually ensures failure at conventional living in the free world.

Security Without Deception or Violence

The second characteristic of mature coping is addressing problems without resort to deception or violence, except when necessary for self-defense. Deception and violence are primitive behaviors. Except when engaged in to prevent immediate physical harm—itself a primitive self-defense situation[6] —deception and violence represent gross and reprehensible violations of the integrity of other human beings. Regrettably, deception and violence flourish in dangerous and unstable environments, where there is a chronic absence of trust in oneself and others, and preemptive strikes—hurting someone first and asking questions later—masquerade under the mantle of practical wisdom. Thus in prisons and on slum streets, deception and violence are a regular feature of daily life and adjustment; they are seen as normal, even desirable behaviors.

Deception in one's dealings with others is, of course, a possibility in any social circumstance. It is apparently the case that the possibility of deception, which greatly complicates human social interaction, has been an important force in the evolution of the human psyche. The psyche must be attuned not only to peoples' words and deeds, but also to the thoughts behind those words and deeds: to the thoughts people have about how others think as interactions unfold (Allman, 1994).[7] To be sure, deception is a possibility in any interaction, and in some cases, unlike violence, deception can be harmless—as when one passes along false compliments meant to put someone at ease. But as a general rule, deception of others is a destructive force because it impedes cooperation and undermines solidarity. It is therefore of crucial significance that deception is a *central* feature of prison culture (see Clemmer, 1940). Indeed, Empey (1982:251) reminds us, "deception is the name of the game" in prison. "Among officials as well as among inmates," Empey (1982:251) continues, "it will be the most skillful manipulator who most often gets what he wants."

To be sure, manipulation is also "the name of the game" on slum streets and in other areas marked by poverty and crime. In these settings, as in prisons, cooperation is comparatively rare and hence honesty has limited adaptive value in public social encounters (Suttles, 1968; Hannerz, 1969; Anderson, 1994). (Here, as in prisons, people are expected, at the very least, to be cagey. Telling the truth as a matter of course implies gross naïveté, and may be the equivalent of revealing one's hand in a game of poker before the game is over.) Violence, moreover, is met with explicit approbation in these same milieus and is considered a hallmark, if not *the* hallmark, of manliness and respect (see Anderson, 1994; Earley, 1992).

The operating premise on slum streets as well as prison yards would appear to be that lying to or physically harming others are but behavioral cousins on a continuum of adaptive abuse. Whether on slum streets or in prison, the world is populated by victimizers who exploit others and a host of prospective victims variously known as "punks, chumps, pigeons, or fags" (Schwendinger & Schwendinger, 1967:98). Even one's friends are presumed to be less than fully trustworthy, and thus are potential candidates for exploitation (Nettler, 1984:209). Since others are devalued, they become fair game. The authorities (police or guards) are seen as impotent and irrelevant; people are on their own, forced to make their own way (see Earley, 1992; Anderson, 1994). In what amounts to a social jungle, it is the weak versus the strong, with no holds barred (Walters, 1990:86–87; Anderson, 1994). Bonds of trust built on words have little value. Small wonder so many people arm themselves in these environments. For them, a knife (in prison) or a gun (on the streets) is "like an American Express card . . . you don't leave home without it" (Montgomery, 1994:A4).[8]

The primitive quality of prison life comes across clearly in the comments of a prisoner in Leavenworth, a prison noted for a hard-core convict culture of violence. "I don't respect the law," this convict explained to Earley (1992:211),

> because laws are for people who are weak and need them. If someone comes into my house and takes something, I'm not going to call a cop, I'm going to deal with it, and if I'm not man enough to get it back, then

that guy has a right to take whatever he wants because I don't really deserve to own it. That's how society should be. If justice needs to be applied, I will apply it, and the reason that I have a right to apply it is because I have the power to do it. Having the power gives me permission.

Indeed, not to take advantage of others is to show a kind of moral weakness, to advertise a potentially fateful failure of nerve in a social jungle. Correspondingly, not to be ready for violence at any time is a fateful—and often deadly—departure from prison norms.

> The first day I was in prison, two dudes busted in on this guy in the cell next to mine and stuck him twenty-six times with shanks. He was sitting on the crapper when they killed him, and he couldn't fight back because his pants were wrapped around his legs. Stupid bastard. Anyone who don't know better than to take a leg out of his pants in prison before he sits down on a toilet deserves to die. Something you learn in here. (Earley, 1992:50)

This cynical and ultimately adolescent view of life—where there are no shades of grey, no tempered emotions, no feelings of concern or sadness for the "stupid bastard" butchered in the cell next door—is common on slum streets. It is at the very heart of prison culture, however, in which anger and fear are the dominant emotions (see Walters, in Earley, 1992:50). In one prisoner's words,

> when you're in the joint you deal with people different than you do on the street. I mean your language and your actions. You just take a more aggressive posture. It's all body language. You learn to deal with people in jail. You learn to spot weakness there and you learn to hide it. . . . [Y]ou can do anything you want to a guy who's not ready to stand up by himself and fight for it. . . .
>
> In jail you blow up more. You're not scared to blow up. If you bump into someone in jail, you can turn around and say, "Watch out, goof, or I'll tear your face off." But if you say that to someone on the street, you've got a good chance of the guy callin' the cops. (Liaison, 1984:8)

Perceptions of this sort are perhaps the major reason why the prison is, to quote Gresham Sykes (1966:105), "a gigantic playground—a place where blustering and brawling push life in the direction of a state of anomy." In prison, anomy translates into a lack of norms dictating that one must help others in need. Here, perhaps for the first time in one's life, the person is very much on his own. Explains prison psychologist Glenn Walters (1990:68),

> Most of us are never pushed into a corner during our lives. . . . When you are small and need help, you run to your parents. When you get older, you run to a priest, a minister, a psychologist. If you have a legal problem, you hire an attorney. If someone threatens you, you call a cop. In prison there is no one to turn to, no one to solve your problems for you. If you go to

the guards, you will be known as a snitch and that can get you killed. So you are on your own, perhaps for the first time in your life, and you are forced to deal with your own problems. Believe me, the guy demanding that you drop your drawers isn't going to be a good sport and simply let you walk away. You must either be willing to fight or you must give in.

The result of living on these terms is tragically predictable: "Prison's survivors become tougher, more pugnacious, and less able to feel for themselves or others, while its nonsurvivors become weaker, more susceptible, and less able to control their lives" (Johnson & Toch, 1988:19–20). Increasingly, others are seen in dehumanized terms, as mere fodder for unbridled fantasies of aggression. In the words of one such prisoner,

> Being in here gets to you, day after day after day. Sometimes, I think about what it would be like to just go into a bank and blow the head off the first teller I see. I know that I am capable of that; I mean, any criminal is capable of that . . . you are around the dregs so much and for so long that you forget the worth of a human life. (Earley, 1992:25)

For this man, civilians are mere "cartoon characters" who people his violent fantasies (Earley, 1992:25). As a solid figure in the convict world of Leavenworth, his experiences graphically reinforce the general observation that neither the winners nor the losers leave the prison's playground better prepared for adult civilian life.

Caring for Self and Others: Self-Actualization Through Human Relationships

The third characteristic of mature coping is making an effort to empathize with and assist others in need, to act as though we are indeed members of a human community who can work together to create a more secure and gratifying existence. The point is that one can achieve autonomy and security—that is, control of one's life—through relatedness to others. "Deep individual connections to others and the experience of benevolent persons and institutions result in feelings of safety and trust" (Staub, 1989:265). With trust in ourselves and in the world, "both individuals and groups can acquire confidence in their ability to gain security and fulfill essential motives through connection and cooperation" (Staub, 1989:265).

One such essential motive is control. Trust, in other words, can replace power as a mode of problem solving. Generally, power strategies operate destructively; power expresses itself in manipulation, deception and violence, which in turn spawn division and dissension. Trust allows people to feel secure enough to relate to others openly and honestly, and to cooperate with them in the resolution of difficulties. Ultimately, such cooperative relations hold out the prospect of self-actualization. As Staub makes clear, self-actualization can occur "in relationship to other people, as part of a community" (Staub, 1989:269). Self-actualization, then, need not be a solitary feat. Indeed,

Staub maintains, "The full evolution of the self, the full use of the human potential, *requires* relationships and the development of deep connections and
community" (Staub, 1989:269; emphasis added). Prison poet Henry Johnson
makes a similar point: "To live unloved, makes us cold; cruel; remote" (in
Bruchac, 1989:149). We need to think of ourselves—of our *selves,* if you
will—as persons-in-a-social-context, never fully alone, never fully submerged
in the group, loved, ideally, but not suffocated by others. In the balancing of
self and relations to others is to be found the most harmonious route to personal development.

Relatedness is not some idealistic panacea. At issue here is neither romantic
love nor pure altruism. The notion of a selfless community of human beings is
hopelessly romantic, particularly for people who have led hard lives. Nor is
calculated relationship, in which one aims to establish a debt, sufficient to en-
gender community. Rather, what is needed is "altruistic egotism," in which the
objective is to help others, with the selfish *and* selfless motive of "*deserving* their
help in return" (Selye, 1975:72) (emphasis added). In prison and in hardscrab-
ble environments like urban ghettos, those who deserve and receive support
feel well loved.

Life would be implacably combative and unstable without altruistic egotism. The pure egotist, the selfish, hasty hedonist who seeks his own gratification at the expense of others, is planting the seeds of his own destruction. He
is breeding anger and ill-will in others, who will merely bide their time until
they have the opportunity to pay him back. This is why such persons can never
really trust others. They live in a world of enemies, who have it in for them.
Since they must always be on the defensive, they turn the Golden Rule on its
head and hurt others as a matter of course.

The person who follows the dictates of altruistic egotism, in contrast,

> admits to being self-centered and acts primarily for his own good; he
> greedily collects a fortune to assure his personal freedom and capacity for
> survival under the most satisfying conditions, but he does so through
> *amassing an army of friends.* No one will make personal enemies if his ego-
> tism ... manifests itself only by inciting love, goodwill, gratitude, respect,
> and all other positive feelings that render him useful and often indispens-
> able to his neighbors. (Selye, 1975:120) (emphasis added)

One of the more touching manifestations of altruistic egotism is revealed in
the "gift relationship" (Mauss, 1969), particularly when such vital gifts as food
and clothing are given to those who are destitute and vulnerable. The gift relationship was a fundamental social institution among concentration camp inmates. Here, as in the general case, the goal "is not to bribe or acquire, but to
establish relations" (Des Pres, 1977:163). The result is that "self-interest turns
to goodwill, and the gift relation becomes one of the constitutive structures of
social being" (Des Pres, 1977:163).

Altruistic egotists are generous but they are not saints. They take other people seriously and hold them accountable for their conduct. If gifts are repeatedly spurned, for example, altruistic egotists are not constrained to continue

acting charitably toward an ungrateful neighbor. Nor are they impelled to love a neighbor who regularly abuses them. In practice, they follow a strategy of living that closely resembles the computer game strategy of "tit for tat." Tit for tat is the "strategy of starting with cooperation, and thereafter doing what the other player [person] did on the previous move [encounter]" (Axelrod, 1984:viii). This strategy, particularly when the notion of "starting with cooperation" is generously construed, is ideally suited for cultivating cooperation. The other person is given at least one chance to behave cooperatively; if he persists in behaving abusively, he is treated abusively in turn. (In this context, deception and violence are species of justified self-defense. Even nice guys have to be tough when the situations call for it. See Allman, 1994.) If the other person reconsiders and then offers to cooperate, prior offenses are forgiven and the errant person is met with cooperation. Commonly, mutual coopera-tion emerges as the most sensible strategy of living. It becomes apparent that one's egotistical needs are best satisfied by altruistic endeavors.

Tit for tat's success in generating cooperation, notes Axelrod, "is due to being nice, provokable, forgiving, and clear." Elaborating, Axelrod observes that tit for tat's

> niceness means that it is never the first to [act uncooperatively], and this property prevents it from getting into unnecessary trouble. Its retaliation discourages the other side from persisting whenever [uncooperative ac-tion] is tried. Its forgiveness helps restore mutual cooperation. And its clarity makes its behavioral pattern easy to recognize; and once recog-nized, it is easy to perceive that the best way of dealing with tit for tat is to cooperate with it. (Axelrod, 1984:176)

Tit for tat is not so much a strategy for winning as it is a strategy for better liv-ing. The person need not retaliate exactly in kind against an uncooperative opponent, for example, for doing so, although justifiable on ethical grounds, might escalate tensions. Retaliation need only approximate the original injury. The objective of retaliation in a tit-for-tat scenario is twofold: to communi-cate that one is not a pushover, and to open the door for interactions that fur-ther downplay hostility. The person following a tit-for-tat strategy is advised to be quick to anger when abused—so that he will be taken seriously—but also quick to forgive, so that cooperative relations may be established (see Allman, 1994:82–83). The tit-for-tat strategy is the peacemaker's strategy; reconcilia-tion is a valued goal. It is crucial to appreciate that "tit for tat succeeds without doing better than anyone with whom it interacts. It succeeds by eliciting co-operation from others, not by defeating them" (Axelrod, 1984:189–90).

The tit-for-tat strategy can prove successful even in an environment filled with predators. The key is for the altruistic types to "selectively interact with each other," in effect forming niches within otherwise hostile milieus that both shelter them from harm and offer safe havens to predators who want to "defect" from violent relations and embrace cooperation (see Allman, 1994:91). In computer simulations, at least, the eventual result is that coopera-tion often spreads gradually throughout an environment, setting up new norms of conduct for entire populations. There is some evidence that organizational reforms—like the introduction of functional units, to be discussed at length in Chapter Nine—can create formal niches in which climates of cooperation and nonviolence permeate prisons, or at least portions of prisons (see, for example, Toch, 1977; Herrick, 1989:8).[9]

Prisoners generally are admonished to live by a predatory code of ethics and to avoid cooperation other than in the conduct of illicit activities. They are enjoined not to cultivate generosity, connectedness and cooperation but to suppress these attributes by being cold, unfeeling, and hedonistically self-centered in their dealings with others, both in the free world and in the prison. They do not take people seriously but instead treat them as objects to be used to further their own ends. (More often than not, gifts are the opening gambit in a seduction or ruse; the person who offers to cooperate is taken to be an easy mark.) Their code of ethics is a product of inconsistent, harsh, and even defective nurturing. Bonds to others are, as a result, weak and unreliable. In some instances, social ties may be missing altogether.

We come into this world with an innate capacity to develop a conscience and hence to establish responsible social relationships (Hoffman, 1981; Nettler, 1984). This capacity may, for genetic reasons, be less pronounced in some of us than in others (see Wilson & Herrnstein, 1985); but it is present in some degree in all of us, and can be promoted or retarded by environmental forces. Warm, supportive environments promote the development of conscience. Such environments feature affection, responsiveness to feelings and concerns, the use of reasoning to resolve conflicts, inculcation of moral standards and, above all, an explicit concern for helping others in need. Morality, in other words, is learned by precept, example, and action—by doing good (see Staub, 1989:280). Doing good, in turn, makes us feel good about ourselves and others. Forgoing the pleasures of the moment for a future good—which generally means taking into account the welfare of others—is part and parcel of what it means to have a conscience. Were it not for guilt and anxiety, the hallmarks of conscience, we would all live selfishly in the present (Allman, 1994:97–99).

Harsh, repressive environments, in contrast, suppress the development of conscience and promote selfish, short-run hedonism. "Without nurturing," Nettler (1984:289) reminds us,

> the human animal grows up wild. It behaves violently. It destroys what it has not been trained to appreciate. It does not understand "right and wrong" except as greater and lesser might. As a consequence, what offends the conscience of socialized persons cannot offend the conscience of the unsocialized. There is nothing to offend.

Nurturing may not merely be absent; there may be active attempts to inculcate guilt-free violence. As one Scottish life-sentence prisoner observed, "The only rule in our home was fear: fear of pain and violence. It was just endless. Endless and senseless" (Parker, 1990:84).

In homes such as this, violence is the normal thing. Violence, even brutal violence, is

taken for granted, part and parcel of everyday life. It's normal: what would
be abnormal would be if violence wasn't in your life. . . . I was brought up
with it, I was brought up to it. My father carried a knife, my brothers
carried knives, everyone: you wore a shirt and trousers and shoes, and a
knife. You weren't properly dressed without one. (Parker, 1990:86–87)

This man, together with his brothers and father, shared the status of "hard
men," which is to say, men who could mete out violence casually, as if it were
natural. To be such a man made his father proud. "That was the greatest thing
in the world you could be" (Parker, 1990:87). Family outings featured forays
from pub to pub, looking for people to assault.

Conscience is not the only victim of defective socialization. Without nurturing, the development of empathy is also stunted. Empathy, like conscience,
appears to be promoted by "relatively benign, nonpunitive socialization experiences" (Hoffman, 1982:306). This is particularly true of those socialization
experiences that stress role taking, so one is encouraged to see the other person's point of view; and affection, so one's own needs are satisfied, and thus do
not interfere with one's seeing and acting on the needs of others.

Single-parent homes have long been known to be a source of delinquency
and other social disabilities (see Hirschi, 1994; McLanahan & Sandefur, 1995).
More such homes are found in inner-city slums, especially black ghettos, than
elsewhere in America, but the criminogenic dynamics operating in such homes
are universal. In any case, single-parent, low-income, disorganized homes are
becoming more prevalent in white communities as well.[10] Recently, attention
has been focused on the prevalence of neglect and abuse among low-income
families, particularly those run by single parents. In New York City, for example, Legal Aid Society figures indicate that abuse and neglect cases have increased by a factor of eight—from roughly 3,000 to 24,000—in the five-year
period from 1984–1989 (Will, 1994:C7). The probable culprit: crack cocaine,
which "produces volatility, or stupor, that causes loss of emotional contact with
children" (Will, 1994:C7). Though only a tiny fraction of our nation's children
grow up in abusive homes, these homes are the formative environments for
many chronic offenders, especially chronic violent offenders.[11]

Children raised in abusive homes are treated like commodities. On one
hand, they are often abandoned to the television set as youngsters, allowed to
watch enormous amounts of violent programming because it holds their attention. There is now no doubt that heavy exposure to television among al-
ready-troubled children produces increased propensities to violence, even if
viewing habits change later in life. (Adult viewing habits do not appear to influence violent behavior. For better or worse, this makes the TV a benign distraction in the prison.) Children of the poor are especially prone to watch excessive amounts of television, especially violence-oriented television. For poor
children more than for other children, the television is in effect a substitute
parent that models and reinforces violence as a normal and even preferred way
of relating to others. Cross-cultural research suggests that the coming of age of
the first "television generations" here and abroad was a major factor in the

phenomenal growth of violence in so many contemporary societies (see generally, Donnerstein & Linz, 1994).

These children are also treated like commodities in the sense that their parents or guardians store them like so many parcels rather than care for them like human beings who crave loving attention. "What strikes me is how many of our young black men were never held as babies," states Jasper Ormond, a drug treatment counselor for the D.C. Department of Corrections who was interviewed by Courtland Milloy, a columnist with *The Washington Post* (Milloy, 1991:D3). Ormand goes on:

> So many of them never bonded to another human being. When they put a gun to somebody's head and pull the trigger, they don't see the victims as people. They don't even see themselves as part of the human family. (Milloy, 1991:D3)

These children, Ormand concludes, "are being socialized as pure individuals, with no empathy for others. What is missing is love, and what has emerged is a tremendous amount of self-hate" (Milloy, 1991:D3).[12] These children see no future, no hope. They live each day in a state of psychological trauma. The pain and isolation of daily life is such that they would rather face death, which promises escape, than disrespect and the endless humiliation it entails (see Anderson, 1994; Kotlowitz, 1991).

Lives devoid of love and contaminated by self-hatred virtually propel people into crime, especially violent crime. If conscience and empathy somehow survive in the face of harsh and punitive socialization experiences, such as those decried by Ormond, they are too impoverished to exercise any moral restraints on self-serving conduct (Sykes & Matza, 1957; Goldstein, 1975). Thus, whether by outright lack of human morality or by facile rationalization, others are seen and treated as so many objects to be used for one's selfish purposes.

In the free world, poor social bonds are expressed in a routine distrust of others, especially strangers. But even the worst slum has room for civility and relationships. There is, in other words, a "social order" that has its roots in the expectation of minimal standards of conscience and community (Suttles, 1968). That social order is less robust these days, given the inroads made by guns and violence in low-income areas, including in inner-city schools, but it remains the case that the "decent" people still outnumber the "street" people and hold out to each other and their children the prospect of a civil life in slum communities (see Anderson, 1994).[13]

In prison, by contrast, men are explicitly and almost unanimously encouraged to be uncivil and amoral, that is, "'to do their own time' and ignore the suffering and inhumanity that surround them" (Johnson & Toch, 1988:20). To be sure, there are a few permissible exceptions. One may have relationships with one's "main man" or a fellow gang member, though these and other such arrangements seem at least in part to reflect calculated efforts to assure one's personal protection and further one's criminal objectives (Jacobs, 1977; Carroll, 1988). Be this as it may, the prison's version of decorum calls for restraint bordering on suppression in matters of affection and concern for others in the prison world (Sykes, 1966:101; Toch, 1975:6). There are, as a result, few real friendships in prison. There are even fewer Good Samaritans (who surely would deserve "an army of friends") and none who will own up to this rather egregious lapse from manliness. In the words of one prisoner, "you've got to keep in mind that [another man's problem] doesn't concern you. . . . You want to help the guy, but prison is no place to be a Good Samaritan if you want to come out in one piece" (Lerner, 1984:17).

The prison community is quite different from any free world community. Relations there are distinctly calculating and transient. "In prison there are," notes Seymour,

> no primary ties, few alliances that extend beyond the immediate situation, and few norms that transcend the bounds of one's immediate relationships. Adjusting means the ability to survive and cope with each other's company. Membership in groups is temporary and artificial, and where groups may be friendly, there are few friends. Mutual aid is given, but with an emphasis on reciprocity, not altruism. Cultural dissension is part of a perceived war of prisoners against each other, and sitting out the war is a major goal. (Seymour, 1977:195–96)

To "make it" as an inmate one must live in the present, ever suspicious and alert to the depredations of others, drawing what little sustenance one can from the meager and often exploitive emotional ties available in the prison community (Cordilia, 1983:25–27). Our prisons are moral cesspools, then, as much because of the callous disregard for others they promote as for the overt abuse that takes place there. Naturally, to the extent prisoners are permitted (by officials) and encouraged (by their peers) to treat others in need with indifference and even contempt, the greater will be their willingness to victimize others when it suits their interests.

PRISON ADJUSTMENT AND PERSONAL REFORM: RECONCILING PUBLIC AND PRIVATE CULTURES

Mature coping contradicts standard cultural prescriptions about appropriate prisoner deportment. The public culture of the prison has norms that dictate behavior "on the yard" and in other public areas of the prison such as mess halls, gyms, and the larger program and work sites. This culture emphasizes an almost automatic use of hostility and manipulation in one's relations with fellow inmates and especially with the staff, and makes friendly and caring behavior, again especially with respect to the staff, look servile and silly.

Thus, it is not surprising that prisoners often value roles that are, from the point of view of the larger society, distinctly antisocial. Goodstein's (1979) research, for example, reveals that most inmates (43.5 percent of the maximum-security prisoners in her sample) would like to think of themselves as tough and rebellious in their dealings with staff; as "right guys" who take no guff from the "wrong guys," their keepers. Another 34.7 percent claim to value deception in their relations with staff, which they view as a legitimate, even mandatory, tactic in winning early release from confinement. A few prisoners (5.4 percent) take pride in being institutionalized; they punctuate leisure time with work at easy, high-status prison jobs, all the while studiously avoiding programs and other activities that might have rehabilitative value upon their release from prison. Only 16.3 percent expressly attempt to maintain a "generally positive attitude toward [their] environment" (Goodstein, 1979:253). This type of inmate "accepts the authority of the prison's official social system but maintains his commitment to life outside the institution" (Goodstein, 1979:253). While many inmates privately value this adjustment (see Glaser, 1969, and Toch, 1977), the only men who publicly admit to these beliefs are the much-maligned "square johns" no self-respecting convict would be caught dead with on the yard.

There are few success stories in prison, few real winners. The predatory convicts who dominate the prison yard are stereotypes of adolescent immaturity. They have been described (by means of psychological tests) as "individuals who adhere to procriminal attitudes, who are self-centered, exploitive of others, easily led [by peers], and anxious to please [peers]; they recidivate at high rates (Gendreau, Grant & Leipciger, 1979), particularly when the prison experience has boosted their self-esteem (Wormith, 1984:612–13) and when their exploitive behavior features violence (Quay, 1984:48)—when they have become, in other words, hardened criminals (see generally, Bonta & Gendreau, 1991). Their recidivism is sometimes obscured by the fact that they may appear to make the transition back to civilian life fairly well (Goodstein, 1979). Like Goffman's prisoners who follow an "intransigent line," they attempt to deny the reality of prison and behave behind bars as though they are not really subject to the rules and restrictions of the prison (Goffman, 1961). For example, they break institutional rules with regularity (Goodstein, 1979), and are openly hostile to the authorities and the prison the authorities represent (Thomas & Zingraff, 1978; Alpert, 1979). When they leave prison, they can pick up civilian life fairly readily since they live in a way that is, psychologically speaking, a continuation of their prison adjustment.

Before long, however, their proclivity to victimize others as a routine feature of daily life gets them in trouble with the law. Citizens, known derisively as square johns, do not play prison games. On release, hard-core convicts find that ploys that work in the prison fail miserably in the free world. In the words of one such predatory convict interviewed by Earley:

> "I can walk into any prison in this country, any prison, and know immediately what's happening. I can deal with this crazy prison environment, with the so-called worst of the worst convicts in Marion and the so-called prison predators and all that baloney," he explained. "But in the outside world, I'm always getting tripped up. Every time I mess with a Square

John, I end up getting fucked because you people have no concept of jailhouse respect and absolutely no honor. . . . You see," he continued, "in here, I know how to play all the games and play them well, but out on the streets, the deck always seems to be stacked against me. (1992:249–50)

Such encounters may imperil the precarious sense of self that many convicts develop from their criminal exploits, adding urgency to the need to dominate and control the ebb and flow of prison life. Given the significance of predatory convicts in today's prisons, their adjustments will be discussed in detail in Chapter Six.

Some convicts mellow over time and become "institutionalized," or, in Goffman's terms, "colonized." They serve many prison sentences, and eventually come to make the prison their "home away from home." One finds evidence for this adjustment in all types of prisons, including penitentiaries. "To many," states one penitentiary inmate, "there is no place so *natural* and so much like home as a prison" (Thompson, 1847/1969:349; emphasis in original). States another penitentiary prisoner, "They find themselves naturally, at home, in a prison—and they cannot conceal their perfect acquaintance with its habits, and their familiarity with the incidents of a prison life" (Coffey, 1823:65). One result is that levity rather than long-faced suffering was the order of the day among the more institutionalized convicts of the penitentiary.

"It was always to my mind a horrid place, and I naturally expected to find every visage sad, every eye sunk, every cheek pale, and every heart among convicts, uncommonly depressed. The severity of punishment—the solitude of adversity—the bleakness of their prospects—the agony of their destitution—the horrid result of their crimes—I assuredly thought, were fully calculated to produce such appearance. But I was entirely mistaken. There was nothing to be seen, but unbounded levity. Cheerfulness and contentment played upon their cheeks; quietude of mind was visible in their actions. (Coffey, 1823:20–21)

Contemporary prison accounts surface their fair share of institutionalized convicts. Fleisher found a number of Lompoc inmates who had adopted an institutionalized adjustment. For them, captivity is the norm, freedom the anomaly. They prefer prison to the free world because they have found, through hard experience, that freedom "means freedom to be out of work, freedom to be out of money, freedom to be without clean clothes, freedom to be without an apartment, and freedom to resume an alcohol or drug dependency, or both" (Fleisher, 1989:22–23). Prison, in contrast, means relative security. One's needs are taken care of, and one's reputation as a tough character is assured by a history of prison survival. Institutionalized prisoners can assume menacing postures, and may flaunt their indifference to the pains of imprisonment, but they are, in the final analysis, pathetic figures whose self-doubt and personal inadequacy consign them to a life of prison (see Toch and Adams, 1989:225).

Like their more combative comrades, institutionalized convicts win their battle with the prison but lose the larger war of survival in the free world. Since institutionalized prisoners are veterans of the prison, they "know the ropes" and can "play the angles"; after years of hard experience, they have enough sense to "keep their noses clean." They lead a manipulative and calculating existence, and usually have what is, by prison standards, a materially comfortable life behind bars. They are "model prisoners," not in the sense that they exemplify the staff's version of the ideal prisoner—they do not—but because being a prisoner is what they do best. Where the predatory convicts simmer with hostility and yearn for freedom, these prisoners have become so acclimated to the prison routine that they become dependent upon it for a sense of security and self-esteem. This dependency is a double-edged sword, however, because it entails a loss of personal control that in turn promotes "higher levels of stress" than experienced by inmates who adapt to prison on their own terms (MacKenzie, Goodstein, & Blouin, 1987:63). An even more telling legacy of institutional dependency is the reduced ability to cope in situations where one must rely on one's own initiative. Accordingly, institutionalized prisoners find it very difficult to make the transition to the free world. For if they cannot rely on the dictates of authorities, on an explicit code of conduct, and on preordained schedules, they recidivate almost immediately (Goodstein, 1979).

In terms of the norms and mores that make up the public culture of the prison, the undisputed losers of prison games are known as "inmates," a term that in this context is meant to set the run-of-the-mill prisoners—the "masses"—apart from the more savvy convicts (see Irwin, 1980). Yet most inmates get by; they are neither victims (of the convicts) nor victimizers (like the convicts). Some of the more sophisticated ones become institutionalized, usually by carving out a narrow but safe round of life in conformity with the officials' view of prison decorum. (It is these men, as we shall see in Chapter Six, who are the prison's model inmates.) But from the larger population of inmates are drawn such low-status types as "punks," "dings," and "scapegoats." These inmates are often devastated psychologically by the prison experience. Bowker (1980) provides a melancholy catalog of their fate in prison; Quay (1984:48) demonstrates that the more dependent among these prisoners are unusually prone to recidivate. These men are both impaired for the purposes of adjustment in the free world and prone to escalating traumas should they return to prison (Toch, 1975).

Yet mature behavior, and hence the prospect of successful adjustment upon release, can be found in prison on a more regular basis than might first be supposed. One reason is that "the actions available to inmates are constrained, and many of the ineffective, diversionary, or destructive actions they might take on the outside are precluded" (Zamble, Porporino & Kalotay, 1984:69–70). In prison, one cannot normally turn to hard drugs or heavy drinking to escape one's problems; nor can one beat one's spouse or children to let off steam. It is also much harder to deny problems.

While an inmate can still . . . deal with [a problem] ineffectively, it is difficult to avoid dealing with it in some fashion, because the institutional
world is so confined and restricted. An inmate's problems are inevitably
part of his daily life, and they must be encountered regularly. (Zamble,
Porporino & Kalotay, 1984:70)

Confinement also promotes an increase in introspection and critical examination of one's actions (Zamble, Porporino & Kalotay, 1984:81). As one Canadian prisoner aptly observed, with perhaps a hint of irony, "I'm glad to be here
because I had the opportunity to think a lot. You are alone and you learn about
yourself. When I'm outside, I haven't the time for that. I'm too busy" (quoted
in Besozzi, 1993:37). It can thus be the case that "the constraints of imprisonment can paradoxically make it easier for inmates to cope relatively more effectively with problems," at least with respect to the daily adjustment difficulties that surface behind bars (Zamble, Porporino & Kalotay, 1984:69–70).

The adjustment of lifers (life-sentence prisoners) often reflects the legacy of
improved coping created by the constraints of prison. Ethnographic accounts of
prison adjustment among lifers, from the penitentiary to contemporary prisons,
emphasize that they tend to see prison as a home—an involuntary one, to be
sure—but still a domestic world in which they have an investment; they care
about such things as the level of cleanliness, the quality of the food, the variety
of activities, and even relations with their keepers (see Elgar, 1886:6; Anonymous, 1871:376; Flanagan, 1988; Johnson, 1990:160). In contrast, these concerned citizens of the prison community see their short-sentence counterparts
as rude visitors or disruptive tourists who have nothing to lose. Lifers, who feel
they have everything to lose since prison is all they have, strive to make the
most of the resources available in prison. As a result, they obey the rules and
generally stay out of trouble, secure good jobs, participate in programs, involve
themselves in organized clubs and recreation, and generally fill their days with
structured activities—all so that they might live fully in the present and give as
little thought as possible to the world they left behind.

A recent longitudinal study by Zamble reinforces these observations, and
traces the emergence of improved coping among a sample of twenty-five
Canadian long-termers over a seven-year study period. Zamble documents
that these long-termers did not suffer "generalized emotional damage" as was
speculated by some early penologists and critics of the prison (Zamble,
1992:410; see also, Flanagan, 1988). Confirming early ethnographic studies,
Zamble found that these long-termers tended to fill their days with "structured activities and regular routines, such as those of preferred institutional
employment" (Zamble, 1992a:13–14). They were correspondingly "less interested in the unstructured or aimless activities that typify institutional socialization" (Zamble, 1992a:13–14).

Those "unstructured or aimless activities" avoided by long-termers are
often at the heart of the prison's public culture. It is this life in the prison
yard that often pushed prisoners into destructive activities and, ultimately,

contributed to high rates of recidivism (see Zamble & Porporino, 1990:59). Lifers saw clearly that trouble would reduce the quality of their prison lives.

> Unlike the very weak contingencies between behavior and consequences that the system presents to most prisoners, long-term inmates learn that misbehavior results in tangible diminution of the quality of their lives. Even if the contingencies are only inconsistently enforced, over a period of years the consequences of maladaptive behaviors are sure to be triggered. (Zamble, 1992:423)

Lifers shared the perception that "short-termers were irresponsible and rowdy, and that mixing with them was likely to lead to trouble" (Zamble, 1992a:29). Short-termers had little to lose, and the link between their behavior and deprivations while in prison was weak. Lifers had much to lose, and over time this became quite clear to them. In general, they learned that they had to be more careful and controlled about prison living.

Zamble's long-termers, unlike short-termers, exploited constraints available in the prison community so that they could lead structured, controlled, and ultimately autonomous lives. For example, they explicitly and consciously chose the cell over the yard as the main arena for their daily life in prison. They did this because they could control the routine in the cell. Life in the sheltered confines of the cell was more autonomous than life elsewhere in the prison.

> [W]hen they had the choice of whether to go out onto the range [yard] or stay in their cells, they increasingly chose the latter. . . . The most frequent reason given for this was the choice of activities that could be done better in their cell, such as studying, hobbycraft, or watching television. . . . Thus, over time subjects' lives had become more regulated by routines of their own choice and devising. (Zamble, 1992:414)

Life in the cell and away from the yard offered a sensible withdrawal from the myriad emotional and interpersonal problems, and resulting problems with authorities, that present themselves in the public world of prison. The prisoners developed a few relationships with others facing long terms, for support and protection, but they consciously held themselves back from involvement in the regular prison social life, which featured "confusion and uncertainties" and, in general, trouble (Zamble, 1992:415).

> The majority of subjects largely withdrew from much of the diffuse and casual social networks that are typical of inmate interactions. Instead, they spent much of their discretionary time in their cells, and when they did socialize it was primarily with one or two close friends. Their socialization was centered more on these interactions, or on relationships with people on the outside, than on involvement with inmate social networks. (Zamble, 1992a:33)

Here we see, then, a healthy and constructive focus on relations with others as they are available within the constraints of the prison world.

None of Zamble's long-sentence prisoners mentioned concerns about their personal safety, even though they were directly queried on this point. It would appear that the prison under study was relatively safe and that, perhaps more importantly, they had been able to successfully remove themselves from the predatory relations that exist in all prisons to some degree. "In effect," states Zamble, "they sometimes seemed to be living within a world of their own, inside the prison but separate and apart from its ordinary discourse" (1992a:34). Their orientation was not to the present as represented in the prison yard but to the future, as captured in educational and other programs that would help them gain release and, in their view, successful readjustment in the outside world. Once again, we see these prisoners using prison resources, notably educational programs, to constrain and direct their behavior.

Consistently, Zamble's lifers showed improvements in coping competence as their sentences unfolded. Their behavior became more controlled and more reflective. They were more likely to seek social support and to deal with problems rather than avoid them.

> The changes in coping modes are generally in the direction toward more normal and mature ways. . . . Thus, in general there seems to have been some improvement in subjects' coping abilities over time in prison. . . . [T]hey were working more at controlling their behavior in problem situations, seeking solace and advice from others more than before, and were less likely to avoid dealing with problems. Although the statistical evidence is weak, more of them may also have been monitoring, analyzing, and planning their responses. As a result, their efforts seemed more effective in dealing with problems, with lower risk of exacerbation. (Zamble, 1992a:20)

Better coping produced a host of benefits. There was, for example, an increase in prosocial attitudes (Zamble, 1992a:23) and a decrease in disciplinary problems over time (Zamble, 1992a:26). Prisoners suffered less distress, as revealed in "a decrease over time in stress-related medical symptomology," including a decrease in anxiety and depression, as well as "some improvement in measures of general health" (Zamble, 1992a:22; for further evidence on improved physical health among prisoners, see Bonta and Gendreau, 1990:356). Daily emotions tied to situational pressures within the prison remained constant since the pressures themselves were unchanged. Hence, emotional states like anger, boredom, or loneliness were unaffected by improved coping skills. Nor did the prisoners see themselves as happy or beset with fewer problems (Zamble, 1992a:22). They coped better, then, and suffered fewer impairments, but prison life remained difficult.

One reason prisoners cope better over time is that the stresses of prison life, though high at the outset, tend to level out as time passes. Prison life then becomes fairly predictable. Continuity of prison conditions is largely assured because prison offers a life marked by routines; prison thus offers many opportunities for acclimatization and adjustment. As a result, almost all prisoners, though especially long-termers, cope better over time with the problems and pressures of imprisonment. That is, they become acclimated to the prison environment (Toch & Adams, 1989:210). These inmates learn to live with predictable constraints. Accordingly, they lead "compromise existences in which they achieve compromise goals, operating within available constraints" that are fixed by recurrent features of prison life (Toch & Adams, 1989:254).

Some of the constraints on behavior imposed by prison can be circumvented, and this, in turn, can undermine constructive efforts at coping. The public prison culture might be seen as a means of doing just that, under the guise of ameliorating the pains of imprisonment (Sykes, 1966). The "right guy," for example, can readily obtain contraband, sometimes including hard drugs. Moreover, as the putative model of prison deportment, the right guy would seem by definition to be free of the need for critical introspection. Certainly the right guy lives on the yard, in the middle of the prison fray, not sequestered in his cell. He scorns programs as the refuge of the weak or effeminate. Nevertheless, most inmates are not right guys and, judging by what they do as distinct from what they say, they do not aspire to that role. Instead, they disavow the mainline prison culture and the destructive behavior it promotes. These inmates may or may not subscribe, on a verbal level, to the convict code; they may or may not claim that "doing time" and "sticking together against the screws" are the wellsprings of prison life. What is important is that they show, through their actions, that they wish to avoid contact with the so-called prison community. Desire to avoid the mainline prison culture appears in some instances to be a source of deterrence (Kassebaum, Ward & Wilner, 1971), and presumably can be converted to a motive for personal reform (Toch, 1988).

Disaffection from the public prison culture is not unexpected. The values so saliently reflected in this culture landed these men in prison, a setting that has been known to give many a hasty hedonist a moment's pause. Moreover, most inmates see the dominant or public prison culture as causing more problems than it solves in the here-and-now world of the prison, a direct and immediate relationship between behavior and consequences that even the hastiest and least reflective of hedonists can appreciate (Seymour, 1988). As a result, most prisoners, and not only lifers, want to shelter themselves from this culture, not immerse themselves in its adolescent games (Toch, 1977). This often means passing for a convict in one's public dealings with prisoners and staff (which one judiciously attempts to minimize), but evolving a markedly different lifestyle in one's private prison life.

Thus the actual "day-to-day concerns" of the typical prisoner "do not revolve around status, power, or honor in the prison world" (Seymour, 1988:268). Most prisoners attempt to carve out a private prison world composed of niches or sanctuaries, offering sheltered settings and benign activities that insulate them from the mainline prison. Lifers seem especially likely to secure niches. Too, prisoners characterized by an internal locus of control and a corresponding sense of self-efficacy seem to "hold the advantage in obtaining, and maintaining, niches" (Goodstein and Wright, 1989:245). The larger point, however, is that the adjustment efforts of virtually all prisoners reveal a range of ecological options that support life "off the yard," in the relative privacy of the cell or, more exotically, in the physical and social settings that form the backwaters and byways of penal institutions.

The maximum-security prison, in other words, is not a monolith. (Even the penitentiary, which was in many respects monolithic, afforded some sanctuaries for harried prisoners. See, for example, Anonymous, 1871:78–79 & 94.) Today's prisons, moreover, provide substantial ecological diversity in the form of "varying degrees of privacy from irritants such as noise or crowding, safety from insult or attack, structure and consistency of procedures, support services that facilitate self-improvement, feedback or emotional support, activity to fill time, and freedom from circumscription of one's autonomy" (Johnson & Toch, 1988:18). Prisoners who use this environmental diversity to create niches live not as role types or stereotypes parading about the prison yard but as individuals within small and manageable worlds, often, as with Zamble's lifers, built around their private cell activities. Moreover, these prisoners treat their peers and officers, some of whom have helped them in their adjustment efforts, as specific individuals who in some instances deserve a measure of respect and even affection, not as anonymous "cons" or "hacks" who are, by definition, candidates for abuse (see Seymour, 1988).

Those prisoners who live outside the mainstream of prison culture have created for themselves a mosaic of prison worlds and adjustments in which stress is reduced and in which mature coping is possible. One option is to use niches as sanctuaries from stress and nothing more; in effect, to take prison life one day at a time and go about business as usual. This is probably the most common mode of prison adjustment, especially among those serving short sentences, but it has obvious drawbacks.

> If inmates anesthetize themselves against the pains of imprisonment—or of life—by narrowing their vision, they are truly taking a short-sighted approach. In helping to deal with the present they are cutting themselves off from most of the possibilities of future improvement. (Zamble, Porporino & Kalotay, 1984:80)

A better strategy is to use niches as arenas for constructive social learning, that is to say, as places where one feels secure enough to respond maturely to stress instead of avoiding it. It is reasonable to suppose that prisoners who adapt in this fashion, like those studied by Zamble, may be more likely to handle general life stresses in mature ways when they leave prison. They may be able, in other words, to honor the minimal obligations of citizenship, which amount to navigating life's difficulties without preying upon or otherwise exploiting others (Conrad, 1981). A central correctional task, then, to which we shall return when we consider the matter of prison reform in Chapter Nine, is to arrange prison environments that promote mature coping as an exercise in citizenship and as a desirable alternative to the immature response fostered by the public inmate culture.

GENERAL DYNAMICS OF ADJUSTMENT

Now at first blush, it sounds painfully naive to postulate a direct and positive link between prison adjustment and subsequent adjustment in the free world. To use the language of formal psychology, the "behavior contingencies" of prisons and the free world are markedly different. What one learns in prison should have little direct relevance to free-world situations, "where one must structure one's own life, conditions are more varied, choices are required, and the range of possible behaviors is greatly enlarged" (Zamble, Porporino & Kalotay, 1984:136). Still, contingencies or "reinforcement schedules" in prisons can be altered to more closely approximate those in the free community. (Reforms of this sort will be discussed in Chapter Nine.) Such reforms would increase the usefulness of specific coping lessons learned in prison and later applied in the free world.

Independent of such reforms, however, there is and always has been a general similarity between the adjustment problems posed in prison and those in the outside world. For there is an important sense in which prison life and life in general are related. Prison problems are essentially exaggerated—though sometimes greatly exaggerated—versions of problems experienced in normal life. As a former inmate once observed, "The pain of imprisonment is offset by the discovery that you are strong enough to take it" (Gates, 1991:68). And because essentially "the same system of pain and reward" operates both in prison and "in the outside world, you realize that you can succeed there, too" (Gates, 1991:68)

Imprisonment is painful because it deprives one of liberty, goods and services, heterosexual contacts, autonomy, and security (Sykes, 1966). It also puts an enormous strain on personal relationships with loved ones outside the walls, and suspends or even ruins any notion of a conventional occupational career (Toch, 1975). Yet all of us suffer these pains to some degree. None of us is as free as we would like, has all the goods and services we'd like, is completely satisfied by our sexual outlets, or is as autonomous or secure as we'd like. None of us is free from strain in our personal and family lives, in our jobs or careers. It is also true that all of us must cope with time.

> [T]ime transcends the conventional social order. Prisoners can be snatched from that order but not from time. Time imprisons us all. When the prisoner returns to society after serving his time, in an important sense he's never been away. (Wideman, 1984:36)

Certainly the correspondence between general life problems and prison problems is especially salient for the lower-class men who make up the vast bulk of our prison populations. Indeed, we know that many of these men come from urban slums that are, in some respects at least, as harsh and depriving as the prisons they wind up in! "Doing time" in one ghetto or another is a familiar if uncongenial experience in the lives of these men.

Thus it can plausibly be argued that the inmate who learns to cope maturely with the stresses posed by confinement is learning to cope maturely with the stresses of life (Toch, 1988:37). Moreover, while immature coping typically complicates problems (even the most proficient predator must contemplate the army of enemies he is cultivating), mature coping enables one to solve problems or at least make them more manageable. These successes in coping are apt to build self-confidence and encourage more ambitious behavior, such as taking on new challenges, learning new skills, and generally engaging the world rather than running from opportunities or exploding when pressure mounts (Toch, 1988:37). At this juncture, the prisoner is no longer embroiled full time in a dog-eat-dog fight for survival or trapped in a cycle of personal failure and defeat. He is thus more likely to sample traditional correctional programs in an effort to remedy personal deficiencies. More generally, he is ready to tackle the hard job of rebuilding his life.

Central to this thesis is the notion that self-esteem mediates coping behavior in any environment and must be enhanced if mature behavior is to occur (see Stotland 1975:3). The psychological sequence underlying this adaptive process has been identified by Toch, and can be paraphrased as follows:

1. Mature problem-solving efforts are likely to succeed, and this builds self-esteem and encourages more mature behavior.

2. A history of successful mature coping efforts produces a confident, resilient person who can learn from occasional failures rather than be demoralized or even traumatized by them; in short, success breeds success and makes failure manageable.

3. Immature behavior generally produces failure, which, in turn, lowers self-esteem and further inhibits effective problem solving.

4. A history of failure produces chronically low self-esteem, with the result that the person spends more time nursing hurt feelings and less time attending to the environment; stated differently, failure breeds failure and, eventually, crippling self-doubt.

Given this sequence, we cannot "engage in stress amelioration without being involved in rehabilitating people (inmates) or in developing them (staff)" (Toch, 1988:37–38). We find, in Zamble's words, "a self-reinforcing cycle of improvement" that sparks continuing efforts at "monitoring and controlling" dysfunctional behavior (1991:34).

The easy logical flow of this psychological sequence should not lead us to believe that building self-esteem is, in practice, a simple business. Bandura (1977:200–202) reminds us that people sometimes go to great lengths to defend their negative self-images and to discount the implications of successful experiences. They may do this, he tells us, by limiting the perceived import of successful experiences to idiosyncratic or highly circumscribed or trivial events, or by ascribing success to luck or fate rather than to their own ability or effort. It is also true that change must feature cognitive, behavioral and moral dimensions (see Walters, 1990:171–72). For offenders to go straight, in other words, we must help them learn to (a) think clearly, (b) take responsibility for their actions, and (c) create for themselves a plan for living that respects the needs and rights of others. Nevertheless, a history of successes, as indicated by

Toch (and concurred in by Bandura), will almost invariably build self-esteem and improve coping proficiency.

Stress management and personal reform, then, are linked in direct if sometimes complicated ways, and this connection forms the core of the correctional agenda. For stress, more than any other aspect of the prison experience, defines the quality of life and adjustment behind bars. As Toch and I have noted,

> Stress is an important feature of prison life, and indeed may be the central feature of prison life as it is experienced by the prisoners themselves. Stress can contaminate programs, undermine adjustment efforts, and leave a residue of bitterness and resentment among inmates. It can make the prison a destructive and debilitating institution; to ignore stress is to relegate prisons to the business of warehousing spoiled (and spoiling) human resources. Stress must be controlled if prisons are to become environments in which the work of corrections, in any sense of the word, can take place. (Johnson & Toch, 1988:20)

Ultimately, the prison itself must deal competently, meaning *maturely,* with stress. Porporino and Zamble (1984:403) are surely correct when they maintain that

> there is a general consensus that imprisonment should not be damaging. Prisons should not change individuals for the worse. Social objectives [of imprisonment] are not met to the extent that imprisonment serves to exacerbate psychological vulnerabilities and emotional difficulties, reinforce pro-criminal attitudes and aggressive behavior patterns, or curtail the development of coping skills needed to function in the outside world.

Stated positively, prisons must be "resilient environments, settings orchestrated by line and managerial staff to meet the adjustment needs of prisoners" (Johnson & Toch, 1988:20). The premise is that "even environments of stress such as prisons can become settings for survival and milieus for personal growth" (Toch, 1975:326). Even maximum-security prisons, in other words, can promote mature adjustment, and they must do just that if they are to play a viable role in the correctional process.

To make informed policy suggestions based on the connection between prison adjustment and personal reform, we must understand in detail how prisoners (Chapters Five and Six) and their keepers (Chapters Seven and Eight) come to terms with life in the contemporary prison world. It is to these matters that we next turn. In the final chapter of the book (Chapter Nine), we examine a correctional agenda that adapts the social realities of prison life to the demands of mature coping and personal reform.

NOTES

1. In some situations, in normal life as well as in prison, opportunities for control are entirely absent. Problems cannot be met directly because they are out of one's control. Examples include patients facing life-or-death surgery or advanced terminal illness. In both instances, patients can only await their fate. Given their objective and complete helplessness, "[d]istorted perceptions of reality through denial and rationalization" can be quite effective as strategies of adjustment (Porporino & Zamble, 1984:411).

2. Osgood et al., (1985:76), reporting on a study "conducted at four correctional institutions for adolescents in a large Midwestern state" housing "males between the ages of 13 and 18", emphasized the value of autonomy in the constructive adjustment of the young offenders. Findings revealed that reduced autonomy among inmates led to increased support for the inmate subculture, much as Sykes has suggested; these boys stood in more or less unified opposition to the staff and the programs the staff offered, and generally made trouble for the institution. In contrast, enhanced autonomy led to increased support for institutional goals. Of particular note, young offenders granted autonomy felt more secure and were more willing to participate in rehabilitation programs. Overall, enhanced autonomy produced "a more orderly and humane setting" (1985:87).

3. The adaptive qualities of ghetto lifestyles are not usually captured in psychological measurements, which tend to draw upon an implicitly middle-class view of the world and the kind of ego it supports (Toch, 1971). For example, the most popular means of measuring sense of control over one's world, Rotter's (1966) Internal/External Locus of Control Scale, does not reliably assess the ego strengths of low-income persons and prisoners. Rotter's scale items feature a number of general statements about whether one perceives one's place and experience in the world as subject to internal (personal) or external (impersonal) control. For slum dwellers and prisoners, many of these items refer to outcomes that for them are in large measure objectively determined by external forces and are hence only partly subject to their personal control. The implications of the test scores are not adjusted to reflect the accuracy of perceptions.

Rotter's scale also focuses on narrowly middle-class concerns, such as the equity of academic grades or the rationality of politics, concerns that are largely irrelevant to more needy populations (see Miller, 1958; Toch, 1971). It is not at all clear how these items are read by respondents with respect to their own environments. Do prisoners who see an ambiguous and unresponsive larger society also see urban street corners and prison yards as alien and beyond their control? Even if they do—and surely many do not—the test tells us nothing about their perception of their own competency to cope in these environments. As Bandura (1977:204) has noted, "Rotter's conceptual scheme is primarily concerned with causal beliefs about action-outcome contingencies rather than with personal efficacy. Perceived self-efficacy and beliefs about the locus of causality must be distinguished. . . . "

4. This 1984 monograph was expanded and subsequently published as a book. The book, *Coping, Behavior, and Adaptation in Prison Inmates* (Zamble & Porporino, 1988) is highly recommended. Since I read the original monograph with some care, I have retained my references to that work in this book.

5. One pitfall of ethnographic work with criminals is taking their stories about crime at face value. On the one hand, criminals in prison often tell inflated tales of bloodthirsty violence to impress others with their machismo. Toch (1990:581) has suggested that Fleisher, in his enthnographic study of Lompoc prison, may well have fallen for such tall tales. On the other hand, criminals on the streets often adopt the pose of persons unjustly arrested and confined for behavior of little consequence. In my view, Irwin and Austin appear to accept without question such

statements by their interviewees (see Irwin & Austin, 1994:40–49).

One interviewee, for example, related to Irwin and Austin that police questioned him because he resembled a suspected offender. "The police asked what was I doing over there. I wrestled with him and his gun fell out of his holster. I kicked it and ran. They got me later." The interviewee expressed a sense of injustice that he was charged for "taking [the officer's] gun." How the encounter with the police officer went from the officer asking questions to the interviewee wrestling with him and at least dislodging the officer's gun is never broached, though it is possible, even likely, that the interviewee committed some species of assault. Irwin and Austin discuss this case as an instance of someone ending up in prison simply because he was "around crime" and had not himself committed a crime. I do not wish to entirely discount their larger point—that the behavior of offenders is often less heinous than offense labels would imply—but the accounts of offender often err in the other direction, minimizing the seriousness of the behavior that has landed them in trouble. Minimizing one's personality responsibility is one of a number of strategies of rationalization people can use to prevent themselves from facing and resolving serious personal problems.

6. Some people will take exception to my use of the term *primitive* in this way, but substantial anthropological evidence bears me out. The work of Lawrence Keeley, for example, makes it clear that violent death rates were, at a minimum, more than fifty times higher among ancient peoples than among people in the modern world. Some very ancient societies had violent death rates thousands of times higher than current violent death rates. Violent death rates drop as societies become more civilized, Keeley observes, because less violent means of dispute resolution become institutionalized (Keeley, 1995).

7. Deception requires what Allman has termed "a theory of mind about others" so that one can try to manipulate what others are thinking and hence deceive them. "The human ability to develop a theory of mind about others appears to be a specialized feature of the brain that operates independently of other mental activities typically associated with intelligence." (Allman, 1994:67)

8. Montgomery is quoting defense attorney Bill Lane, one of the lawyers arguing the "urban survival" theory in defense of Daimion Osby, a black man who shot two other black men who were menacing him. The defense for Osby's violence: "'the fear that black people have of other black people' in the nation's most dangerous urban areas" (Montgomery, 1994:A4), a fear so great it leaves no alternative but to use preemptive violence when confronted with problems involving young black men, described by one expert at the trial as "the most dangerous people in America" (Montgomery, 1994:A4). The fears are often real enough, and presumably are greatly enhanced in prison, which gathers together the most dangerous felons in one environment. Nevertheless, the notion that the legally recognized remedy to this situation can be summary violence on the streets or in prisons would only make matters worse in these already troubled environments.

9. A more visible if not more common problem, however, is for a perversion of tit-for-tat logic to run amuck in already dangerous environments, such as slum communities marked by a robust drug trade. Here, the violence of the drug trade spread outward into the community, raising the ante in encounters featuring conflict. We see graphic evidence for this in many inner-city communities, especially from 1985 to the present, during which time there has been a tremendous growth of gun-related homicides among ghetto youths. As Blumstein (1994:412–13) has observed,

The nature of the [drug] industry has made guns a necessary tool of the trade for those who participate in it, and use of violence a standard means of dispute resolution as well as self-defense. Since that industry is often quite pervasive in many communities, it is inevitable that others in those communities will also arm themselves, at least as a self-defensive measure, and possibly also as a means of enhancing their status among their peers. The presence of violence in that industry . . . undoubtedly sets a tone in the community, undoubtedly generates a greater inurement to violence generally, and so stimulates violence by others. This leads to an escalation of violence. . . .

The District of Columbia provides a telling case in point. As US Attorney Eric H. Holder, Jr. has observed, the drug trade in the District fueled an explosion of violence that has persisted, indeed grown worse, even as drug activities have declined. Holder's point, paraphrased by *Washington Post* reporter Lewis, was that

[W]hen drug-dealing began to decline [in D.C.], the guns remained. Instead of protecting drug supplies and prime sales locations . . . the guns were used to rob the remaining drug dealers and, more recently, to rob random victims. (Lewis, 1994:A24)

The guns not only remained but proliferated in the District, at least among the young, as Blumstein would have predicted. It is significant that youths in the District "are piling up gun charges at three times the rate of their adult counterparts and are arming themselves at twice the pace they did five years ago," when the drug trade in the District was at a high point (Lewis, 1995:A1). A culture of gun violence, initially given significant impetus by the drug trade, has now become a functionally autonomous phenomenon.

10. Since 1960, there have been dramatic increases in the rates at which children are born to unmarried mothers, particularly among low-income whites. "Back then," notes Samuelson (1994:A23), 22 percent of all black births and only 2 percent of all white births were to unmarried mothers; by 1991, those figures were 68 percent and 22 percent." Most of these children born of out wedlock to poor mothers are raised in single-parent homes and supported by welfare. Children in such homes, as noted above, are more likely to be abused, and this in turn promotes crime, and particularly violent crime. Perhaps unsurprisingly, Samuelson (1994:A23) reminds us that since 1960 and coincident with the growth of "out-of-wedlock births and welfare dependency," the murder rate in America has more than doubled.

11. Estimates are that only "about one-half of 1 percent of all kids in this country grow up in circumstances where neither parents nor other adults adequately care for them. Many of these children are severely abused and neglected by deviant, delinquent, or criminal adults, including their biological parents" (DiIulio, 1995:C2). The "cycle of violence" often perpetuated in such environments has been well documented. As Widom's research has revealed, "being abused or neglected as a child increased the likelihood of arrest as a juvenile by 53 percent, as an adult by 38 percent, and for a violent crime by 38 percent" (1992:1). Diagnoses of antisocial personality disorders are also more prevalent among adults who were abused as children (Luntz & Widom, 1994). As many as three out of four violent juveniles in confinement experienced abuse in the home (DiIulio, 1995:C2). Children raised in abusive environments are crime-prone "because they were raised to be violent, impulsive, self-centered and remorseless by adults who taught these traits by example" (DiIulio, 1995:C2). The obvious policy implication of these findings, as stated bluntly by DiIulio (1995:C1): "remove the children from their homes to other stable settings."

12. Anderson has a somewhat different take on this problem. He notes that these mothers may not know any other way of controlling their children than by resort to violence. He argues that they "love their children dearly" and in effect beat them to make sure they behave decently (Anderson, 1994:83). In any case, they "come up hard," a common term in the ghetto that in this context may have two meanings: their lives are hard, and as a consequence, they are hardened to human feelings. For them, life in the home is a lesson in the use of violence to solve problems or vent frustration.

13. Even so, the decent people must be able to live by the code of the street when they venture from their homes and mingle with others in public settings. This code, which closely resembles the prison code of conduct, emphasizes toughness and a willingness to use violence to defend or avenge oneself (Anderson, 1994:82).

REFERENCES

Allman, W. F. *The Stone Age Present: How Evolution has Shaped Modern Life— From Sex, Violence, and Language to Emotions, Morals, and Communities.* New York: Simon & Schuster, 1994.

Aichhorn, A. *Wayward Youth: A Psychoanalytic Study of Delinquent Children.* New York: Meridian, 1955.

Alpert, G. P. "Patterns of change in prisonization: Longitudinal analysis." *Criminal Justice and Behavior* 6 (3) 1979:159–74.

Anderson, E. "The code of the streets." *Atlantic Monthly* 273 (5) 1994:80–94.

Anonymous. *An Illustrated History and Description of State Prison Life, By One Who Has Been There. Written by a Convict in a Convict's Cell.* Globe Publishing, 1871.

Axelrod, R. *The Evolution of Cooperation.* New York: Basic Books, 1984.

Bandura, A. "Self-efficacy: Toward a unified theory of behavioral change." *Psychological Review* 84 (March 1977):191–215.

Besozzi, C. "Recidivism: How inmates see it." *Forum on Corrections Research* 5 (3) 1993:35–38.

Bonta, J., and P. Gendreau. "Reexamining the cruel and unusual punishment of prison life." *Law and Human Behavior* 14 (4) 1990:347–72.

Bonta, J., and P. Gendreau. "Coping with prison." In P. Suedfeld and P. E. Tetlock (eds.). *Psychology and Public Policy.* New York: Hemisphere, 1991:343–54.

Bowker, L. *Prison Victimization.* New York: Elsevier, 1980.

Brennan, P. A., S. A. Mednick, and J. Volavka. "Biomedical factors in crime." In J. Q. Wilson and J. Petersilia (eds.). *Crime.* San Francisco: ICS Press, 1994:65–90.

Bruchac, J. (ed.). *The Light from Another Country: Poetry from American Prisons.* Greenfield Center, NY: Greenfield Review Press, 1984.

Carroll, L. "Race, ethnicity, and the social order of the prison." In R. Johnson and H. Toch (eds.) *The Pains of Imprisonment.* Prospect Heights, IL: Waveland Press, 1988:181–203.

Clemmer, D. *The Prison Community.* Boston: Christopher Publishing, 1940.

Coffey, W. A. *Inside Out: Or, An Interior View of the New York State Prison; Together with Bibliographic Sketches of the Lives of Several of the Convicts.* New York: Printed for the author, 1823.

Conrad, J. P. "Where there's hope there's life." In D. Fogel and J. Hudson (eds.). *Justice As Fairness.* Cincinnati, OH: Anderson, 1981:3–21.

Cordilia, A. *The Making of an Inmate: Prison as a Way of Life.* Cambridge, MA: Schenkman, 1983.

Des Pres, T. *The Survivor: An Anatomy of Life in the Death Camps.* New York: Pocket Books, 1977.

DiIulio, J. J. "The plain, ugly truth about welfare: Getting kids out of bad homes is the key to lasting reform." *The Washington Post,* January 15, 1995:Outlook Section C1 & C2.

Donnerstein, E., and D. Linz. "The media." In J. Q. Wilson and J. Petersilia (eds.). *Crime.* San Francisco: ICS Press, 1994:237–64.

Earley, P. *The Hot House: Life Inside Leavenworth.* New York: Bantam Books. 1992.

Empey, L. "Implications: A game with no winners." In A. J. Manocchio and J. Dunn. *The Time Game: Two Views of a Prison.* Beverly Hills: Sage, 1982:241–52.

Flanagan, T. J. "Lifers and long-termers: Doing big time." In R. Johnson and H. Toch (eds.). *The Pains of Imprisonment.* Prospect Heights, IL: Waveland Press, 1988:115–45.

Fleischer, M. S. *Warehousing Violence.* Beverly Hills: Sage, 1989.

Foucault, M. *Discipline and Punish: The Birth of the Prison.* New York: Pantheon, 1977.

Freeman, R. B. "The labor market." In J. Q. Wilson and J. Petersilia (eds.).

Crime. San Francisco: ICS Press, 1994:171–91.

Gates, M. "The excavation." American University: Unpublished manuscript, 1991.

Gendreau, P., B. A. Grant, and M. Leipcoger. "Self-esteem, incarceration and recidivism." *Criminal Justice and Behavior* 6 (1) 1979:67–75.

Glaser, D. *The Effectiveness of a Prison and Parole System.* New York: Bobbs-Merrill, 1969.

Goffman, E. *Asylums.* New York: Anchor Book, 1961.

Goldstein, J. H. *Aggression and Crimes of Violence.* New York: Oxford University Press, 1975.

Goodstein, L. "Inmate adjustment to prison and the transition to community life." *Journal of Research in Crime and Delinquency* 16 (2) 1979:246–72.

Goodstein, L., D. L. Mackenzie, and R. L. Shotland. "Personal control and inmate adjustment to prison." *Criminology* 22 (3) 1984:343–69.

Goodstein, L., and K. N. Wright. "Inmate adjustment to prison." In L. Goodstein and D. L. MacKenzie (eds.). *The American Prison: Issues in Research and Policy.* New York: Plenum Press, 1989:229–51.

Halleck, S. *Psychiatry and the Dilemma of Crime.* New York: Harper & Row, 1967.

Hannerz, U. *Soulside.* New York: Columbia University Press, 1969.

Hawkins, R., and G. P. Alpert. *American Prison Systems: Punishment and Justice.* Englewood Cliffs, NJ: Prentice Hall, 1989.

Herrick, E. "The surprising direction of violence in prison." *Corrections Compendium* 14 (6) 1989:1, 4–17.

Herrnstein, R. J. "Criminogenic traits." In J. Q. Wilson and J. Petersilia (eds.). *Crime.* San Francisco: ICS Press, 1994:39–63.

Hirschi, T. "The family." In J. Q. Wilson and J. Petersilia (eds.). *Crime.* San Francisco: ICS Press, 1994:121–40.

Hoffman, M. L. "Is altruism part of human nature?" *Journal of Personality and Social Psychology* 40 1981:121–37.

Hoffman, M. L. "Development of prosocial motivation: Empathy and guilt." In N. Eisenbert (ed.). *The Development of Prosocial Behavior.* New York: Academic Press, 1982:281–313.

Howard, A., and R. A. Scott. "A proposed framework for the analysis of stress in the human organism." *Behavioral Science* 10 (1965):141–60.

Irwin, J. *Prisons in Turmoil.* Boston: Little, Brown, 1980.

Irwin, J., and J. Austin. *It's About Time: America's Imprisonment Binge.* Belmont, CA: Wadsworth, 1994.

Jacobs, J. B. *Stateville: The Penitentiary in Mass Society.* Chicago: University of Chicago Press, 1977.

Johnson, R. *Culture and Crisis in Confinement.* Lexington: Lexington Books, 1976.

Johnson, R. "Crowding and the quality of prison life." In C. Hartjen (ed.). *Correctional Theory and Practice.* Chicago: Nelson-Hall, 1992:139–45.

Johnson, R., and H. Toch. "Introduction." In R. Johnson and H. Toch (eds.). *The Pains of Imprisonment.* Prospect Heights, IL: Waveland Press, 1988:13–21.

Kassebaum, G., D. Ward, and D. Wilner. *Prison Treatment and Parole Survival.* New York: Wiley, 1971.

Katz, J. *Seductions of Crime.* New York: Basic Books, 1988.

Keeley, L. *War Before Civilization.* New York: Oxford University Press, 1995.

Kotlowotz, A. *There Are No Children Here: The Story of Two Boys Growing up in the Other America.* New York: Anchor Books, 1991.

Lerner, S. "Rule of the cruel." *The New Republic* October 15, 1984:17–21.

Lewis, N. "Court cases reveal arms buildup among D.C. youths." *The Washington Post,* January 1, 1995:A1, A24.

Liaiaon (staff author). "The hardest part is getting out." *Liaison* 10 (10) 1984:4–10.

Lombardo, L. X. "Stress, change, and collective violence in prison." In R. Johnson and H. Toch (eds.). *The Pains of Imprisonment.* Prospect Heights, IL: Waveland Press, 1988:77–93.

Luntz, B. K., and C. S. Widom. "Antisocial personality disorder in abused and neglected children grown up." *American Journal of Psychiatry* 151 (5) 1994:670–74.

Mackenzie, D. L., L. I. Goodstein, and D. C. BLOUIN. "Personal control and prisoner adjustment: An empirical test of a proposed model." *Journal of Research in Crime and Delinquency* 24 (1) 1987:49–68.

Mauss, M. *The Gift: Forms and Functions of Exchange in Archaic Societies.* London: Routledge & Kegan Paul, 1969.

McCall, N. *Makes Me Wanna Holler: A Young Black Man in America.* New York: Vintage. 1995.

McLanahan, S., and G. Sandefur. *Growing Up with a Single Parent: What Hurts, What Helps.* Cambridge: Harvard University Press, 1995.

Miller, W. "Lower class culture as a generating milieu of gang delinquency." *Journal of Social Issues* 14 (3), 1958:5–19.

Milloy, C. "For tragedy of black youths, put blame where it belongs." *The Washington Post,* January 3, 1991:D3.

Montgomery, L. "'Urban survival' rules at issue in trial." *The Washington Post,* October 26, 1994:A4.

Mueller, J. "Crime is caused by the young and restless." *Wall Street Journal,* March 6, 1985:18.

Nettler, G. *Explaining Crime.* New York: McGraw-Hill, 1984.

Osgood, D. W., E. Gruber, M. A. Archer and T. M. Newcomb. "Autonomy for inmates: counterculture or cooptation?" *Criminal Justice and Behavior* 12 (1) 1985:71–89.

Parker, T. *Life After Life: Interviews with Twelve Murderers.* London: Secker and Warburg, 1990.

Porporino, F., and E. Zamble, E., "Coping with imprisonment." *Canadian Journal of Criminology* 26 (4) 1984:403–21.

Quay, H. C. *Managing Adult Inmates: Classification for Housing and Program Assignments.* College Park, MD: American Correctional Association, 1984.

Rotter, J. "Generalized expectancies for internal versus external control of reinforcement." *Psychological Monographs* 80 (1966) Whole No. 609.

Samuelson, R. J. "'Bell curve' ballistics." *The Washington Post,* October 26, 1994:A23.

Schwendinger, H., and J. Schwendinger. "Delinquent stereotypes of probable victims." In M. W. Klein (ed.). *Juvenile Gangs in Context: Theory, Research, and Action.* Englewood Cliffs, NJ: Prentice-Hall, 1967.

Selye, H. *Stress Without Distress.* New York: Signet, 1975.

Seymour, J. "Niches in prison." In H. Toch. *Living in Prison: The Ecology of Survival.* New York: Free Press, 1977:179–205.

Seymour, J. "Environmental sanctuaries for susceptible prisoners." In R. Johnson and H. Toch (eds.). *The Pains of Imprisonment.* Prospect Heights, IL: Waveland Press, 1988:267–84.

Smith, D. "Crowding and confinement." In R. Johnson and H. Toch (eds.). *The Pains of Imprisonment.* Prospect Heights, IL: Waveland Press, 1988:45–62.

Staub, E. *The Roots of Evil: The Origins of Genocide and Other Group Violence.* New York: Cambridge University Press, 1989.

Stotland, E. "Self-esteem and stress in police work." In W. H. Kroes and J. J. Hurrell (eds.). *Job Stress and the Police Officer: Identifying Stress Reduction Techniques.* Washington, D.C.: Government Printing Office, 1975.

Suttles, G. D. *The Social Order of the Slum: Ethnicity and Territory in the Inner City.* Chicago: University of Chicago Press, 1968.

Sykes, G. *The Society of Captives*. New York: Atheneum, 1966.

Sykes, G., and D. Matza. "Techniques of neutralization: A theory of delinquency." *American Sociological Review* 22 (1957):664–70.

Thomas, C. and R. Zingraff. "Structural and social psychological correlates of prisonization." *Criminology* 16 (3) 1978:383–93.

Thompson, G. *Prison Life and Reflections*. New York: Negro Universities Press, 1847/1969.

Toch, H. "The delinquent as poor loser." *Seminars in Psychiatry* 3 (3) 1971:386–99.

Toch, H. *Men in Crisis: Human Breakdowns in Prison*. Chicago: Aldine, 1975.

Toch, H. *Living in Prison: The Ecology of Survival*. New York: Free Press, 1977.

Toch, H. "Studying and reducing stress." In R. Johnson and H. Toch (eds.). *The Pains of Imprisonment*. Prospect Heights, IL: Waveland Press, 1988:25–44.

Toch, H. "An anthropologist in the prison.' *Contemporary Psychology* 35 (6) 1990:581.

Toch, H., and K. Adams with J. D. Grant. *Coping: Maladaptation in Prisons*. New Brunswick, NJ: Transaction Publishers, 1989.

Walters, G. D. *The Criminal Lifestyle: Patterns of Serious Criminal Conduct*. Beverly Hills: Sage, 1990.

White, R. W. "Motivation reconsidered: The concept of competence." *Psychological Review* 66 (1959):297–333.

Wideman, J. E. *Brothers and Keepers*. New York: Holt, Rinehart & Winston, 1984.

Widom, C. S. "The cycle of violence." *Research in Brief,* National Institute of Justice (October 1992).

Will, G. *The Washington Post*, May 1, 1994:C7.

Wilson, J. Q. and R. J. Herrnstein. *Crime and Human Nature*. New York: Simon & Schuster, 1985.

Wormith, J. S. "Attitude and behavior change of correctional clientele: A three-year follow-up." *Criminology* 22 (4) 1984:596–618.

Yochelson, S., and S. E. Samenow. *The Criminal Personality*. 3 Vols. New York: Jason Aronson, 1976.

Zamble, E. "Behavioral and psychological considerations in the success of prison reform." In J. W. Murphy and J. E. Dison (eds.). *Are Prisons Any Better?: Twenty Years of Prison Reform*. Newbury Park, CA: Sage, 1990:129–45.

Zamble, E. "Behavior and adaptation in long-term prison inmates: Descriptive longitudinal results." *Criminal Justice and Behavior* 19 (4) 1992:409–25.

Zamble, E. "Personal communication relative to coping patterns among long-term prison inmates." (1992a).

Zamble, E., and F. Porporino. *Coping, Behavior and Adaptation in Prison Inmates*. New York: Springer-Verlag, 1988.

Zamble, E., and F. Porporino. "Coping, imprisonment, and rehabilitation: Some data and their implications." *Criminal Justice and Behavior* 17 1990:5–70.

Zamble, E., F. Porporino, and J. Kalotay. *An Analysis of Coping Behaviour in Prison Inmates*. Ministry of the Solicitor General of Canada: Programs Branch User Report, 1984.

5

Prowling the Yard

The Public Culture
of the Prison

Prisons readily adopt a warehousing posture, particularly in the absence of an explicit reform agenda. The modern prison, which as we have noted originated with the penitentiary, is no exception to this observation. "Once the ideal of prisoner reformation is abandoned," which has happened in most maximum-security prisons in this century, "the penitentiary becomes essentially a kind of storage warehouse for society's rejects" (Stastny & Tyrnauer, 1982:25). The custodial warehouse prison has in fact been described as "the most persistent of any species of prison system" (Stastny & Tyrnauer, 1982:25). This generic prison type both preceded and survived the penitentiary, and warehousing features persist today in at least some segments of virtually all contemporary prisons.

In the warehouse prisons before the penitentiary, storage involved a regime of undiluted idleness inside the walls and total isolation from family, friends, and others in the free world (see Chapter One). Physical brutality and psychological abuse were common. The procedures followed in twentieth-century warehouse prisons have been more accommodating. These prisons, whether they display specific characteristics of the Big House, the correctional institution, or the contemporary violent prison (see Chapter Three), permit some activity and conviviality among the prisoners, as well as fairly regular personal contact with the outside world in the form of visits and, more recently, furloughs and work-release programs. Such prisons are designated as storage enterprises because the limited activities allowed within them are, in the main, considered to be of little or no demonstrable benefit to the prisoner or society.

One might say that they are warehouses more by default than by design: correctional aspirations linger, but no correctional agenda shapes the operation of today's prisons. In the absence of an explicit correctional mission, it is not uncommon for prisoners simply to be housed, clothed, fed, and kept under surveillance (Cobb, 1985).

In its twentieth-century form, the warehouse prison has evolved considerably. What was once a repressive but comparatively safe Big House is now often an unstable and violent social jungle (Irwin, 1980; Irwin & Austin, 1994), though as we shall see (in Chapter Nine) there has been a recent drop in prison violence produced by administrative reforms. The twentieth-century warehouse prison has typically featured a smattering of correctional programs, though these are becoming rarer in today's crowded institutions, even as promising advances in treatment programs are noted by researchers and practitioners (see Chapter Nine). In extreme cases, which happily are few in number, our prisons have served *only* to hold and restrain. In such prisons, staff police the prison's periphery, and inmates "dominate the internal polity," with violence a fact of daily prison life (Stastny & Tyrnauer, 1982:27–28).

In all prisons, power is divided in some measure between the staff and the prisoners. The staff man the walls, at a minimum, and maintain a varying degree of order as inmates go through the formal routine of meals, counts, work, recreation, and sometimes correctional programs that the official prison day contains. The threat and occasional use of force are vivid testimony to the staff's power. Outside the formal schedule—on cell block tiers, in recreation areas, on the yard—the inmate body is ceded a [degree] of self-rule" that may be more or less pronounced in any given prison (Stastny & Tyrnauer, 1982:27–28). Those who exploit this self-rule most visibly and violently are colloquially known as "convicts." They are not to be confused with nondescript inmates who, from the convicts' point of view, comprise a victim pool not unlike that of the general citizenry (Irwin, 1970 & 1980). In the convict world, toughness and the capacity for violence define power, status, and honor. Here, in the public or mainline culture of the prisoners' prison, the worst of society's rejects create a world in which the prospect and often the reality of violence are facts of everyday life.

The convict world, which has its symbolic home on the yard of the maximum-security prison, is the subject of this chapter. Two themes are explored. One is the change in the atmosphere of the convict world from one of violence restrained (in the Big House and, to a lesser extent, the correctional institution) to that of violence unleashed and sometimes out of control (in the contemporary violent prison). This is essentially a study in the evolution of the social system of the prison during this century. The second theme concerns the life and adjustment of state-raised convicts. These men have always been the most violent of the convicts. Whereas once they were a fringe element of the convict group, however, they have increasingly come to dominate today's prisons. In this study of the psychology of prison violence, these themes converge. For all that is immature and destructive about adjustment to the pains of prison life, both in inmate conduct and in the staff response, is shown in relief in the contemporary prison world of the state-raised convict.

THE CONVICT CULTURE OF VIOLENCE

Violence has always been a salient aspect of the convict world. In many of today's prisons, however, the convict culture of violence is unusually pronounced. This was not the case in the Big Houses that dominated the prison scene from the turn of the century until the mid-1960s. There, rigid discipline kept inmate violence under control. Convict violence was also controlled in the penitentiary. In the original nineteenth-century penitentiaries and in twentieth century Big Houses, the staff maintained a heavy-handed and often violent authority, and inmates found their lives closely regulated. Of course, staff control on this order does not necessarily mean that inmates felt secure. It was not uncommon for prisoners to feel vulnerable to abuse by staff.

Crouch and Marquart's account of social control in Texas prisons during most of this century is instructive on this score. Texas featured plantation prisons (as distinct from Big Houses), but their patterns of social control were carefully modeled after those found in Regan's Stateville, a traditional Big House (Crouch & Marquart, 1989:39). This was particularly true in Huntsville Prison, the focus of Crouch and Marquart's study. Using Building Tenders (known as BTs) as a kind of inmate militia, officers in Texas's Huntsville Prison could orchestrate a regime of "relentless supervision" and almost total control (Crouch & Marquart, 1989:41). If anything, the regime at Huntsville was more physically brutal than that found at Stateville, since the BTs were essentially given a free hand to discipline and control errant inmates as they saw fit.

> Building tenders enjoyed near limitless authority to maintain control. Keeping peace in the tanks [cell blocks] often involved 'set ups,' contrived evidence to injure another for some gain, and terrorism. They openly carried, with staff approval, clubs and knives to protect themselves as well as to threaten and intimidate other inmates. (Crouch & Marquart, 1989:88)

The BTs, moreover, explicitly understood themselves to be "organizationally sanctioned" agents of the officials, though no written policies authorized their brutal actions (Crouch & Marquart, 1989:105). Like the BTs, Texas guards, notably the mounted field officers, used corporal punishment at will to maintain order in the fields, where inmates labored like plantation slaves "under the sun and under the gun" in a situation of virtually complete powerlessness (Crouch & Marquart, 1989:71–72). In contrast, the officers at Stateville were more closely supervised and circumscribed, and the conditions of inmate labor, though hard, were considerably less brutal than found in Texas. Nevertheless, the role played by inmates in social control efforts at both prisons—as informants in Stateville and informants and enforcers in Huntsville—produced comparable climates of rigid discipline and suffocating routine.

Prisoners of Big Houses had less reason to fear one another than they do in today's less controlled prisons. Stateville's guards and Huntsville's BTs were successful in holding down the violence of regular inmates in the cell blocks and in the yard, at least by today's standards (see Crouch & Marquart, 1989:46). But many prisoners chafed against these controls and others were reduced to numb submission, as we noted in Chapter Three. Periodically, those who could not suppress their feelings erupted in emotional explosions. Discussing the rigid discipline at Stateville when it qualified as a Big House, Jacobs (1977:31 & 44) notes that "many inmates suffered emotionally and psychologically from this intense supervision. . . . Going 'stir bugs' was an everyday occurrence."

Since inmate violence was relatively uncommon in the Big House, however, this gave the prison a stable and even placid exterior. The high-status convicts were courted by the prison administration and given positions of influence. They were the officers' clerks who could arrange cell transfers and even nightly assignations with "punks" or "queens"; they were also the runners who could move contraband and information around the prison. Troublemakers were routinely "salted away in segregation for as long as a decade" (Jacobs, 1977:50). Both the convict elite and the staff had a vested interest in stability and order. The regular inmate was admonished by guard and peer alike to keep his nose clean and do his own time. Congenial or at least stable accommodations of this sort between staff and prisoners are not as much in evidence today and the social world of the prison has a more unstable and violent climate (Conrad, 1988). As a result, it is considerably harder to do one's own time in our contemporary prisons.

The Big House: Repression and Its Discontents

Stateville penitentiary was a typical Big House from the years of the Depression through the early 1960s. During this time it was run by Joseph Ragen, an authoritarian warden whose penological philosophy was drawn with little modification from the nineteenth-century notion of the prison as a machine of discipline. This philosophy was implemented, appropriately enough, in the only American prison to embody Bentham's panoptical design, a series of circular tiers described by Foucault as the quintessential rendering of an architecture of power, "a dream building" in which surveillance of dependent and docile bodies is achieved in its ideal form (Foucault, 1977:205). Fittingly, observed Jacobs (1977:30),

> Ragen maintained "that if you stress the small things, you will never have to worry about the big ones." Thus, under his fully elaborated system of administration the inmates were subjected to intense supervision under innumerable rules blanketing every aspect of prison life.

As recently as 1960, "the silent system was enforced in the dining room and while marching in lines" (Jacobs, 1977:44). "The entire prison" during this era "functioned with Prussian punctuality" (Jacobs, 1977:44).

The Big House had few pretensions. It promised, and usually delivered, adequate food, hygiene, and housing. Many of these prisons were formally labeled "correctional institutions," particularly after World War II, but little that could pass for rehabilitation occurred within their walls. The Big House did not aim at transforming the character of its prisoners. Yet there was the enduring hope, as in the first congregate penitentiaries, that obedience for its own sake, coupled with regular work, might ensure the conformity of convicts upon their release from prison.

> Ragen reasoned that the strictness of the Stateville regime would coerce the inmate into a conformity that would ultimately produce a respect for the rules. Through obedience to prison rules, the inmate would be resocialized. . . . A cardinal principle . . . [was to] keep every inmate working. (Jacobs, 1977:46)

Attributing correctional benefits to bald custodial control perhaps has always been more a rationalization than a rational correctional agenda. In any case, it simply reinforced the legitimacy of the authoritarian regime.

The formal routine of the Big House was often remarkably rigid and even oppressive. Like the penitentiaries that preceded them, the Big Houses were marked by a bell-ringing punctuality that made life there stiff and formal. However, in conjunction with the scheduled and ordered official prison world, "a complex, subtle, informal prisoner world with several subworlds was also operating" (Irwin, 1980: 11). This prisoner world had a code of conduct, prescribed social roles, and preferred ways of living. Its norms for correct deportment "pivoted around the convict code," which "could be translated into three rules: Do not inform, do not openly interact or cooperate with the guards or the administration, and do your own time" (Irwin, 1980:11–12). Prisoners assumed stylized roles that reflected the values of the convict code and "were arranged in a hierarchy of prestige, power, and privilege" (Irwin, 1980:12). The typical mode of adjustment was "to do your own time." This meant, above all,

> avoiding trouble . . . [and] avoiding "hard time." To avoid hard time, prisoners stayed active in sports, hobbies, or reading; secured as many luxuries as possible without bringing on trouble; and formed a group of close friends with whom to share resources and leisure hours and to rely on for help and protection. (Irwin, 1980:14)

The model inmate was the right guy, a convict who stuck by his friends and did his time with a stoic and even exemplary calm. He embodied the notion that

> The rigors of the inmate's world are to be met with a certain self-containment and excessive display of emotion is to be avoided at all costs. The prisoner should speak slowly and deliberately and he should move in the same fashion. Curiosity, anxiety, surprise—all are to be carefully curbed. Even too great a show of humor must be checked since there is the danger of being thought a clown or a buffoon. The prisoner, in short, is urged to "play it cool," to control all affect in a hard silent stoicism which finds

its apotheosis in the legendary figure of the cowboy or the gangster.
(Sykes, 1966:101)

Yet the informal prisoner world of the Big House was not uniformly populated
with right guys who pulled their time like real men. This social role was an
ideal rather than a reflection of daily prison living. Victor Nelson, an inmate in
a Big House prison, describes the most common type as a boorishly self-centered figure who played the role of the adolescent bad boy at play in the prison:

> The egocentricity of the average prisoner is revealed in the most startling
> as well as in the most amusing ways. It is apparent in his brash loudness of
> voice, his pushing forward of himself and his views at every opportunity.
> When he is in line, he will crowd and shove his fellows (unless they are
> bigger than he is); at the table he will reach impolitely across his neigh-
> bor's place and grab the biggest or best portions of whatever is in sight; at
> the table he is inconsiderate and coarse, belching, feeding noisily, and
> generally revealing the table manners of a healthy pig. (Nelson,
> 1936:133–34)

Nelson states emphatically that his porcine contemporaries displayed an "amaz-
ing callowness" and indeed were even "infantile" in their daily deportment,
which departed sharply from the inmate code:

> It goes without saying, of course, that in most prisons the admirable part
> of this code is more honored in the breach than in the observance. Men
> of high ideals, men with a personal code which is rigorously lived up to,
> are infinitely more scarce in prison than they are anywhere else. (Nelson,
> 1936:118)

Honor was notable for its absence in culture of the Big House. "There is,"
writes Nelson a bit wistfully,

> very little of that "honor among thieves" of which so much has been writ-
> ten. Thieves are, for the most part, pretty treacherous, double-dealing
> wretches, without a trace of glamour, and very different from the "gentle-
> man thief", "Raffles", and other types beloved of crime-fiction writers
> and sentimentalists. The average convict, as a matter of fact, however
> loudly he may assert his adherence to the prison code, usually deems it
> proper to violate it if he can do so without getting caught and if in so
> doing he can advance his own interests. (Nelson, 1936:119)

Loyalty, too, was scarce among the Big House convicts. "There are," states Nelson, "perhaps fifty or sixty inmates in the population of nine hundred who
have any [but the] faintest notion of loyalty to their kind. (Nelson, 1936:130).
A fair number of inmates were sufficiently disloyal to become informants, a
role that is the antithesis of the right guy and entails flagrant violation of the
convict code. Indeed, the prevalence of "rats" in Stateville prison gave substance to Regan's celebrated claim, "Whenever you see three inmates standing
together, two of them are mine."

The Big House, though possessed of an orderly social regime, displayed a fairly robust if controlled culture of violence. In a fight, Nelson makes clear, the aim was to win at any cost.

> When the average prisoner has an argument or fight with another inmate, he generally feels called upon to be as vindictive as possible, considering it a sign of weakness and efficacy to shake hands afterwards and make up the peace with his enemy.... There is very little good sportsmanship or sense of fair play, it being considered the essence of folly and weakness to give an enemy an even break. The idea is to win, to gain the advantage—no matter how. (Nelson, 1936:126–27)

Such violence was tolerated and even encouraged by the convict code. The central tenet of the code—that prisoners should "do their own time"—meant that prisoners were to mind their own business when others were being attacked or exploited; this injunction even prohibited victims from invoking the aid of staff. The convict code thus served the interests of the elite and made it easier for them to ride roughshod over the other prisoners.

Prisoners who were not among the convict elite were open game for exploitation, and this included not only hustles and cons but also sexual and other kinds of coercion and violence. Seductions of young convicts would occur in open view; "wolves" would prowl the yard unimpeded by fellow convicts or guards. Nelson recounts the telling case of Dreegan, the undisputed "champion wolf" of Auburn Prison in the thirties:

> Now, whereas most "wolves" have the grace to be more or less discreet in their activity, Dreegan was quite frankly what he was. He went boldly after any young and good-looking inmate whom it was his desire to seduce. That he got a punch in the eye for his pains every so often, and was more than once knifed by boys defending themselves from his vigorous assaults did not disturb Dreegan for very long. He outrageously flattered the objects of his lust; he gave them cigarettes, candy, money, or whatever else he possessed which might serve to break down their powers of resistance.... Once the boy had been seduced, if he proved satisfactory, Dreegan would go the whole hog, like a Wall Street broker with a Broadway chorus-girl mistress, and squander all of his possessions on the boy of the moment. In this Dreegan was different from the average "wolf" only in the brazen directness of his conduct. (Nelson, 1936:158–59)

Violence, ever a threat in these situations—to Dreegan, in this instance, but to unyielding targets in the case of other, less genteel "wolves"—was thoroughly unremarkable in the world of the Big House.

Most of the roles associated with this convict culture involved exploitation that was backed, explicitly or implicitly, by violence (Bowker, 1988).[1] There were also periodic disturbances and riots, sometimes involving tremendous violence (Sykes, 1966). There was often an active market in illicit drugs, which would spur violence among groups to control markets or among individuals to secure drugs to ease their addictions. The presence of drugs, Nelson notes, results in a great deal of friction among the prisoners themselves. Various cliques try to get control of the intramural drug trade. There are fights, often bloody and terrible to behold, not only among the professional vendors, but between prison addicts who accuse one another of "holding out" on the secret supply of drugs. (Nelson, 1936:187–88)

Drugs not only corrupted the prisoner community, if you will, they were also a source of corruption among officers. Poorly paid, the officers would take bribes to smuggle drugs into prison. This would "weaken the defenses of the prison" by reducing the independence and effectiveness of individual officers (Nelson, 1936:188). Beholden to drug dealers, they would turn a blind eye to all manner of deviance in the prison community (Nelson, 1936:188–89). Newspaper accounts and periodic scandals suggest that drug-related corruption, though by no means the norm in our contemporary prisons, may be worse today than during the Big House era.

The Big House was a setting of repressed and controlled behavior, and hence violence there had a patterned and sometimes even ritualized flavor. One could not wander through the cell blocks knifing people, as reportedly occurs in some prisons today, because one didn't wander through the cell blocks at all! But one did carry weapons and sometimes used them, both in self-defense and to intimidate, control, and harm other prisoners. One could also menace and often successfully exploit others through carefully calculated postures and stares. Thus, violence and the threat of violence were key ingredients of prison life, and the capacity to stand up under the pressure this created was the substance of which real men ultimately were made.

The Decline of the Big House

The disciplined routine that both shaped and restrained overt violence in the Big House was periodically put to one side in favor of prison reform efforts, most notably in the self-governance experiments of Osborne and Gill (see Murton, 1976). (These reforms were implemented at the turn of the century during the heyday of the Big House. They produced an orderly prison, to be sure, but an order based on commitment rather than coercion.) When these reforms were scuttled, usually as a result of social and political forces unrelated to their penological merits, standard discipline was resumed.

The demise of the "repressive but reasonably safe" Big House had many causes (Conrad, 1988:320). One was the "rise of professional administration" (Jacobs, 1977:138). Professional administrators began to enter the prison service as early as the 1930s, though their impact was not fully felt until as late as the 1950s and 60s, with their influence extending through the mid-1970s. Typically, they were committed to the trappings, though not the substance, of rehabilitation (Jacobs, 1977:138). They sought to infuse penal institutions with their own distinctive correctional ambiance. Often, they did little more than take the discipline out of the Big Houses they inherited.

The management approach of correctional professionals emphasized human relations and sought a relaxed and—ideally—almost collegial atmosphere.

However, nowhere were these changes in prison climate backed by a regime of meaningful programs or opportunities for involvement in prison governance. It would seem that many of these administrators meant to make prisons less oppressive and nothing more, as if a lax prison regime were somehow also a humane one. As a result, reforms undertaken in the name of rehabilitation served to undermine the rigid discipline essential to the operation of the Big House prison, but they did not replace this discipline with a new basis for order. In the context of a correctional treatment climate, discipline appeared punitive and antitherapeutic. Yet in the absence of correctional treatment, there was no reason for inmates to follow the dictates of their keepers.

Another factor in the decline of the Big House was "the intrusion of the courts" (Jacobs, 1977:138). Again primarily in the 1960s and 70s, but continuing today in such prison systems as those of Texas and New Mexico, court rulings further restricted the use of authoritarian control strategies. As DiIulio (1991:148) has made clear,

> the doctrinal wall of separation between the judge's chambers and the prison's corridors has crumbled. The courts have intervened on a wide range of prison and jail issues, including crowding, food services, sanitation, health care, due process protections for inmates, and the constitutionality of prison and jail conditions "in their totality."

The discipline of the Big House fell to a court-sanctioned revolt: inmates demanded—and to some extent won—more rights and freedoms, particularly in the areas of expression and association. The holdings in specific cases are not the issue; often these court decisions were "quite modest and even conservative" (Jacobs, 1977:107). Judges have been quite cautious in this matter. Even the most liberal reform judges, notes DiIulio (1991:151), have

> approached institutional penal reform cases in the spirit evoked by these words from a federal circuit court decision handed down in 1988: "Judges are not wardens, but we must act as wardens to the limited extent that unconstitutional prison conditions force us to intervene when those responsible for the conditions have failed to act." Almost without exception, the judges have approached intervention as a necessary evil, not as a positive good.

The larger point, however, is that court rulings gave "legitimacy to inmate protest against authoritarian rule" and hence "provided the ideological basis for a frontal attack upon the entire regime" (Jacobs, 1977:118; see also Rothman & Engel, 1983), an attack that continues, though in muted form, even today. Court holdings have thus contributed substantially to the erosion of custodial control of the prison. As such, they were—and are—resented by most correctional officers and administrators alike (see, for example Stojkovic, 1995:68)

The advent of professional administration and court intervention had immediate effects on some systems and delayed effects on others. For example, Texas prisons were able to maintain many of the Big House trappings even into the early 1980s. (In English prisons, the essentials of the Big House were still in place as recently as 1992.)[2] Today, however, the rigid custodial routine that marked the operation of the Big House is a thing of the past in the vast majority of American prisons.[3] Today's prisons are, in the main, more relaxed in their discipline but often more dangerous in their daily operation. The iron hand of the custodian has all too often given way to a "rule of the cruel," with the hard-core convicts now setting the tone of prison life (see Lerner, 1984).

Corrections Contained, Violence Unleashed

Most beleaguered prison officials fought to maintain order by resisting reha-bilitation and prisoners' rights. Such negative tactics occurred to some degree in all prisons, but were not the only means of maintaining order during the increasingly turbulent 1960s and 70s. Officials could have embraced these agendas and created a basis for a civil order in the prison. Correctional pro-grams worth their salt can hold a man's attention and give him something constructive to do with his time. What a correctional system loses in exter-nally imposed discipline can be compensated for by the self-discipline of those who are working for their own reform. Similarly, newly enfranchised inmates could be given a constructive role in shaping the conditions of their confine-ment; for instance, by means of experiments in self-governance. Again, inmate self-discipline would replace or supplement prison discipline. As a practical matter, however, few correctional programs of any substance emerged in these institutions, nor was there any broad-scale attempt to work with inmates to give them some sense of responsibility for the quality of prison life. The promise of corrections—breached almost from the outset—produced a dis-tinctive sense of injustice, and ultimately rage, directed at a prison system that was perceived to be patently hypocritical and manipulative (Irwin, 1980).

Thus, when rules and discipline were played down in most American pris-ons, ostensibly in the name of correctional treatment and out of respect for rights, what resulted was not a new order but a collapse of the old order. Guard morale and effectiveness fell, predatory behavior among inmates rose; there was a general decline in the conditions of prison life. It is indeed both tragic and ironic that the rehabilitative ideal and prisoners' rights, as implemented in most prisons during this period, "resulted in more violence, worse general liv-ing conditions, and fewer programmatic opportunities. The food was worse. There was more fear, more violence, and more sexual assault . . . inmates did more cell time" (Jacobs, 1977:86–87; see also Rothman & Engel, 1983).

Together, relaxed discipline and increased rights reduced some of the pres-sures of daily life in the typical American prison and made that institution more responsive to individual concerns (see Jacobs, 1983). The deadening routine of the Big House was gone, for instance, and with it went the "pressure cooker" atmosphere that had made prison life so tense and occasionally explosive. But as we have noted, these changes also produced a crisis of custodial authority and provided an opportunity for inmates to vent their frustration and anger at the failed correctional system. This crisis of authority and general climate of inmate aggressiveness gave predatory prisoners a free hand to exploit their neighbors. It also set the stage for the emergence of large and often violent gangs and militant groups (which have since proliferated).[4] Explaining rampant gang activity at Stateville during the late 1960s and early 70s, Jacobs (1977:138) observed:

> The abandonment [by the courts] of the "hands-off" doctrine exposed an authoritarian regime to outside accountability, limited the institution's recourse to coercive sanctions and provided the inmates with a legitimate means of expression with which to challenge the system of social control. The rise of professional administration, informed by the rehabilitative ideal and the human relations model of management, led to intrastaff conflict, a decline in the morale of the guard force, and ultimately to the deterioration of the organization's capacity to meet basic control and maintenance goals. It was only in the context of this organizational crisis that the gangs were able to organize, recruit, and achieve dominance.

Similar organizational forces were at work at other prisons.[5] New York prisons, for example, followed a pattern like that of Stateville and the California prisons. Indeed, the infamous Attica riot of 1971 can be traced to failed correctional promises coupled with enhanced inmate freedoms and diminished custodial control. This explosive riot was not caused by the pressures of living in the Big House, but rather by the pressures that came in the wake of the Big House (Lombardo, 1988). Nor did subsequent reforms restore order to the troubled prisons. Sheehan (1978) notes that liberal "After Attica" reforms were implemented in New York State prisons between 1971 and 1976 in an effort to create a better correctional treatment climate and to make the institutions more responsive to prisoners' rights. These reforms did in fact make the prisons increasingly less custodial—any traces of the Big House in the New York State prisons of this time were largely obliterated—but they did not make these prisons over into truly correctional institutions. As at Stateville and elsewhere (most notably in California prisons), there was an outraged sense of injustice that could not be contained by a weakened guard force. Again, there was an exploitation of this climate of aggression by the predators. Again, correctional reforms made the prisons considerably more dangerous. The result was, in Sheehan's words, a "breakdown of control" (1978:147).

The growth of the black prisoner population in the 1960s and 70s added a racial element to prison tensions (Irwin, 1980). This was a time when "black rage" (Grier & Cobbs, 1968) had surfaced in social movements in the free world, first in muted form in the civil rights movement, later in more virulent form in the black power movement (Carmichael & Hamilton, 1967). Many prisoners drew inspiration from their angriest brethren on the streets, some of whom were subsequently incarcerated for standard felonies but who assumed the status of self-proclaimed political prisoners. The failure of correctional programs took on an almost conspiratorial tone; the larger "system" was rigged against the down-and-outs, the logic ran, and so was the correctional system (see Dorin & Johnson, 1978). Prisoner militancy and black power became synonymous at the outset of what has come to be known as "the prison movement." Clashes between militant black prisoners and the largely white prison authorities became increasingly commonplace. Violence against the staff took on an ominous character.

> Because of the prison movement, many more prisoners openly defied and physically attacked guards than in any period in the history of our prisons. In past eras, violence against guards or other staff members was extremely rare. Also, it was less random. When prisoners attacked guards, it invariably followed some hostile interaction between them. During the prison movement, guards were often randomly selected for attack. Defiance—which was always present, but had been more subtle or covert—became open and bold. (Irwin, 1980: 110)

Violence against fellow inmates, formerly "more subtle or covert," also became "open and bold." Militant prisoners were often not the dedicated and selfless revolutionaries they made themselves out to be (Irwin, 1980; Carroll, 1974, 1988). More often than not, their commitment, like that of gang members and lone predators, was to violence and survival and not to radical social change (Johnson & Dorin, 1978).[6] As prisons became less controlled, these prisoners assaulted their peers as well as the staff.

As order yielded to disorder, violence and fear fed upon one another, producing a climate of terror. These forces were shown in the relief in Walpole State Prison in Massachusetts in the early 1970s and, a decade later, in Texas prisons. In Walpole, a reform commissioner, riding the crest of legal changes in the rights of inmates, advocated civilian involvement in the monitoring of the prison. The notion that civilians could roam the cell blocks, observing and reporting on the behavior of officers, would have been entirely inconceivable during the Big House era, and was a stunning blow to the morale of the line officers. Discredited from above by the commissioner and their warden (who supported this curious venture), and pressured by newly empowered convicts, the authority of the guards was profoundly compromised. The effectiveness of the officer force plummeted. The result was a drop in living conditions (the prison became deploringly dirty) and a rise in violence among inmates and between inmates and staff. Kauffman provides a telling description of the gruesome violence that became the order of the day at Walpole:

> While the inmates were locked in their cells for the night, one inmate began throwing flammable liquid on another inmate who had been asleep in the adjacent cell. For nearly fifteen minutes screams filled the block while the man methodically reached through the bars and doused his terrified quarry. On the undermanned night shift, no officers were in the area, only civilian observers. A frantic effort was made to find someone with keys to open the cells, or at least some fire extinguisher (there were none in the institution). Just as help finally arrived, the inmate tossed lighted matches through the cell door, instantly incinerating his victim and filling the block with smoke.
>
> Four days later an inmate was stabbed twenty times and his body flung from the second tier onto the concrete flats below. More assaults and attempted murders followed. . . . [T]wo inmates reportedly attempted to

hang themselves, four others slashed themselves in an apparent bid to be transferred out of the prison, and one inmate and two officers were assaulted. That night a sizable number of inmates refused to be locked in their cells in [a] dispute over shakedowns. State police were . . . asked to stand by. (Kauffman, 1988:13)

"Walpole prison," Kauffman concluded, "was in a state of virtual anarchy" (Kauffman, 1988: 13). Officer and inmate alike lived in fear.

A similar state of affairs could be found in the Texas prison system following legal reforms undermining its custodial model of social control. The Ruiz decision, handed down in 1972 but resisted by obstinate prison officials for nearly a decade, eventually resulted in the demise of the notorious Building Tender system, and the imposition of sharp and carefully enforced limits on use of force by officers. Almost immediately, "the highly ordered inmate society began to crumble" (Crouch & Marquart, 1989:188). The quality of life dropped; dirt and disorder became the norm (Crouch & Marquart, 1989:188). Inmate-on-inmate violence was so common that extortion became a kind of cottage industry, replete with the equivalent of service contracts. " 'We had one prison,' a Texas official observed, 'where we found actual written protection policies. $49 a month for complete security, $29 a month for cuts and bruises, that sort of thing' " (Crouch & Marquart, 1989:189). Inmates without such protection were left to their own devices. Said one Texas inmate,

> Today there's no more protection without the BTs. You're on your own. You're either gonna survive or perish. No matter which way, it's up to you. . . . You take care of yourself. That's how a convict makes it here. (Crouch & Marquart, 1989:190)

Once again officers too lived in fear, since in the absence of BTs they had to deal directly with restive and hostile inmates.

Increasingly, violence among inmates took on racial connotations, with formerly repressed black inmates rising to positions of dominance within the prison culture. This reversal of white convict dominance, evident at virtually every prison of this era and continuing today (see Jacobs, 1976; Carroll, 1974; McCall, 1995), was particularly salient in the Texas prison system.

> Once the BTs were removed . . . [the] status quo among prisoners changed. Long-repressed racial animosities and hatreds rose to the surface of everyday interactions as minority prisoners began to exert themselves. Blacks, for example, soon dictated television programming and controlled the benches and the domino tables in the dayrooms. Not only did blacks effectively take over in many cellblocks, but they also began to exploit white prisoners. (Crouch & Marquart, 1989:192)

During this period, the guards in the trenches of our nation's prisons, the vast majority of whom were white, refrained from enforcing the rules in order to avoid conflict; others intervened in aggressive and insensitive ways, including resort to outright violence and brutality, which served merely to escalate tensions (Colvin, 1982 & 1992; Carroll, 1988; Crouch & Marquart, 1989:175;

Kauffman, 1988:34). Officers with seniority (and presumably the competence to mediate those conflicts properly) elected administrative assignments or retreated to the towers on the prison walls, far from the dangers of the cell blocks and the yard (Sheehan, 1978:142–43; Cressey, 1982:xx; Crouch & Marquart, 1989:175). "A general maxim about Walpole," Kauffman (1988:34) observed, "would have been the greater an officer's experience, the less he had to do with inmates." This maxim would have applied to many other prisons as well, notably those in New York, California, and Texas.

The inexperienced officers running these violent prisons were disproportionately drawn from the ranks of women and minorities, who had been newly recruited to prison work. These guards entered prisons during a period of turmoil, and were resisted by white male officers along with other changes imposed from outside the prison. In fact, the arrival of female and minority officers (including, of course, some female minority officers) was seen as part of the general loss of power to the courts and to central offices of increasingly bureaucratic prison systems. In the words of one disgruntled officer, mixing racism and sexism with raw alienation:

> What will they think of next? They've lowered the standards so anybody can get in. First they brought in these minorities; some of them can hardly sign their name. Now we've got these women who can't even protect themselves. How do they expect us to run a prison? Next thing you know, they'll be bringing kids in here to control inmates. We might as well give the inmates the keys to the place and go home. (Zimmer, 1986:59)

Informal accommodations between staff and inmates broke down during the prisons of this time, in part because seasoned officers were nowhere in evidence. The absence of such officers undermined the various licit and illicit opportunity systems, noted above, that had given stability to the convict culture of the Big House. With little reason to conform to staff directives or even to negotiate compromise solutions to problems with the frightened novice officers manning the cell blocks and yards, violence became the order of the day and the preferred mode of adjustment among the convicts (Colvin, 1982:456 & 1992).[7]

For their part, regular inmates (who now included some prisoners who would have counted themselves among the convicts of earlier days) assiduously avoided the public areas of the prison (Irwin, 1980). Many fled to protective custody cells, which were filled in record numbers (Barak, 1978; Conrad, 1988). In effect, the prison was given over to the most predatory convicts, who often prowled the yard in gangs. Gone was the notion that prisoners should be "right guys" who did their time in the company of a few "main men" and who respected like-minded "regulars." The violent convict and his clique of thugs became the leaders of the yard.

> Today the respected public prison figure—the convict or hog—stands ready to kill to protect himself, maintains strong loyalties to some small group of other convicts (invariably of his own race), and will rob and attack or at least tolerate his friends' robbing and attacking other weak

independents or their foes. He openly and stubbornly opposes the administration, even if this results in harsh punishment. Finally, he is extremely assertive of his masculine sexuality. . . . To circulate in this world, the convict world, one must act like a convict and, with a few exceptions, have some type of affiliation with a powerful racial clique or gang. (Irwin, 1980:192–95)[8]

If it is true that a society gets the criminals it deserves, it is also true that we get the prisons we deserve. Years of turmoil and violence within our prisons have been met by the larger society with indifference and neglect. Unsurprisingly, we find ourselves the reluctant landlords of prisons that harbor a frightening potential for mean-spirited and unregenerate violence. As Colvin (1992) makes clear, the Penitentiary of New Mexico is just such a prison today. The riot at that prison at the close of the violent 1970s, which claimed the lives of thirty-four prisoners and resulted in serious physical injuries for another two hundred inmates, as well as seven of the twelve officers taken hostage (Colvin, 1992:192), has come to symbolize modern prisons at their worst. Events over the intervening years since that riot serve to confirm New Mexico's image as a tough, violent prison.

Corrections can and often does run prisons that are better, much better, than the Penitentiary at New Mexico, and we will explore a host of viable prison reforms in the concluding section of this book. But as Colvin points out, apathy and indecision—and then, frustration and rage—too often guide prison policy. The larger social forces constraining the prison can be formidable, and this, in turn, can leave prison administrators feeling there is little they can do to run a decent prison. An economy with a declining base of working-class jobs seems almost to demand warehouse prisons, whose agenda is merely to contain surplus and essentially useless unskilled and unmotivated workers. As the body count rises and the cell blocks become more and more crowded, those prisons are too readily treated like political footballs—courts may confer rights and professionals may promise treatment, but disorder too often overcomes good intentions, yielding grim environments marked by violence and fear. Tales of abuse flourish, but few people outside the prison hear or care. An increasingly punitive public captures the attention of politicians, who lengthen sentences, shorten bottom lines, and call for increasingly spartan prison regimes. Resources shrink, frustrations mount, conditions worsen. Staff have low morale, inmates little cohesion, and few people—staff or inmate—treat anyone with simple human compassion. Everyone lives in fear, and rage lurks just beneath the surface of daily prison life. Ultimately, the rage explodes forth, exploiting preexisting breaches in prison security to foment raw anarchy and violent death in the time-honored ritual of the prison riot. Sadly, prison riots occur these days at an unprecedented rate (Useem and Kimball, 1989).

This last point—that riots exploit preexisting weaknesses in the prison security—is mundane but important. Scholars like DiIulio discount the value of studying the social structure of inmate and staff relations (not to mention the larger societal context in which prisons operate), maintaining that prison problems such as individual and collective violence are *caused* by failures of prison security (see DiIulio, 1991). Prisons hold bad people, so the logic runs, and they will behave badly if we let them. If we run a tight ship, the logic continues, prisons will run smoothly.

Colvin puts this simplistic view to rest. The Penitentiary at New Mexico has always been plagued by poor management and lapses in basic security procedures, but relations between staff and inmates were, for much of the prison's history, quite orderly. For much of the history of the Penitentiary of New Mexico, staff were willing to accommodate reasonable inmate demands, and inmates were able to achieve a fairly high level of organization, which they used to maintain order and stability within the prison community. (Violence among inmates occurred, of course, but it was sporadic; inmate leaders, out of self-interest, tried to keep such violence to a minimum. This connection between inmate cohesion and social order has been noted by others, particularly Gresham Sykes, and is artfully documented by Colvin.) Staff relations with inmates turned coercive at the Penitentiary of New Mexico over the course of the 1970s, but only after informal sources of order eroded and finally broke down, mostly along the general lines described by Irwin for other American prisons during this period of turmoil (discussed above). The effect of coercive staff behavior was to divide but not conquer the now-restive convicts. Instead, heavy-handed approaches by the staff, often featuring violence, were mirrored within the increasingly fragmented prisoner society. Staff coercion, in other words, bred coercion among the inmates and, ultimately, between inmates and staff. Violence, in particular, proved contagious. When invoked by the staff as a substitute for social control, violence did not produce conformity; it fed on itself, producing more violence in turn. In this explosive context, failures of security became fatal organizational flaws.

The convict culture of violence, so evident in the Penitentiary at New Mexico, may be more or less prevalent in any particular prison today. Its coercive power may be supplemented by other types of power available to inmates, Stojkovic (1984) makes clear, most notably that associated with resources (such as drugs), expertise (jailhouse lawyers and writ-writers), and ego building (by means of ethnic and religious awareness groups). Nevertheless, this culture of violence is always present in some degree and always shapes the daily life and adjustment of prisoners. State-raised convicts—men reared on rejection and abuse in orphanages, detention centers, training schools, and youth prisons—have come to epitomize this culture of violence.

PRISON VIOLENCE AND THE
STATE-RAISED CONVICT

State-raised convicts have always been bitter and prone to violence. In the Big House, their violence was held largely in check by discipline. Many of these prisoners adapted by being cagey and cool—by becoming institutionalized, and saving their overt violence for their periodic excursions to the free world. Jimmy Dunn, a state-raised convict who served his time during the Big House era, is typical of this class of prisoner:

I want nothing from the state that they want to give me. All I want is the opportunity to hate them and to destroy everything they stand for and everyone who gets in my way. . . . I'm going to do everything I can, all my life, to beat them, rob them, lie, and con them. I'm going to beat them at their own game. I'll play it like they want it while they've got their eyes on me; but as soon as they turn their backs, or can't see me, I'll kill something that someone thinks is good. (Manocchio & Dunn, 1982:35)

Dunn plays the prison game, biding his time until he gets out from under the heel of authority, whereupon he can be the hasty and destructive hedonist he longs to be. It is telling that even his reveries of life in the free world have a violent edge to them. On release, says he,

I'm going to kill them out there! All that good money from bad women or bad money from good women, it don't make no difference. I'm going to rip-and-tear and have a ball. I'm going to shoot junk, pimp whores, and tear holes in business roofs and live life the way it was meant to be lived. The world's mine and I'm going to kill them dead. (Manocchio & Dunn, 1982:238).

State-raised convicts like Dunn are less easily controlled today.[9] Those who, like Dunn, spent their formative years in Big House prisons are also less able to adapt to today's prisons. It is telling that upon his return to confinement in the late 1960s, Dunn found California's prisons, then racked with gang- and other group-related forms of violence, to be unlivable. Out of place in a prison that was so different from the more controlled prisons he had known, Dunn took his life.

It is almost certainly the case that at least some state-raised convicts adapt to today's prison's nonviolently, presumably by becoming institutionalized, much like their predecessors in Big House prisons. Over time, these prisoners, like virtually all prisoners, find themselves better suited to prison life than to life on the outside, and are able to get by with less effort and less trouble (see Toch & Adams, 1988). State-raised convicts who are serving long terms, for example, often adapt as do the vast majority of lifers, by making the most of the legitimate resources and lifestyles available within the prison community.

It is primarily the aggressive and, if you will, unpacified state-raised convicts who have displaced the tough but accommodating "right guy" as the hero of the prison yard (Irwin, 1980), and it is this group of state-raised convicts that will be the subject of our analysis in the remainder of this chapter. They typically come to prison as angry young men; over time, their anger remains unmollified, though it may be punctuated by periods of depression and boredom (see, for example, Porporino, 1991:6–7). Angry, disgruntled, and alienated from the legitimate options such as work and education offered in the prison, these prisoners make their home on the prison yard, where they come to yield considerable—and violence-suffused—power among their fellow prisoners (Colvin, 1982). They have made today's prison a dangerous place for staff and fellow prisoner alike. It is they who, by their violence, intimidate other prisoners and who, again through violence, find themselves embroiled with the custodial staff. They are the prison's bastard children, and this unhappy status brings out the worst in both the prisoners and the prison. They are easily provoked to violence by the stresses of prison life, and in turn they provoke the prison staff to use violence and even brutality to maintain law and order behind bars. Predictably, they find themselves, to quote one of their more famous members, "in the belly of the beast."

Life in the Belly of the Beast

Sociological portraits of the state-raised convict depict him as a man at home in the prison, inured to its abuses and coldly dispensing violence to achieve his selfish ends. He typically moves in predatory cliques, but whether alone or in gangs he is adept at exploiting the weak and defenseless. He finds sexual gratification in the violation of other men; paradoxically, these encounters prove his manliness. He succeeds as a convict because the prison is the only world he knows.

> He was raised in a world where "punks" and "queens" have replaced women, "bonaroos" [specially pressed prison outfits] are the only fashionable clothing, and cigarettes are money. This is a world where disputes are settled with a pipe or a knife, and the individual must form tight cliques for protection. His senses are attuned to iron doors banging, locks turning, shakedowns, and long lines of [uniformed] convicts. He knows how to survive, in fact prosper, in this world, how to get a cell change and a good work assignment, how to score for nutmeg, cough syrup, or other narcotics. More important, he knows hundreds of youths like himself who grew up in the youth prisons and are now in the adult prisons. (Irwin, 1970:74)

State-raised convicts adapt to prison life and even dominate the public culture of the prison, but they are by no means immune to the pains and deprivations of confinement. In fact, many of these men are deeply scarred by a life of imprisonment, and these wounds are apparent in the lives they lead in the prison world.

The most striking thing about state-raised convicts is their facade of adult maturity, their veneer of cool, hard manliness. Yet this demeanor and their sometimes casual use of violence are not badges of strength, but tragic testimony to the violence prison has done to them. They were reared in a world where they were susceptible to flagrant abuse. More than other prisoners, they know in their guts what it means to be locked up—to be "helpless and vulnerable" and hence at the "matrix of disaster" while in the arms of the law. In the words of Jack Abbott (1981:12), in many ways a prototype of the state-raised convict,

> He who is state-raised—reared by the state from an early age after he is taken from what the state calls a "broken home"—learns over and over and all the days of his life that people in society can do anything to him

and not be punished by the law. Do anything to him with the full force of
the state behind them.

Abbott speaks with some authority in this matter for, sad to say, Abbott's
credentials as a state-raised youth are unimpeachable.[10] His life is a study in neglect and abuse, in the free world and in the prison (see Nusser, 1982). His
parents separated when he was quite young, breaking up what was a turbulent
and no doubt abusive home. He was passed from one foster home to another
over a period of years, during which time he was physically beaten and sexually abused. He dropped out of school after the sixth grade. Within a year, "he
was committed to the Utah State Industrial School for Boys for 'failing to adjust.' He was twelve years old. He stayed there until his release at age eighteen"
(Nusser, 1982:560). His adjustment never improved. If anything, his lengthy
stay in training school—most juveniles serve short terms—indicates that his
adjustment worsened over time.

Abbott's marginal adjustment to life continued into adulthood. On release
he developed a drinking problem. He issued fraudulent checks, for which he
was sent to prison. In prison, as a young adult, he appears to have fully cultivated his propensity to violence.

> While serving his court-imposed sentence, Abbott stabbed another inmate
> to death for informing on him. He was convicted and sent back to prison
> with an additional twenty years, but not before throwing a water pitcher
> at the judge and trying to choke one of the jurors. (Nusser, 1982:560)

At one point Abbott escaped from prison briefly, robbed a bank, and was confined once again with an additional nineteen years to serve. At this point his
fate was sealed. He was truly a state-raised man, a product of institutions. "Uncaring and impersonal, each of these institutions compounded and passed on
responsibility for the problem" (Nusser, 1982:560).

A substantial part of "the problem" in Abbott, and in other state-raised
convicts, is chronic defensiveness. Abbott assumes a tough and menacing pose
because he is angry and frightened, and because he sees no other way to keep
a hostile and rejecting world at bay. And because this world is almost a caricature of the abusive worlds that spawn the chronic felons who later come to
share adult prisons with him (see Chapter Four), the state-raised convict typically becomes the most impulsive of prison's hasty hedonists, the most cun-
ning and lethal of its jungle cats.

The state-raised convict's predatory pose has a distinctively adolescent
character. And for good reason. Prison life equates the normal dependency of
childhood with vulnerability and makes adult independence impossible. Life
on these terms is likely to leave the prisoner emotionally stunted, a perpetual,
impulsive adolescent. "You hear a lot about 'arrested adolescence' nowadays,"
observes Abbott (1981:13), "and I believe this concept touches the nub of the
instability of prisoners like myself." The state-raised prisoner, Abbott continues, does not have a chance to mature normally. "As a boy in reform school,
he is punished for being a little boy. In prison, he is punished for trying to be a

man" (Abbott, 1981:14). At best, "he is treated as an adolescent in prison" (Abbott, 1981:15).

Abbott's point has been made before, notably by Sing Sing's Warden Lawes, who quotes an English penal authority who observed that "the trouble with the American Reformatory idea"—an idea that shaped many of the prisons that shaped Abbott—"was that it made youths out of adults and adults out of youths, subjecting both to all the odious and cruel oppressions that prevailed in prisons for men steeped in crime and viciousness" (Lawes, 1932:36). More recently, Zamble, Porporino, and Kalotay's research supports Abbott's analysis of the chronic prisoner's adolescent character. "Imprisonment," they found,

> deprives people of the usual experience necessary for the development of coping, and in this way it freezes development at the point when a person enters the institution. Thus, we can see why the behavior of habitual offenders resembles that of adolescents in many ways, e.g., in the dependence on peer groups, emphasis on physical dominance, and [a] generally impulsive behavioral style. It also follows that imprisonment at an early age will have more effect on subsequent behavior than at a later time, since that is when the greater development is normally occurring. Finally, we can also predict that those who have spent the most time in prison will be those who cope most poorly when they are on the outside. (Zamble, Porporino & Kalotay, 1984:137)

The result for the state-raised convict, in Abbott's (1981:15) words, is that "he lacks experience and, hence, maturity. His judgment is untempered, rash; his emotions are impulsive, raw, unmellowed" (see also Myers & Levy, 1978; Higgins & Thies, 1981).

The "raw" emotions of the state-raised convict are not those of the typical adolescent, however. Unlike adolescents in the free world, prison's adolescents have never been taken seriously or cared for as individuals. These prisoners, then, are not only consigned to a lifetime of adolescence, a painful experience in itself, but are also burdened with chronic self-doubt, the often crippling corollary of rejection that reads, "I must be unlovable if I am unloved; I must be bad to be treated badly." Moreover, it is likely that this self-doubt will escalate over time and become personally disabling. A lifetime in prison means emotional and sometimes physical abuse. These experiences produce a legacy of impotent rage (because one is helpless to defend oneself) and ultimately self-hatred (a product of one's sense of shame and contamination). The result, in Abbott's view, is a kind of "prison paranoia" that reduces one's life to a daily struggle to maintain sanity and self-control.

> When I walk past a glass window in the corridor and happen to see my reflection, I get angry on impulse. I feel shame and hatred at such times. When I'm forced by circumstances to be in a crowd of prisoners, it's all I can do to refrain from attack. I feel such hostility, such hatred, I can't help this anger. All these years I have felt it. Paranoid. I can control it. I never seek a confrontation. I have to intentionally gauge my voice in a conversation to

cover up the anger I feel, the chaos and pain just beneath the surface of what we commonly recognize as reality. Paranoia is an illness I contracted in institutions. It is not the reason for my sentences to reform school and prison. It is the effect, not the cause. (1981:5)

To my knowledge, Abbott has never been diagnosed as a paranoid psychotic, though this diagnosis is unusually common among prison populations.[11] Yet Abbott is, like all paranoids, profoundly self-centered; his fragile sense of self is always hanging in the balance. His personality is marred by suspicion of others, doubt in himself, and an ugly festering rage and hate that touch virtually everything and everyone in his world. There is no rest for Abbott, no chance to let his defenses down. His image in the mirror is simply a poignant reflection of the continuing struggle he must wage against the pain of the prison world and the hurt he carries within himself.

Prisons thus raise men who are as much at war with themselves as with the world around them. On both fronts they are threatened: internally, with the knowledge of their inadequacy; externally, with the knowledge of their vulnerability. Failure in social encounters, even the slightest hint of defeat, at once exposes their weaknesses to themselves and others. To guard against this, they must avenge even the slightest insult that might cast doubt on their manliness, brook any authority that would curtail their sense of self. To do less, as they see it, is to be demeaned as a man (see Abbott, 1981:78– 79).

The difficulty is that encounters in which such a fragile notion of dignity might be shattered are quite common in prison. Prisoners vie for status and routinely make invidious comparisons among themselves; guards issue and enforce countless orders every day. Under this continuing assault upon their self-esteem—for state-raised convicts, such encounters feel like personal attacks—state-raised convicts readily come to see themselves as innocent victims of an arbitrary world who have no choice but to strike out in their own defense. Their behavior is, for the most part, wildly disproportionate to the objective pressures at hand. Sadly, their justifications for their conduct are transparently false and self-serving to everyone but themselves.

Perhaps the root of the problem with state-raised convicts, and why so many of them appear as pathetic but dangerous adolescents, is that they simply cannot see the world from the other person's point of view. At best, others emerge as pale reflections of their own inner worlds, as persons distorted by the same forces that shaped and ultimately distorted the prisoners themselves. Thus Abbott sees others as contemptible, just as he holds himself in contempt, and as sources of danger, just as he knows the danger within himself. The state-raised youth's dealings with others routinely involve manipulation and deception; that is, he believes, what others deserve and what is required to succeed in life. Yet these stratagems typically fail, at least in one's dealings with other savvy state-raised convicts, and hence one must fall back on violence as the final measure of worth.

Prisoners like Abbott are all the more dangerous, moreover, because the lesson they learn from their redundant interpersonal failures is that violence is in fact their *only* means of becoming men of consequence who are taken seriously. Life is reduced to an either/or proposition: either you or me. As a result, these men have a personal stake in violence, and they protect it jealously. Thus Abbott (1981: 15 & 149–50) speaks almost reverently of

> the high esteem we naturally have for violence, force. It is what makes us effective, men whose judgment impinges on others, on the world: Dangerous killers who act alone and without emotion, who act with calculation and principles, to avenge themselves, establish and defend their principles with acts of murder that usually evade prosecution by law; this is the state-raised convicts' conception of manhood, in the highest sense. . . .
> Here in prison the most respected and honored men among us are those who have killed other men. . . . It is not merely fear, but respect.

One such prisoner bragged to a television reporter about the raw, brutal violence he had used to kill a guard, who had been chosen at random, merely to impress other convicts. He concluded by saying, on camera, "This has just begun for me. I'm only thirty-one years old. I got a lot of bodies to collect yet" (Earley, 1992:305).

Abbott sees his violence as a dignified, one might almost say solemn, obligation of manhood. This self-serving view is no doubt shared by other convicts and helps them to glorify their explosive tantrums. (If this sounds harsh, remember that Abbott himself traced the "nub" of his character to "arrested adolescence.") This violence does in fact command respect from other prisoners, but on the grounds that its authors are the most unrestrained, emotionally immature, and hence dangerous men in the institution. There is even an awareness among the prisoners that this behavior reflects a kind of mental instability not far from Abbott's conception of prison paranoia. In the words of Schroeder (1976:23), an ex-inmate,

> if you clearly didn't care, if you could convince inmates and guards that you had absolutely nothing to lose and that your countermeasures to even the most trivial provocation would be totally unrestrained and pursued to the utmost of your abilities—then you were given respect and a wide berth, and people looked to you for leadership and advice. "He's crazy," they'd say admiringly, even longingly, when the name came up. "He's just totally, completely insane."

Hence it is that the prisoners who are least equipped for life in the civil world set the tone of adjustment on the prison yard.

The threat of violence, even lethal violence, is a salient norm in the convict world. It begins at the point of entry into the prison, when the young convict must protect himself from the predations of others. But the use of violence to establish one's manly image never stops here, even if one humiliates one's opponents (see Abbott, 1981:93–94). Violence continues because there is no mechanism within the convict culture that allows prisoners to make peace with one another, to break with the violence of the past and embark on a nonviolent future. Convicts, ever on the defensive, feel they must draw lines in the prison yard, as it were, demarcating that point beyond which others cannot cross for fear of retaliatory violence; to do less is to live without principle or honor in the prison community (see Earley, 1992:186). The difficulty is that for many convicts, the very presence of such lines is an open invitation to test the prisoner's mettle, to see if he will in fact defend himself. The drawing and crossing of lines of permissible behavior occur endlessly in the prison community, leaving in their wake a history of insult and retaliation that seems endless.

That past hurts and slights live on, crying out for revenge, is the theme of a poem, written by Ed Lipman, a prisoner, and aptly entitled "Because Our Past Lives Every Day" (see Bruchac, 1984: 193). Frank, the protagonist, lives in a world in which time is a seamless, suffocating web and in which violence lives and breathes in the prison yard, waiting to pounce on a man to avenge acts he'd like to leave behind him:

> They wrapped Big Frank in plaster
> and put him on a bed
> to heal
> & watch
> each approaching stranger
> with dangerous eyes . . .
> The cops assigned
> to guard his door
> can't understand
> that what's become
> the past to them
> can be heard breathing
> softly on The Yard
> thru the eerie quiet
> of this prison hospital
> early in the dawn.

> But Frank knows better;
> he's learned today
> is as much a part
> of yesterday as is tomorrow;
> and that there are
> no innocent bystanders . . .

The convict world is populated by men who doubt their worth as human beings, and who feel they must constantly find occasions to "prove" themselves. In this world, there is no such thing as an accident, and hence "there are no innocent bystanders." Here, Lipman continues, "paranoia is nothing more than increased awareness" (Bruchac, 1984:193). While an apology may often suffice to resolve a conflict among regular inmates (see Cooley, 1992:36), being a convict is, apparently, never having to say you are sorry, and certainly never accepting an apology at face value because it is almost certainly a ploy, a trick. For convicts, every insult is premeditated, a planned assault demanding a vengeful response that provides tangible evidence of one's worth. The only proofs of worth that matter in this context are those that entail the subjugation of other men.

The convict world is a world of continuing—and generally escalating—conflict. Aggrieved parties cannot afford to back down, for then they are seen as weak and hence vulnerable to more abuse. Violence in the convict world establishes one's competence as a man who can survive in a human jungle. The ultimate paradox of this world is that only lethal violence can truly assure one's peace of mind:

> To a prisoner it is an insult to grapple hand-to-hand with anyone. If someone ever strikes him with his hand (another prisoner), he has to kill him with a knife. If he doesn't, he will be fistfighting with him everyday. He might be killed. . . . All violence in prison is geared for murder, nothing else. You can't have someone with ill feelings for you walking around. He could drop a knife in you any day. . . . [Y]ou are not killing in physical self-defense. You're killing someone in order to live respectably in prison. Moral self-defense. (Abbott, 1981:88–89)

As simple and straightforward as this code of violence may be, the notion that when in doubt, one should hurt or kill one's neighbor produces a bleak and solitary prison "community" in which "most prisoners fear almost every other prisoner around them" (Abbott, 1981:85). In fact, in the convict world,

> *Everyone* is afraid. It is not an emotional, psychological fear. It is a practical matter. If you do not threaten someone at the very least someone will threaten you. When you walk across the yard or down the tier to your cell, you stand out like a sore thumb if you do not appear either callously unconcerned or cold and ready to kill. Many times you have to "prey" on someone, or you will be "preyed" on yourself. After so many years, *you are not bluffing*. No one is. (Abbott, 1981:144)

In the convict world, day-to-day relations among prisoners are at best distant and tense, with simple coexistence a major achievement. One is vividly reminded of Sartre's notion of hell as a circumscribed world with "no exit," and hence no escape from people you hold in contempt.

> You don't comfort one another; you humor one another. You extend that confusion about this reality of one another by lying to one another. You can't stand the sight of each other and yet you are doomed to stand and face one another every moment of every day for years without end. You must bathe together, defecate and urinate together, eat and sleep together, talk together, work together. (Abbott, 1981:102)

To be sure, other prisoners may feel less bitter than Abbott, but the quality of their interpersonal relations with fellow prisoners is often much the same (see Chapter Four).

Relations between convicts and staff are, if anything, even worse. (There is no exit here either.) Convicts' perceptions of guards are suffused with resentment. Officers are hacks who comprise a monolithic caste of oppressors; the convicts are their hapless victims. The standard notion that is "us" against "them" doesn't fully capture the animosity the state-raised convict feels toward his keepers. "Us" against "that" comes closer to the mark.

> Among themselves, the guards are human. Among themselves, the prisoners are human. Yet between these two the relationship is not human. *It is animal.* Only in reflection—subjective reflection—do they acknowledge sharing a common consciousness. What is that common consciousness? It is the consciousness that we belong to a *common species* of life. But this is not the consciousness of society. It is not humanistic; *it is animalistic.*
>
> What I am saying is that the prisoner is closer to humanity than the guard: because he is *deprived* by the guard. That is why I say that evil exists—not in the prisoner, but in the guard. Intentions play none but an illusory role. *In fact*, the guard is evil. His *society* is demonic. I don't care if he likes the same food I do or the same music—or whatever: this is the illusory role intentions play. Animals can enjoy the same music or food we do. (Abbott, 1981:70–71)

It is almost as if the state-raised convict is impelled into destructive encounters with his keepers. When they treat him in a standard but impersonal way, this is an affront. When they vary their treatment of prisoners, they are revealed as arbitrary tyrants (see Abbott, 1981:65–66). One senses that guards, by the very exercise of authority, imperil the state-raised convict's tenuous sense of autonomy. The prisoner's only course of action, then, is to rebel and deny the possibility of legitimate prison authority—to "beat the man" by breaking every rule you can, all the while nurturing an unremitting hatred for them and everything they stand for (see Earley, 1992:282–83). This stance has both tragic and comic elements, and both are grasped by Abbott.

> It's impossible. I'm the kind of fool who, facing Caesar and his starving lions, need only retract a statement to walk away scot-free but instead cannot suppress saying "fuck you" to Caesar—knowing full well the consequences. What is more, *I refuse to be martyred*; I don't accept the consequences, and whine all the way to my death. A death, it seems, that I chose.
>
> If I *could* please Caesar, I would, I gladly would. It's a fucked-up world, but it's all I got. (Abbott, 1981:18)

The punishment system within the prison that is invoked to handle these degenerating encounters is, as the state-raised convict sees it, by definition a sham, a mockery of any notion of justice (see Abbott, 1981:139–40). The prisoner knows himself to be helpless before a powerful and malevolent opponent whose goal is to crush one's manhood. Still, he rebels and gets the worst punishments prisons have to offer. This includes, in at least some instances, flagrant acts of brutality.

Abbott, for instance, records a litany of punishments comprised of lengthy solitary confinement, mind-altering drugs, and overt physical violence

(1981:44–45). These punishments have almost certainly been embellished with time, but the more important point is that in no instance can Abbott see his own role in precipitating these abuses, even though he freely admits to insulting and even attacking "the pigs" at will. Nor can he put himself in the shoes of his punishers or even acknowledge the pain and rage that move them to primitive violence. Always he is utterly innocent; always they are unremittingly brutal. He suffers—and he does suffer—but somehow they only mete out pain. If he errs at all, as Abbott sees things, it is in being too stubbornly faithful to the convict code of manliness even as he nurses his wounds.

> There is a saying: *The first cut is the deepest.* Do not believe that. The first cut is nothing. You can spit in my face once or twice and it is nothing. You can take something away that belongs to me and I can learn to live without it.
>
> But you cannot spit in my face every day for ten thousand days; you cannot take all that belongs to me, one thing at a time, until you have gotten down to reaching for my eyes, my voice, my hands, my heart. You can't do this and say it is nothing.
>
> I have been made oversensitive—my very *flesh* has been made to suffer sensations and longings I never had before. I have been chopped to pieces by a life of deprivation of sensations; by beatings so frequent I am now a piece of meat and bone; by lies and by drugs that attack my nervous system. I have had my mind turned into steel by the endless smelter of *time* in confinement.
>
> I have been twisted by justice the way other men can be twisted by love. (Abbott, 1981:44–45)

The hurt generated by these encounters seems endless, and still there is no effort on Abbott's part to learn from them, to approach problems differently in the future.

THE PATHOS OF PRISON VIOLENCE

State-raised convicts like Jack Abbott live in a bleak and threatening prison world. Mostly, these men simply endure the various indignities and slights that make up their daily round of prison life. When the opportunity arises, they abuse others in turn, perpetuating the very cycle of violence that has marred their lives. They do not learn new and constructive ways of confronting problems. They bend because they have to, and are weakened in the process. In the end, they meet the prison world on its own terms, by suppressing their feelings and acting tough.

Yet their tough-guy stance is really just a facade. As McCall has observed, drawing on his own prison experience, even the toughest guys on the yard, with rare exceptions, are "really frightened boys, bluffing, trying to mask their fear of the world behind muscular frames" (1995:209). Beneath the hard exterior is a tender core of vulnerability and pain. In Abbot's words,

> So we can all hold up like good soldiers and harden ourselves in prison. But if you do that for too long, you lose yourself. Because there is something helpless and weak and innocent—something like an infant deep inside us all that really suffers in ways we would never permit an insect to suffer. That is how prison is tearing me up inside. It hurts every day. Every day takes me further from life. And I am not even conscious of how my dissolution is coming about. Therefore, I cannot stop it. (1981:5)

But prison officials can and must stop the process of decay. This core of humanity, which state-raised convicts share with other prisoners and with the rest of us, must be preserved and ultimately enriched. Correction means nothing at all if it does not mean preserving humanity, and it is not worth striving for if the humanity we preserve is not that of a mature adult.

Abbott, our poster child for the state-raised convict, is ferociously committed to immaturity. Consequently, he presents himself as a substantial obstacle to the creation of civilized and civilizing prisons. Ironically, though he wishes to reject the prison and everything associated with it, Abbott adopts the lifestyle of the institutions in which he was reared, particularly the prison. As fellow inmate Gary McGivern (1982:562) has noted, Abbott "used his talents to justify a lifestyle as callous in its exchanges as the social institutions about which he wrote." A victim, in prison and out, he felt entitled to victimize others in turn. "He felt it was his 'right' to continue the abuses to which he had been subjected," observed McGivern (1982:562), but in point of fact "He had no such right." Abbott, it seems, could never comprehend this crucial point.

Abbott was released soon after the publication of his book, though the reasons are unclear. Some contend that he was set free because of his literary talent, and because of the support of Norman Mailer, who had become his mentor of sorts. Others contend that Abbott informed on other inmates, and was rewarded by the state with early release (see Nusser, 1982). In either case, on release, he was imprisoned by his deficiencies and utterly unprepared for life in the free world. In the words of fellow inmate Tommy R. Mason (1982:564),

> Abbott emerged from prison a celebrity, yet he remained dependent, no more than a child. Even in walking out of prison he did not 'go free,' because the prison was inside him. The minute he encountered pressure, he reacted with the fury and destructiveness cultivated in that prison.

Abbott had described himself in these very terms in his book, as a dangerous man-child, prone to vengeful violence. Within weeks of his release, Abbott killed a waiter in a New York restaurant. The waiter, also an aspiring actor, had insulted Abbott—remember that Abbott is extremely thin-skinned—and Abbott stabbed him, chillingly, using a technique found in Abbott's book, *Life in the Belly of the Beast*. Abbott then fled, taking refuge for a time in the Louisiana oil fields, only to be apprehended, returned to New York, and sentenced to a lengthy prison term.

Some years after his conviction, the widow of Abbott's victim sued to collect damages. Abbott represented himself. At various points in the trial he berated the widow, claiming her evident feelings of sadness were trumped up to impress the jury and win a healthy settlement. How could Abbott imagine real sadness at the loss of a loved one? No one, after all, had ever expressed sadness about the tragic happenings in his life. At one point Abbott claimed that his victim was lucky to have been killed by one such as himself, an acknowledged expert with a knife, who could do the job quickly and well, with little or no pain. So much for empathy.

It is unlikely Abbott will ever see the free light of day again. Our concern must be not only for Abbott, but for the other would-be Abbotts who are working their way through our system. For them, violent convicts like Abbott are heroes, the rest of us villains; as state-raised youths, embarking on a life of prison, they *aspire* to be thugs (see Earley, 1992:281). We must break this cycle by breaking with violence. As one prison poet observed, "the prison knows how to handle me when I use my right hand in anger but they have to think twice when I use my head" (Dessus, in Bruchac, 1984:86). Prison officials must think twice as a matter policy in their dealings with prisoners. The goal must be to meet the violence of prisoners with empathy and reason, and to provide opportunities for mature living that reverse the experiences of failure and rejection upon which the prisoners' violence feeds. The adolescent violence these prisoners engage in, and too often elicit in the staff, has no place in a civilized prison system.

NOTES

1. Bowker (1982:63) draws this figure from Sykes's classic study of Trenton State Prison in the mid-1950s, reminding us that "fully three-fourths of the prisoners he studied played predatory social roles." We need reminding because this is not something Sykes himself emphasized. The implications of this fact for daily prison living are, if anything, played down in Sykes's book, and in most other accounts of the social world of the prison during the Big House era, in favor of a more harmonious "social systems" perspective on prison adjustment.

2. As recently as 1992, British prisons were described as Big Houses marked by spartan and repressive regimes. Since that time, a host of liberal reforms have been introduced, which have produced more relaxed regimes. The relaxation of Big House discipline has produced internal problems, including an increase in violence, much as occurred in America in the late 1960s and on through the early 1980s (see Cavadino and Dignan, 1992; lectures on prison reform by Vivian Stern and Adam Sampson, the Comparative Corrections Institute, sponsored by The American University and held at the University of London in the summer of 1994). As in America, part of the problem is that correctional officials do not quite know how to occupy prisoners with considerable amounts of free time on their hands.

3. Aspects of Big House discipline, sometimes augmented by sophisticated modern technology, can be found in so-called super-max or maxi-maxi prisons, reserved for disruptive prisoners, and in short-term boot camp prisons, which are reserved primarily for "young adult offenders convicted of nonviolent crimes who are serving their first prison terms" MacKenzie, 1993:21). Facilities such as these are

becoming more common, but they are by no means typical American prisons.

4. See Krajick, 1980; Fong, Vogel & Buentello, 1992. See also *The Prison Journal* 71 (2) (Fall/Winter 1991), the entire body of which deals with prison gangs. For a discussion of Stateville Prison today as a "gang-entrenched" facility, see Brown (1995:7).

5. A parallel process was at work in our public schools during this time and, as is the case in many prisons, continues today. In both settings, order has become *a* dominant (if not *the*) dominant concern, and violence or the threat of violence are facts of daily life (see Toby, 1994:152–58).

6. Radical rhetoric, which emphasized the systemic oppression of the poor and the need for organized violence to secure social change, was common in the prisons of the late 1960s and early 70s, but there were few committed revolutionaries. There are many reasons for this (see Irwin, 1980; Carroll, 1982). Perhaps the primary reason is that the stance of the prison revolutionary is flagrantly self-destructive.

The radicalized prisoner, after all, stipulates the existence of a monolithic power structure that is purposely arranged to wreak damage upon him as a helpless member of the underclass. There is . . . the concession of personal impotence in the face of such threats and the view that the only way out is through a violent mass insurrection. While there is, in theory, an army of similarly alienated persons ripe for conscription, most of these potential recruits have suffered at the hands of their fellow convicts and have come to view them with suspicion. To engage in revolutionary action, the prospective militant must develop faith in an unimpressive group of peers, and must then gird himself for what may easily degenerate into a Pyrrhic victory—short-term ascendance following a bloody prison riot. And if our rebel is prisonwise, he may well fear the reign of the inmates and the backlash from guards more than the disturbance itself. (Johnson & Dorin, 1978:45)

7. Analyzing the growth of violence in the New Mexico State Penitentiary over the decade of the 1970s that culminated in a savage riot in 1980, Colvin argues that "removal of legitimate (program) and illegitimate (drug trafficking) opportunities in the prison created a new opportunity structure that produced the 'hero' or 'new breed' role" discussed by Irwin (Colvin, 1982:456).

8. Irwin's observations are confirmed in the research of Abdul-Mu'Min (1981) and Colvin (1982 & 1992), and most recently Silberman (1995).

9. There is no evidence that the growing influence of state-raised convicts stems from a lower class of criminal confined in today's prison. Prisoners of this type are not statistically more prevalent in today's prisons, nor has there been an increase in the proportion of violent offenders making up prison populations (Colvin, 1982). Instead, they have become a dominant force in today's prisons because today's prisons are less controlled.

10. Many of the more telling and tragic observations made by Abbott about the life of the state-raised youth are confirmed and amplified in the work of Dwight Edgar Abbot (1991).

11. The prison is "rigidly hierarchical and routinized, cold and impersonal" (Johnson, 1976:111). As such, it "parallels the classic paranoid image of conspiratorial control" (Johnson, 1976:111). Psychiatric research reveals that prison attracts a disproportionate number of people with paranoid dispositions and then reinforces their suspicious worldview. Prison also independently creates this disposition. Diagnosis and treatment of prison paranoia are therefore difficult, because the adaptive and maladaptive aspects of paranoid views may be hard to separate (see Thurrell, Halleck & Johnson, 1965; and Hamburger, 1967).

REFERENCES

Abbot, D. E. *I Cried, You Didn't Listen: A Survivor's Exposé of the California Youth Authority*. Portland, OR: Feral House, 1991.

Abbott, J. H. *In the Belly of the Beast*. New York: Vintage, 1981.

Abdul-Mu'Min, E. M. *Power and Survival: The Role and Structure of Religious Fellowships, Self-Help Groups and Gangs in a California Prison*. Ann Arbor, MI: University Microfilms International, 1981.

Barak, I. L. *Punishment to Protection: Solitary Confinement in Washington State Penitentiary, 1966–1975*. Ann Arbor, MI: University Microfilms International, 1978.

Bowker, L. H. "Victimizers and victims in American correctional institutions." In R. Johnson and H. Toch (eds.). *The Pains of Imprisonment*. Prospect Heights, IL: Waveland Press 1988:63–76.

Brown, M. "Stateville Correctional Center: A neophyte's view." *The Keeper's Voice* 16 (1) 1995:5–8.

Bruchac, J. (ed.). *The Light From Another Country: Poetry From American Prisons*. New York: Greenfield Review Press, 1984.

Camp, G., and C. Camp. *The Corrections Yearbook*. South Salem, NY: Criminal Justice Institute, 1984.

Carmichael, S., and C. Hamilton. *Black Power*. New York: Random House, 1967.

Carroll, L. *Hacks, Blacks and Cons*. Lexington: Lexington Books, 1974.

Carroll, L. "Race, ethnicity, and the social order of the prison." In R. Johnson and H. Toch (eds.). *The Pains of Imprisonment*. Prospect Heights, IL: Waveland Press, 1988:181–203.

Cavadino M., and J. Dignan. *The Penal System: An Introduction*. London: Sage, 1992.

Cobb, A., Jr. "Home truths about prison overcrowding." *The Annals of the American Academy of Political and Social Science* 478, (March 1985):73–85.

Colvin, M. "The 1980 New Mexico prison riot." *Social Problems* 29 (5) 1982:449–63.

Colvin, M. *The Penitentiary in Crisis: From Accommodation to Riot in New Mexico*. Albany: SUNY Press, 1992.

Conrad, J. P. "What do the undeserving deserve?" In R. Johnson and H. Toch (eds.). *The Pains of Imprisonment*. Prospect Heights, IL: Waveland Press, 1988:313–30.

Cooley, D. "Prison victimization and the informal rules of social control." *Forum on Corrections Research* 4 (3) 1992:31–36.

Cressey, D. R. "Foreword." In F. Cullen and K. E. Gilbert. *Reaffirming Rehabilitation*. Cincinnati, OH: Anderson, 1982.

Crouch, B. M., and J. W. Marquart. *An Appeal to Justice*. Austin: University of Texas Press, 1989.

DiIulio, J. J. *No Escape: The Future of American Corrections*. New York: Basic Books, 1991.

Dorin, D. D., and R. Johnson. "Violence and survival in prison: The case of George Jackson." In J. Inciardi and A. Potheger (eds.). *Violent Crime: Historical and Contemporary Issues*. Beverly Hills, CA: Sage, 1978:125–42.

Earley, P. *The Hot House: Life Inside Leavenworth*. New York: Bantam Books, 1992.

Fitzgerald, M., and J. Sim. *British Prisons*. Oxford: Blackwell, 1982.

Fong, R. S., R. E. Vogel and S. Buentello. "Prison gang dynamics: A look inside the Texas department of corrections." In P. J. Benekos and A. V. Merlo (eds.). *Corrections: Dilemmas and Directions*. Beverly Hills, CA: Sage, 1992:55–77.

Foucault, M. *Discipline and Punish*. New York: Pantheon, 1977.

Grier, W., and P. Cobbs. *Black Rage*. New York: Basic Books, 1968.

Hamburger, E. "The penitentiary and paranoia." *Correctional Psychiatry and*

Journal of Social Therapy 13 (4) 1967:225–30.

Higgins, J. P., and A. P. Thies. "Social effectiveness and problem-solving thinking of reformatory inmates." *Journal of Offender Counseling, Services & Rehabilitation* 5(3/4) 1981:93–98.

Irwin, J. *The Felon.* Englewood Cliffs, NJ: Prentice-Hall, 1970.

Irwin, J. *Prisons in Turmoil.* Boston: Little, Brown, 1980.

Irwin, J. amd J. Austin. *It's About Time: Imprisonment Binge.* Belmont, CA: Wadsworth, 1994.

Jacobs, J. B. *Stateville: The Penitentiary in Mass Society.* Chicago: University of Chicago Press, 1977.

Jacobs, J. B. "The prisoners' rights movement and its impacts." In J. B. Jacobs. *New Perspectives on Prisons and Imprisonment.* Ithaca, NY: Cornell University Press, 1983:33–60.

Johnson, R. *Culture and Crisis in Confinement.* Lexington: Lexington Books, 1976.

Johnson R., and D. D. Dorin. "Dysfunctional ideology: The black revolutionary in prison." In D. Szabo and S. Katzenelson (eds.). *Offenders and Corrections.* New York: Praeger 1978:31–52.

Kauffman, K. *Prison Officers and Their World.* Cambridge; Harvard University Press, 1988.

Krajick, K. "Profile Texas." *Corrections Magazine* 4 (1) 1978:4–25.

Krajick, K. "At Stateville, the calm is tense." *Corrections Magazine* 6 (3) 1980:6–19.

Lawes. L. E. *Twenty Thousand Years in Sing Sing.* New York: Ray Long and Richard R. Smith, 1932.

Lerner, S. "Rule of the cruel." *The New Republic* (October 15, 1984):17–21.

Lombardo, L. X. "Stress, change, and collective violence in prison." In R. Johnson and H. Toch (eds.). *The Pains of Imprisonment.* Prospect Heights, IL: Waveland Press, 1988:77–93.

McCall, N. *Makes Me Wanna Holler: A*

Young Black Man in America. New York: Vintage, 1995.

MacKenzie, d. L. "Boot camp prisons in 1993." *National Institute of Justice Journal* (November 1993):21–28.

Manocchio, A. J., and J. Dunn. *The Time Game: Two Views of a Prison.* Beverly Hills, CA: Sage, 1982.

Marquart, J. W., and B. M. Crouch. "Judicial reform and prisoner control: The impact of Ruiz v. Estelle on a Texas penitentiary." *Law and Society Review* 19 (4) 1985:557–86.

Mason, T. R. "The epitome of failure: Jack Abbott." *Crime and Delinquency* 28 (4) 1982:557–66. (Note that various inmate writers are featured in this article.)

McGivern, G. "The epitome of failure: Jack Abbott." *Crime and Delinquency* 28 (4) 1982:557–66. (Note that various inmate writers are featured in this article.)

Morris, T., and P. Morris. *Pentonville: A Sociological Study of an English Prison.* London: Routledge & Kegan Paul, 1963.

Murton, T. *The Dilemma of Prison Reform.* New York: Holt, Rinehart & Winston, 1976.

Myers, L., and G. W. Levy. "Description and prediction of the intractable inmate." *Journal of Research in Crime and Delinquency* 15 (2) 1978:214–28.

Nelson, V. F. *Prison Days and Nights.* New York: Garden City Publishing, 1936.

Nusser, N. "The epitome of failure: Jack Abbott." *Crime and Delinquency* 28 (4) 1982:557–66. (Note that various inmate writers are featured in this article.)

Porporino, F. "Differences in response to long-term imprisonment: Implications for the management of long-term offenders." *Research Report No. 10.* Research and Statistics Branch, The Correctional Service of Canada, 1991:1–15.

Rothman, S., and K. Engel. "Prison violence and the paradox of reform." *The Public Interest* (fall 1983):91–105.

Schroeder, A. *Shaking It Rough*. Garden City, NY: Doubleday, 1976:23.

Sheehan, S. *A Prison and a Prisoner*. Boston: Houghton Mifflin, 1978.

Silberman, M. *A World of Violence: Corrections in America*. Belmont, CA: Wadsworth, 1995.

Stastny, C., and G. Tyrnauer. *Who Rules the Joint?* Lexington: Lexington Books, 1982.

Stojkovic, S. "Social bases of power and control mechanisms among prisoners in a prison organization." *Justice Quarterly* 1 (4) 1984:511–28.

Stojkovic, S. "Correctional administrators' accounts of their work worlds." *The Howard Journal of Criminal Justice* 34(1) 1995:64–80.

Sykes, G. *The Society of Captives*. New York:Atheneum, 1966.

Thurrell, R. J., S. L. Halleckm and A. F. Johnson. "Psychosis in prison." *The Journal of Criminology and Police Science* 56 (3) 1965:271–76.

Toby, J. "The schools." In J. Q. Wilson and J. Petersilia (eds.). *Crime* San Francisco: ICS Press, 1994:141–70.

Toch, H., and K. Adams with J. D. Grant. *Coping: Maladaptation in Prisons*. New Brunswick, NJ: Transaction Publishers, 1989.

Useem, B., and P. Kimball. *States of Siege: U.S. Prison Riots 1971–1986*. New York: Oxford University Press, 1989.

Zamble, E., F. Porporino and J. Kalotay. *An Analysis of Coping Behavior in Prison Inmates*. Ministry of the Solicitor General of Canada: Programs Branch User Report, 1984.

Zimmer, L. E. *Women Guarding Men*. Chicago: University of Chicago Press, 1986.

6

Living in Prison

The Private Culture
of the Prison

L iving well may be the best revenge against social rejection. Each day's
pleasure belies the basic premise of rejection, namely, that the person ostracized must suffer as a result. Prisoners feel a particularly urgent need to
"reject their rejectors," to live as though the pains of imprisonment are of no
consequence to them (McCorkle & Korn, 1954). Prisons are monuments to
social rejection. Prisoners are nothing in the eyes of the public, and they know
it. To cope with the hurt that would normally accompany ostracism, many
prisoners minimize the pains of confinement, even claiming that prison is easier, better, more accommodating than the outside world. Such "manliness
myths" promote the view that tough convicts feel no pain. Where others—
regular citizens—would wilt in prison, convicts blossom and thrive. They are,
then, in myth if not in reality, above punishment.

Among those who count themselves as convicts, the rejection of society
and the adoption of a prison-centered worldview is raised to an article of faith.
"As the years go by and you get older," one convict told Earley (1992:89),

> you realize more and more that your life is considered a failure by society's
> standards. . . . You are a jailbird. You don't have any money, no house, no
> job, no status. In society's eyes you're a worthless piece of shit. Now, you
> can buy into what society says and decide you really are a piece of shit or
> you can say, "Fuck society, I'll live by my own rules." That's what I did. I
> decided to live by my own standards and rules. They aren't society's but
> they are mine and that's what I've done. In your society, I may not be
> anybody, but in here, I am.

This attitude may explain why so many prisoners flaunt big tattoos and even bigger muscles. To the outside world, the flamboyant body art of the prison iron man (weight lifter) marks the convict as "a circus sideshow freak," yet in prison these seeming stigmata are "badges of honor" (Earley, 1992:14).

The impression made by such prisoners, to be sure, is suitably impressive and even intimidating, at least to newcomers on the prison scene. As one Lompoc prisoner observed, "ink scares new pigs," meaning that tattoos frighten new officers (Fleisher, 1989:122). In this prisoner's view, the effect can prove useful.

> They think the more ink you have, the longer you been in the joint, and the badder you are. It works. I walk by the office at night with my shirt off when a fish is working, and I can tell he's scared. If new fish cops are scared, they leave us alone. (Fleisher, 1989:122)

So called "fish"—newcomers—include new prisoners. They, too, may well find their tattooed neighbors frightening, but they at least have the option of decorating themselves, if you will, using tattoos of their own as camouflage to blend into the prison community. (Officers, of course, may sport tattoos, but they can never blend into the prison community.)

One might fairly conclude from all of this that prisoners are mocking the conventional world, graphically illustrating how domesticated and weak is the society that must cage its manly outlaws. Yet however comforting such beliefs may be, prisoners have little hope of cultivating an enviable lifestyle behind bars. Prisoners do not live well. Nobody envies their lot. For many men, prison life is a stage in a theater of survival. In the words of one prisoner,

> Turning the corner into the prison yard for the first time is like stepping onto the set of a Cecil B. DeMille spectacular where most of the extras are black. Everyone has a yard image. Still there are no plush trimmings, trumpet fanfares or superstars. The only Herculean act performed is survival. (Washington, 1981:9)

If the truth be told, the prison yard features a motley crew of social misfits, some frightening, others frightened, a few merely outlandish; all, after a fashion, a little pathetic. The setting offers limited options. At best, prisoners "choose not a way of life" within their involuntary and largely sterile habitat, "but a way to live" (Seymour, 1977:179). Their modest but difficult task is to "create, seemingly from rocklike or diaphanous material, a fabric of life" (Seymour, 1977:179). Simply "living in prison"—getting by from day to day, surviving—may be the only revenge they can take on the prison (Toch, 1977).

And some prisoners, tragically, are denied even that small pleasure, experiencing psychological breakdowns while confined (Toch, 1975 & 1992). Others die behind bars, either at their own hands or at the hands of others (Bowker, 1980; Lester & Danto, 1993). A few, sentenced to die, are executed each year (see Johnson, 1990). Most prisoners, of course, are more fortunate. The sentence passes, if not quickly or easily, at least without crisis or trauma (Bonta & Gendreau, 1990). Yet the vast majority of prisoners, as we observed in Chapter Four, grapple ineffectually with their problems, and emerge to take up barren and uninviting lives. A few learn something constructive. They live in prison, and subsequently in the free world, in mature and rewarding ways. One might say they have fully avenged themselves, to their benefit and ours.

LIVING IN PRISON

The "fabric of life" most prisoners weave is quite prosaic. It bears little resemblance to the violent and even dramatic convict culture reviewed in the last chapter. The plain fact is that most inmates are not members of the convict culture and do not subscribe to its rules for living. To be sure, they pay lip service to its code and deference to its heroes, but they do not want to live as convicts. They want, instead, to get along without trouble while in prison, and they even hope to go straight upon release.

That most inmates want to do their own time and steer clear of prison after they are released is simply common sense. It is also supported by research. Glaser (1964:118) observed of federal prisoners during the early 1960s, "Our findings from several different types of inquiry indicated that inmates have a predominant interest in adjusting to the demands of the institution and that they have strong noncriminal aspirations." Toch's research, conducted with state prisoners in the mid-1970s, confirms Glaser's point. Though Toch and his associates interviewed prisoners during the peak period of custodial crisis and convict violence (see Chapter Five), the central finding was that today's inmates do indeed want to "live in prison" and make a conventional life for themselves upon release (Toch, 1977). Zamble, Porporino & Kalotay (1984:66), reporting on more recent research with Canadian prisoners, tell us that "examination of subjects' plans for their terms does indicate some attempts to change and improve themselves. Eighty percent said that they had a goal to accomplish during the term, with 75 percent of these specifying either education or job training." Fully half of their sample considered self-improvement to be the main objective of their prison adjustment strategies (Zamble, Porporino & Kalotay, 1984:66 & 67).

And more prisoners may succeed in reforming themselves than first meets the eye. Though most studies tell us that between one-half and three-quarters of ex-prisoners return to crime—that is, they are arrested, though not necessarily sent back to prison, for one or more crimes[1]—it is worth remembering that very few first offenders go to prison. Virtually all ex-prisoners, in other words, were recidivists before they were incarcerated. That from 25 to 50 percent of them avoid arrest after release from prison suggests that they either refrained from criminal activity or engaged in criminal activity that was less serious or repetitive than was the case prior to their confinement (see Nettler, 1984). Moreover, the fact that most persons arrested for crimes after release from prison are not reconfined—between 30 and 40 percent go back to prison (Wallerstedt, 1984; Beck & Shipley, 1989:1)—suggests that they, too, engaged in criminal activity that was less serious or repetitive than before their confinement (see Nettler, 1984).

These partial successes may indicate no more than the effects of aging or discouragement (Hoffman & Beck, 1984), or indeed may reflect the limited ability of law enforcement officers to apprehend criminals (Bennett, 1983:pt. 1). But they may also tell us that some offenders improve themselves while behind bars, and hence are able to forge more conventional lives upon release from prison. Megargee and Cadow, reporting on the impact of life in a comparatively program-rich, medium-security federal prison for men, provide data that strongly suggest this possibility.

> When interviewed prior to leaving, 84 percent of the 643 inmates queried reported they had changed for the better. Comparisons of personality test scores and profiles obtained upon entrance and departure showed improvement was much more common than deterioration. A followup study of 1,008 offenders who had been released on the average 3 1/2 years showed that 45 percent had no subsequent arrests, 71 percent had no subsequent convictions and 72 percent had not been returned to prison for any reason. (Megargee & Cadow, 1980:36)

It is reasonable to conclude that, when given an accommodating correctional milieu, many offenders will make a bona fide effort to use the prison experience to improve themselves and hence to improve their chances for a decent life upon release. (In the last chapter of this book, we will consider how maximum-security prisons can be arranged to encourage this result.)

Prisoners who want to live peacefully in prison and go straight upon release are, for the most part, neither voluble nor eloquent in expressing their beliefs. It is quite likely that they overestimate the prevalence and ferocity of the convicts and consider themselves the minority. They are not. The "masses" of inmates have always done their time and avoided "the general prison social activities" dominated by the convicts (Irwin, 1980:14). This important observation was recently confirmed in an ethnographic study of Leavenworth prison, which revealed that roughly 80 percent of the prisoners "try to avoid trouble and simply do their time as easily as possible" (Earley, 1992:44). Many of these inmates, to be sure, return to living on release. They simply avoid prison's dangers but do little to confront and solve the problems that brought them to prison. Yet they are not troublesome prisoners. The mundane world of daily life and adjustment shared by this "silent majority" is and has always been the foundation of stability upon which the prison rests.

Even the convict world, which places a premium on violence, ultimately must reach an accommodation with the masses of inmates who inhabit the institution and the prison officials who run it. Even on the yard there is at least a degree of order to prison life, though in many of today's institutions it is often a "dangerous and tentative order" (Irwin, 1980:212). And it is worth remembering that even convict gang members need some stability in their lives. They are not continuously embroiled in conflict. They also need nurturance now and again, not to mention support for wounded egos.

Violent men cannot live by violence alone and have no desire to do so (Toch, 1980). This means that gangs and other predatory groups must be more than convenient vehicles for exploiting others. To serve the normal human needs of their members, they must also be safe harbors within the lonely and dangerous prison world, providing a kind of extended psychological support system. Jacobs's account of black prison gangs in Stateville prison, for example, underscores their role as a psychological haven of acceptance for prisoners all too familiar with rejection.

> By far the most important function the gangs provide their members at Stateville is psychological support. . . . [Said one gang member] "these guys . . . are closer to me than my own family. Anything I do around them is accepted—for stuff that my parents would put me down for, these guys elevate me to a pedestal." Every inmate informant expressed this opinion—that the organizations give to the members a sense of identification, a feeling of belonging, an air of importance. . . . Time and again gang members explained that, whether on the street or in the prison, the gang "allows you to feel like a man": it is a family with which you can identify. Many times young members have soberly stated that the organization is something, the only thing, they would die for. (Jacobs, 1977:150–53)

The supportive function of gangs may be even more pronounced for Latin prisoners. Davidson (1974:21), for example, has described Chicano prison gangs, which often involve relatives and friends of relatives, as playing the role of a "mother" providing aid for "her child through the long process of enculturation" to prison. Loosely known as "the Family," these gangs offer an unconditionally supportive context in which a man's "machismo" rests assured (Davidson, 1974:84). Certainly gangs are flagrantly criminogenic. They "elevate" men, as Jacobs's informant would have it, for some fairly primitive behavior and reinforce an almost paranoid view of the world. Nevertheless, these gangs ensure the psychological survival of their members (see Carroll, 1988).

Most prisoners are not members of gangs or other predatory groups, however, and do not try to work out a livable arrangement on the prison yard. Their adjustment reveals that the options for nonviolent and potentially constructive ways of living in prison are more diverse than one would first suppose. Prisons have a uniformly cold and forbidding exterior, giving the impression that life within their walls must be consistently harsh, a continuing war of all against all (or gang against gang) for such scarce commodities as status and respect. These battles are indeed fought by some prisoners, mainly the convicts, though these are not the only battles the convicts fight, as the inner turmoil and loneliness of Jack Abbott and others like him clearly reveal. Moreover, the prison accommodates a wide range of nonviolent lifestyles that are sought, and usually found, by the masses of prisoners who studiously avoid the world of the convicts and who, for the most part, survive prison on their own terms.

THE ECOLOGY OF PRISON SURVIVAL

To say that prisons support a variety of lifestyles is not to imply that they are in any way inviting. At issue here is not the so-called country club prison. That mythical institution has been likened to the Loch Ness Monster: "many people believe in it," remarks Levinson (1988:242), "but nobody has ever seen one." Actually, the "arenas that prison provides for action are, in free-world terms, small, poorly equipped, and frequently threatening" (Seymour, 1988:268). Nevertheless, these environments do possess a "remarkable variability" (Seymour, 1982:268). This variability is the product of a transactional process in which the adjustment efforts of prisoners shape, and are shaped by, prison environments. As researched and codified by Hans Toch, this transactional process reveals seven ecological dimensions that express the preferences and needs of prisoners. These dimensions, according to Toch (1977), are as follows:

1. **Activity**   *"A concern about understimulation; a need for maximizing the opportunity to be occupied and to fill time; a need for distraction"* (17). Physical or mental activity, Toch tells us, "can be functional for its own sake—for energy and attention it consumes, for feelings it challenges, for distracting or anesthetizing effects. For such purposes, the nature or content of the activity is irrelevant" (25). Activities that are themselves "meaningful and engrossing," however, offer not just distraction but a degree of personal fulfillment (25).

2. **Privacy**   *"A concern about social and physical overstimulation; a preference for isolation, peace and quiet, absence of environmental irritants such as noise and crowding"* (16). Privacy is in many respects the opposite of activity. "Where activity is a means of enriching experience through self-stimulation, privacy involves *reducing* external stimuli to streamline experience and to make purposive adjustment a simpler task" (27). Privacy-oriented persons are content when they are left alone. States Toch, "the intensely private person lives at peace with himself when he is left to himself. He feels harassed when others demand attention, response or social contact from him" (28). When he is granted privacy, the main rewards for the prisoner are peace and relaxation, and the feeling that the environment is simpler and more easily managed.

3. **Safety**   *"A concern about one's physical safety; a preference for social and physical settings that provide protection and that minimize the chances of being attacked"* (16). While the privacy-oriented person seeks sanctuary from a wide range of noxious stimuli, the safety-oriented person seeks sanctuary from a particular type of pressure, that of violence, which he sees around him in the prison world and feels within himself. The person concerned with safety is apt to label his environment as "tense" or "explosive," characteristics that apply both to himself and his world. "Violence and its control become," for this inmate, "the main theme of the inner and outer environment" (50).

4. **Emotional feedback**   *"A concern about being loved, appreciated and cared for; a desire for intimate relationships that provide emotional sustenance and empathy"*

(17). Persons concerned with emotional feedback want "warm" and "responsive" environments populated by "people who care" (52). Prison can be a direct source of emotional feedback, providing inmate friends, concerned staff, or programs that offer the hope of a better future. For many prisoners, emotional feedback is found in the daily round of talk that helps make bearable the typical prison day.

> Prison is an oral place. There's not much to look at in a cell, so inmates do a lot of talking. Talking to your neighbor, or the guy locked five cells away, two above, or one below. And when no one else will give any rap, you talk to yourself.
>
> Even in the yard, it's an oral place. Jiving. Joking. Shouting. Laughing. Crying. Often just plain lying. And when there's no one who will listen, you always have yourself.
>
> Inmates will rap about anything, to anyone, to keep the tension off. (Washington, 1981:16)

The prison can be a mediator between the prisoner and his loved ones outside the walls, facilitating or impeding mail or visits; or it can provide other kinds of contacts with the outside world, such as furloughs. The problem of loneliness in prison, whatever its source, is a problem of inadequate emotional feedback.

5. **Support** *"A concern about reliable, tangible assistance from persons and settings, and about services that facilitate self-advancement and self-improvement"* (16). Some inmates make use of the reintegrative or rehabilitative services available in prison. These are persons who "see themselves having a future and social role, and can thus relate environmental opportunities" like vocational or educational programs "to ends that they prize" (70). Many trace their past failures to deficiencies in their education or training, and eagerly embrace prison programs that promise to remedy those deficiencies and afford opportunities for a new life.

6. **Structure** *"A concern about environmental stability and predictability; a preference for consistency, clear-cut rules, orderly and scheduled events and impingements"* (16). An environment affords structure "to the extent to which it furnishes reliable guides for action" (81). Inmates for whom structure is important want a road map of the prison. "Persons concerned with structure have a need to know. . . . The structure person must know where he stands; this knowledge tells him how the outside environment is arranged and what he must do to cope with it" (93).

7. **Freedom** *"A concern about circumscription of one's autonomy; a need for minimal restriction and for maximum opportunity to govern one's own conduct"* (17). The freedom dimension relates authority and dependence in complex and subtle ways. Psychologically speaking, authorities put their subjects in a position of dependency and helplessness, and thus are obligated to protect and serve them as well as to control them. For some men, particularly those raised in inhospitable settings like urban slums and penal institutions,

authority figures have operated almost exclusively as sources of control and almost never as sources of protection or nurturance. (Certainly Abbott and other state-raised convicts are cases in point.) As a result, these men are forced to mature without the support and guidance of caring authority figures. Orders issued by a guard thus are presumed to constitute abuse (control for its own sake) or disrespect (treating one like a child), not an effort to arrange social affairs in an equitable or even responsive manner. An order becomes, then, an occasion to test wills and measure strength, to see who can dominate the other (98). The process is painful for both parties but particularly for prisoners, who almost always come out on the bottom. Freedom means the ability to maintain a degree of autonomy and yet avoid or minimize these abrasive encounters.

Naturally, inmates vary in terms of their needs and preferences. Older prisoners, for example, often seek privacy; younger men are inclined to value freedom and activity. The young and naive are often preoccupied with safety. So, too, the availability of the seven ecological dimensions of prison life is not uniform; a host of demographic and criminal justice variables influence the distribution of ecological concerns (see Toch, 1977:123–40). Some institutions are more structured than others or permit more freedom; one facility may offer more support services or be safer than another. Prisons are marked by internal variation as well: the ecological climates of different living quarters, for instance, are not interchangeable. The experiences of a Georgia prisoner are instructive in this regard:

> Recently I moved from one of [the] violent dormitories to a new unit where I had my own cell. It was like moving out of a junkyard into a Hilton or Holiday Inn: the atmosphere was as different as could be. The noise level went to zero, whereas in the 140-inmate dormitories, the two television sets were always going full blast, as were fifty radios, all on different stations. In the dormitories people talked only about parole, radios, cinnamon rolls—that is, sweet bagels—picture shows, and the like, whereas in the new units there were some conversations about programs, going to college, and other means of self-help. The new units housed only 27 inmates, each in a separate cell, and administration and inmates alike made an effort to keep noise to a minimum. There were, moreover, resources to keep the units well maintained. (Cobb, 1985:74)

Of course, cell blocks need not necessarily be superior to dormitories; there are plenty of noisy and dangerous cell blocks in prison. By the same token, there are some prisons in which dormitories are seen as sanctuaries. Lorton prison, which holds District of Columbia prisoners but is located in Northern Virginia, is a case in point. For many prisoners, the dorms in Lorton offer a niche featuring emotional feedback:

> Now most of the dormitories in Lorton are like small families. As you walk around, you'll see some of your friends. If they good enough friends

of yours, you can get in the dorm with them, the same guys you hung out with on the street.

Officers are rarely in evidence in the Lorton dorms.

> An officer may come into the dormitory and take a look around, but basically he only stay two or three minutes in there. Don't no dormitory hold no officer. Don't no officers stay in no dormitory all day. For no reason. (Blecker, 1990:212)

When officers are present, in the dorms and elsewhere in the prison compound, their general attitude is one of laissez-faire: live and let live. Many of the younger inmates like this, because they can do their time as they see fit. For them, the absence of officers connotes freedom. Said one such inmate to a ranking officer, as he refused to get up from his bed, "Judge said I get ten-to-thirty years. He didn't say I got to get out of bed to serve it" (Blecker, 1990:244). The older inmates, however, often feel abandoned in this situation. In the words of one older inmate, "If you read the commitment paper, all it says is 'hold the body.' . . . That's all they care about, to hold my body." (Blecker, 1990:244)

For older prisoners, the absence of officers may also translate into concerns for safety. They report that younger inmates prowl the prison yard in gangs, sometimes invading unprotected dorms. "They wear masks and attack in groups," said one such prisoner (Blecker, 1990:214–15). To many older inmates, Lorton offers neither emotional feedback nor freedom, but is instead a death trap:

> Almost uniformly the older inmates condemn Lorton Central as a "death-trap." "You can get killed because you have no protection. . . . You can't go to a dark room; you can't take a bucket and wash your clothes without realizing it's possible you might not come out. It's no such place as that you're guaranteed to see tomorrow. You go to bed with a nightmare, and the only peace that you ever get is not waking up at all.

The larger point of this discussion is that prison environments—dorms, cells, work areas, even yards—are not stamped from one mold. Nor do objectively comparable prison environments have uniform impacts on their inhabitants. One man's niche can be another man's nightmare, as Lorton's dorms so vividly illustrate. There is, in other words, more to prison than the buildings and schedules that mark its official world, and there is more to prison adjustment than a one-way process of people adapting to environments. Always, there is a person–environment transaction in which people and settings interact and shape one another in an ongoing, mutual process (see Toch, 1977:2). There is, then, the prospect of diverse forms of life and adjustment after one moves beyond the convict world and the prison yard.

Prison Life, Prison Niches

The inmate, confronted with a diversity of prison environments, usually is able to "arrange a microcosm" or "niche" within the larger prison, a world to which he can adapt at least partly on his own terms (Seymour, 1977:180). Described most broadly, a niche is

> a functional subsetting containing objects, space, resources, people, and relationships between people. A niche is perceived as ameliorative; it is seen as a potential instrument for the relaxation of stress and the realization of required ends. It is this quality of niches that stimulates the creative process of niche search and niche identification. Niche search is usually an explorative process in which a person seeks a specific setting because adjustment appears easier there. . . . These settings in prison may be work assignments, living units, or programs, and they may feature any combination among privacy, safety, structure, freedom, support, activity, [and] emotional feedback. . . . (Seymour, 1977:181)

Niches serve as "defenses of the boundaries of self" (Seymour, 1977:188). Though life in a niche "rarely guarantees happiness" or, for that matter, personal reform, it "usually guarantees survival" (Seymour, 1977:188). The prisoner in the process of adapting to prison

> can selectively perceive elements of the prison milieu that either defy his needs or reflect a potential for meeting them. The more salient features of the prison environment—its walls and gates, overlapping security nets, bars and cells, those aspects that have the impact of theater—can fade into psychological insignificance. The inmates attend to a series of invisible subenvironments, with various degrees of movement in or out, population sizes, inmate types, degrees of control and supervision, activities, routines, rules and regulations, behaviors permitted or restrained. (Seymour, 1977:180)

Evidence of these adaptive processes at work can be found in accounts of life in virtually any prison, including the original penitentiaries. Prisoners of these ostensibly monolithic penal environments came to see at least a degree of ecological variability around them. Incoming prisoners of the penitentiaries would be "tested" by peers (Anonymous, 1871:60), news of life inside the prison would travel on a "grapevine" (Anonymous, 1871:244), and at least some prisoners were able to secure niches, either in cells or work settings (Anonymous, 1871:78–79). Prison tiers could be distinguished, at least in a limited way, in terms of social climate (Anonymous, 1871:94), apparently as a function of the supervising officer's style of guarding or of the ethnic or racial composition of the inhabitants (see Coffey, 1823:105). Differential adjustment and survival were features of prison life, even in the most barren of penitentiaries (see Coffey, 1823:116).

One can make the generalization, then, that out of the raw material of the prison—virtually any prison—the prisoner normally fashions a round of life that enhances his ability to negotiate the stresses of prison. The focus of adjustment is on ameliorating those stressors that are of greatest concern to him, variously permitting *activity*—a life in the gym or in which one is otherwise on the run; *privacy*—working in the library or simply spending time alone in one's cell; *safety*—staying close to guards or friends; living in protective custody; *emotional feedback*—preserving one's ties to loved ones, building new ties within the prison with fellow inmates or staff; *support*—a program or activity that offers something of value and hence promises a better future upon release from prison; *structure*—a routine of work and recreation one follows closely so one always knows what is expected; a shop or housing area that is run "by the book"; or *freedom*—a work assignment that requires minimal supervision; a cell block that is run in a relaxed manner.

Men in niches try to live as individuals, not as role types or anonymous members of collectivities. Their goal is to find a routine that meets their basic needs and provides, as much as possible, a "slice of home" in an otherwise alien environment.

> Normally, in the free world, we carry off a surprising number of roles—husband, handyman, father, worker—and we can shape and discard roles. In prison one's world is more limited. But even though one cannot use the blueprint of one's former life and former roles to construct a way of living in confinement, one uses what is familiar. Though the world of job and street is gone, one of assignment and block can be substituted. Often an inmate creatively alters his space for living to follow old modes as closely as possible. (Seymour, 1977:184)

The gang member from the slums may join the prison chapter of his gang and use it as a niche—to make it possible for him to operate on the yard, to avoid exposure to its dangers, or simply to secure companionship and support. The ubiquitous "street hustler," whether in association with others or alone, may simply take up his hustle once again in the prison, thus following "old modes" of living "as closely as possible" within the constraints of the prison situation. As one prisoner told Susan Sheehan, when asked how he got by in prison, "I hustle, I swag, same as on the street" (1978:95).[2]

A DAY IN THE LIFE

The greater part of Sheehan's book, *A Prison and a Prisoner*, is an account of the daily life of a self-proclaimed "professional prisoner." The prisoner, whom Sheehan dubbed George Malinow, is more adept at prison living than most prisoners. He is able to arrange his affairs to approximate a conventional domestic life and work schedule. This is revealed in a diary kept at Sheehan's (1978:96) request, cataloging "four ordinary days of swagging and spinning out time." Here is one such day.

Tuesday, August 10, 1976

6:30 A.M.   Bell rings very loud and long. A certain C.O. [correction officer, or guard] does this (rings bell long) whenever he comes on duty, and I and many other inmates here would like to hit him with a shoe, as he seems to do this on purpose!

God—I hate to get up, I feel so tired!! Serves me right for staying up doing glass painting till 1:55 this morning. But—get up I must and do so. Wash up, shave and get dressed in my work clothes which is green regulation issued pants and shirt and work shoes. Put on water to be boiled for my coffee. Have coffee and 2 do-nuts. Smoke a cigarette and listen to the news, via earphones.

7:15 A.M.   Doors open up. I immediately rush off to the mess hall entrance area on the West Side entrance, being I'm one of the first inmates up—no one is near that area at this time of the morning. Terry, a friend of mine (inmate) who works in the kitchen, is there awaiting me. He hands me a large card board box which contains 20 dozen eggs (fresh ones), about 20 pounds of raw bacon, and about 20 pounds macaroni, 20 to 30 oranges, 2 large cans orange juice and one large can of olive oil for cooking. I immediately rush back to my cell, to avoid the other inmates about due to start going to the mess hall for their breakfast.

Hide all said foods items in my cell and my friend Andy's cell. Andy is just at this time up and washing. We joke together about our sudden good windfall from our friend.

7:40 A.M.   Andy and I proceed to go to work, the parole-clothing department located at the basement of the Administration Building. Terry stops us to ask us to please get him some shorts, 2 white shirts and black socks. We tell him that we'll give it to him next morning. We reach the check point gate of the Administration Building, get pat frisked and we sign the logbook at the desk to verify at what time we arrived to work. Also left our institutional passes at this check point with the C.O. assigned there, as must be done.

We arrive at the basement parole-clothing area where we work. C.O.s Stevens and Barton are there already. Stevens works the 7:20 to 3:20 shift. Barton does not usually arrive this early because he works the 9:45 to 5:45 shift but today he is working extra early over-time as he has been assigned to drive one of the inmates to an outside hospital for a medical appointment.

The coffee pot is ready as C.O. Stevens always plugs in this pot early as he arrives about 20 minutes to 7, each morning. So Andy, I and Stevens all have coffee and cake. C.O. Barton is busy with the checking of papers for the inmate he is due to take to the hospital so he doesn't join us. We have the radio playing and listening to the local news broadcast. Meanwhile, there are 4 men going home on parole this morning and they just arrived and are getting dressed. Andy and I both help and make certain that all these 4 inmates going home, have all their clothes and personal property packages they may own. They have cups of coffee and relax in casual and happy conversation—about the steaks, drinks and women they'll soon enjoy out there, etc.

Andy and I, both at times, have been asked by many persons—does seeing men talk like this and seeing them go home each day bother us? We don't see it that way as Andy and I, feel very glad to see as many as possible leave any prison as prison represents "hell" in all respects!!

7:50 A.M. All the men due to go home now, leave with C.O. Stevens, to go upstairs to an office where they'll all receive their $40 gate money and whatever's in their inmate account and their release papers. Then C.O. Stevens will escort them out and drive them in the prison van bus to Hopewell jct. station where they will board a bus for N.Y. City. I sorted out all their state issued clothing they turned in to our dept. and also gathered all the earphones they brought to our dept. upon departure. Bagged all state clothes to be sent to State Shop, their final destination.

8:05 A.M. We have an extra relief C.O. to stay with us, as C.O.s Stevens & Barton are out on assignments. Said relief C.O.s name is Officer Dover (works in officers' mess from 10 A.M. onward), who is one of the best natured officers in all respects that I have ever come across. Good sense of humor, always smiling & happy go lucky. Very well mannered, fair and easy to relate with. Should be made a warden.

Andy and I, go to our kitchen room at our basement job area and have another cup of coffee and do-nuts. We relax and talk about general topics on the outside.

8:30 A.M. Another 3 inmates that work with us now arrive to work also. They are Danny, Benno, and Ned.

This morning—we have to take a full inventory of all the stock garments we have and record each item in our general inventory stock so we will know what to order, we are short of. After Danny, Ned, and Benno all have their coffee and buns, all 5 of us get ready to do the inventory.

8:50 A.M. Andy and I, start counting the jackets, slacks, socks, handkerchiefs, belts, shoes and shirts. Danny and Ned start to count the ties, topcoats and the other apparel that the men wear to go out on furloughs, death visits and to courts.

10:35 A.M. We all are caught up on our inventory and go to have coffee again and relax. During all this time of inventory taking, Benno sat at the desk to answer all phone calls of general inquiry and also, made up lists for calling men the next day—that have to be fitted out with civilian clothes for their due release dates soon.

11:05 A.M. Benno starts to prepare the foods that he will cook for our lunch as we are not going to go to the mess hall as there is only franks for lunch. Benno is making steaks, fried onions, French fried potatoes, sauce gravy and sweet green peas for our lunch meal. Benno is an exceptional cook! When he cooks, we all leave the kitchen to be out of his way and also, not to distract him then. One or more of us are available to help him—if he calls us, but most times he does it all by himself.

Of course, he cooks—so all others of us do the cleaning up and wash the pots & dishes.

11:40 A.M. We are just about ready to start eating. We all are in conversation about how good Benno cooked the steaks, the high price of food outside, etc. The radio is playing a late song hit and we all are enjoying the food and are in a good mood.

12:25 P.M. We are done eating—so Andy, Danny and I all take out the dishes, silver ware, pots to the sink area away from the kitchen and wash & dry all. Meantime, Ned swept out kitchen while Benno went to his desk to relax.

12:45 P.M. No inmates to dress this afternoon so Danny and I, recheck all the men due to go home the next morning—on our out going releases sheet. We line up all the clothing outfits and their personal packages containing personal property at the benches where they will get dressed in the morning.

1:15 P.M. We all now sit around the desks and are in conversation about many topics. The parole board's unjust decisions, rehabilitation, politics and prison mismanagement, etc.

2:05 P.M. Phone rings and we have to go to the store house to pick up 6 large cases containing jackets and slacks. Andy, Danny and I, all take a strong push wagon and check out from the check out gate at the administration area, get pat frisked and proceed to go to the store house. Along the way, we stop off at E block, on the East Side, to find out if 2 of the men locking there will be at our Jaycee's meeting tonight? They said they will. We leave for the store house.

We arrive at the store house, load our wagon with all the large cases and pick up a copy of the order-form. We arrive at the front administration check point and again are pat frisked. We start sliding the boxes, one at a time, down the stairs to the basement where we work at. We get all boxes to the rack area. We open all boxes, take out garments and count them. The total checks out correctly. C.O. Stevens signs the receipt form copy and I take it back to the store house civilian clerk. When I return, Andy, Danny, Benno, and Ned are about half way done placing the slacks on the shelfs in their respective sizes, and the jackets on the line racks, in their respective sizes.

I join them in doing this and I sort the jackets. We stop this work at 2:45 P.M. I check and pull out coffee pot plug, stove plug, radio plug and toaster plug. Meanwhile—Andy dumps out all the trash into plastic trash bags due to go out to the dump area, via truck, in the morning. Benno dumps out all water from wash pails in kitchen. Danny washes out coffee pot and prepares it for next morning's use.

2:55 P.M. All of us leave our job area in basement, get pat frisked again at check out gate, pick up our passes and proceed to our cells in C block, all except Ned as he locks in J block.

3:05 P.M. I arrive at my cell, change clothes, wash up and go to the wash room on my gallery's end, to wash out and hang up the clothes I left there to soak yesterday.

3:25 P.M. Returned to cell, put water on for my thermos bottle to make my coffee. Layed down, smoked a cigar and relaxed listening to some soft music via earphones.

4:10 P.M. Got up, made cup of coffee, had a ham and Swiss cheese sandwich. Cleaned up table, brushed teeth and started to get all the necessary materials ready to do my glass painting. Worked on glass painting until lock in.

5:05 P.M. Bell rings—lock in time. Doors close and 2 C.O.s walk by & check the doors & count as they walk past my cell. I continue on working on the glass pictures.

5:25 P.M. C.O. stops at my cell and hands me 8 letters (personal), 2 more business letters and 1 magazine on real estate. C.O. continues on handing out mail to other cells.

Read 3 of these letters which come from the Philippines. One from my sweetheart, one from her sister & the 3rd from her mother. Finish reading all mail and lay down to catch the prison phone bulletin announcements on prison news.

5:55 P.M. Get up, wash up, brush teeth and get all my papers and materials ready for my Jaycees meeting due tonight at the school class building at J block, from 6 to 8:30 P.M.

6:00 P.M. Doors open up. I proceed to block door exit where many other men are waiting to go to different night classes and program classes. The block C.O. checks each one of us out on his master sheet.

I arrive at my Jaycee class room and start writing out on the black board the agenda for tonight's meeting. An outside male Jaycee coordinator arrives and our Jaycee meeting starts. We discuss various project possibilities. One project involves bringing boys from the high schools within a few miles of Green Haven to the prison to see what it is like so that they will never want to commit crimes and will never wind up in prison. We also form committees for each project. Meeting ends at 8:25 P.M. and all of us leave to return to our blocks.

8:35 P.M. Returned to cell. Wash and make cup of coffee & smoke 2 cigarettes. Start to work again on my glass pictures and continue until 10 P.M. I stop to eat a salami & cheese with lettuce & tomatoe sandwich. Smoke 2 cigarettes and relax on my bed.

I start to think of my sweetheart in the Philippines. What's she doing, etc.? That's rather silly cause since it is a 12 hour difference in time from

N.Y. City, it goes without saying it has to be about 10 A.M. there so of course, she can't be sleeping.

10:20 P.M. I start working on my glass pictures again. I accidently spill over the bottle of drawing paint all over my glass and I am angry as hell at myself for my carelessness! Finally get that particular portion on my glass cleaned and I have to re-draw that part of the picture again.

10:55 P.M. The bell rings and that means it's time to lock in for the night. Doors close and the 2 C.O.s again check the doors & take the count. I continue on working on the glass pictures. I feel very tired tonight so I stop working on these pictures at 11:40 P.M. I clean up all paint brushes, table and put away to a safe area, the glass paintings to dry during the night. Have a fast cup of coffee, then wash up, brush teeth and get undressed.

11:55 P.M. Put on only small night lamp, put on phones to catch midnight news. Light up cigarette and listen to the news on phones. Music (Western songs) comes on by some local Poughkeepsie disc jockey and I listen to it until 12:30 A.M.

12:35 A.M. I put out light, pull out phone plug and go to sleep.

Malinow's routine is an unusually comfortable one for a maximum-security prisoner, and is a testament to his savvy as a "professional." He does seem to live reasonably well if one focuses on the rudimentary material aspects of his existence. Elsewhere in the book, Malinow makes it clear that he was not able to live comfortably when he was young and more rebellious. In those days he worked at less appealing prison jobs and ate his meals in the mess hall. He also had to prove himself to other prisoners, had his share of run-ins with the authorities, and spent a considerable amount of time in segregation. As he aged he became more modest in his goals and more successful at carving out a life that met his needs. Where once he rebelled against prison authority and raged at the deprivations and hurts he suffered, now a life of "assignment and block" is enough. The larger world of freedom, family, respect, and variety are fading memories that cause little pain. He has been institutionalized, shaped to fit the prison and to live at ease within the girdle of security provided by its walls and routines.

Most prisoners do not become institutionalized, however, nor do they live like Malinow. Statistically more typical is the cell block hustler who swags for a living and marks time on the prison yard. Still, these prisoners, like Malinow, "understand how hard it is to lose one's freedom" and all the pleasures that go with it (Sheehan, 1978:130–31). They know, too, "how hard it is to endure the daily humiliations of prison life," such as having an inmate number and submitting to constant searches (Sheehan, 1978:130–31). There is, moreover, identity between Malinow's prison life and that of the young man who hustles on the cell blocks, shoots baskets all day in the yard, and smokes dope at night in his cell (when he can get it), all the while hungering for freedom (both in prison and out), and doing all he can to safely vent the frustration that builds up within him during the normal prison day. The differences between him and Malinow are those of particular skills and needs, and thus they move in different prison environments. But each has shaped a life in prison more or less on his own terms. Each lives in a prison niche of his choosing.

PRISON LIFE ON ONE'S OWN TERMS: CHALLENGES AND SOLUTIONS

The fact that there is a diversity of niches that accommodates various lifestyles does not mean that prisoners necessarily find the living arrangements they need. Malinow, for example, was a resourceful inmate who over the years had proven his ability to find a routine to his liking. Less experienced or less competent prisoners, who may be more in need of the oasis Malinow found in the parole-clothing shop, are unlikely to secure these positions. Others, who would prefer the drugs and activity enjoyed by the basketball-playing hustler or gang member, might be afraid to go out into the yard. The prison, like the free world, is more accommodating to some prisoners than to others. More often than not, those who are vulnerable and in need of help are forced to fend for themselves.

The diversity of niches within the prison does not assure a man that his needs will be met. As we noted earlier, one man's niche (for example, a gang in which he feels both autonomous and secure) can be a source of indifference to another man (because the gangs leave him alone) or a source of considerable anxiety (because the presence of gangs introduces, at a minimum, fear and uncertainty into the world of many nongang members). When the various worlds that operate within prison collide, stress and sometimes conflict are the result. Freedom-oriented inmates, some of whom Malinow mocks for being impetuous youngsters and Abbott admires for being real men, are both a nuisance and a danger to those seeking structure and safety. The freedom to move about the prison and to congregate in one's neighbors' cells (two liberal reforms of the 1960s and 70s) provide occasions for both conviviality with one's friends and exploitation of others—activities that converge, with tragic consequences, in the instance of gang rapes (Bowker, 1980:4-6). There is also a perennial though less dramatic conflict when activity- and privacy-oriented prisoners come into contact with one another.

> You see, down here everybody wants to get familiar with you, and like, myself, I want to just be left alone and do my bit—let the administration leave me alone and in general [be left alone] by the population. I got my little game with my [homemade] jewelry now, and I get my frustrations off with my active sports, and I just want to be left alone, but it is getting to a point now where you can't even play solitaire by yourself. Guys are always bullshitting and hanging around in and around your cell. . . . And these are the type of guys that when you are taking a crap or something,

they want to talk to you and they want to know everything you are doing. (Toch, 1977:37)

Under these conditions, otherwise reclusive men are driven to distraction and sometimes to violence.

Niches reflect the diversity of needs of the prisoners who create or stumble upon them or are lucky enough to be formally assigned to them. While it is true that all niches have the psychological connotation of a haven from stress, what constitutes a safe place for a given person may be intensely personal. One inmate of a federal prison maintained that he had to envision a secure world, drawing on his personal life; once the mental image was in place, he could arrange a prison routine that met his needs:

> The psychological niche may be the first and most difficult to achieve. I imagined the hiding place that I wanted to find. The mental picture that I drew was of an area, surrounded by latticework, under the small back-porch stairs of a house. When I created the niche in my mind that I wanted, the niches that were, in reality, available fell into place: the job in the prison industries, the housing that was the most appropriate, and even the volunteer work that I did with the suicide patients. (Gates, 1991:75)

For this man, and perhaps for most men, "The real niches became the outward manifestations of the internal, personal, and psychological niches" (Gates, 1991:75).

There is, then, no typical niche, just as there is no typical prisoner. Increasingly, however, niches have one thing in common: they are ways of avoiding the convict culture, of finding shelter from the mainline prison. McCorkle's research on adjustment in a maximum-security prison in Tennessee bears out this point. Fully 300 prisoners filled out questionnaires on prison adjustment. Of that substantial group, over three in four (77.7 percent) indicated that they kept to themselves, living as loners, to avoid victimization. Four of every ten inmates "avoided certain areas of the prison," notably such public areas as the mess hall, housing units other than their own, recreation areas, and the prison yard (McCorkle, 1992:10). While most prisoners in McCorkle's sample were by no means immobilized by fear, "A substantial proportion of respondents live with the perception that their personal safety is in constant jeopardy" (McCorkle, 1993:87). Cooley's research on prison victimization—featuring interviews "with 117 inmates in five prisons, spanning three security levels in one region" of Canada—provides a similar picture of prison adjustment. At these institutions, "informal rules of social control" emphasized withdrawal from the public world of the prison, expressed in such admonitions as minding one's own business, avoiding the prison economy (which is dominated by the convicts), trusting no one and, when one must engage others, going to considerable lengths to show respect and avoid giving offense (see Cooley, 1992:33–34). These days, then, the real and often frightening prospect of victimization shapes adjustment. The safest and potentially most rewarding way to live in our threatening prisons is to avoid the predatory world of the convicts and evolve a smaller and more congenial world of one's own.

Convicts are, to be sure, a statistical minority of any prison population, but they are unpredictable and dangerous. These prisoners do not retreat into solitary niches. They move about in the public areas of the prison, often ostentatiously. They seek to deter violence by arming themselves with weapons and lifting weights to beef up their strength. When pressured, they respond with aggression (see McCorkle, 1992:10). As we know from Abbott, state-raised convicts often go on the attack to avoid being attacked themselves (see Chapter Five). Consequently, the threat posed by their presence and their periodic predations shapes the adjustments of other prisoners. After all, one knife-wielding convict is not a gang, but he certainly can intimidate others and discourage them from wandering about "his" yard or dining in "his" mess hall. An actual gang of such men is a positive deterrent to venturing far from one's cell block or work area. Scrupulous avoidance of these convicts, Irwin observes, is a goal shared by the vast majority of inmates in today's violent prisons. More than ever, states Irwin,

> prisoners are shying away from public settings and avoiding the activities of the convict world. Although they occasionally buy from the racketeers, place bets with gamblers, trade commodities with other unaffiliated prisoners, or sell contraband on a very small scale, they stay away from the rackets and any large-scale economic enterprises. They dissociate themselves from the violent cliques and gangs, spend as little time as possible in the yard and other public places where gangs hang out, and avoid gang members, even though they may have been friends with some of them in earlier years. They stick to a few friends whom they meet in the cell blocks, at work, through shared interests, in other prisons, or on the outside (home boys). With their friends they eat, work, attend meetings of various clubs and formal organizations that have abounded in the prison, and participate in leisure time activities together. Collectively, they have withdrawn from the convict world. (Irwin, 1980:197)

This retreat from the yard may not be a completely honorable one, at least as convicts measure honor, but for most inmates it is workable. "The convicts disrespect those who withdraw," notes Irwin (1980:202), "but usually ignore them." Of course, being ignored is just what inmates strive for, and it is why they keep to themselves as they go about their daily prison lives (McCorkle, 1992:10).

The first step in arranging a niche away from the convict world is to find a friend or two, or at least an acquaintance one can call upon in a pinch, on the assumption that one cannot afford to be alone and hence easy prey for the tougher convicts. This process of developing protective ties is quite explicitly undertaken by new prisoners.

> The first thing you needed was allies, and that as quickly as possible. The procedure tended to begin as soon as you were taken from court to the

precinct jail, where they gathered the sentenced offenders and handcuffed them two by two for transport to maximum security. You sized up the guy you were handcuffed to and let your instincts do the rest; if he looked like a useful sort, you started up a conversation and established a rapport. You kept this procedure up until you knew enough people to generally cover the territory you were going to run in (e.g., your tier, the exercise yard, your place of work, the gym) and then you chose your friends and chose them carefully, keeping in mind that anything they were involved in would inescapably involve you too. Most of these maneuverings didn't happen as mechanically as this may sound, but the rationale behind them was unavoidably clear and few could afford to ignore the routine. A loner or loser in prison was a goner more often than not. (Schroeder, 1976:30)

Armed with potential allies, one then constructs a narrow and predictable round of life. This structured existence serves as an antidote to the instability introduced by the violence of the convicts and the sometimes overbearing and even violent control efforts of the staff who do combat with those prisoners. (The "hacks" who do battle with the "cons" are discussed in the next chapter.)

For many inmates, however, allies prove hard to find. Trust, as noted above, is a scarce commodity in prison. Men who are unable to find a reliable "part-ner" or gain acceptance with a supportive group are left to their own devices in the event that trouble ensues (see Cooley, 1992:34). Because they are un-willing to venture alone into the public prison world, life for many of these solitary inmates virtually begins and ends in the cell. For example, almost four in ten of the Tennessee prisoners (39.5 percent) surveyed by McCorkle (1992:10) reported that they "spent more time in the cell" as an explicit means of avoiding victimization. (Presumably, many of these inmates also avoided public areas of the prison when they *did* leave their cells, but McCorkle's study does not address this matter.) At least one inmate in a Georgia prison has ar-gued that extended cell time is a maxim for prison living. "Certain skills are needed to survive" our dangerous prisons, says he, "the best being the one that enables you to remain in your cell, or on your bunk, 20 to 22 hours a day, year in, year out. It is this ability, above all, that you must acquire if you wish to re-main alive and return to the outside" (Cobb, 1985:74). Inside the cell, prison-ers like this man find a degree of safety and privacy; alone in their cells, they experience moments of autonomy, however limited and fleeting. Outside the cell they see lurking an intrusive public culture that is at once monotonous and dangerous. For them, then, the cell offers a kind of liberation from prison. The yard and the cell blocks, in contrast, offer only a drab, repetitive, demoral-izing routine, which for them epitomizes the constraints of prison life.

Prisoners who log long hours in the cell often describe themselves as alone but not lonely. Paradoxically, when they leave the world they have fashioned in the cell, they may find themselves captive to the lonely crowds that roam the prison world. "Always a lot of fools and crazy people surrounding you," observed Robbie Wideman (1985:230), "so you ain't never alone but you always lonely." Coping means escape from these lonely and sometimes dangerous crowds.

Longer I spend in here, the more I back away. Even back away from hang-out time with the fellas on the range. I got to find my own space. Even if it's tiny. See in your cell you ain't got nobody else to worry about but your ownself. It's one of the few safe places in here. Course people been offed in they cells. Ain't no place really safe, but least you can be alone, be in your cell with your own stink and your own little bit of stuff and your own thoughts and do. Cause outside your cell ain't nothing going on but the same ole shit. That's what gets to you after a while. Repetition. Same ole, same ole all the time. Same bullshit on the hangout corner. Same slop at breakfast. Same nasty guards. One day just like the other. Same simple cats doing the same dumb numbers. Day in and day out, every day. It gets to you. It surely does. (Wideman, 1985:230)

Inmates for whom the cell is a niche are inclined to decorate their cells with care, to fashion them into homes away from home. Said one such inmate, a lifer I interviewed at a Maryland penitentiary,

I just took a memory and where I could apply it from my house or even my mother's house, and I got something in that cell that reminds me of those things. For instance, the bookshelf reminds me of a wall unit my mother has in her home. The rug on the floor makes me reminisce about the rug in me and my wife's bedroom, the same color pattern and that kind of a thing. (Personal Communication, 1988)

Many of these men face long prison terms, including life terms, as we noted in Chapter Four (see, generally, Zamble, 1992). They know they are going to live in their cells for a considerable time, and they strive to make the cell a living environment (see, for example, McCall, 1995:171). In the words of the Maryland prisoner,

A lot of people say that when you decorate your cell like that, it means you've moved in permanently. I think in a sense that's true. You wouldn't take the time to do all that if you thought you was going someplace. You want to make it liveable, cause you're going to live there. (Personal Communication, 1988)

These same men are inclined to develop jobs that, like their cells, offer them a routine that takes them away from the public culture of the prison. The Maryland prisoner, for example, described his job (as a clerk) as a career that absorbed so much time and energy that he felt removed from daily prison life. For instance, he worked late into the evening on a daily basis, "primarily because I just don't have anything else to do."

Prison, for this man, amounted to cell time or work time. The same can be said for Robbie Wideman. As he makes clear, both cell and work offer a respite from the mainline prison culture.

Most of my time away from my cell is in the hospital. My schedule's kind of different from most people's behind me working there. I like my job. Get to be around the nurses, for one thing. You know I dig that. Being around anybody who ain't locked up is a real pleasure, don't care who it is. It's nice too cause in the hospital ain't no guards in my face all day. Sometimes I carry the meals up to the hospital so I can eat in there too. Food ain't no different but it sure do taste better when you ain't sitting with them nuts in the mess hall. (Wideman, 1985:232)

For others, the insulation and liberation provided by the cell is achieved through activities that absorb their energy and spirit, transporting them from the confines of the prison. "You know," said one prison poet, "when I'm writing, I'm not in prison." (Klein, 1988:15). Telander, speaking of a dedicated weight lifter nicknamed Beetle, who had just lifted the equivalent of the "front end of a small car," observed that "for an instant there, Beetle looked as if he were free" (Telander, 1988:4) Robert B. Smith, a prison poet, writes of the literal liberation—release from prison by court order—sought by prison's writ writers. They work obsessively, devoted to law as if it were an instrument of magic, "more potent than ram's horn," able to breach prison walls with a single phrase or incantation.

> They search by sunlight, by lamplight,
> by no light,
> knowing the day will, must, come
> when from a sudden page a key
> comes rising, a gold sword from a lake of milk,
> setting them free from the manacles
> that couple them to this desperation, this life.

(Smith, in Bruchac, 1984:298)

More often than not, these writ writers lose their appeals but find a psychological escape in the form of hope. For them, the medium of the law is the message: they can be free within the confines of the prison, psychologically if not physically shorn of "the manacles that couple them to this desperation, this life."

These various inmates adjust by removing themselves from the public prison culture. Yet others, perhaps fewer in number these days, revel in the culture of the prison yard, with its street culture and its communal rhythms of life. Prison poet Raymond Ringo Fernandez, in his "poem for the conguero in D-yard," captures aspects of the public prison culture that are as alien to convicts like Abbott as they are to inmates like Malinow. For Fernandez, the infamous D yard in Attica, home to a terrible riot and symbol for many of the ferocity of prison life, can at times provide the freedom of a warm summer night in his native Central Park.

> on warm summer evenings
> i hear the tumbao   [rhythm]
> of your blue conga
> declamando   [declaring]
> carrying your inspiration
> over the wall

like a refreshing
caribbean wind

if it wasn't for
the culturally deprived minds
in the gun towers
i'd swear
i was in central park
chilling out
by the fountain
con un yerbo and a cold   [with a joint]
can of bud
or
haciendo coro
at un bembe   [singing in a group]
on a 110th street
where even the children
understand the clave: [beat]
          cla-cla / cla-cla-cla
repica vida conguero   [alive with bongos]
contratiempo con el tiempo   [as time passes]
que with each slap
on the congas skin
you bring me closer
to home . . . .

(Fernandez, in Bruchac, 1984:95)

Fernandez shows us that at least some inmates some of the time—and maybe many inmates at least on occasion—can find slices of home in the very hustle and bustle of music and talk and leisure that is part and parcel of the larger prison culture.

Of course, Malinow wants nothing to do with congo music in the prison yard. He would describe Fernandez's prison yard party as trouble waiting to happen. For him, Fernandez represents "the new element," mostly urban minority inmates, that is ruining today's prisons. Malinow seeks a niche far from the hostile battlefield Fernandez equates with a congenial urban park. Thus Malinow's routine featured cell activities (mostly writing and hobbycrafts), a job, and a daily routine that was expressly calculated to keep him away from the public areas of the prison. For Malinow, venturing into such areas as the mess hall and the yard meant risking confrontations with guards he didn't know and convicts he didn't want to know. The predictable result of mingling in the convict world was either that one responded to their threats or insults and got into trouble, or one backed down and was further belittled and abused.

It isn't just the uninspiring food and the fact that he can manage to eat well enough on his job and in his cell, it is also the atmosphere of the mess hall that keeps Malinow from going there. Like many experienced inmates at Green Haven, he leads a circumscribed life, avoiding crowds and cutting down on his chances of being hassled by officers and inmates he doesn't know. He dislikes the long walk to the mess hall, the waiting in line, and the possibility he may inadvertently wind up at a table next to some inmates he describes as "the new element," by which he means young black drug addicts. "If one of the new element jumps in line ahead of me or makes a remark about honkies and he knows I've heard it, I'd have to hit him and that would get me into trouble," he said. "I don't need trouble. But I can't let such a remark go by. I'm not from a blue-blooded family, I don't have a million dollars. All I have is my image, how I'm re-garded in prison, how I carry myself. Some inmates won't react—you can call their mothers or fathers anything—but from then on they're consid-ered trash, and they're treated accordingly. They'll let a remark go by, and the next thing you know they'll be standing in the yard in front of the TV set and some guy standing behind them will say, 'Hey, creep, get out of here,' and they'll have to go. . . ." Malinow rarely goes to the yard. He no longer participates in sports, says he has outgrown idle prison conversa-tions about past and future Cadillacs and women, and considers the yard another place to avoid the new element. (Sheehan, 1978:83–85)

The new element Malinow strives to avoid poses different problems for different prisoners. When Malinow and other, usually older, inmates of con-temporary prisons demand a structured and predictable routine, "it is not chaos that they bemoan, it is the prison's failure to control things that need control-ling" (Seymour, 1977:188).[3] Malinow, for instance, quite explicitly prizes an ordered prison life and speaks nostalgically about the rigorous and disciplined prisons he has known in his time. Foremost among these is Clinton prison in upstate New York, a prison that to this day is known for its regimentation.

At Clinton, you always knew where you stood. . . . You got up in the morning and went through your daily routine like a robot. You even set yourself a precise schedule for your daily chores, like rinsing out your clothes on Tuesdays and Thursdays from four-thirty to five. . . . Those seven years at Clinton under rigid conditions went by very quickly . . . Some of the old-timers, men who had been sentenced in the 1920s, when sen-tences were much longer—thirty to sixty years for first-degree robbery wasn't uncommon—taught me the trick of doing time. They told me never to think of my sentence as a whole but to do one day at a time. They said that if you concentrated on the day you were up, soon the many days and years ahead of you would be behind you. They were right. The seven years went by like three and a half. (Sheehan, 1978:199 & 205)

Jimmy Dunn, a man who served a number of lengthy prison terms in regi-mented Big Houses, explains the salutary connection between having a rou-tine and taking one day at a time:

So I'll get up this morning, like every other morning, and I'll go through the routine, because the routine is what saves me. The days are all the

same. Each one exactly like the one preceding it and like the one following it. They're all the same—just a blur—and looking back a year ago
when I got this jolt, it seems like only yesterday because yesterday was just
like it was a year ago. (Manocchio & Dunn, 1982:33)

A structured, circumscribed life need not be an especially barren or lonely
one, at least as these terms have meaning in the prison. Years of a robotlike
regimentation are preferable to the worse alternative of chronic anxiety about
one's reputation or safety. As it happens, Malinow and many of the other prisoners who live highly structured lives off the yard and away from militant
groups and gangs have their own networks of support. While one is not show-
ered with spontaneous displays of affection, one is at least provided for on a
regular basis.

Within a few minutes [of his arrival at the prison], runners came up to
him bringing large bags of groceries and thermoses filled with coffee,
compliments of the many friends he had made during his stay [at other
prisons]. "I was very appreciative that people thought of me even before I
was in the place an hour," he says. "Old-timers know it can be hard in a
new prison the first day or two. Sometimes you don't get your personal
property immediately, and you don't get to the commissary right away."
(Sheehan, 1978:238)

There are alternatives to Malinow's comparatively monastic existence that
provide structure and predictability, even if his routine is not as barren as one
would suppose. Some inmates join formal prisoner clubs or organizations.
These groups, officially sanctioned and closely supervised by prison authorities, are an important aspect of the prison ecology. In some prisons, as many as
half of the inmates maintain such affiliations (Fox, 1982:141; see also Stojkovic,
1984). As Fox (1982:88) observed of the contemporary violent prison, "while
an increasing number of prisoners have adopted a hardened posture toward
their fellow prisoners and prison officials, many prisoners sought traditional or
legitimate solutions to problems of personal and social adjustment in prison."
Most of these prisoners, Fox (1982:106) continues, "accept the legitimacy of
authority used in their apprehension, conviction, and incarceration." They turn
to authorized formal groups to solve adjustment problems because they now
have greater rights of association as well as a greater need for shelter against
the tempestuous prison yard.

These organizations serve a variety of needs for both prisoners and staff.
For prisoners, the diversity of living and program arrangements is supplemented by a host of voluntarily selected group activities relating to cultural
awareness, religion, self-help, and various special interests such as community
service (for example, through a prison chapter of the Jaycees like the one to
which Malinow belonged) (Fox, 1982:141; see also Stojkovic, 1984). Some of
these groups serve clearly rehabilitative goals for their members. Given the
void many inmates report in their lives, both in the free world and the prison
(see Chapter Four), the appeal of these rehabilitative groups would seem to be

almost existential, giving meaning and direction to an otherwise empty existence. Other prisoner organizations provide protection to their members, or serve as arenas for benign forms of recreation. (A few groups, notably some of the cultural or ethnic awareness organizations, serve as covers for convict gang activities, but they are the exception rather than the rule.) These prisoner groups assure the staff that the prison "masses" now operate to a great extent under their authority and supervision. Officials grant charters to these organizations, approve their activities, and provide the space and administrative support (including security) needed to carry out their various missions. Prisoners are thus more readily served and controlled by virtue of these groups (Fox, 1982:138; see also Stojkovic, 1984). The "tentative order" Irwin described in today's prisons is in no small part due to the civil relationships that bind these groups and the prison authorities.

Some prisoners have an especially hard time securing a niche in the regular prison population. Younger, inexperienced inmates, for instance, are more vulnerable to prison predators than Malinow and his associates, and have fewer avenues of adjustment open to them (see, for example, McCorkle, 1993:87). Naive white inmates are apt to be particularly vulnerable because, more often than not, black prisoners have assumed positions of dominance in the prison community. Simple civility will mark them as targets. A seasoned white convict at Leavenworth makes this point, with evident contempt for white victims and black victimizers.

> Most whites fuck up right away when they come into prison, because they try to be friendly. . . . Let's say a white dude is put in a cell with maybe fifteen niggers. If he says hello or even nods to them, then he's already doomed. You see, half of them will think he is just being polite and treating them with respect, but the other half will know he is weak and afraid, because they know that a white man isn't even going to acknowledge them if he's been in prison before, because whites don't speak to niggers in prison. These niggers are going to move on that guy as soon as the hack disappears. (Earley, 1992:419)

Some vulnerable prisoners may be too fearful to join formal prisoner organizations or, having joined one, may find that their fellow Jaycees cannot protect them from predatory convicts. They find that they cannot simply retreat from the public areas of the prison as Malinow and some club members do, because they are actively pursued by aggressors. Often they are friendless, either because they are new to prison or because other inmates avoid them for fear of being targeted by aggressors. (As Schroeder reminds us, in prison one picks one's associates carefully, "keeping in mind that anything they were involved in would inescapably involve you too." The implication is that only prospective victims would gravitate to one another, but even here, fear keeps would-be supporters apart, each trying to maintain a low profile.) Nor can vulnerable inmates turn to staff. The convict code, which regular inmates respect out of fear, all but precludes a target from enlisting the aid of staff. As Lockwood (1977:215) has observed, referring to targets of sexual aggression, the prisoner who " 'rats' on those who make aggressive advances to him is a 'sissy,' because he is an object of sexual attention, a 'punk' because he will not fight, and a 'snitch' because he has told a staff member about his problem." He is very much in jeopardy. "Above all, vulnerable inmates learn that no amount of supervision, no physical barriers, can prevent their being the object of threats and advances ranging from simple pleas to physical violence" (Lockwood, 1977:216).

For "young and effeminate prisoners," then, "segregation may be their only safe niche" (Irwin, 1980:202). Here, structure serves the need for safety to the virtual exclusion of other living requirements. Inmates who seek what is known as "protective segregation," "protection company," "protection," or simply "PC" are housed

> under conditions similar to those found in disciplinary segregation: they are isolated from the rest of the prison population; they are confined to their cells for all but a small part of the day; they are not able to participate in institutional activities. Indeed, some officials fail to distinguish between disciplinary and protective segregation. As the judge in one case involving sexual assault recently noted, "a threatened inmate can go to the hole." (Lockwood, 1977:206; see also Brodsky, 1984)

Only in protection are men in fact "truly protected from other inmates" (Lockwood, 1977:208). Still, they pay a high price for this service.

> In exchange for safety, they sacrificed the freedom of movement that is available to other prisoners, the opportunity to participate in school, and the access to other prison programs. They relinquished their weekly movies and the sports in the yard. In exchange for their safety they lived in quarantine, spending twenty-two hours a day in their cell. (Lockwood, 1977:208)

Sadly, the price of safety includes more than discomfort and boredom. For many offenders, living in isolation produces psychological harms as well. In Brodsky's words,

> the PC living experience deprive[s] the inmates of the opportunity to engage in behaviors that allow each of us to define who we are. Without a sense of accomplishment, most people cannot maintain self-esteem. Without interpersonal stimulation, we narrow emotionally. Without the exercise of our emotional and intellectual skills, we become stagnant and lose mastery of ordinary abilities to concentrate and to attend. . . . These constrictions become magnified further in the context of fear and perceived harassment. . . . [As a result,] for up to two-thirds of . . . confined men in the more typical institutions, the PC living experience is harmful in ways that interfere with their mental health and well-being. (Brodsky, 1984:21; see also Toch, 1975; Burtch & Ericson, 1979.)

And these inmates are likely to remain in quarantine for long periods of time, often for their entire sentence. The reason: they are now visibly labeled as weak, and hence as fair game for predators. It is for this reason that protective custody has been variously called "an escape hatch with a boomerang" and "a sanctuary from which there is no return" (Lockwood, 1977:211).

Yet it is crucial to appreciate that protective custody "is generally liked by its residents," even though it is uncomfortable and sometimes psychologically disabling (Lockwood, 1977:221). These men, unlike the convicts such as Abbott who populate disciplinary segregation, are in all likelihood traumatized by their experiences of victimization and hence in full retreat from the prison world. Victims in prison tend to be drawn disproportionately from among the young and the socially isolated; for all prison victims, but for the young and the isolated in particular, "victimizations that occur in prison are much more 'fear-provoking' than those which occur in the free world" (McCorkle, 1993:87). As a result, vulnerable prisoners, for whom the threat if not the reality of victimization is a daily fact of life, have "a preponderant need for safety, and/or a consuming desire for privacy" (Lockwood, 1977:223). These concerns are at least minimally satisfied in protective custody, while the convicts' obsession with freedom is flagrantly violated by the same regime. Fearful prisoners prefer "sanctuary in protection to life in a prison population" (Lockwood, 1977:223). They "perceive themselves as having made a free and knowledgeable choice" among the range of admittedly unappealing options open to them (Lockwood, 1977:223). While it may seem odd from a free-world perspective, given the harsh realities of life in prison, "one shudders at the fate of these men should the alternative of protection not be available to them" (Lockwood, 1977:223).[4]

MORE THAN SURVIVAL

Prisons provide stressful and sometimes disabling experiences. There are frightened, vulnerable, lonely inmates who fail to secure protection or support in any form. Cut adrift in a viciously rejecting world, they find no niche, no respite. For them, in the words of prison poet J. A. Hines,

> There is no escape
> not in dreams
> not in death
> not in dreams of death
> not even in the death of dreams
>
> (Hines, in Bruchac, 1984:127)

These inmates run a substantial risk of suicide, hoping perhaps to secure the final escape of physical death and the oblivion it seems to promise.[5] Typically, however, confinement is endured without breakdowns or lasting psychological harm. Even in protective custody, an admittedly barren "last-ditch niche," there is life and adjustment (Lockwood, 1977:207). Morale is low, but most men somehow make do in the prison.

The challenge for prison administrators is to translate occasions of stress into opportunities for growth. Men in niches typically avoid problems, whether they be problems with authorities, fear of peers, anxiety in social situations, or feelings of inadequacy when separated from loved ones. Avoidance is, of course, one aspect of a competent coping strategy: religions have long counseled that one should avoid occasions of sin, and there is merit in this advice. But one cannot avoid all problems, and some methods of avoidance, such as manipulation and deception, are harmful to others. Thus, skills for responsibly circumventing problems must be supplemented with problem-solving skills.

Prisoners who have found a niche are, in a sense, hiding in and from the prison, and they are not likely to come out of hiding unless we offer support and encouragement. The security of the niche, in other words, is unlikely to be given up unless we make the prisoners a better offer. Yet that same sense of security provides an opening for change. As one man observed, the prisoner who is secure in his adjustment evokes confidence in others, who in turn are more likely to see him as a fellow human being who is a worthy candidate for help and support:

> If you find your niche, the others sense that you feel less threatened and feel less threatened by you. The self-confidence that you gain from feeling secure enables others to have confidence in you. Thus, the staff in particular, because of their heightened ability to do so, and the other inmates, in their more limited and sometimes more profound way, will tend to view you as someone upon whom help will not be wasted. And, because you feel secure in the niche, you are able to accept the help. (Gates, 1991: 75–76).

For this man, and perhaps for most men in prison, "the best help . . . always included letting you know that you were a regular human being" and not a mere criminal or inmate.

The vast majority of prisoners survive confinement in the sense that they make compromises and get by. But corrections must be more than this, must mean more than simply making do. Corrections means addressing the problems of confinement with all of the human and environmental resources at our disposal. To do this, relations in the prison world must embody exchanges between and among full-blooded human beings whose aspirations and concerns are taken seriously. Problems in living experienced by the human beings who populate our prisons include those suffered by the convicts as well as by the other prisoners. Among the key actors in the correctional process are the line staff. The adjustments of the line staff to the various pressures of prison life, and the roles they play in shaping the institutional world that is inhabited by the prisoners, are the subjects of the next two chapters.

NOTES

1. See Renzema, 1988:161, Note 1 and Beck and Shipley, 1989 for recidivism among American ex-prisoners; see Bonta, Lipinski & Martin (1992) for recidivism among Canadian ex-prisoners. The latest recidivism research reports on a sample of 16,000 prisoners released from confinement in eleven states in 1983 and followed for a three-year period. We learn that "62.5 percent were rearrested for a felony or serious misdemeanor within three years, 46.8 percent were reconvicted, and 41.4 percent returned to prison or jail" (Beck & Shipley, 1989:1). A sizable minority (about 37 percent) were neither rearrested nor reconfined for a felony or a serious misdemeaner. As a group, this cohort of releasees were active criminals *before* confinement, having been "arrested and charged with an average of more than twelve offenses each" (Beck & Shipley, 1989:1). Interestingly, about two-thirds of these prisoners had been confined before; this is about the same confinement rate as displayed after release from prison, suggesting that incarceration had not, on average, increased criminality among this group. Chronic offenders, in particular young chronic offenders, were exceedingly active in crime before and after their imprisonment; fully "94.1 percent of prisoners age eighteen to twenty-four with eleven or more prior arrests were rearrested within three years" (Beck & Shipley, 1989:1).

2. As Zamble, Porporino, and Kalotay (1984:66) have noted in their research with Canadian prisoners, "despite differences from the outside, the environment in the penitentiary allowed inmates to reestablish on the inside much of the pattern of their outside lives." Leo Carroll has been kind enough to remind me that this observation holds for gang members, who are apt to view at least some of the functions and activities of their gangs in ameliorative terms. That is, gang members are apt to see their gangs as niches (Carroll, personal communication).

3. Elaborating, Seymour (1977:188) notes, *Older inmates may feel a particular need for environmental stability, in light of changes in the composition of prison populations. Given a shift in the inmate subculture, from a respected coping style of emotional distance and coolness, to one that includes militancy, confrontation, and testing, new needs for stability are generated.*

4. Though protection may be a niche of sorts under current arrangements, this does not mean that more accommodating living conditions cannot be developed to afford protection cases the privacy and safety they require. Brodsky (1984) studied one such PC unit, and reported adequate adjustment among its residents.

5. Suicidal behavior is a low-rate phenomenon in all environments. Comparatively speaking, however, suicide is common in confinement. The suicide rate for prison inmates in the United States is 17.5 per 100,000, which is roughly 50 percent higher than that of free citizens, for whom the rate is 11 per 100,000. This figure has remained constant for fully twenty years (Bonta & Gendreau, 1990:356). The suicide rate for jail inmates, for whom the stresses of transition from free world to confinement are great and the supports in the environment few, are anywhere from five to nine times higher than in the free world (see Hayes, 1983; Gibbs, 1988; Hayes & Rowan, 1988). Suicide rates are lower in prison than in jail because prisoners face a less abrupt transition than does the jail inmate (the prisoner comes from a jail rather than the free world), and the prison generally offers a more stable environment than the jail. Self-mutilation, again a low-rate behavior, occurs among inmates of jails and prisons at an even more disproportionate rate than do suicides (Toch, 1975 & 1992). Once again, rates of self-mutilation are substantially higher in jail than in prison, and for the same reasons.

REFERENCES

Anonymous. *An Illustrated History and Description of State Prison Life, By One Who Has Been There. Written by a Convict in a Convict's Cell.* Globe Publishing, 1871.

Beck, A. J., and B. E. Shipley. "Recidivism of prisoners released in 1983." Washington, D.C.: Bureau of Justice Statistics, 1989.

Bennett, R. R. (ed.). *Police At Work: Policy Issues and Analysis.* Beverly Hills, CA: Sage, 1983.

Blecker, R. "Haven or hell? Inside Lorton Central Prison: Experiences of punishment justified." *Stanford University Law Review* 42 (May 1990):1149–249.

Bonta, J., and P. Gendreau. "Reexamining the cruel and unusual punishment of prison life." *Law and Human Behavior* 14 (4) 1990:347–72.

Bonta, J., S. Lipinski, and M. Martin. "Characteristics of federal inmates who recidivate." Ottawa: Statistics Canada, 1992.

Bowker, L. *Prison Victimization.* New York: Elsevier, 1980.

Brodsky, S. L. "Inmates in protective custody: First data on emotional effects." Presidential Address, Division 18, Annual Meeting of the American Psychological Association; Toronto, Canada, 1984.

Burtch, B. E., and R. V. Ericson. "The silent system: An inquiry into prisoners who suicide and an annotated bibliography." Toronto: University of Toronto Centre of Criminology, 1979.

Carroll, L. "Race, ethnicity, and the social order of the prison." In R. Johnson and H. Toch (eds.). *The Pains of Imprisonment.* Prospect Heights, IL: Waveland Press, 1988:181–203.

Cobb, A., Jr., "Home truths about prison overcrowding." *The Annals of the American Academy of Political and Social Science* 478 (March 1985):73–85.

Coffey, W. A. *Inside Out: Or, An Interior View of the New York State Prison; Together with Bibliographic Sketches of the Lives of Several of the Convicts.* New York, 1823:Printed for the author.

Cooley, D. "Prison victimization and the informal rules of social control." *Forum on Corrections Research* 4 (3) 1992:31–36.

Davidson, R. T. *Chicano Prisoners: The Key to San Quentin.* New York: Holt, Rinehart & Winston, 1974.

Earley, P. *The Hot House: Life Inside Leavenworth.* New York: Bantam Books, 1992.

Fernandez, R. R. "Poem for the conguero in D-Yard." In J. Bruchac (ed.). *The Light from Another Country: Poetry from American Prisons.* Greenfield Center, NY: Greenfield Review Press, 1984:95.

Fleischer, M. S. *Warehousing Violence.* Beverly Hills, CA: Sage, 1989.

Fox, J. G. *Organizational and Racial Conflict in Maximum-Security Prisons.* Lexington: Lexington Books, 1982.

Gates, M. "The excavation." American University: Unpublished manuscript, 1991.

Gibbs, J. J. "The first cut is the deepest: Psychological breakdown and survival in the detention setting." In R. Johnson and H. Toch (eds). *The Pains of Imprisonment.* Prospect Heights, IL: Waveland Press, 1988:97–114.

Glaser, D. *The Effectiveness of Prison and Parole Systems.* Indianapolis: Bobbs-Merrill, 1964.

Hayes, L. M. "And darkness closes in . . . A national study of jail suicides." *Criminal Justice and Behavior* 10 (4) 1983: 461–84.

Hayes, L., and J. R. Rowan. *National Study of Jail Suicides: Seven Years Later.* Alexandria, VA: National Center for Institutions and Alternatives, February 1988.

Hines, J. A. "Cancel my subscription." In J. Bruchac (ed.). *The Light from Another Country: Poetry from American*

Prisons. Greenfield Center, NY: Greenfield Review Press, 1984:127.

Hoffman, P. B., and J. L. Beck. "Burnout-age at release from prison and recidivism." *Journal of Criminal Justice* 12 (6) 1984:617–23.

Irwin, J. *Prisons in Turmoil.* Boston: Little, Brown, 1980.

Jacobs, J. *Stateville: The Penitentiary in Mass Society.* Chicago: University of Chicago Press, 1977.

Johnson, R. *Death Work: A Study of the Modern Execution Process.* Belmont, CA: Wadsworth, 1990.

Klein, R. "Molding a cry and a song: American prisoners as poets." *Commonweal* 115 (1) 1988:14–18.

Lester, D. and B. L. Danto. *Suicide Behind Bars: Prediction and Prevention.* Philadelphia: The Charles Press, 1993.

Levinson, R. "Try softer." In R. Johnson and H. Toch (eds.). *The Pains of Imprisonment.* Prospect Heights, IL: Waveland Press, 1988:241–56.

Lockwood, D. "Living in protection." In H. Toch. *Living in Prison: The Ecology of Survival.* New York: Free Press, 1977:206–23.

Manocchio, A. J., and J. Dunn. *The Time Game: Two Views of a Prison.* Beverly Hills, CA: Sage, 1982.

McCall, N. *Makes Me Wanna Holler: A Young Black Man in America.* New York: Vintage, 1995.

McCorkle, L. W., Jr., and R. Korn. "Re-socialization within walls." *The Annals of the Academy of Political and Social Science* 293 (May 1995):88–98.

McCorkle, R. C. "Institutional violence: How do inmates respond?" *Forum on Corrections Research* 4 (3) 1992:9–11. (This is a summary of McCorkle's "Personal precautions to violence in prison," *Criminal Justice and Behavior* 19 (2) 1992:160–73.)

McCorkle, R. C. "Living on the edge: Fear in a maximum-security prison." *Journal of Offender Rehabilitation* 20 (1/2) 1993:73–91.

Megargee, F. I., and B. Cadow. "The ex-offender and the 'monster' myth." *Federal Probation* 44 (1) 1980:24–37.

Nettler, G. *Explaining Crime.* New York: McGraw Hill, 1984.

Renzema, M. "The stress comes later." In R. Johnson and H. Toch (eds.). *The Pains of Imprisonment.* Prospect Heights, IL: Waveland Press, 1988:147–62.

Schroeder, A. *Shaking It Rough.* Garden City, NY: Doubleday, 1976.

Seymour, J. "Niches in prison." In H. Toch. *Living in Prison: The Ecology of Survival.* New York: Free Press, 1977:179–205.

Seymour, J. "Environmental sanctuaries for susceptible prisoners." In R. Johnson and H. Toch (eds.). *The Pains of Imprisonment.* Prospect Heights, IL: Waveland Press, 1988:267–84.

Sheehan, S. *A Prison and a Prisoner.* Boston: Houghton Mifflin, 1978.

Smith, R. B. "Jailhouse lawyers." In J. Bruchac (eds.). *The Light from Another Country: Poetry from American Prisons.* Greenfield Center, NY: Greenfield Review Press, 1984:298.

Stojkovic, S. "Social bases of power and control mechanisms among prisoners in a prison organization." *Justice Quarterly* 1 (4) 1984:511–28.

Telander, R. "Sports behind the walls." *Sports Illustrated* 69 (17) 1988:82–96.

Toch, H. *Men in Crisis: Human Breakdowns in Prison.* Chicago: Aldine, 1975.

Toch, H. *Living in Prison: The Ecology of Survival.* New York: Free Press, 1977.

Toch, H. *Violent Men.* Cambridge: Schenkman, 1980.

Toch, H. *Mosaic of Despair: Human Breakdowns in Prison.* Washington, D.C.: American Psychological Association, 1992.

Wallerstedt, J. F. "Returning to prison." Special Report of the Bureau of Justice Statistics, November 1984 (NCJ-95700).

Washington, J. *A Bright Spot in the Yard: Notes and Stories from a Prison Journal.* Trumansburg, NY: Crossing Press, 1981.

Zamble, E., F. Porporino and J. Kalotay. *An Analysis of Coping Behavior in Prison Inmates.* Ministry of the Solicitor General of Canada; Programs Branch User Report, 1984.

Zamble, E. "Behavior and adaptation in long-term prison inmates: Descriptive longitudinal results." *Criminal Justice and Behavior* 19 (4) 1992:409–25.

7

To Have and to Hold

The Prison Officer's Public (Custodial) Agenda

Like the prisoners they supervise, guards adapt to prison life in the context of both public and private worlds. The public world of the prison guard is reflected—and distorted—in images of the officer as a mindless and brutal custodian. Yet this stereotype fits some officers. These guards, dubbed "smug hacks" or "subcultural custodians" by Toch and Klofas (1982), typically account for about a quarter of the guard force. They are custodial officers in the pejorative sense of the term. They seek order at any price, and violence—their own or that of inmate allies—is one of the tools of their trade. Their stance of toughness is exalted in the guard subculture, and is the public image (though not the private reality) adopted by most officers. Smug hacks find their counterparts in the convicts of the prison yard. The combative relations that ensue between these groups account for much of the abuse and even brutality that occurs in the prison.

The private world of the prison guard is the subject of the next chapter (Chapter Eight). There the focus is on the various ways individuals take an alienating role and shape it to meet their personal needs as well as those of the inmates under their control. Some officers try to enrich their jobs. They fight alienation by expanding their roles and making them rewarding; they do not succumb to alienation by reducing their work to the bare bones of the custodial role. These guards are correctional officers in the best sense of the term. Their objective is to provide the human services necessary to make the prison a place where inmates can live as mature adults and perhaps graduate to conventional lives in the free world. They find their counterparts in the many inmates who struggle to carve out niches for themselves in the hope that they can emerge from the prison no worse, and perhaps a little better, than when they went in. Constructive personal relations between these groups account for much of the correctional work that takes place behind prison walls.

THE PRISON GUARD AS HACK

For prison guards, the line between being a figure of authority and an authoritarian figure is sometimes exceedingly slim. The history of prisons "includes the most arbitrary and sadistic, the most bestial abuses of power of which men—in the guise of debased authority—are capable" (Toch, 1977:98). Responsibility for such abuses has been placed with the staff, particularly the guards, who can be most readily identified as having trafficked in "debased authority." The resulting image of guards assumes incompetence and brutality.

Accounts by inmates of penitentiaries and Big Houses are replete with references to brutal officers. Some officers, indeed, appear in the eyes of their charges as living caricatures of humanity, as atavisms in action. In the words of an anonymous inmate of Southern Indiana State Penitentiary, writing in the 1860s,

> I heard some one approaching with a shuffling gate, and soon there appeared at the door a short, burly, bow-legged man, with arms dangling nearly to his knees, and having the most villainous countenance it has ever been my misfortune to look upon. You would have known at once that the devil was his master by his unsightly squint and satanic grin. His head was turned slightly to one side as he leered at me from under his shaggy eye-brows. I at once read my fate in his demoniac smile. (Anonymous, 1871:28)

If many officers qualify as servants of Satan, a few—a very few—are portrayed as handmaids of humaneness, agents, as it were, of the angels. An inmate of New York State Penitentiary, writing in 1823, had this to say about a ranking officer of the prison, who transcended the evil that surrounded him in the penitentiary.

> In the midst of all the inhumanity of the prison, like a pyramid in the desert, surrounded by nothing but bleakness and ruin, there was one heart that still retained, all the grandeur—all the sincerity—all the elevated sympathy, of our nature. It is to Mr. John Gibson, the Deputy Keeper, that I allude. Upwards of Fifteen years have glided away, since he entered the prison as a Keeper. He has seen every odious picture, in the gallery of depravity;—he has taken the most sickening view of the character of many;—and still he is sympathetic—still he is sensitive—still he is humane. With him, the mere stripedness or texture of a man's garment, makes but little difference; he looks at the heart. Every well meaning convict, finds in him a valuable friend. (Coffey, 1823:179)

Most often, stereotypical views of officers, and indeed of all prison staff members, cast them as uncaring. "From the warden down," observed Nelson, a prisoner in Sing Sing in the 1920s and 30s, "chaplains and all, they're a pretty lousy outfit." As the Big House was a creature of discipline, symbolized in the count, so too were its agents. "All they care about is if the count is right and to have no riots" (Nelson, 1936:25). An orderly, quiet, surface routine was all that mattered. "[O]utside of that, we could all rot to death, and they wouldn't give a fiddler's so-and-so for us" (Nelson, 1936:25).

Prisons today are, in the main, less harsh and depriving than their predecessors of even a generation ago, and guards are better trained and supervised. Discipline is less extreme, and is almost never an end in itself.[1] Routines must be explained and justified. Abuses by officers are less common, and tend to occur when the authority of the staff has been directly (and often violently) challenged (Bowker, 1980:104). Still, the image of the subhuman and senselessly brutal custodian lives on, as if the modern prison were frozen in time as a relic of the penitentiary or the Big House.

Inmates, for instance, use the symbolic figure of the brutal guard as a rallying point for their public identity as "cons" who despise "hacks," regardless of what their personal experiences with individual prison officers may have been.

> For a prisoner, of course, a guard is possibly the lowest imaginable form of humanoid life, a species somewhere about the level of the gorilla and often rather easily mistaken for one. He's called a bull, a pig, a wethead or a screw, and it's understood he'd rather shoot you than give you the time of day, stick you in the back rather than give you a crust of bread. . . . The intriguing aspect of this view of guards, however, is that no inmate I've ever met came by it through his own experience—at least not initially. It's an opinion a prisoner automatically picks up at the door along with his issue of prison clothes and his government-issued toothbrush, and from that point on he simply looks for incidents to confirm the view. Without having to discuss it, he understands instinctively that such an opinion goes along with his khaki shirt and his cheap boots, that it's wise to establish one's loyalties clearly and that guard-hating is an act which clearly confirms such a loyalty to the inmate cause. It's expressly part of the function of being a prisoner. (Schroeder, 1976:151–52)

There is, to be sure, a corresponding stereotype of inmates—the convict as thug—that is embraced by many officers, at least when the officers are nurturing their public identities as tough and unfeeling hacks. "In metaphoric imagery and folklore," states Fleisher (1989:230),

> convicts have these features: They are hard and emotionless; they are faceless, but have dark, coal-like eyes; they are muscular, very strong, and rather clever; they can sometimes be pleasant, but they are always deceptive and potentially violent; and if one dies, another will be along to take its place. That is a thug.

None of these stereotypes is accurate. The point is that self-righteous convicts like Abbott, working more or less in concert with smug hacks (who don't write books and hence remain nameless), make it their business to provide the incidents of abuse and violence that confirm the stereotypes, in their eyes and in the eyes of others in their groups. The result is a caricature of prison life that deceives and divides some inmates and officers, and it would appear, some of the scholars who have made it their business to study the prison community.

Prison scholars, many of them penologists trained in the social sciences, have been almost as prone as the more hard-boiled convicts to assume "automatically" the incompetence and malevolence of officers and to focus upon unrepresentative incidents. (Violence is almost always only a small part of even a violent person's behavior; to adjudge an officer violent and nothing more is thus to misrepresent him.) It is as though such beliefs were "expressly part of the function" of the penologist's role as well. Certainly this view was not derived from research into the guard's life and adjustment in prison.

The only research that purports to document the inherently negative character of the prison officer focuses not on guards at all, but on college students assigned to play this role in a simulated jail populated by other students acting as inmates (see Haney, Banks & Zimbardo, 1981). However, the students who participated in the "Stanford Prison Experiment," as the study has come to be called, were implicitly encouraged to play out stereotypical conceptions of guard and inmate roles. The student/guards were given no training or guidance. Instead, they were issued uniforms reminiscent of a southern state trooper, complete with silver "Cool Hand Luke" reflective sunglasses and long nightsticks, and then given blanket authorization to run the prison as they saw fit. (Be advised that correctional officers in many states wear slacks and sport coats; officers who come into contact with inmates almost invariably carry no weapons of any kind.) By contrast, the student/inmates wore sacklike dresses. As if this weren't enough, they had bracelets for their ankles and stocking caps for their heads. (Real male inmates sometimes wear unflattering uniforms, but their attire is decidedly masculine in appearance.) Can anyone doubt that the student/guards felt it was appropriate to play the tough-guy role with the emasculated student/inmates over whom they held complete power?

What *is* surprising about this study is that only about one in three of the "guards" did in fact behave abusively. The majority were noted to be fair and even friendly. Interestingly, the decent officers were blamed for perpetuating the negativity of prison. They were alleged to seduce inmates into acceptance of oppressive conditions against which they might otherwise have rebelled. At the same time, the abusive behavior of some student/officers was taken to be prototypical of guard behavior in the real world, as indicative of a pathology built into guarding and into the prison itself. The notion of the guard role as naturally corrupt appears to be widely accepted among penologists. One can gain some comfort from the fact that no one other than the researchers confused the depression shown by the lonely, confused, and frightened student/inmates with the typical inmate's reaction to confinement. In the real prison world, inmate adjustment is quite diverse and, in most cases, oriented to action and denial rather than to passivity and depression (see Chapter Four).

Beyond this study, investigative journalism has resulted in articles that constitute a collage of unmitigated (and usually gratuitous) abuse of the "debased authority" that is seen as the hallmark of prison management. The result is that "much of the material that is available" from prison critics

> presents a stereotypical picture of the guard as a harsh (if not sadistic), power-hungry illiterate—an ignorant, rigid, authoritarian individual who is vigorous only when demanding inmate compliance, when opposing inmate's rights, when criticizing management policies or when scuttling rehabilitation programs. Whereas some prison analysts have described them as thugs, others have viewed them as clones or zombies—an amorphous mass of uniformed automatons, indistinguishable one from the other, performing routine, mundane and mindless tasks which anyone could do, which permit no individual excellence, and require no notable skills. (Ross, 1981:3)

There is no indication, moreover, that the market for this literature is drying up. Guards have been recently characterized by John Irwin, a prominent penologist who should know better, as stupid, bigoted hayseeds who can't even learn the byways of their own institution! In Irwin's (1980:125) words,

> guards are more racially prejudiced than the average citizen. . . . Guards' racism takes three forms. First, they do not like, and in fact often hate, nonwhites. . . . Moreover, most white guards believe that nonwhites are inferior. . . . Finally, the guard force, with a rural background and poor education, misunderstand the perspectives or subcultures of most prisoners.

If it is any consolation to the officers, their colleagues among the professional treatment staff fare little better. "It has been my impression," says Irwin (1980:130), "that the type of staff person who filled the treatment ranks tended to be the less intelligent, less creative, and less ambitious college graduates with B.A.'s in the social sciences or social welfare." Irwin concedes that a few good men (and women) may start out in these ranks, but contends that they become demoralized and leave. The result, in Irwin's view, is that only the dregs of the college educated stay behind to fill treatment roles in the prison. The impression with which one is left after reading Irwin is that the treatment staff and the guards deserve one another's bad company, but that the inmates certainly deserve better!

Yet there is no evidence that guards as a group are distinctively prejudiced or authoritarian, or indeed share any personality type at all (Hawkins, 1976:86-87). (Treatment professionals no doubt are also a psychologically heterogeneous group, though I know of no research on this point.) Guards are neither congenital sadists, rabid racists, nor ex-military officers looking for another uniform and more men to boss around. "Most line staff are," in DiIulio's view, "living rebuttals to the popular stereotypes of prisons workers" (1991:51). Unlike many of their fellow citizens, observes DiIulio (1991:52), line staff separate "the criminal from the crime" and strive to treat inmates even-handedly in terms of their prison adjustment. If the attitudes of officers toward prisoners have anything in common, they are "characterized not by hostility or dislike but rather by despair and disappointment" (Hawkins, 1976:87). "It is the fact that prisoners recidivate" observe Morris and Morris (1963:255–56), "that the staff find intolerable." Many guards care about recidivism because they view themselves as part of the correctional enterprise. They do more than the "mundane and mindless tasks" associated with custody, and hence recidivism is an indictment of their correctional skills as well as a reflection on the inmates.

Nor must persons who play a guard role inevitably do so in an authoritarian way. The National Guard of Wisconsin, for instance, was able to take over a maximum-security prison during a guard strike and run the institution with a respect for the prisoners' individuality. The inmates responded in kind. In one prisoner's words, "The National Guard came inside and treated us like men and human beings—and we reciprocated" (League of Women Voters of Wisconsin, 1981:175). These officers arrived with hostile expectations of criminals—and perhaps with the assumption that they would have to use a heavy-handed authority—but were able to relinquish their stereotypes and evolve a more relaxed style of control after face-to-face contact with the prisoners. This natural experiment, moreover, lasted three weeks, three times longer than the Stanford prison simulation that supposedly established the pathology of the guard role.

Many real prison guards come to treat inmates as individuals, a fact that will be explored in some detail in the next chapter. Suffice it here to say that, like the National Guardsmen assigned to the Wisconsin prison, they start out with false images of inmates but often are quickly disabused of them. This may occur right at the beginning of the officer's career. The following interview excerpt provides a telling case in point.

> When I started [in 1970], after seeing prison movies, I was scared shitless. I started on a Saturday as a temporary employee. I thought they were criminals and that's it.
>
> Did you find what you expected?
>
> They all looked like people. I couldn't tell them from people on the street. The guy that broke me in in the mess hall was a murderer. You couldn't work for a nicer guy. When I started, the inmates checked everything out in the mess hall to see if things were clean. An inmate broke me in. Inmates trained officers. Really! He told me to stand back and he showed me how and where to frisk. He hit the table top to sound it out. Rap the bars to see if they were solid. Many times when you're running companies, or you're a new officer in a factory, there's an inmate that shows you the right way. On Sunday they let out the wing waiter to mop and clean cells. Now they have four or five at a time. The wing waiter guided you right so there's no confusion. An inmate doesn't want to have any more problems than he has. (Lombardo, 1981:32–33)

Over the years since Lombardo conducted the survey of prison officers from which this excerpt is drawn, the level of order in prison has declined. Entering officers today have, if anything, more reason to be "scared shitless." They must contend with more disorder and less respect than was the case in 1970, the period referred to by Lombardo's interviewee. On the other hand, today's officers are better trained, know more about the diverse human beings who comprise the prison population, and enter the guard force with more confidence in their ability to manage objectively the difficult social world that is the modern prison.

The larger point is this: The keepers and the kept are not necessarily at odds with one another; they are not inevitably locked into oppositional roles. Nor are officers sadists who skulk into prison looking for victims and eager to team up with others of their despicable ilk. It is more accurate to say, in the words of one ex-offender, that many of the officers "simply answered all the want-ads and Corrections gave them a job" (Schroeder, 1976:153). As a rule, they know little about what they are getting into, even if they have grown up in such notable prison towns as Auburn, New York, the home of the first congregate penitentiary.[2] According to Lombardo (1981:36),

> As the naive citizens of Auburn became the guards of the prison community, they accepted jobs but did not readily identify with their new titles. They quickly learned to identify with and appreciate the convicts over whom they would stand guard and learned that convicts had to be judged by behavior and not as stereotypes.

As we enter the guards' world, the goal is that they too "be judged by behavior and not as stereotypes."

ALIENATION AND ITS CONSEQUENCES

Stereotypes often contain a grain of truth. The problem is that this truth is blown out of proportion; a theme becomes the whole story, a single note a symphony. The grain of truth in the stereotypes of prison guards is that the guard's job is an alienating one (see Seeman, 1959). In recent surveys, for example, roughly two-thirds of the officers sampled indicated that they had second thoughts about their career choice and would rather be in a different job (Cullen et al., 1989:97; Toch & Grant, 1982:199). The average satisfaction score for the officers as a group was "lower than every other occupation category" for which data were available; the list of occupations included a range of "traditional working class occupations" (Cullen et al., 1989:101). Furthermore, there was evidence that "job satisfaction may be decreasing among correctional officers" (Cullen et al., 1989:97).

The role of the prison officer is one that is hard to identify with, to see as an extension of one's self, because it can be demeaning, dangerous, and lonely (Poole & Regoli, 1981). For most officers, alienation translates into stress and stress-related problems.[3] Some, usually a minority, respond with violence to alienation. The sources of alienation among prison officers, and the link between alienation and violence, will be considered in turn.

Dimensions of Alienation

There are many reasons why the guard's job is alienating. One is that guards are sometimes treated no better than inmates, a fact the officers take to be unjust since they have committed no crimes. Both guards and inmates may be subjected to searches, for instance, upon entering or leaving the prison. Both may be publicly "dressed down" and disciplined by superior officers. For guards who live on the prison compound, living quarters are often comparable to those for prisoners. In fact, it wasn't so long ago that the officers' quarters were subjected to the same thorough searches as inmates' cells. If their "rooms" didn't pass muster, the water and electricity might be turned off (Jacobs, 1977:40).

Guards at work share the prison environment with the inmates. Specific work assignments pose many of the same adjustment problems for officers as they do for inmates. Though it may not be obvious, for example, the segregation officer is, like his charges, isolated from the rest of the prison, with comparatively little freedom of movement or variety in his daily regime.

> It's confined, this block. It's too small a place. After a while, even the officers start arguing with themselves. It happens every day. Any old thing sets the officers off. Out in [the general prison] population at least you're walking around, you got space out there. Or you have the yard duty or you go on transportation, or hospital detail or something. But down at [segregation]. Where you goin'? Upstairs, downstairs, that's it. We're bangin' into one another. (May, 1981a: 13)

More generally, when prison conditions are grim, they affect staff as well as inmates. Prison conditions deteriorated dramatically in places like Stateville and Walpole following the demise of prison discipline in the mid-1970s (see Chapter Five). Guards, like the inmates, were directly affected. Kauffman notes that the guards "recognized Walpole for the 'rats' nest, garbage hole' that it was. They had to work daily in the filth, and they hated it" (Kauffman, 1988:81).

The similarities between the guards' situation and the inmates' lead many guards to think of themselves merely as "uniformed prisoners." Moreover, guards know that others are tempted to see them in this light; to think of guarding as the kind of job one would naturally fill with men and women of the caliber of uniformed prisoners. From the average citizen's vantage point, far from prison yards and cell blocks, guarding would seem to be a sinecure, a matter of merely watching, filing an incident report now and again, and issuing a few orders. If one subscribes fully to the stereotypical image of the guard, one envisions him (or her) indulging in an occasional unprovoked beating. Tower guards do in fact have primitive mandates of this sort; they do simply watch and wait, though they decidedly do not engage in recreational assaults (Toch, 1981). Most officers have more challenging assignments.

Officers usually must apply abstract rules to a wide variety of concrete situations involving persons who are, for the most part, resentful of authority. They are asked to make daily judgments covering an enormous range of inmate conduct, from the appropriateness of a prisoner's clothing, hair length, and demeanor, to his patterns of movement, level of noise in his cell, and any disputes he may have with fellow inmates or even other officers. Most of their decisions involve discretion. No official rulebook can cover all the contingencies. What does one do, for instance, when an inmate breaks a minor rule, such as the requirement that one's clothing be "presentable" at all times when out of the cell, but the violation occurs in a highly public context such as the mess hall? How about an altercation (short of an actual fight) that takes place in the yard, with hundreds of prisoners watching? Does one intervene at all? If so, what does one do? Whether defining the subtleties of what constitutes presentable dress or nonbelligerent conduct, or deciding how to handle the less egregious departures from these standards, there are few informal norms to follow, since unguided discretion generally produces a hodgepodge of conflicting interpretations of what is proper policy.

In effect, each officer has to make his own judgments and sometimes his own rules, but his formal authority makes little or no provision for such ambitious uses of discretion. (The officer may be told to use "common sense" in applying rules, but this injunction is as vague as some of the rules that must be applied.) As a result, the guard often feels he is out on a limb, subject to being second-guessed after every decision. The notion that one is "damned if you do, damned if you don't"—and likely to be thought incompetent in either case—applies with a special urgency to the guard's situation. In the words of one officer,

> Never mind what the rule book says . . . the fact is that you've got to work it out for yourself. . . . One day this is O.K. and the next day it's not O.K. And the next day . . . well, maybe it's O.K. There are no rules, no regulations for the correctional officer himself. . . . There is no direction and he more or less fends for himself. . . . You're expected to think for yourself in certain situations. If it turns out fine, all's well and good. If you make a decision they expect of you and it doesn't turn out right . . . even if it might not have been the wrong decision but it just didn't work out right . . . then you're an asshole. After a while, if you're called an asshole enough by the inmates, and you're called an asshole enough by the brass and, from what you read in the newspapers, [by] the vocal minority [those fighting for prison reform] . . . well, after a while you begin to feel like one. Who's the asshole? Me for staying, or the guy who left? (May, 1981b:25–26)

This officer's concerns are shared by most other officers and even some supervisors; they are a source of serious and sometimes disabling stress.[4] Cheek and Miller (1983), analyzing a survey of prison officer stress, report that the typical guard faces a double-bind situation. The problem is precisely the same as that identified by our officer: lack of clear guidelines for guarding along with lack of autonomy invested in the role, which leave the officer chronically vulnerable to making errors because of factors beyond his control.

The difficulty for guards, then, is not one of being confused over treatment or custodial functions. This confusion exists mainly in the minds of penologists. As Lombardo has made clear,

> From the guard's perspective, prison guard tasks have nothing to do with rehabilitation, just desserts, corrections or punishments. These are issues for the policy planner and program designer—issues that focus upon the inmate's past or attempt to prepare him for the future. For the prison guard going about his day-to-day business, it is the immediate present that matters, life as it is lived and passes *within the prison community;* the outside has little relevance. . . . Faced with a work environment laden with fear, mental tension, uncertainty, isolation, inconsistency and boredom, correction officers are more motivated to develop strategies to cope with these conditions than to pursue management goals. (Lombardo, 1981:55 & 165)

The problem for officers is one of doing one's custodial job adequately, of knowing what to do so one is not an "asshole" (Poole & Regoli, 1980; Willet, 1982). A complicating factor is that each of the officer's audiences within the prison demands something different: administrators look to officers to lead inmates rather than relate to them or otherwise deal with them in interpersonally skillful ways; inmates value interpersonal skills in officers, especially as these relate to problem solving in everyday prison life, and are suspicious of efforts to lead them (see Wahler & Gendreau, 1990:265). Conflicting demands such as these leave many officers feeling alienated from everyone around them. It is Cheek and Miller's (1983:119) conclusion that "the officer gets no respect from anyone." As one officer told Stojkovic (1990:215), "We are the screws no one really cares about." To many officers, it seems that failure—in the eyes of administrators, inmates, or both groups—is virtually unavoidable.

Concerns of this sort may have been muted in the penitentiary and later in the Big House. In those settings, a disciplined regime and harsh punishment kept shows of discontent among the inmates to a minimum; line staff had considerable authority, and staff as a whole exhibited a more united front in opposition to the prisoners. Lewis Lawes, destined to become a famous prison warden, started out as a prison guard in 1905 in Clinton Prison in upstate New York. He recalls the clear role he was given, in an era when, for officers, might made right:

> "Tread softly and carry a big stick," was my first lesson in penology, on my arrival at Clinton Prison on March 1st, 1905. It was to be followed literally. When I reported for duty that night, I was handed a pair of sneakers and a club. The sneakers, to enable the guard to make his rounds noiselessly, so as not to disturb the sleeping forms within the dark cells, and the club to be used in emergencies should any of those forms become unduly active (Lawes, 1932:12).

Lawes was admonished to wield his club early and often, so as to establish his authority. As he later confessed, "I looked for trouble. I found it soon" (Lawes, 1932:24). Decades later, sitting securely in his warden's chair, Lawes marvelled at how normal violence seemed in the yards and cell blocks of the reformatories and prisons of the Big House era, where an officer, in broad daylight and in the middle of the yard, could knock a prisoner out as a disciplinary measure, and have the prisoner take it as a perfectly normal state of affairs! In Lawes's words,

> in order to properly impress the offender, I landed him one on the chin and knocked him out. We worked on him and he was as good as ever in a few moments. The fellow didn't resent my act. He took it for granted. (Lawes, 1932:39).

Evidence suggests that Lawes's experience was typical of officers in all prisons run on the Big House model, whether those prisons were of the traditional factory-based or plantation varieties. Crouch and Marquart described the officer subculture of Texas prisons, for example, dating from roughly 1920 through 1970. These prisons were staffed by quintessential hacks who were virtually unrestrained in their authority. Mounted field officers, who would supervise inmates at work at slave labor in fields and on road gangs, were said to epitomize this officer subculture. Crouch and Marquart offer a revealing description of one such officer, as seen through the eyes of an inmate under his dominion:

> When he raised his head enough so the brim no longer hid his sinister-looking face, I quickly squinted a peek at his eyes. Their icy-blue color contrasted his heavily tanned weathered skin. He seldom blinked, roving his eyes over us. "I'm gonna tell ya'll one time, and one time alone how I'm gonna deal. First off, if airy one uv you tries to run off, I'm gonna kill ya. If airy one uv you 'sputes my word, I'm gonna kill ya. If airy one uv you don' do lak I tell ya, I'm gonna kill ya. If you lay th' hammer down under me [refuse to work], I'm gonna kill ya. And if I jes take a notion to, I'm gonna kill ya." (Crouch & Marquart, 1989:59)

Guards like this were so dominant that they could name and rename inmates at will (based on their physical appearance or attributes as workers) and could command a "highly stylized" etiquette featuring servile submission to their every order. Thus, prisoners demeaned by degrading (and often racist) nicknames would be forced to further demean themselves in order to carry out the most rudimentary functions, such as urinating or smoking a cigarette. "If an inmate wanted to stop for a cigarette, he said, "Lightin' it up, Boss?' and to urinate, he said, 'Pourin' it out, Boss?' The boss' permission would come as 'Light it' and 'Pour it out.'" (Crouch & Marquart, 1989:73)

No one questioned the competence of officers like Lawes's or his Texas counterparts. Everyone knew who was in control. Concerns about the competence of officers are pronounced in today's prisons, however, where inmates have more autonomy and discipline is more difficult to maintain. Officers are no longer encouraged, or indeed even allowed, to club recalcitrant inmates into submission or even to threaten them with harm. Guards can still punish, but only indirectly, through the issuance of reports that must be reviewed by disciplinary committees. These reports can be rejected by their peers, and though this may not occur often, such rejections of the officer's limited power to punish do occur; in the face of growing due process rights, such rejections are probably occurring at an increasing rate these days. Small wonder that the occupational concerns of contemporary prison guards center on powerlessness: in their dealings with the administration (which many feel has abandoned the rank-and-file officer in the name of inmate rights), as well as in their efforts to control prisoners who claim rights and seek to negotiate the conditions of social control (Fox, 1982:42–47; see also Fitzgerald & Sim, 1982:132 and Kauffman, 1988). Nor is it surprising that safety is the next most salient concern (Fox, 1982:51; Kauffman, 1988). Officers feel vulnerable because they work with increasingly restive and demanding prisoners and, in the main, can expect little support from their superiors in controlling these men. It almost goes without saying that the officer's round of life within the prison community can be an exceedingly lonely one. Perhaps it is to be expected that some officers will express their discontent in behavior that flagrantly contravenes modern penal policy—namely, by being abusive, and sometimes violently abusive, toward the more obstreperous convicts, the offending group that is nearest at hand.

Alienation and Violence

Violence can occur as a function of organizational norms or institutional procedures (see Johnson, 1986). When Lawes resorted to his club in Sing Sing prison at the turn of the century, he was following norms that were central to the functioning of that institution. By his own account, he was not in the least bit alienated. The same holds true for Texas officers throughout most of this century; their morale was high, in part because they took pride in their effective use of coercion and violence to maintain a high level in order in Texas prisons. The psychology of violence changes when violence is formally prohibited by the institution, as is the case in all modern prisons. Today, violence has become a tool of alienated officers, who feel abandoned or betrayed by the institution and come to feel authorized to make their own rules.

Some alienated officers work on their own, as freelance agents of violence, if you will, but most work in a group or with some degree of group support. Group norms supporting violence among the alienated typically emerge because people who feel alienated often band together for reassurance and protection. Life seems simpler and more manageable if it is "us" against "them." There is also security in this polarization: the alienated go to great lengths to cover for their own. If exposed in their dealings with inmates, some staff draw battle lines and dig in for a fight. Prisoners, especially the convicts like Abbott, see themselves as in the same boat and do likewise. The result is an "implicit combat and warfare model" in which

> staff and clients tend to view each other as enemies and to see their peers as trench-mates. Breaks in client and staff ranks are seen as openings to the enemy. Although a peer may be violent, he is also a comrade-in-arms who

deserves protection or silence. Questions of solidarity, of maintaining a common front, become strong concerns. Exaggerations of enemy militance and malevolence become supports for morale. (Toch, 1977a:8)

Staff who adopt a trench-warfare model of prison work do their custodial duties but no more. Few words are wasted and no back talk is taken. At best, one is cool and aloof. At worst, one is looking for trouble, in order to prove who's in control. It is as if these officers seek to turn back the clock, to return to the "good old days" of repressive prison control such as those extolled in the Big House.

In this context, the guard's heroes are the "goon squad" officers or other officers informally assigned the duty of physically coercing or even assaulting recalcitrant prisoners (see Marquart, 1984). Usually the smuggest of smug hacks, these are the men who "get the job done" without recourse to such unmanly considerations as tact or persuasion. Bowker's description of goon squad activities highlights the role of force and the image of efficacy these officers project.

> The goon squads are groups of physically powerful correctional officers who "enjoy a good fight" and who are called upon to rush to any area of the prison where it is felt that muscle power will restore the status quo. If a prisoner is ripping up things in his cell and refuses to be quiet, the goon squad may be called and three or four of these correctional officers will forcibly quiet him, administering a number of damaging blows to the head and body. If there is a fight between two prisoners, the goon squad may break it up. Should a prisoner refuse to report to the hospital when he is ordered to do so, he may be dragged from his cell and deposited in the hospital waiting room. Mentally ill prisoners who are acting out are almost always initially dealt with by goon squads rather than by qualified therapeutic personnel or even by orderlies under the direction of such personnel. (Bowker, 1980:102)

Some officers no doubt join goon squads or other violent cliques for reasons unrelated to alienation or a proclivity for violence. Conrad points out that goon squad officers may see this assignment "as a more interesting job than passing out towels at the shower baths or sitting in a tower" (personal communication). Still, whatever their motives for taking the job, the activities of these men are a dramatic reflection of "alienation or an absence of community" with prisoners (Toch, 1977a:123) as well as with their nonviolent fellow officers (Marquart, 1984).

Violence, moreover, is apt to promote or accentuate alienation because it precludes more constructive dealings with inmates and fellow officers. As a result, "the loyalty of such men," either from the outset or after involvement in violence, "is to their own kind, no matter how individually reprehensible they are" (Toch, 1977a: 123; see also Marquart, 1984). Given their attitudes and behavior, "the larger setting is seen as impersonal and threatening" (Toch, 1977a:123). Understandably, the violent officers "feel they have no real stake in the larger community, and they see themselves as having much to lose and little to gain by trying to relate to the world at large" (Toch, 1977a:123). These officers create for themselves a subculture of violence and may go to great lengths to exclude nonviolent officers from their ranks (Marquart, 1984; Kauffman, 1988). Perversely, violence may be a source of high morale and even, in the more explicitly punishment-oriented prisons, a route to professional advancement (see Marquart, 1984 & Kauffman, 1988).

Walpole prison during much of the 1970s provides a vivid illustration of a prison in which alienation ran high, and in which a clique of smug hacks—a goon squad—banded together to create a subculture of violence. As Kauffman's research makes clear, officers at Walpole were overwhelmed by the inmate violence that had swamped the prison and demoralized by their inability to control that violence. They felt fearful and inadequate. "The possibility of serious injury, even death, at the hands of inmates was very real to them" (Kauffman, 1988:123–24). At the root of the problem, in the eyes of the officers, was a weak prison administration. Officers felt abandoned and betrayed by both the warden of Walpole and the state's commissioner of corrections, whose policies sought to placate violent inmates rather than sanction them. At one point, as we have noted, untrained civilian monitors were actually placed throughout Walpole as a kind of United Nations peacekeeping force. The officers felt that the administration was monitoring them rather than the inmates and, in the process, humiliating them and compromising their already limited authority. As one officer told Kauffman (1988:35), "We're alone. We have only each other. The administration does not give a shit for us."

Officers at Walpole felt they had virtually no powers of formal punishment. This perception stemmed from court rulings, which did in fact limit their authority, but more centrally their perceived powerless was due to the deeply held belief that the administration would not back them up. As a result, Kauffman's research reveals that many if not most guards at Walpole bypassed the formal punishment system, resorting to petty abuses and illicit sanctions in an effort to harass and control unruly convicts.

> Guy wants to make a phone call? You can make him wait ten, twenty minutes. Guy wants some writing paper? Tell him you don't have any. Guy wants some matches? You can have a drawer full of matches, "I don't have any matches," you tell him. Just things like that. And they know. . . . And there's the ways that you can screw around with his property when he's not around. . . . One inmate . . . he gave another officer a hard time. . . . This particular inmate loves plants. . . . And he had about . . . two dozen plants. . . . He woke up the next morning and every one of them plants was dead. . . . Say a guy works with the woodworking stuff. Just put scratch in his furniture or something. He know how it got there. He knows why it was put there. But there's nothing he can do about it. . . . There's so many ways you can get these guys. (Kauffman, 1988:66)

Only a minority of officers at Walpole turned to violence, though that violence could be quite ferocious. These officers were real "hard asses" in the lingo of Walpole, men "coldly indifferent to inmates and to the violence and sadism around them" (Kauffman, 1988:244). In the view of the nonviolent officers at Walpole, these officers were little more than bullies and thugs. "They are just like an inmate," said one fellow officer (Kauffman, 1988:153). "They're the type like Hogan's Heroes," said another, "kick heads and ask questions later" (Kauffman, 1988:139). As is generally the case when violence occurs in contravention of official policy, these officers operated primarily on the 3–11 shift, when administrative officials "and other 'outsiders' were gone and the institution was inhabited almost exclusively by inmates and officers" (Kauffman, 1988:139; see also Marquart, 1984 for a discussion of a similarly situated subculture of officer violence in a Texas prison). But since they had the tacit support of the shift supervisor, their violence appeared to be authorized and legitimate, and served as an example that was followed—or at least not opposed—by other officers. The result: the false impression of "majority support" for officer violence, at least on the evening shift (Kauffman, 1988:140).

For an alienated guard, goon squad member or not, violence can become a badge of honor earned in self-defense. Even flagrant overreactions may be excused. To shoot first and ask questions later makes sense in a battlefield. Prisons in the throes of violence become, like battlefields, totally, isolated and isolating worlds (see Kauffman, 1988:238–39). In Kauffman's words, soldiers

> go to war and they say, "Well, I killed this gook and I shot this commie." Officers went to prison and they spoke of maggots killing each other, of inmates bleeding and dying, not men. "What happens here to the inmates does not bother me now in the least. I have no compassion for the inmates as a group. . . . I used to pass out at the sight of blood. Now it doesn't bother me. It's inmate blood." (Kauffman, 1988:231)

For the officers at Walpole, the prison had become a separate moral realm, to which normal human sentiments and sympathies did not fully or readily apply (see Kauffman, 1988:212).[5] They struggled to see inmates not as fellow human beings in distress but as dehumanized creatures beyond the reach of care or compassion. Violence merely shed "inmate blood," over which little sleep was lost.

Numb to the plight of their charges, officers working prisons like Walpole might readily overreact with violence or underreact and, by inaction, leave vulnerable men unprotected. Such behaviors are reprehensible, but under warlike prison conditions, it is only natural that other officers stick by their beleaguered colleagues. At the very least, others maintain a discreet silence, because tomorrow they may be the "assholes" in need of protection and support. Perhaps they think they can do the job better and without recourse to violence, but who are they to judge those who must react quickly under pressure?

The conditions that create alienation and violence may well foster not only dehumanized views of inmates but also anxiety and self-doubt about one's failure to run a decent prison. All inmates some of the time will appear to guards to be palpably human; some inmates all of the time will command human compassion from officers. Dehumanization is a mechanism of self-defense, but like all defenses, it is an imperfect one. For most officers there will be, then, at least on occasion, a desperately felt desire to do something, any-thing, to stem the violence and secure order for the human beings under their authority. Certainly this proved true at Walpole prison:

> Many officers expressed frustration in the interviews over their inability to protect inmates in their charge, even a sense of guilt over deaths or serious injuries they had been unable to prevent. There were officers who felt a personal stake in ensuring the safety of at least some of the inmates. "I can think of some (inmates) up there that if they happen to get hurt or if they were being pushed around (or) something it would affect me greatly. I would do *almost anything* I could to stop it or make sure that didn't hap-pen again." (Kauffman, 1988:120; emphasis added)

Willingness to do *almost anything* can readily extend to include a willingness to tolerate others doing *virtually anything*, assuming that they, like yourself, oper-ate from a presumption of good will—in this case, the desire to secure an or-derly prison. And who can confidently question the motives of one's col-leagues—or better, in a prison war zone, one's comrades-in-arms? Unsure of the value of their own work, officers are hesitant to judge others; better not to judge, and to be immune from judgment in return.

The officers most likely to embrace violence—and to do so with little or no ambivalence—are the "smug hacks," officers who find satisfaction in the exercise of coercive power. Though they typically are a statistical minority of the guard force, they are (smugly) confident that they are the vanguard of the officer force. And they may have good reason for believing this. After all, there are prisons in which they *are* a kind of vanguard, at least for some officers, dur-ing periods of turmoil (see Marquart, 1984; Kauffman, 1988). Even officers who eschew violence will embrace a tough-guy or hard-ass demeanor to help them cope with the stresses of work in a violent prison.

> The facade most officers adopt at prisons like Walpole is that of the "Hard Ass", coldly indifferent to inmates and to the violence and sadism around them. "We all change a little bit when we come in the front door for roll call. You put on your cap and assume a different disguise for eight hours a day. . . . You got to kind of knuckle down and be the tough guy." They seek to maintain that "disguise" regardless of the circumstances they are in or the company they are keeping (Kauffman, 1988:244–45).

More commonly, the smug hacks will merely look like model officers because the style of control one is most likely to see exercised by peers is that associ-ated with the management of inmates in public places like mess halls, gymna-siums, and yards. In these contexts, whether a given prison is violent or calm, guards deal with prisoners en masse and hence are little more than anonymous figures of authority. A formal, distant, tough-minded discipline, sometimes spiced with profanity, bluster, and the implicit threat of violence, is in fact the norm in these contexts (Crouch & Marquart, 1980; Lombardo, 1981).[6] One is also apt to *hear about* a skewed sample of officer-inmate encounters. Those that feature violence, for instance, are the ones that will not only draw attention when they occur but will make up the lore, lovingly retold to novice officers and naive civilians, of The Embattled Guard Who Keeps Ferocious Convicts at Bay. Smug hacks may thus come to see themselves as superior officers because they are the men with the nerve to use violence when the chips are down.

The notion that authority means toughness and dominance—the strong coercing the weak—is intuitively appealing to many officers, who appear to confuse authoritarian with authoritative uses of their power. (The subject of authoritative correctional officer behavior is covered in the next chapter.) Thus it is that new officers are encouraged to control inmates not by the force of their personalities or the merits of their judgment (that is, by authoritative behavior), but by being aloof, cynical, and intimidating (by authoritarian behavior). That one should cow or deceive convicts to gain compliance—to "mess with their minds" and "keep them off balance" (Crouch & Marquart, 1980:88)—may seem quite natural to officers who have been schooled in the public version of guard authority.

Crouch and Marquart (1980) provide a number of revealing instances of this bogus notion of authority, drawn from their research on Texas prisons. One involved "acting crazy," which "means the guard responds to the inmate in ways quite unrelated to the inmate's question or problem; in this way the inmate is put off and becomes uncertain himself" (Crouch & Marquart, 1980:88). Alternatively, the officer is admonished to go out of his way to make the prisoner feel ashamed or vulnerable. One method involved

> confronting an unsuspecting inmate with feigned seriousness and asking about something which may make the inmate uncomfortable. For example . . . an officer asked an inmate if he was the one who *slumbered* in bed. The inmate paused, looked at the officer, his feet . . . then replied: "I don't know uh–I–maybe–uh–you mean do I sno'?" The officer asked about slumbering again and got a similar reply. The inmate admitted he did not know what slumber meant and by not knowing appeared inferior to all present and to himself since everyone but him clearly knew the term. (Crouch & Marquart, 1980:88–89)

"A more aggressive tactic," Crouch and Marquart (1980:89) continue,

> involves prolonged staring at selected inmates. After a time, the inmate will notice the stare and become increasingly nervous and uncertain. Although the staring is not necessarily prompted by official suspicion of any wrong doing, the inmate does not know this and thus worries about what he has done or what the guard really knows.

The logical outgrowth of the conception of authority underlying these control strategies is to coerce physically (in the extreme, to beat into submission) those who cannot be manipulated or conned into compliance by the officials. One reason is that authoritarian control strategies evoke defensiveness among inmates, and indeed move inmates to violence against their keepers (see Light, 1991:258). Inmate resistance, and particularly violent resistance, in turn sparks more repression on the part of authoritarian officers. Reporting on the behavior of a clique of authoritarian officers not unlike those operating at Walpole, Marquart (1984) provides a telling example of escalating strategies of coercion that moved from insulting "verbal assaults" on inmates to more physically abusive "tune-ups," and finally to overtly violent "ass-whippings" and "severe beatings." Inmates who mouthed off or fought back against officers were likely to be punished with the more extreme forms of retaliatory violence.

Primitive uses of authority do not normally reach the extremes observed by Marquart in Texas or Kauffman in Massachusetts. Even officers trapped in violent prisons—and these officers do feel trapped in such prisons (see, for example, Kauffman, 1988:240)—yearn for training and support for more constructive roles. As one Walpole officer told Kauffman (1988:229) plaintively, "If there was any other way open to us, we'd take it." Moreover, even in the absence of training, abusive control strategies are often relinquished as officers "mellow" with experience. They learn to control inmates through more constructive "presentations of self," based primarily on an image of competence in solving problems (Crouch & Marquart, 1980:91) and trustworthiness in personal relationships (Lombardo, 1981:63). Seasoned officers, for example, typically feel less constrained to issue a disciplinary report simply because the prisoner has broken a rule. These officers feel confident in overlooking minor infractions where discretion is the greater part of wisdom or valor (Poole & Regoli, 1980). They also feel competent to resolve conflicts informally, drawing upon their experience and their personal relationships with the men under their care (Lombardo, 1981:74–75). These changes in the officers' use of authority are subtle, however, and are not likely to be obvious in public encounters. The result is that most officers rate their colleagues as more custody-oriented and violence-prone than is actually the case (Klofas & Toch, 1982; Kauffman, 1988:248). In effect, then, the smug custodians personify the guard's public role and set the tone for officer behavior in the public areas of the prison, much as the convicts (who are, as Abbott makes clear, also quite smug) determine the public image of the prisoner and the social climate on the prison yard.

Many officers put on a tough facade to appease the smug hacks just as the inmates act tough to keep at a distance those whom they presume to be predatory convicts. This is particularly true in violent prisons, but it is true to some degree in all prisons. What emerges might be called parallel instances of pluralistic ignorance; substantial segments of both the guard and inmate populations are putting on a front to impress peers who are doing the very same thing for their benefit! The possibilities for confusion and conflict are many. Small wonder, for example, that many officers feel they are misunderstood and disrespected even by their colleagues (Poole & Regoli, 1981) and that "interactions with fellow officers heighten stress" (Cullen et al., 1985:518). Problems are compounded, moreover, because the real hacks and cons of the prison world often gravitate toward one another with violent and sometimes tragic results, since they compete for the same space, often with the same methods. These encounters are relatively uncommon, but they are the stuff of which stereotypes of all officers and inmates are made. It is here that one finds the battles

that comprise the prison war, and they are of the making of a small and essentially self-selected sample of officers and inmates.

Organizational Sources of Alienation and Violence

The psychology of warfare in prison is reinforced by official regulations pro-
hibiting staff from developing relationships with inmates. Guards in New York
State prisons, for example, are expressly forbidden to

> engage in any conversation, communication, dealing, transaction, associa-
> tion, or relationships with any inmate or former inmate or any visitor,
> friends or relative of any inmate or former inmate in any manner or form
> which is not necessary or proper for the discharge of the employee's du-
> ties. (cited in Toch, 1977a:67)

These strictures may not be literally enforced, but they "translate into subcultural norms among guards that are counterparts to the 'never talk to a screw'
rule of inmates" (Toch, 1977a:67). These norms are espoused by the smug hacks
and honored, at least in public encounters, by other officers. This means that officers and inmates meet in public places like the yard as role players rather than
as individuals. Hostility is common, and hard to address and resolve since no
one admits to sentiments that do not fit their respective tough-guy roles.

Yet if officers and inmates do not talk openly in their public encounters,
they never discover a common ground for order in the prison community. At
best they collude with one another for mutual benefit, with manipulation, deceit, and the threat or use of force as the only means to resolve conflicts of interest. One such collusive relationship involves officers and other officials using
"snitches" or "rats" as sources of information about the inmate population. Informants are variously threatened and rewarded to secure their cooperation,
and the inmate troublemakers they betray to the staff are punished (see Stojkovic, 1986).

Rats are thought to be an important source of information for the staff, and
information in the prison is a key source of power. As one ranking officer at
Lompoc told Fleischer (1989:194), "If it weren't for the snitches and the snitches
who snitch on snitches, the prison wouldn't be able to run." The supposed
prevalence of rats in prison is also a source of humor in some prison circles.
Washington, a prisoner and a writer, tells an apocryphal tale on this subject:

> The last time we tried a hunger strike the warden stormed into the Mess
> Hall and ordered us to eat. When no one made a move to break our soli-
> darity by eating, the warden dragged a large chalkboard into the middle of
> the Mess Hall.
>
> "This is your last chance," the warden shouted as he held up a piece of
> chalk for all to see, then prepared to write. "If you men don't start eating
> right now," the warden screamed, "I'm going to write the names of every
> informer, snitch and rat in the prison."
>
> Before the chalk touched the board nearly every plate was clean.
> (Washington, 1981:21)

Yet there is reason to doubt the power and prevalence of prisoners who inform on their peers. In real life, as opposed to fiction or myth, informants often are marginal members of the prison community, so the value of any information they might provide is probably quite limited. And given the source, if you will, one must question the veracity of some informants, whose motives are not above suspicion. Moreover, many so-called rats are not informants at all. They are men who, by virtue of limited coping competence, have been stigmatized by their peers (see Johnson, 1961). The term "rat" thus is often an epithet, not a description of informing behavior. The fact that this degrading and often misleading label is bandied about so casually in prison is one measure of the failure of community within the prison's walls.

The quintessential collusive relationship, often called "corrupt favoritism" in the prison literature (see Sykes, 1966), is the antithesis of ratting. Corrupt favoritism pits the prisoner elite against their fellow inmates. It works like this: If the elite "keeps the place quiet" they receive special privileges, including immunity from sanction for most rule infractions, and they are generally free to use whatever methods they choose to preserve the status quo. They protect the good order of the prison because it is in their best interests to do so. Social control becomes an exercise in coercion and violence orchestrated in large measure by the prisoners themselves. The guards' authority is debased more by default than by overt action.

Collusive relationships, particularly of the type involving the prisoner elite, have been common historically. In the Big House they involved high-status prisoners, "right guys" who controlled other inmates partly by example and partly by threat (Sykes, 1966; Irwin, 1980:22–24). In some contemporary prisons, gangs and other groups of convicts sometimes perform this function, and the impression is that they do so by regular recourse to violence (Jacobs, 1977; Irwin, 1980).

Recently, Stojkovic has examined patterns of corrupt favoritism in a midwestern prison, highlighting the informal relationships officers develop (for example, with older, more reliable inmates) to aid them in carrying out daily tasks (such as counts) and generally to assist them in maintaining order (by discouraging younger inmates from making trouble, for example). These relations have a functional side to them in that officers, and perhaps some inmates, have less trouble to worry about. Some aspects of the social order, in other words, may be improved as a function of these arrangements. But Stojkovic's thoughtful work also identifies a tendency of these officers, perhaps *because* their authority is corrupted by these relationships, to shrink back from enforcing rules in dangerous situations—indeed in precisely those situations one would suppose officers are hired to police. Thus the officers point out that situations involving sex or drugs are quite dangerous, to inmates as well as to officers themselves. As one officer told Stojkovic (1990:225–26), speaking about the reluctance to intervene to stop illicit sex or to break up a drug deal, "If I got in the middle of that shit, I would be crazy because I will either get seriously hurt or killed. It would be plain stupid." As a general matter, officers considered themselves wise enough to expressly avoid inmate transactions involving sex or drugs. Though the officers claimed to intervene when weaker inmates were victims of abuse, the claims rang hollow. If one is busy avoiding these situations, how can one draw fine lines distinguishing coercive and noncoercive encounters in an environment in which those distinctions are subtle at best? How can inmates feel secure in such an environment?

In southern prisons, collusive relationships were until quite recently a formal part of the organizational chain of command. Trusted prisoners acted as a kind of deputized force, like an inmate goon squad, with a remarkably free hand in the use of violence. The building tenders of the Texas system are an instructive case in point. Called "BTs," these men operated as a shadow police force in Texas prisons until late 1981, when, over the objections of prison officials, they were abolished by court order. (The abolition of the BTs is thought to have contributed significantly to the decline of order recently noted in some Texas prisons. See Chapter Five.) These men were, as a rule, older recidivists doing big time. They were armed (though not with guns, as in some other southern prisons as recently as the early 1970s), and immune from normal disciplinary procedures. Formally selected by ranking security officers, these prisoners were given apprenticeships before assuming the role of the BT. They were even assigned assistants ("runners") to do the errands and other scut work that was beneath the dignity of a full-fledged BT. They proved themselves by maintaining order and by protecting officers from inmate violence. Regular duties assigned to these quasi-officials called for the threat or use of violence. Thus, each BT

> learned the script for orienting new inmates in the tank. That is, he noted and developed his own version of: "mind your own business" and "keep the noise down," "I'll cut you slack the first time and maybe the second, but if you screw up again, we'll go down to the wash room and get your heart straight." (Marquart & Crouch, 1984:504)

Under riot conditions, the BTs became a volunteer militia at the disposal of the staff. The following narrative, which refers to a riot that took place in the fall of 1981, is a revealing account of their collusive and violence-suffused relationship with the staff.

> The riot began when inmates . . . started several fires and broke windows in the nearby gymnasium by throwing rocks and other debris. Within a relatively short period, officers and approximately 150 BTs and runners converged in the gymnasium. While the officers were armed with riot batons, the BTs had brought clubs and pipes and several wielded long wooden toilet brushes. One inmate even passed out blackjacks from a paper sack. When all the "troops" were assembled, the warden addressed the inmates: "Anyone who don't want to kick ass can just go on back to his house (cell)." The inmates cheered in support of the warden's declaration and waved their weapons in the air. The door to the gymnasium was then opened and officers and inmate elites (who identified themselves by wearing red bandannas) attacked the 200 or so rioters. . . . Most of the

rioting prisoners were injured in some way, many quite seriously. (Marquart & Crouch, 1984:502)

The BT system has been dismantled, though it is possible that some of these men continue to play violent roles in the informal accommodations linking staff and inmates in the Texas prisons.

The passing of the BT system produced, for a time, a less orderly prison regime. Official records revealed an increase in violent attacks of inmates against one another and against officers. As noted in Chapter Five, the general quality of life declined dramatically. Paradoxically, the average prisoner did not feel less secure in these troubled institutions. The explanation for this paradox is that inmates felt unsafe under the reign of hard-nosed hacks and lawless BTs, just as most inmates feel insecure under any corrupt prison regime. During the transition from an essentially corrupt system to a modern, trained guard force, inmates experienced Texas prisons as dangerous, to be sure, but no more dangerous than during earlier days—the difference was primarily that threat emanated from inmate gangs that had emerged to fill the power vacuum left by the BTs rather than from staff and their inmate henchmen. After a few years of turmoil, the new officer force gained legitimate control of Texas prisons. This they did by learning to wield authority, primarily in the form of cultivating such bureaucratic skills as effective incident report writing (incident reports can land a prisoner in segregation and may even add time to his sentence by removing "good time"), and effective and restrained uses of force rather than violence. In today's Texas prisons, Crouch and Marquart (1989:216) conclude, most prisoners feel "much safer" than ever before.

CUSTODIAL VIOLENCE IN PERSPECTIVE

Officers must sometimes use force to defend themselves or protect others from harm. The proper response features restraint, on the order of the tit-for-tat strategy enunciated in Chapter Four as a feature of mature coping. At Lompoc, a federal prison, the notion of "equal force for equal force" is explicitly endorsed by the officers (Fleischer, 1989:218). The sole object of force is to gain control over the prisoner. Accordingly, Lompoc officers subscribe to the proposition that "once a convict is [under] control, don't use force" (Fleischer, 1989:218). Restrained force thus serves to constrain, not to punish or abuse.

The periodic need to use force in prison reminds us that officers must be tough enough, for want of a better word, to fight inmates when the need arises. As one seasoned officer observed, with a hint of irony,

> I think I would make a good convict. I have the qualities you need—toughness, not being afraid of violence. I can handle that. But there is one big difference that separates us. Convicts are predators. They hurt other people. They take advantage of other people. They really only care about themselves. They don't attack the strong, they prey off the weak and helpless in our society and they destroy lives (Earley, 1992:305–306)

A good officer, in contrast, is never a predator, "and that is what separates us from them. We don't cross that line" (Earley, 1992:306).

Regrettably, some officers are—or become—predators. With them, force is used for its own sake, because it is convenient or easy, and that amounts to violence pure and simple. Violence in service of social control represents a failure of coping, a giving in to alienation. This violence occurs with some regularity in prison, but it is neither as common as suggested by guard stereotypes nor as inevitable as the smug hacks and convicts make it out to be. Guard violence, moreover, is avoidable. Officers can be provided with a range of nonviolent problem-solving skills so that they need not rule by intimidation and threat. As Toch has observed, "Men with more options" when faced with stress and conflict "feel more secure." As a result,

> They are less apt to be trapped into responding to challenges, taunts, baiting, and "tests" of "manhood." They are less likely than some of our present-day staff . . . to play unseemly games with unworthy opponents at everyone else's expense. (Toch, 1977a:135)

Walpole officers provide a revealing, if negative, case study of Toch's proposition. New officer recruits at Walpole, generally sympathetic to the plight of inmates, were routinely posted to the cell blocks, which had been abandoned by seasoned officers in search of safe assignments. These officers were, in Kauffman's words, "left virtually at the mercy of inmates" during a period of almost anarchic violence (Kauffman, 1988:190). The officers were traumatized and, as a result, embittered. "Whatever sympathetic attitudes an officer had held toward inmates on entering the institution were quickly, and permanently, extinguished" (Kauffman, 1988:194). For many of these officers, Toch's "unseemly games with unworthy opponents" became the only games in town.

Yet things could have been different for the Walpole officers, given adequate training and deployment. And things are in fact different for most officers in most prisons. Most officers develop constructive, competent ways of carrying out their jobs. Some develop skills and confidence in human relations training, which is increasingly available as part of standard correctional training programs (Frank, 1966; Cohen, 1979). Many others cultivate these interpersonal skills on the job (Johnson, 1977 & 1981; Lombardo, 1981). Others develop expertise in matters of correctional policy and practice, which makes them on-line bureaucrats who can facilitate problem solving for inmates confronting increasingly bureaucratic correctional systems (see Lombardo, 1989).

Most officers, whatever the source of their competence, are not impelled to use violence to carry out their jobs, either directly or through collusive relationships. They do not aspire to a berth in the trenches occupied by some of their colleagues. Like most inmates, most guards would rather sit out the prison war. They make an effort to meet alienation head on and to make their job worthy of the time and attention it commands. In effect, these officers attempt to respond maturely to the challenge of alienation, rather than merely sulking or striking out in frustration. These officers, the real correctional officers in our prisons, are the subject of the next chapter.

NOTES

1. Boot camps may be a notable exception to this observation, but boot camps are by no means typical prisons.

2. It is commonly thought that people who live in prison towns and who take prison jobs have already been socialized to their roles—and usually to a negative version of those roles—through their association with guards in their families and among their friends. This was not true for the Auburn officers Lombardo studied. "Many officers whose fathers were guards reported that their fathers almost never talked to them about their work, at least until the sons became officers. Then, as one officer put it, 'That's all we did talk about'" (Lombardo, 1981:23).

3. Cheek and Miller (1983:116) confirm that "correction officers experience considerable stress on the job." (See also Cullen et al., 1985.) This stress is associated with "high rates of divorce and serious health problems . . . such as hypertension, ulcers, and heart disease . . . [which] are even higher than those of police officers previously identified as a highly stressed occupational group. Moreover, the corrections officers, like police, perceive many stress-related physical and emotional problems in their fellow workers" (Cheek & Miller, 1983:116). Though the problem has been less thoroughly studied, correctional managers are stressed as well. They feel overworked on their jobs, limited in their authority and control over situations, and unappreciated by those above and below them in the organization (American Correctional Association, 1984:15).

4. Research indicates that "Seven out of ten officers agree with statements such as 'we're damned if we do, and damned if we don't.' One out of four hold such alienated views strongly" (Toch & Grant, 1982:199).

5. For a more general discussion of the dynamics of dehumanization as it relates to violence, see Johnson, 1986.

6. Block officers or work assignment officers, who conduct many of their activities away from the gaze of peers and often deal with inmates on a one-to-one basis, may be understanding in their dealings with their men. "In the yard," by contrast, where one deals with prisoners in groups and under the view of one's colleagues or superiors, "displays of understanding are apt to be interpreted as weakness"—by inmate and officer alike (Lombardo, 1981:105–106).

REFERENCES

American Correctional Association. *Stress Management for Correctional Officers and Their Families*. 1984.

Anonymous. *An Illustrated History and Description of State Prison Life, By One Who Has Been There. Written by a Convict in a Convict's Cell*. Globe Publishing, 1871.

Bowker, L. *Prison Victimization*. New York: Elsevier, 1980.

Cheek, F. E., and M. D. S. Miller. "The experience of stress for correction officers: A double-bind theory of correctional stress." *Journal of Criminal Justice* 11 (1983):105–20.

Coffey, W. A. *Inside Out: Or, An Interior View of the New York State Prison; Together with Bibliographic Sketches of the Lives of Several of the Convicts*. New York: Printed for the author, 1823.

Cohen, J. "The correction academy." *Crime & Delinquency* 25 (2) 1979:177–99.

Crouch, B. M., and J. W. Marquart. "On becoming a prison guard." In B. M. Crouch (ed.). *The Keepers: Prison Guards and Contemporary Corrections*. Springfield, IL: Charles C. Thomas, 1980:63–105.

Crouch, B. M. and J. W. Marquart. *An Appeal to Justice*. Austin: University of Texas Press, 1989.

Cullen, F. T., B. G. Link, N. T. Wolfe and J. Frank. "The social dimensions of correctional officer stress." *Justice Quarterly* 2 (4) 1985:505–33.

Cullen, F. T., B. G. Link, J. B. Cullen and N. T. Wolfe. "How satisfying is prison work? A comparative occupational approach." *Journal of Offender Counseling, Services & Rehabilitation* 14 (2) 1989:89–108.

DiIulio, J. J. *No Escape: The Future of American Corrections*. New York: Basic Books, 1991.

Earley, P. *The Hot House: Life Inside Leavenworth*. New York: Bantam Books, 1992.

Fitzgerald, M. and J. Sim. *British Prisons*. Oxford: Blackwell, 1982.

Fleischer, M. S., *Warehousing Violence*. Beverly Hills, CA: Sage, 1989.

Fox, J. G. *Organizational and Racial Conflicts in Maximum-Security Prisons*. Lexington: Lexington Books, 1982.

Frank, B. "The emerging professionalism of the correctional officer." *Crime & Delinquency* 12 (3) 1966:272–76.

Haney, C., C. Banks and P. Zimbardo. "Interpersonal dynamics in a simulated prison." In R. R. Ross (ed.). *Prison Guard/Correctional Officer*. Canada: Butterworth, 1981:137–68. (Originally published in the *International Journal of Criminology and Penology,* 1973.)

Hawkins, G. *The Prison: Policy and Practice*. Chicago: University of Chicago Press, 1976.

Irwin, J. *Prisons in Turmoil*. Boston: Little, Brown, 1980.

Jacobs, J. *Stateville: The Penitentiary in Mass Society*. Chicago: University of Chicago Press, 1977.

Johnson, E. "Sociology of confinement: Assimilation and the prison 'rat.'" *Journal of Criminal Law, Criminology, and Police Science* 51 (1961):228–33.

Johnson, R. "Ameliorating prison stress: Some helping roles for custodial personnel." *International Journal of Criminology and Penology* 5 (3) 1977:263–73.

Johnson, R. "Informal helping networks in prison: The shape of grass-roots correctional intervention." In R. R. Ross (ed.). *Prison Guard/Correctional Officer*. Canada: Butterworth, 1981:105–25. (Originally published in *The Journal of Criminal Justice,* 1979.)

Johnson, R. "Institutions and the promotion of violence." In A. Campbell and J. J. Gibbs (eds). *Violent Transactions: the Limits of Personality*. Oxford: Basil Blackwell, 1986:181–205.

Kauffman, K. *Prison Officers and Their World*. Cambridge, MA: Harvard University Press, 1988.

Klofas, J., amd H. Toch. "The guard subculture myth." *Journal of Research in Crime and Delinquency* 19 (2) 1982:238–54.

Lawes, L. L. *Twenty Thousand Years in Sing Sing*. New York: Ray Long & Richard R. Smith, 1932.

League of Woman Voters of Wisconsin. "Changing of the guard: Citizen soldiers in Wisconsin correctional institutions." In R. R. Ross (ed.). *Prison Guard/Correctional Officer*. Canada: Butterworth, 1981:169–89. (Originally published by the League of Women Voters of Wisconsin, 1979.)

Light, S. C. "Assaults on prison officers: Interactional themes." *Justice Quarterly* 8 (2) 1991:243–61.

Lombardo, L. X. *Guards Imprisoned: Correctional Officers at Work*. New York: Elsevier, 1981.

Lombardo, L. X. *Guards Imprisoned: Correctional Officers at Work,* Second Edition. Cincinnati, OH: Anderson Publishing, 1989.

Marquart, J. W. "Prison guards and the use of physical coercion as a mechanism of prisoner control." Paper presented at Annual Meeting of the American Sociological Association, August 1984.

Marquart, J. W., and B. M. Crouch. "Coopting the kept: Using inmates for social control in a southern prison." *Justice Quarterly* 1 (4) 1984:491–509.

May, E. "A day on the job—in prison." In R. R. Ross (ed.). *Prison Guard/Correctional Officer.* Canada: Butterworth, 1981:9–18 (1981a). (Originally published in *Corrections Magazine,* 1976.)

May, E. "Prison guards in America–the inside story." In R. R. Ross (ed.). *Prison Guard/Correctional Officer.* Canada: Butterworth, 1981:19–40 (1981b). (Originally published in *Corrections Magazine,* 1976.)

Morris, T., and P. Morris. *Pentonville: A Sociological Study of an English Prison.* London: Routledge & Kegan Paul, 1963.

Nelson, V. F. *Prison Days and Nights.* Garden City, NY: Garden City Publishing, 1936.

Poole, E. D., and R. M. Regoli. "Role stress, custody orientation, and disciplinary actions: A study of prison guards." *Criminology* 18 (2) 1980:215–26.

Poole, E. D., and R. M. Regoli. "Alienation in prison: An examination of the work relations of prison guards." *Criminology* 19 (2) 1981:251–70.

Ross, R. R. "Introduction." In R. R. Ross (ed.). *Prison Guard/Correctional Officer.* Canada: Butterworth, 1981:1–5.

Ruiz vs. McKaskle, Civil Action No. H-78-987, 1984.

Schroeder, A. *Shaking It Rough.* New York: Doubleday, 1976.

Seeman, M. "On the meaning of alienation." *American Sociological Review* 24 (6) 1959:783–90.

Stojkovic, S. "An examination of compliance structures in a prison organization: A study of the types of correctional power." Paper presented at Annual Meeting of ACJS, March 1984.

Stojkovic, S. "Social bases of power and control mechanisms among correctional administrators in a prison organization." *Journal of Criminal Justice* 14 (2) 1986:157–66.

Stojkovic, S. "Accounts of prison work: Corrections officers' portrayals of their work worlds." *Perspectives on Social Problems* 2 (1990):211–30.

Sykes, G. *The Society of Captives.* New York: Atheneum, 1966.

Toch, H. *Living in Prison: The Ecology of Survival.* New York: Free Press, 1977.

Toch, H. *Police, Prisons, and the Problem of Violence.* (DHEW Publication No. (ADM) 76–364, 1977a.

Toch, H. "Is a 'correctional officer' by any other name, a 'screw'?" In R. R. Ross (ed.). *Prison Guard/Correctional Officer.* Canada: Butterworth, 1981:87–104. (Originally published in *Criminal Justice Review,* 1978.)

Toch, H., and J. D. Grant. *Reforming Human Services: Change Through Participation.* Beverly Hills, CA: Sage, 1982.

Toch, H., and J. Klofas. "Alienation and desire for job enrichment among correction officers." *Federal Probation* 46 (1982):35–44.

Wahler, C., and P. Gendreau. "Perceived characteristics of effective correctional officers by officers, supervisors, and inmates across three different types of institutions." *Canadian Journal of Criminology* (April 1990):265–77.

Washington, J. *A Bright Spot in the Yard: Notes and Stories from a Prison Journal.* Trumansburg, NY: Crossing Press, 1981.

Willet, T. C. "Report to the commissioner of the correctional service of Canada on a follow-up study of correctional officers and their partners in 1981." Ottowa, Ontario: Correctional Service of Canada, 1982.

8

❖

To Protect and to Serve

The Prison Officer's Private (Correctional) Agenda

Prison guards are, for the most part, an alienated and at times even embittered lot. This is not surprising since they are imprisoned by unflattering stereotypes and have limited autonomy in their job (see Lombardo, 1981). Yet alienation does not demand a negative or destructive response; officers need not wallow in bitterness and resentment. Many try to come to grips with their situation and find it possible to do something about it.

It is by helping prisoners—by promoting secure and, ideally, responsive prison regimes—that some officers rise above the limitations of their formal custodial role. They use their authority to help inmates cope with prison life; they provide human service rather than custodial repression. They do the best they can with the resources at their disposal to make the prison a better place in which to live and work. In contrast to their merely custodial colleagues, these officers cope maturely with their own problems as well as with the problems experienced by prisoners. They serve, by their helping activities and by example, as true correctional officers.

CORRECTIONAL AUTHORITY:
A MATTER OF HUMAN SERVICE

Officers who assume correctional roles are authority figures in the full sense of the term. It is often assumed that authority must have negative connotations; that it exists, particularly in settings like the prison, as a pretext for domination of others. Yet "an essential ingredient of authority," observes Sennett (1981:17), is possessed by someone "who has strength and uses it to guide others through disciplining them, changing how they act by reference to a higher standard." Guidance, in turn, requires nurturance, a fact we too often deny or distort in our prisons (Toch, 1975 & 1977) and other social institutions (Sennett, 1981). Punishment administered by authorities, then, must serve a constructive end and be administered by people who care. Punishment can be justified as a proper expression of authority only when it "can be shown to be a good for the wrongdoer," that is to say, when it is "an attempt, by someone who cares, to improve a wayward person" (Hampton, 1984:238).

It is among the ranks of the line officer that we are most likely to find authorities who care enough to work, day in and day out, for the correction of prisoners. And line officers have much to contribute to the well-being of inmates and the correctional mission of the prison. These officers find that to be of real service, however, they must emphasize the constructive side of their jobs or at least deemphasize the negative, alienating aspects of their work. It is telling that the similarities of situations that make some officers—the hacks—hostile to inmates, draw others—the correctional officers—together with inmates in a shared way of life. For correctional officers, being "uniformed prisoners" is an insult that is made into an asset; at least they are, by virtue of their hybrid status in this otherwise rigid caste system, very much a part of life and adjustment in the prison community.[1]

Many officers see correctional work as an intrinsically worthwhile endeavor (see Jurik, 1985). They hunger for opportunities to improve the quality of life in the prison community and grasp them when they can. Like most of us, they want to be people who matter. In the prison, the skills that matter are human relations and human services skills. These are the skills that can be used to develop relationships and hence to reduce tension, defuse crises, and conduct daily business in a civilized (and potentially civilizing) manner. This point is often obscured by the macho-worship of the smug hack, but is nevertheless reaffirmed daily in the successful nonviolent interventions on the part of some officers. As one prison officer observed,

> I am almost ashamed to say it in public, but the key to being a good correctional officer is having a caring attitude. Now that sounds to most staff here as being weak and not very macho. . . . It sounds like you are giving in to the inmates—or at least, that is how the staff interprets it, anyway—but it is not the same at all. (Earley, 1992:269)

To be a professional, this man maintained, means "letting your conscience be your guide," and caring enough about inmates and about yourself to do the job in a responsive way. Violence has no place in such a role, and force is used only as a last resort.

These observations resonate especially well among female officers, who began working in men's prisons in the early 1970s. One of San Quentin's female officers assures us, for example, that the presence of women in the guard force produces "a calmer setting" (Owen, 1985:158). The presence of women in the prison trenches, she continues, also

> forces male officers not to act as "big, bad and tough" because here they
> have this little 5'2" 115 lb. woman standing beside them, putting a guy
> that is 6'4", 230 lbs. in cuffs . . . saying, "Come on now, act right," and not
> having any problem doing it. Whereas he might have to go in there with 2
> or 3 other guys and tackle him down to cuff him. It also forces them to
> recognize that they can't go home and talk about how bad and mean they
> are and what a tough day they have had because some little chickie can do
> the same thing that he is doing. (Owen, 1985:158)

This officer's observations are borne out by research. Female guards in men's prisons are likely to take a human relations view of the correctional officer job. Though they do not necessarily have a more positive view of inmates and in fact approach the correctional role in a diversity of ways (Jurik, 1986; Zimmer, 1986), female officers tend to exert a "softening" influence on the prison environments in which they work, making them more livable and less violent (Kissell & Katsampes, 1980; Owen, 1985). (They are also likely to be ostracized by their more custodial male peers. See Crouch, 1985; Jurik, 1986; and Zimmer, 1986).[2] Though female officers constitute only a fraction of the overall guard force in most men's prisons, their numbers are growing. This fact augurs well for life and adjustment in prisons of the future.

To be sure, human relations are not the exclusive province of women. Long before women worked as guards in men's prisons, Glaser (1969:84–85) could state with confidence, "There is ample evidence that control can be achieved by staff without a hostile or superior attitude, and that positive leadership and influence is difficult to achieve without at least a minimum of friendliness and respect." Indeed, as Glaser (1969:87) made clear, officers who are fair and friendly—who relate to inmates as fellow human beings—are liked best and obeyed most readily. More recently, Stojkovic (1984:13 & 19–20) has noted that, in the eyes of the officers themselves, "consistency, fairness, and flexibility in the enforcement of rules were what made a good officer," and that "effective officers are able to develop a sense of respect with inmates by being fair and consistent."

Male or female officers who cultivate personal relationships with inmates are a critical human resource in conflict-ridden prison environments. "It is not merely the officer's physical presence as an authority figure which serves to check inmates in their conflicts with one another," writes Lombardo (1981:53),

> but the relationships that develop between an officer and an inmate. A
> positive relationship allows the inmate to approach the officer when a

problem is developing, allowing the officer time to defuse it. Thus one finds a connection between the officer's abilities to maintain order and personal relationships between officers and inmates.

The link between relationships and control even holds during riot situations. At these critical junctures, an officer's familiarity with a prisoner offers the prospect of negotiating life-and-death conflicts. Thus Guenther and Guenther (1980:172) report that

> officers often emphasized their interest in establishing and maintaining working relationships with inmates . . . for they felt that their ultimate control over inmates during crises was a close function of these associations. The smallest personal knowledge, such as an inmate's name or the job he has in the institution, can be used by an officer to initiate a verbal exchange suggesting trust and a fair settlement.

Further, research reveals that human service officers have more authority and are more satisfied with their jobs. As Hepburn has observed, "the level of institutional authority appears to be greatest among those guards who also have a less punitive and less custodial orientation, who maintain a lower degree of social distance from inmates, and who express a higher level of job satisfaction" (1984:584). These important findings have been replicated and extended by Hepburn in a recent study of custodial and correctional officers in Arizona. The Arizona correctional system "is unique in having a two-track career for correctional officers: one in correctional custody and one in correctional counselling and treatment" (Hepburn & Knepper, 1993:320). Comparing these groups, Hepburn and Knepper state: "We find that job satisfaction is significantly greater among Arizona's more human services-oriented correctional program officers than among the traditional, custody-oriented correctional security officers" (1993:331). Moreover, this seminal study reveals that human service officers experience less role strain than custody officers, even though their job is objectively more complex and therefore more subject to role conflict than is that of their custodial colleagues. Finally, this research supports the key observation that human service officers have greater authority than custodial officers, who tend to see their credibility as a function of the uniforms they wear rather than the services they provide. As a general matter, it would appear that human service officers have more autonomy, and hence are able to adapt more flexibly to the technical and interpersonal demands of the job than is the case with custodial officers. It is fair to say that correctional authority—the ability to protect and to serve, and, ultimately, to influence—rests in those officers who develop personal relationships rather than with those who play aloof custodial roles.

The personal relationships at the heart of correctional authority are valuable not only because they preserve a civil order behind bars and suggest that problems can be solved in a civilized manner, but also because they demonstrate respect for the people under one's authority. As one former inmate observed, "the best help that I was offered came in the form that always included letting you know that you were a regular human being" (Gates, 1991:76). Respect for one's basic humanity matters enormously to inmates. By and large, prisoners "have had a long history of failure, rejection, and ego deflation"; as a result, they "are especially appreciative of attention, encouragement, and compliments from staff" (Glaser, 1969:92). When the prison operates as a correctional institution, perhaps the key lesson it teaches prisoners is that they are valuable human beings in their own right, even if they have offended against the society and deserve punishment (Glaser, 1969:84). Hence it is that

> The common element in the testimonials [of reformed prisoners] is the
> self-respect that was given to the inmates by the officers whom these men
> credited as having been rehabilitative influences. This did not mean that
> the officers were unusually lenient, lax or permissive; it meant only that
> they treated the men with a personal interest and without pretension or
> condescension. The officers were friendly in a way that inspired confi-
> dence and respect rather than contempt; they were frank, fair and consid-
> erate. (Glaser, 1969:92–93)

The rehabilitated inmates reciprocated, treating officers with respect and consideration. In these relationships we see a bridge, constructed of human ties, that links prisoners to the larger society.

> These [inmates], previously treated as though members of an untouchable
> caste, were accepted in prison in long periods of daily contact, by persons
> who were secure and content in respected status groups. Gradually, this
> contact seems to have given the offenders the ability to identify with per-
> sons in socially accepted, conventional groups, and this new self-image
> replaced that image which caused them to think of themselves as a distinct
> criminal group rejected by the noncriminal world. (Glaser, 1969:94)

These relationships, and the constructive lives they sometimes help set in motion, are vivid reminders that "conscience rests not on fear but on the more solid emotional foundation of loyalty and gratitude" (Lasch, 1984:203).

Human service and personal relationships would not seem to be the stock in trade of the "typical" guard, but officers can be quite voluble in expressing their preference for these correctional activities. Reporting on a nationwide survey of prison guards conducted for *Corrections Magazine* in the mid-1970s, a turbulent period in American prisons, May observes,

> Many resent what they believe is their too limited role as jailors of Amer-
> ica's convicts as well as the lack of encouragement from administration to
> work more actively with inmates.... You've got to show that he (the offi-
> cer) is needed," one of them says. "You've got to show that we're doing
> something that's worthwhile ... but how in the world can you feel worth-
> while if you're just opening and closing doors?"
>
> Everywhere *Corrections Magazine* interviewed officers, they defined the
> "worthwhile" aspects of their jobs in highly personal anecdotes of inmates
> they believe they may have helped: Unscrambling administrative snarls for

an inmate who may not have received what was due him . . . the isolated success stories of those who "made it on the street," job assignments they urged for a man who later used the newly learned skill "on the outside." (May, 1981:37–38)

In these kinds of observations (which recur in many other studies of guards at work), we see alienation countered by a desire for job enrichment. The fact that officers want to develop constructive relationships with inmates, to be agents of human service rather than custodial repression, belies guard stereotypes. Even more enlightening is the distribution of this concern. Research has revealed that "officers are disaffected" but, at the same time, "desire for job enrichment tends to be high," especially among such unlikely groups as older, rural guards (Toch & Grant, 1982:199–200). We learn that a "'human service' orientation increases steadily with seniority": fully 75 percent of the officers with twenty or more years of experience think guards should be involved in providing rehabilitative program services, and 85 percent of this veteran group feels that "it's important . . . to have compassion" for prisoners (Toch & Grant, 1982:202). (Jurik's research also tells us that "older officers appear to have more optimistic attitudes towards inmates." See Jurik, 1985:534.) Of equal significance, fully two of every three of the younger, urban, less experienced, and more alienated guards still acknowledge the importance of compassion in one's dealings with inmates (Toch & Grant, 1982:202). Those officers who emphasize human service and compassion, moreover, tend to cope better with the stresses of correctional work and to be more satisfied with their jobs (Cullen et al., 1985). It would seem that smug hacks—and those who think of them as typical guards—have precious little to be smug about. As Cullen and his associates have noted, this body of research leads to the ironic conclusion

> that the very people used by criminologists to arrive at the image of the brutalized, unhappy prison guard—white, relatively uneducated officers—may be the most satisfied segment of the custodial force, while "newcomers" to the correctional arena such as black and college educated guards may be the least satisfied. (1989:105)

Job enrichment calls for expanded definitions of the guard's job, changing it from a custodial to a human service occupation. This highlights the healthy interdependence of officer and inmate and points to constructive alternatives to the collusive relationships reviewed in Chapter Seven. Just as prisoners want to live in prison in ways that meet their basic needs and hold out the prospect of meaningful activity, guards want to work in prison in ways that satisfy their basic needs and give them a meaningful role to play. "Like inmates," Lombardo (1981:46) tells us,

> officers prefer job assignments that "match" their needs for special kinds of social environments. There is also a discernible tendency for officers who have special motivational concerns to prefer specific job locations. Block jobs, for example, are [more] likely to be associated with activity or the desire to help inmates than with any other need.

Though the link between officer needs and work assignment preferences has not been studied in any detail, this would seem to be a fruitful direction for future research.

We know more about the relationship of officer needs and the guard role, independent of any particular work assignment. The main needs expressed by officers are for activity, autonomy, and a chance to contribute "to the well-being of the inmates or to the overall running of the institution" (Lombardo, 1981:46; see also Lasky & Gordon, 1986). Thus, officers usually want time to pass in fast and familiar ways, with opportunities to be useful. More often than not, they satisfy these needs by relinquishing a custodial pose and becoming "human service workers dealing with the inmates' personal and institutional adjustment, assisting inmates to cope with the pains of imprisonment" (Lombardo, 1981:55). Their search is not just for a comfortable and safe routine—the proverbial rut one assumes guards fall into—but for a constructive work niche. The business of officers who are oriented toward human service is corrections, not custody. They traffic not in debased authority but in human concern, and their helping activities range "from offering advice about routine difficulties in negotiating the prison bureaucracy to nursing the private traumas prison can breed" (Johnson & Price, 1981:352).

THE CORRECTIONAL OFFICER AT WORK

Human service activities undertaken by concerned guards on behalf of prisoners include: (1) providing goods and services; (2) acting as referral agents or advocates; and (3) helping with institutional adjustment problems. An officer may specialize in any one of these activities, or engage in each of them as the situation requires (Lombardo, 1988).

Goods and Services

When prison guards provide such mundane goods and services as food, clothing, shelter, and medication, they are making certain that the prisoners' basic needs are met. Of course, even the most disgruntled hacks are required to provide necessities as a matter of course. However, by providing these goods and services in a regular and responsive manner, officers satisfy a legitimate concern of many prisoners for stability or predictability in their dealings with the prison system (Lombardo, 1981).

The regular and responsive delivery of goods and services in turn prevents the accumulation of tension among inmates as a consequence of arbitrary and even degrading deprivations. It is nothing less than a gratuitous insult to be forced to go without such basic supplies as soap or toilet paper or to have simple requests for help ignored. Some officers are quick to prevent or redress such problems. They have empathy for the man in the cell and appreciate the significance of the problem-solving role they can play.

I often put myself in the inmate's position. If I was locked up and the door was locked up and my only contact with authorities would be the officer walking by, it would be frustrating if I couldn't get him to listen to the problems I have. There is nothing worse than being in need of something and not being able to supply it yourself and having the man who can supply it ignore you: This almost makes me explode inside. (Jacobs & Retsky, 1981:68)

Officers who conscientiously deliver basic goods and services are taking care of the routine business of the institution. The result is a minimally habitable environment. They provide other essential services through the enforcement of rules. In the custodial image of prison guards, rule enforcement almost by definition is an exercise in oppression. Yet a prison without rules, or with rules that are enforced in unpredictable ways, is a chaotic, arbitrary, and dangerous place to live.

Even the most service-oriented officer cannot entirely avoid the ambiguity that surrounds prison rules (see Chapter Seven). However, these officers minimize such difficulties by enforcing rules with an eye to improving the quality of life in prison. They seek, often at the request of inmates, to maintain a comparatively clean, quiet, and orderly prison environment, approximating normal domestic life in the cell blocks and normal civil life in the shops and recreation areas (Lombardo, 1981; Johnson & Price, 1981). These officers also enforce rules in an effort to promote a sense of basic fairness or justice, to communicate that conflicts are resolved and resources distributed in an equitable manner.[3] Perhaps the most valuable human service function of rule enforcement is security. A New York State prison officer who saw security as a human service rather than a custodial commodity put the matter this way:

Security doesn't mean keep them from going over the wall. It means you try to make the guy feel secure, that he's not going to get killed or hurt. You make it so an inmate can sit next to another inmate in the mess hall or auditorium and feel comfortable. So he doesn't have to worry about something happening. (Lombardo, 1988:293)

Significantly, officers who define their role as a matter of making prisoners "feel secure" hold views of inmates that parallel those of officers who define their role as more explicitly oriented toward human service—who want more directly to help prisoners adjust (Jurik, 1985). By contrast, officers who see correctional work in extrinsic ways, as a means to a paycheck rather than a job with value in itself, hold considerably more negative views of inmates (Jurik, 1985). From the ranks of the extrinsically motivated officers may be recruited the disgruntled hacks discussed in Chapter Seven.

Various goods and services are essential to a civilized prison existence. Officers who provide them, whether they see their work primarily as a matter of security or service, show that they care—for themselves, as self-respecting professionals, and for the inmates who depend on them to maintain a decent standard of life behind bars. In the words a prison officer,

> If an inmate hasn't had a change of underwear in two weeks, you should care enough to get him a change of underwear. If he hasn't had a shower in a week, you should care enough to get him a shower. You shouldn't have to wait for someone to tell you to do that or have some regulation tell you. (Earley, 1992:269)

Service provision can, and perhaps should, assume a taken-for-granted connotation to the officer. As one officer observed, a bit crudely,

> People make this job harder than it is. If an inmate has something coming—his mail, a blanket, whatever—you give it to him. If he don't, you tell him. And most importantly, if an inmate ain't going over the fence or thumping somebody, then you just leave him the fuck alone. (Earley, 1992:107)

Officers maintain that what an inmate has coming to him is a blend of regulations tempered by common sense and human decency (see Earley, 1992; Lombardo, 1981 & 1989; and Glaser, 1969). No inmate has a right to privacy in prison, for example, either in law or prison policy. Nevertheless, the notion that a prisoner who behaves well should be treated well—which means, in many instances, granted a degree of privacy—is a central tenet of prison wisdom. Officers who commit themselves to the timely delivery of basic goods and services, including such subjective goods as privacy, work on a daily basis to make prisons more responsive living environments. They warrant and often receive the respect and support of the prisoners under their care.

Referrals and Advocacy

Many prison guards act as referral agents and advocates for prisoners. Prisons are cumbersome bureaucracies, and inmates are largely powerless to negotiate directly with the institution on their own behalf. Many inmates therefore turn to the guard for help when the formal bureaucracy fails them. Short of filing legal suits over the daily minutiae of prison life—though a few prisoners do this; suits have been filed over the type of peanut butter available in the prison mess hall—there is nothing else they can do at this juncture. In this context "the officer [can] aid the inmate in a variety of ways, such as by setting up appointments with counsellors or by calling the correspondence office or commissary to check on the status of an inmate account" (Lombardo, 1988:290). Yet assistance of this sort is technically beyond the scope of the officer's formal duties. The officer who undertakes these helping activities may be met with resistance and even abuse from guards and other prison personnel who hew more closely to the custodial line.

Consider the following case. The officer wants to help one man get his prescribed medication, another his proper assignment. Each service is ostensibly simple to perform. Yet to get them done, the officer must battle not only an unresponsive bureaucracy but also fellow guards as well.

> There's times when a guy's been out of pills, I don't have to do it, I could say piss on you, wait till fill-up day and get them yourself or go over and

see the doctor and get them. [But instead] I'll make the trip over and I'll go get them. One or two pills, whatever, to cover the guy for the day. Because I've done it myself, I'm counting out pills or something and I'll drop them on the floor. I could shove it back in the bottle, but I destroy it, and I have to enter it in the book destroyed. There's times when the pharmacy will send over pills that says 28 in a bottle, there's 27, right off the bat I'm one short. So in the course of the week I have to go over and get that extra pill so that we're not short. Especially so that the night shift has got a pill to give the guy. Mainly this man with the sleeping problem and our epileptics. It's mandatory that they have the medication. . . . You go over there to get some pills, they say, "what the fuck you doing over here." "I'm over to check this out." "That's what you got a hospital runner for." "Fuck it, I want to take care of it.". . . Four days ago, an epileptic, way down on the end, had fits, he hadn't been moved yet. So he come up, and he's givin' me static. This is the guy I was telling you, he's a Jew and he called me a Nazi and all this kind of shit. So I said "all right, I'll check into it." So I went over to the hospital, I was over there 2 hours, running this fucking thing down. Come to find out, the only thing that was holding it up was his job classification. You can't put a man on invalid company unless he's a grade four, no job. He can't work, he's medically unfit to work. That was all that was wrong, because they had him marked as a grade one. Grade one, you're going to work. And that was all that was holding it up, and they had to have a written order on it. That the man was changed from one to four; it took me 2 hours to get it. And I got static over that. So the guy will be moving today, everything's kosher. (Toch, 1981:94–95)

The point here is not the specific goods or services the officer secures. Other examples could have been examined focusing, for example, on interpersonal problems and the need to mobilize the professional treatment staff (see Toch, 1981). What is important in these situations is that the officer acts as an intermediary and advocate—and is sometimes an extraordinarily dedicated and persistent one at that—between the prisoner and some segment of the prison bureaucracy.

Help of this kind is mundane but important. By observing that some guards go out of their way to ensure that legitimate needs are met, inmates find that they are not alone and powerless. They have allies among the correctional officers who support them and give them a degree of control over their prison lives.

Officers and Inmate Adjustment

Officers commonly attempt to play a direct role in solving inmate problems. And there are, of course, many problems experienced by inmates. It is fair to say that virtually all prisoners, in varying degrees, feel (1) powerless, and therefore frustrated and resentful, (2) vulnerable, and therefore anxious and afraid, and (3) alone, and therefore lonely and depressed. For most inmates, these are difficult but manageable problems. For some, these concerns spark personal crises (Toch, 1975). Crises become a way of life for a few, whom we think of as psychiatric casualties (Toch, 1982). For many prisoners, however, the officer is able to recognize problems and crises as they unfold and to play a role in their management.

Consider a scenario encountered by officers. A resentful inmate refuses to leave his cell and threatens harm to anyone who tries to make him. His potential for violence invites attention from the smug hack, who deals out such repressive measures as restraint and segregation, perhaps including the use of physical force. These measures will certainly get the man out of the cell, though the prisoner as well as a few officers may be hurt. Moreover, there are likely to be future problems with this prisoner because custodial measures only accentuate the feelings of powerlessness and vulnerability that underlie his pugnacious stance. The prisoner may also become defensive because he feels alone in the impersonal world of the prison—a shrinking world, as he sees it, of him against the hacks. Custodial measures will only aggravate this problem as well.[4]

In contrast, the officer who is oriented toward human service sees this same volatile situation as one that calls for interpersonal skills and collaborative action. He opts for problem solving rather than problem suppression. His aim is to build trust, and to use this as a means to explore nonviolent solutions to the problem.

> The sergeant called me in and said "go upstairs and move a man downstairs." So right away I assumed that the man was causing some problems because we had all these other officers with us. So we approached the cell, we had about 5 or 6 officers plus the sergeant. The inmate was a young Puerto Rican about 6'2", very, very angry, obviously scared to death. The sergeant says "come on, we'll take you downstairs." He said, "no man, I'm not going to come out, because as soon as I come out you're going to really kick my ass and I don't want anything to do with that." He says "I know I'm going to get hurt but I'm going to take some of you guys with me.". . . I asked if I could speak to him. The sergeant says "yeah, go ahead." So I walked in and said "hey, look, nobody wants to hurt you. I think I understand what your problem is." He says, "what's that?" I said "you're putting yourself under a lot of peer pressure up here. Here you've been spouting off to all the other inmates in the gallery how tough you are. Now you want to prove something. You know and I know that we can take you out of here if we have to, but we don't want to hurt you. And why don't you just come along with me and I'll take you downstairs and nothing's going to happen to you." So after a few moments of saying I was lying to him and everything I guess he really decided what the heck else did he have to lose? He says "you mean to tell me that you are going to take me out of here and nobody else is going to lay a hand on me?" I said "yeah, you got my word. You'll go down to my area and I'll keep you down there and see how you behave yourself." So he agrees to do so. When we walked out of the cell naturally he's waiting for somebody to jump on him and romp around on him a little bit, but to his surprise nobody laid a hand on him. (Toch, 1981:96)

Encounters such as this one produce a host of benefits. They go a long way to undo damage done by less constructive involvements with authority figures.

> He said "I was scared to death. After all, you come to prison, you hear all kinds of stories." He said, "I've had a couple of occasions where [guards have] kicked me around a little bit, I thought the same thing was going to happen to me." In fact he made a statement that surprised me the following day. He said, "you know what, I'm afraid of you." I said "why are you afraid of me?" He said "you're too cool." I said "well, did I lie to you?" He said "no, I thought about that." He says "but you're either tough as hell or you got to be crazy." I said "why?" He said "well, you walked in the cell, obviously I was mad enough to hurt somebody." I said "well, I figured if you're going to hurt somebody you're not going to hurt me too bad because I had enough help there to back me up." But I said "I couldn't see you getting hurt from being stupid, and hurting somebody else." So he thought that was pretty good reasoning and we daily built a pretty good relationship.
>
> Did he mention other things that had got him upset and made him act the way he was acting?
>
> Well, he said he was lied to.
>
> By whom?
>
> By other officers. I know another thing that upset him greatly too. I guess when he came in they took some personal property away from him he felt they shouldn't have taken. So I asked him what it was and I found that an officer made a mistake on two items and I got them back for him. So that sort of reassured him that everybody wasn't trying to be unjust to him. (Toch, 1981:97)

Encounters of this nature can also promote long-term personal relationships that in turn permit the officer to become a continuing source of advice and support for his formerly rebellious ward.

> His anger turned into making me more or less a father-image in his behalf. So on a daily basis I talked to this guy, any time he had a problem he'd come to me. . . . I talked to him several times in the yard. He said "what about this peer pressure thing, explain that to me." So I tried to sit down and tell him the term and just what it meant to him and everybody else and he said "gee, that's very interesting, I never looked at it that way." So then we got talking, and we'd sit down and talk about marriage and the problems he'd had with his children and that type of thing. We got along pretty good. (Toch, 1981:96)

Correctional officers have much to offer inmates with all sorts of problems, including those pursued by predatory peers. Officers can, for instance, make it clear that they are "paying special attention" to known aggressors and thereby deter at least some of them (Lockwood, 1980:134). They can also make it clear that they are available to assist potential victims. A prisoner at Attica who personally benefited from this sort of special assistance and surveillance described his experience in the following words:

> As I came through the Times Square, this officer must have realized that I was terribly green and terribly frightened, because he pulled me aside and talked to me. He said, "You look frightened, and if there's anything that I can do to help, or if you want to talk to me, or you have any problem, tell the officer down there to let you come up. If there's something I can help you with." So apparently, from what I understood later, he called the block and talked to the night officer. So therefore the officers were looking out for me. So they kept an eye on me for four or five days. . . . And then later the hall captain talked with me, because he was always a nice guy. And he seen that I was having a problem. He always managed to make sure that I was alone in my cell, because there they could put two guys in one cell. And unless they got into a desperate situation that they were really filled up, he always left me by myself. (Toch, 1977:168)

Helping fearful inmates is a risky business. Frightened men are billed as cowards, and an officer's assistance may inadvertently reinforce this stigmatizing image. Yet the alternative, which is to let them fight and "prove" themselves, is inappropriate and even irresponsible in some cases. On occasion the guard may have no choice but to step in to avert a catastrophe.

> He was a little guy who was afraid of everything and everybody and then all of a sudden in a day's time he started standing up, which he knew was foolish, but he started standing up to some of the roughest guys in the division. And it just wasn't him. And I was afraid that he was going to get hurt because these guys don't take that kind of stuff. It was a complete reversal.
>
> So it just stood out to you—there's a meek guy acting like a tiger.
>
> And plus it was all in a day's time. One day he was a meek guy and the next day he was on the move and he had just changed like that. . . . The kid was actually serious. He wasn't putting it on. It was actually a serious thing. He actually, if it came right down to it, would have taken these guys on. Regardless of . . . the consequences. This is what I feel anyway, and I knew he would get hurt. . . . So, you know, I had to step in and stop this. (Johnson, 1981a:120)

Where the officer can do nothing to help, the best advice he can offer may be that a man seek protective custody. This advice may be gratefully accepted by a frightened and confused prisoner. In the words of one such man,

> So that was the thing, when the officer came down here one night, I told him what was happening, because I was worried. They wouldn't leave me alone, and they wanted to borrow this and that. And I would give it to them, because I was scared and I didn't want anything to happen. So then this officer came down one night, and he talked to me, and he said, "You

know, you should go into protection. I know what's happening and I know that these guys have things that they do to the other inmates, it's happened. And you'll find yourself in real trouble." (Toch, 1977:169)

Loneliness may be the most pervasive and insidious form of prison stress (Toch, 1975; Johnson, 1981b). This problem is particularly acute for men who are abandoned by loved ones or who suffer a death in the family. In cases like this, officers may have to shepherd inmates through periods of enormous stress. Officers who work in cell blocks or in small work areas or shops are the most likely to observe and respond to these crises (Lombardo, 1981). The following account given by an industrial shop officer is a case in point.

> When his grandmother died, he wasn't able to go to the funeral. Now I knew that he couldn't go and he was quite sure that he couldn't, yet he wanted someone to check. So I got ahold of his counselor and we discussed it and I kept the inmate in the office when I did this, so that he would at least know that someone was trying to do something. Then when it was over and he discovered that he couldn't go, the man goes and broke down into tears. And he sat right there and he was crying. And of course the other inmates were going by the office and some of them, you know, had the tendency to snicker a little bit. And just in general conversation with the inmates, I made it plain to them that in my eyes it required some degree of a man to care that much about his family. And I made sure that this particular inmate was there when I said it to kind of reassure him that at least someone in authority didn't consider that crying and concern over a member of the family was childish, was babyish. It was the type of action that one would expect from a sensitive man . . .
>
> I had to keep him busy. I had to keep his mind occupied. But you can't drive a person like that. You have . . . to keep him busy enough to keep his problems off of his mind and at the same time try to communicate to him that . . . you haven't just disregarded him, that you care and you are interested in his problems and what is going on with his family, even though in most cases there is absolutely nothing that I can do about it. All I can do is give him some degree of understanding and try to help him if necessary, try to almost shield him. . . . To give him every hour that you can give him to where he can try to readjust himself with a minimum of pressure. (Johnson, 1981a, 119–20)

Loneliness in prison is not only a matter of missing family or mourning the death of loved ones. Nor is caring about prisoners restricted to situations of personal crisis. Loneliness also reflects the absence of caring relationships within the prison community. Prisoners feel abandoned, forgotten, consigned to serve "dead time." Yet many officers develop "peculiarly intimate" relationships with at least some prisoners, and in doing so they help these men to cope with their loneliness (Webb & Morris, 1980:159). They have the credentials needed to help prisoners with the many painful personal problems that emerge during their confinement.

When I first come to the division I had noticed that he was friendly toward the dudes that was on the floor, the tier boys. And he talked to them
with respect, like, you know, "how was your day today, did you do anything interesting?" It was different for a guard to ask inmates these questions. So when I got on the floor I started rapping to him about my main
interest, which was cars, and he just happens to be another car freak, and
we hit it off really good. And since then he's been a personal friend and
not a guard to me. . . . I talk to him about every problem. I go to him
before I'll come to a chaplain or to a sergeant or something.

   And he's usually pretty helpful?

   Very helpful. He's always got a suggestion. I mean it's not like "do this
and this and this." He'll give me a suggestion and tell me the alternative,
give me another suggestion and tell me another alternative . . .

   Do you ever talk to this guy about very personal things, like your wife
and your child, or what you think of the future, that type of stuff?

   Yeah, almost every night. We have a little chat session every night after
lock-in. He stops by my cell. "Hi, how you doing." And we start from
there, you know. "Did you get a letter from your wife today?" Because he
passes out the mail, he just asks as a joke type thing, you know. And I say
"yeah, I got one." "What'd she have to say?" And I tell him this and that,
and I won't hold nothing back. If she writes in there that she's having
problems with the landlord or something like this, I'll tell it to him, he'll
come up with either a suggestion or relate a story that happened to him
and his wife, that would possibly help me out of my situation.

   So this fellow really treats you as an equal?

   Right, he treats me as an individual, man, not as a group inmate. . . . [I]t
helps people, I don't know how, but when somebody's concerned about
you, you've got the natural instinct to give them something back, whether
it's affection or concern. You know, you've got to give them something
back. And when you've got a contact like this, when you're concerned
about somebody and he's concerned about you back, you've got a relationship going there that brings you above your environment. Brings you
to be what you want to be. If you want to be back out in the world, you
can put yourself to the point to remember when you were there. And
how good it's going to be when you get back out there, not how long it's
going to be. . . . (Toch, 1981:98–100)

The depth of relationships developed between some officers and inmates is
a vivid reminder that prison guards can expand their roles to include the functions of "lay counselors" (Thomas, 1975). Their helping efforts confirm the
observation that the "successful lay counselor is one who can both provide the
individual . . . with the experience of being understood and, at the same time,
serve as a model for him to imitate" (Thomas, 1975:36). The vast majority of
these officers are untrained for their avocation as lay counselors. Many "play it
by ear," fall back on "common sense," and sometimes do no more than "let a

guy blow off steam." The quality of the advice they give varies widely. In general, among untrained helpers "there is a tendency to give the action-oriented solution-type 'Ann Landers' response to almost any situation" (Thomas, 1975:39). This is probably true for many untrained correctional officers, who have been dubbed by Toch (1981:333), with tongue in cheek, as "Meek-but-Sturdy Proletarian Healers of the Disaffected." Still, though the exploration of self at the heart of the counseling process may be shortchanged by many correctional officers, they make an effort to be responsive to the needs of the prisoners. These officers are not "misguided helpers" concerned mostly, even if unconsciously, with helping themselves (see Abbey, Holland, & Wortman, 1980). They *do* listen. Inmates are given a chance to ventilate their concerns and to explore avenues of adjustment. By their example, these officers serve as both models of mature behavior and agents of personal change.

The skills of the lay counselor are useful in addressing a wide range of problems, including those of a delicate personal nature. These skills may even be applicable with prisoners who are (or are becoming) mentally ill. Mentally disturbed prisoners have been called the number one health problem behind bars and identified as a group that recidivates at an unusually high rate (Wiehn, 1988; Toch, 1982). They are, moreover, a growing problem in corrections, yet there is no indication that mental health staffs have grown apace or that treatment practices are adequate.

It is doubtful that more than a handful of prisons will ever have sufficient professional mental health personnel to treat mentally ill prisoners. Prison salaries simply are not competitive with the free-world employment opportunities available to psychiatrists. As a result, psychiatrists are usually available in prisons only on a part-time basis. And during their limited time, they find themselves saddled with mundane bureaucratic functions that cannot be delegated to others. Only psychiatrists can certify the mental health status of prisoners who need formal psychiatric treatment (or confinement in a hospital for the criminally insane) or who are seeking a furlough or parole. Such functions are important, to be sure, but psychiatrists who do little more than that in effect remain tourists, strangers to the life and culture of the prison. Their potential value in the treatment process is never realized.

Another problem, also related to the low salaries offered in prison, is that psychiatric staffs tend to consist of foreign professionals. Many of these psychiatrists accept prison jobs because they cannot command the free-world salaries of their American counterparts. They often find American prisons to be especially alien work environments. This problem is compounded when they work in prison on a part-time basis. The following vignette makes these points with wry humor, though the problem in real life is anything but funny.

> In 1976, Green Haven had no full-time psychiatrists; the New York State Department of Mental Hygiene provided the prison with several part-time psychiatrists, who spent most of their time at Green Haven conducting brief, mandatory pre-parole and pre-furlough interviews, or seeing inmates who had attempted suicide or who had behaved violently. Most

of the psychiatrists are foreigners; the inmates have trouble understanding them and vice versa. In one 1976 pre-parole interview, an Indian psychiatrist, who was obviously more familiar with the street argot of Calcutta than that of New York City, asked an inmate to explain the circumstances of his crime. "Me and these cats were sitting in a bar minding our own business," the inmate began. "We don't talk about cats here, we talk about people," the psychiatrist interrupted. (Sheehan, 1978:52)

As a practical matter, we cannot expect that professional psychiatrists will solve the problems of mentally ill prisoners. Nor can we rely on counselors, even those formally trained in psychiatric social work; these professionals, though competent to help prisoners—including mentally ill prisoners—with a wide range of adjustment problems, also are in short supply (Showalter & Hunsinger, 1983). Disturbed prisoners will have to be managed in ways that capitalize on the lay counseling services of prison officers, which are in more plentiful supply than professional psychiatric services. Interestingly, psychiatry can be understood and practiced in ways that make this proposal quite feasible.

Szasz (1961:255), for instance, defines psychiatry as

the study of personal conduct—of clarifying and "explaining" the kinds of games that people play with each other; how they learned these games; why they like to play them; and so forth. . . . This implies candid recognition that we "treat" . . . not because they are "sick" but rather because: (1) They desire this type of assistance; (2) They have problems in living for which they seek mastery through understanding of the kinds of games which they, and those around them, have been in the habit of playing; and (3) We want and are able to participate in their "education" because this is our professional role.

Szasz's notion of psychiatry as teaching better adjustment games provides a bridge between the counseling activities of correctional officers and more elaborate forms of mental health treatment such as individual or group psychotherapy. Correctional officers, Lombardo (1985:21) states, "learn to interpret and manipulate the rules of 'institutional games'" and therefore can

participate in the "education of inmates" in the playing of such games. This education should help inmates to cope with the problems of living in confinement in a less destructive, if not more constructive, manner. This task should be part of every correctional worker's professional role.

Lombardo is seconded in this view by Thomas (1975:43), who reminds us that

lay people can be as effective as and oftentimes more effective than the professional helper. In our correctional facilities throughout America today, we have a vast reservoir, a natural resource of line staff members who could be trained to complement the efforts of the professional mental health staff.

Helping Networks

Individual prison guards deliver human services to inmates with a wide range of problems. Officers appear to be particularly effective when they collaborate with fellow officers and treatment personnel such as counselors, psychologists, and psychiatrists (Johnson, 1981a). This conforms to Bandura's general observation that

> the most beneficial treatments are generally carried out under professional guidance by persons who have intensive contact with the clients and can therefore serve as powerful mediators of change. They are the ones who exercise substantial influence over the very conditions that govern the behavior to be modified. Unless they too alter their practices, any changes, whether produced by professionals or otherwise, may not endure for long. (quoted in Toch, 1981a:329)

Collaboration of this sort occurs in prisons, but it is typically informal or *sub rosa*. The assumption, particularly among the correctional officers, is that it does not pay to flout custodial norms (Johnson, 1981a).

Members of informal staff groups can describe the benefits of teamwork. A treatment staff member, a counselor referred to as "Mr. G.," observes:

> I have quite a lot of resources to depend on. One of the reasons is they [officers] know that they can come back to me for . . . help when they have a problem. One of the things I find is that we become a team. I even get called about other counselors' people that won't . . . about the people that won't cooperate up there. And I am saying this to you very honestly and I am not saying it boastfully, just gratefully; my concern is for the men that are here. I am employed because I am to help with correction. And these people [officers] know that by the same token that if they have problems, they can call me and, even if it is not my case, I will go and give them information or try to help the situation. (Johnson, 1981a:117)

A correctional officer assigned to a shop corroborates Mr. G.'s account. He tells us that

> Mr. G. and I, we have a working relationship and understanding. It is not an official understanding, but when he does have a man that is assigned to him with a problem—that might have a hard time adjusting or need a little supervision in some areas, such as adjusting to the institution, or perhaps because he is in this particular setting and is away from home and is lonely, or maybe is subject to pressure from his peers within the institution—he sends him to my shop. . . . And up here I take and give the inmates their choice of what they would like to do and I work with them in whatever they choose to do. And in working with him [the man with the problems], I try to keep an eye on his personal [relationships] with each one as I can. . . . And I also tell them that any problems that they have and I can help them with or give advice on, I will help them. And if I don't know the answer, I will find out the answer for them or refer them

to the person who has the answer. And it has worked out very well. (Johnson, 1981a:117)

The payoffs of a team approach can snowball, as friends of team members are inspired to offer their special talents to help with problem-prone inmates. An interview with one such officer (who worked in the cell blocks) was summarized as follows:

Mr. G. on occasion asks him to watch some men or to support them and he will do this. And he gave us an example of a guy Mr. G. told him had a problem and had to get into a good program. And this officer went out of his way to recommend to the prisoner that he try to go into the auto maintenance shop. (Apparently the officer had noted that the prisoner had hot rod magazines in his cell.) The officer also knew the auto maintenance man, knew that the shop was small, wouldn't have pressure, and would be a good setting for the prisoner to work in. So the officer personally went to bat for the man. Now apparently the auto maintenance foreman goes out of his way to respond to recommendations from this officer because they are friends and also because this officer gets his car repaired in that shop, so the shop foreman believes that he would only get serious recommendations from him. As it turned out, the prisoner did beautifully in that shop and seemed to be adjusting very well. (Johnson, 1981a:118)[5]

These teams, whether formally constituted or informally developed over time, expand the pool of services available to prisoners with problems. The immediate result is "more rapid referral, more reliable implementation of treatment plans, more comprehensive follow-up, and the prospect of timely crisis intervention" (Johnson, 1981a:121). The long-term result, it is reasonable to suppose, is a perception among inmates of a correctional staff that is making a concerted effort to run a responsive penal institution on their behalf.

HUMAN SERVICE IN PERSPECTIVE

Many officers, often a sizable minority and sometimes even a majority, go out of their way to promote a humane living environment in the prison (Toch & Grant, 1982). They do this by providing a range of human services that reduce stress and encourage mature adjustment among inmates. They play covert correctional roles in an institution that is a monument to custodial repression.

It is worthwhile to ask why officers do this. Helping is not a requirement of the job. Officers get little or no official recognition or support for their helping efforts. In fact, these officers often act in violation of official regulations that ban fraternization with inmates. (Even when official regulations seem to encourage human services, as in some explicitly reform-oriented prisons, officers may be "sanctioned by colleagues and midmanagement security personnel for emphasizing human service." See Jurik & Musheno, 1986:19). Many officers who stress human service also feel they are violating an unofficial subcultural code that calls for a tough-minded custodial pose rather than a concerned effort to solve inmate problems (see Chapter Seven). Moreover, treatment staff sometimes see correctional officers as encroaching on their professional turf, and thus either ignore or discourage the officers' human service activities (Johnson, 1981a: 108–13). Needless to say, some prisoners (the convicts) routinely reject the ministrations of the "screws" no matter how far they depart from guard stereotypes (see Chapter Five). It should come as no surprise, then, that relatively few officers fly their correctional colors openly. In public encounters they are custodians; in private, they are correctional officers.[6]

Why, then, do some officers persist in activities that take time and effort, are neither recognized nor rewarded by others, and must be hidden or played down for fear of trouble with administrators, peers, treatment staff, or recalcitrant inmates? The reason, as alluded to in the beginning of this chapter, is simply this: human service activities make the officer's job richer, more rewarding, and ultimately less stressful.

Guards, it must be remembered, are typically given no role in the formulation of administrative policy. Nor are they asked to do much of consequence in terms of inmate program services. Even their interpersonal relationships with prisoners are supposed to be superficial, as if the officers themselves were merely props for the authority invested in their roles. The result is that many guards feel powerless, vulnerable, and alone. They show the classic symptoms of alienation. In response, some officers reduce their involvements with inmates while others assume a more aggressive custodial pose (see Chapter Seven).

Many officers, however, try to solve the problem of alienation by expanding their roles and making them more substantial and rewarding. These officers discover that in the process of helping inmates and thereby giving them more autonomy, security, and emotional support, they gain the same benefits: more control over their environment, more security in their daily interactions with prisoners, and a sense of community, however inchoate or ill-defined, with at least some of the men under their care. In solving inmate adjustment problems, in other words, staff solve their own problems as well.

When inmate problems are averted or resolved, everyone can get on with the business of living and working in prison. Problems that are allowed to linger (in prison, fester might be a better word) eventually come home to roost. Officers who neglect their human service obligations are in for trouble. If they are lax in providing the goods and services necessary for an ordered and secure prison life, or if they let personal problems accumulate among the inmates in their care, they are likely to be confronted with a resentful or even explosive population. And if they don't pay for their mistakes, their colleagues will.

Human service officers pride themselves on being responsive to the inmates in their charge. It is critical to note, however, that what constitutes responsive service is not a fixed or set matter. In other words, the correctional officer's role, like the prison in which it is embedded, is not a static entity. Helping activities featuring referral or even informal counseling may be a more or less prominent feature of the officer's role in any given prison system, in part depending on the options open to inmates and the formal roles assigned to staff. Over the last decade, inmates in some prison systems have been afforded ready access to telephones and to extended visits. As a result, these inmates are more autonomous; they can address many personal problems on their own by calling home or taking the matter up at a visit. Again, over the last decade, in some prison systems, counselors' offices have been moved to the cell blocks, making them more readily available to inmates. The need for officers to serve as referral agents in such systems is reduced.

Auburn prison provides a telling case in point. In the mid-1970s, when Lombardo first studied the officers at Auburn, inmates had limited access to telephones and to visits, and counselors were housed away from the cell blocks, in distant administrative quarters. Line officers were readily accessible to inmates and, as a result, were often called upon to play an essential intermediary role between inmates with problems and counselors who could authorize special calls or even arrange emergency visits. Some officers expanded their jobs to include the role of informal counselor. By the mid-1980s, when Lombardo conducted a follow-up study of Auburn officers, the situation of the inmates had changed substantially. They had easy access to telephones and to visits; counselors, now housed in the cell blocks, were on-call for the prisoners. As a result, the officers were less often asked to play a referral role. Their informal counseling role proved less in demand as well. To be sure, officers still handled personal problems—60 percent of Lombardo's sample of officers in the follow-up study said they dealt with personal problems on a regular basis, usually encouraging inmates to take up the matter with a counselor or chaplain—but this function was less salient than it had been a decade earlier. And since the helping function was now seen as part of the formal job description of Auburn officers (even, to a degree, helping networks have been formalized at Auburn), the Auburn officers' helping efforts were seen by inmates as less spontaneous and, in some instances, less genuine (Lombardo, 1989:86–87). Given these factors, the identity of officers was less likely to be tied to helping services.

Other forces operated to change the dynamic of the officer's role at Auburn. Inmates at Auburn, like inmates elsewhere, have more legal rights and hence have a basis for demanding accountability from officers. In response, the officer's role at Auburn has become more fully articulated; formal policies and procedures, generated by administrators in consultation with officers, now cover a wide range of job categories and give a more formal structure to officer-inmate relations. Bound by comparatively clear rules and precise job descriptions, the officers at Auburn are a specialized cadre of correctional bureaucrats, ranging from "friskers" to "packers" to disciplinary hearing officers and special operations team officers, rather than, as but a decade earlier, a conglomerate of undifferentiated line officers with widely varying interests, skills, and patterns of discretionary decision making.

Officers at Auburn and many other prisons are more professional than in days past. One example of prison officer professionalism is the creation of special operations teams, which are the bureaucratic successors of goon squads in better-run prisons. Variously known in most state prisons as CERT teams (Crisis Emergency Response Teams) and in the Federal Bureau of Prisons as SORT teams (Special Operations Response Teams), these teams are comprised of trained officers who are deployed to use controlled force to move recalcitrant inmates, to control and disperse crowds, to free hostages, and to break up riots. (Some of the routines of Lewisburg's SORT team are briefly but accurately portrayed in the documentary *Doing Time: Life Inside The Big House.*) Unlike in prisons where unofficial goon squads still exist, these professional teams are not used to mete out punishments to troublemaking inmates. Another example of prison officer professionalism can be seen in execution teams. In today's prisons, executions are carried out by trained teams of officers whose explicit mission is to conduct executions that are, from the vantage point of officials if not the condemned prisoners, "proper, professional, and dignified" (Johnson, 1990:72).

Security is an increasingly important area of officer accountability in Auburn. If Auburn prisoners in the mid-1980s were more autonomous than their counterparts of a decade earlier, they were also less secure. Auburn in the 1970s was a comparatively nonviolent institution. By the mid-1980s, the forces producing violence in many American prisons were having an impact at Auburn (see Chapter Five). In the words of an officer whose career spanned these changes at Auburn,

> It's changed a lot. It's more violent. The drugs, the extortion. They steal and take from other guys. It will go on 'til the guy fights back or goes to protective custody. Ten years ago if you had a fight, they'd duke it out and then step back. Now with the peer pressure they'll fight and try to kill each other. Ten years ago a guy might go bughouse. Today he might get a knife. With the availability of drugs and other things they get used to it on the street and with the money around they turn to violence. Fights aren't just personal conflicts any more. They're conflicts over extortion, power conflicts, drugs and other things like that. (Lombardo, 1989:166)

Violence, now more common and more calculated, poses a considerable threat to officer and inmate alike. As a result, officers at Auburn have been called upon to provide more security-related services. Such services feature "frisks, drug testing and violence prevention," and are aimed primarily at securing physical rather than psychological survival (Lombardo, 1989:173 & 211).

The Auburn officers report that fear is a salient theme, but competence at security-related tasks helps them keep fear in check. Significantly, these officers are less alienated than their counterparts of a decade ago. They know what to expect as they carry out their specialized tasks, and they know what is expected of them by inmates and administrators. They are less likely than a decade ago to feel caught in the middle, pressured by conflicting demands from above and below. Tense personal encounters with inmates are less frequent; formal recognition of their accomplishments by administrators is more common. Specialization of function has allowed for the development of specialized skills, in which the officers take great pride. A growing administrative bureaucracy, needed to manage a more differentiated officer force, has opened up avenues for advancement (see, generally, Lombardo, 1989).

One can see in Auburn the evolution of a framework for the correctional role that might unite officers with custodial and human service orientations. This role would focus on professional and accountable delivery of basic goods and services. Services would be construed broadly to include justice, which is operationalized at Auburn in a disciplinary system that features clearly defined procedures, with officers assigned as advisors to inmates during hearings; and security, operationalized at Auburn in a phalanx of officers arrayed in a range of specialized security-related positions, sharing a common concern for protecting inmates from physical harm. The experience at Auburn and elsewhere suggests that, with training, even so-called hacks can be equipped to provide basic security services without resort to manipulation or violence.[7] Human service-oriented officers, in turn, can develop security-related specializations that allow them to retain a helping function as a corollary of their commitment to inmate safety. (Remember, security is not solely a matter of physical safety; people must feel secure, and this implies supportive or at least nonthreatening relationships with one's keepers.) As at Auburn, referral responsibilities and helping networks could be formalized; officers could become more or less involved in these activities as dictated by job description and personal disposition. Informal problem-solving efforts by officers would remain just that: informal. Officer involvement in such activities would be entirely voluntary.

Reforms of the sort achieved at Auburn require an organizational culture that is committed to "change rather than stability" (Lombardo, 1989:214). In the face of a changing environment, Lombardo reminds us, institutions must adapt if they are to function effectively. The legal and political environments in which prisons operate have changed dramatically over the past few decades, posing substantial challenges to the adaptive capacities of prisons. To date, Auburn has responded well because it is a prison in which effective leadership[8] committed to innovation has become part of its institutional culture, and officers there have come to expect change as part of their jobs. Problem solving, a key feature of mature coping, has become a component of the prison's culture. At Auburn, changes emanating from without (for example, as a result of legal decisions) and from within (for example, as a result of inmate or officer demands and expectations) are taken as problems to be solved. As such, they are "perceived as part of the institution's internal environment rather than as threats" (Lombardo, 1989:215). The result is adaptive accommodation rather than maladaptive resistance. As we turn to the larger subject of prison reform, the notion of adaptive accommodation—on the part of the prison as well as its prisoners—is one that can fruitfully guide our efforts.

NOTES

1. Usually this is less the case for the various treatment staffs, from counselors and educators through psychologists and psychiatrists, who tend to be removed, both physically and socially, from the daily world of the prison yards and cell blocks shared by officers and inmates.

2. By today's standards, the ostracism faced by female officers in the 70s would be characterized as sexual harassment; much of this abusive behavior was directly sexual in nature or otherwise created a hostile working environment for women. The impression is that ostracism of female officers is less common these days. In the District of Columbia's Department of Corrections, however, the problem of sexual harassment is endemic. Reports Locy (1995:A1), "A jury in U.S. District Court yesterday found that the D.C. Department of Corrections engaged in a pattern of sexual harassment against female employees and created a hostile work environment for women." The problem of sexual harassment in D.C. prisons is by all accounts egregious, and "the verdict is believed to be the first time in the country that a governmental agency has been held responsible in a class-action lawsuit of creating and maintaining a sexually hostile work environment" (Locy, 1995:A1).

3. This goal is summed up in the often-heard statement that officers should be "firm but fair" in their uses of authority. It is also reinforced by grievance mechanisms that permit inmates to have a role in the review of rule enforcement decisions (Rodgers, 1979; Hepburn & Laue, 1980) and in rule enforcement regulations that are clear in themselves and consistently administered (see DiIulio, 1994).

4. It is for reasons such as these that segregation units, the ultimate custodial milieus, are notoriously tense and explosive.

5. This quotation was edited to make references to the various individuals easier to follow.

6. The problem is one of pluralistic ignorance, as noted in Chapter Seven. In some prisons, however, perceptions of guard behavior are more accurate, permitting correctional officers to be more open in their activities (Toch & Grant, 1982:202).

7. In Texas prisons, for example, officers have moved from a largely custodial ethic to one of enforcement of rules in a due process framework in which disciplinary reports have come to replace coercion in daily social control (see Crouch & Marquart, 1989). The federal prison system made this transition some time ago, and indeed serves as a model of the bureaucratic management of disciplinary problems (see DiIulio, 1994).

8. The cultivation of leadership committed to excellence is an important but little-studied feature of the adaptive capabilities of prison organizations. For a seminal work on this topic, directed to scholar and practitioner alike, see Wright, 1994.

REFERENCES

Abbey, A. A., W. Holland, and C. B. Wortman. "The misguided helper: An analysis of people's responses to their loved ones' crises." In D. G. McGuigan (ed.) *Women's Lives: New Theory, Research and Policy.* Ann Arbor: University of Michigan Press, 1980:257–66.

Crouch, B. M. 'Pandora's box: Women guards in men's prisons." *Journal of Criminal Justice* 13 (1985):535–48.

Crouch, B. M. and J. W. Marquart. *An Appeal to Justice.* Austin: University of Texas Press, 1989.

Cullen, F. T., B. G. Link, N. T. Wolfe and J. Frank. "The social dimensions of correctional officer stress." *Justice Quarterly* 2 (4) 1985:505–33.

Cullen, F. T., B. G. Link, J. B. Cullen, and N. T. Wolfe. "How satisfying is prison work? A comparative occupational approach." *Journal of Offender*

Counseling, Services & Rehabilitation 14 (2) 1989:89–108.

DiIulio, J. J. "5270.7 tells the tale." *Federal Prisons Journal* 3 (3) 1994:60–65.

Earley, P. *The Hot House: Life Inside Leavenworth.* New York: Bantam Books, 1992.

Gates, M. "The excavation." American University: Unpublished manuscript, 1991.

Glaser, D. *The Effectiveness of a Prison and Parole System.* Indianapolis, IN: Bobbs-Merrill, 1969.

Guenther, A. L., and M. Q. Guenther. " Screws vs. thugs." In B. M. Crouch, (ed.). *The Keepers: Prison Guards and Contemporary Corrections.* Springfield, IL: Charles C. Thomas, 1980:162–82.

Hampton, J. "The moral education theory of punishment." *Philosophy and Public Affairs* 13 (3) 1984:208–38.

Hepburn, J. R. "The erosion of authority and the perceived legitimacy of inmate social protest: A study of prison guards." *Journal of Criminal Justice* 12 (6) 1984:579–90.

Hepburn, J. R., and P. E. Knepper. "Correctional officers as human service workers: The effect of job satisfaction." *Justice Quarterly* 10 (2) 1993:315–37.

Hepburn, J. R., and J. H. Laue. "Prisoner redress: Analysis of an inmate grievance procedure." *Crime & Delinquency* 26 (2) 1980:162–78.

Jacobs, J., and H. G. Retsky. "Prison guard." In R. R. Ross (ed.). *Prison Guard/Correctional Officer.* Canada: Butterworth, 1981:55–73. (Originally published in *Urban Life,* 1975.)

Johnson, R. "Informal helping networks in prison: The shape of grass-roots correctional intervention." In R. R. Ross (ed.). *Prison Guard/Correctional Officer.* Canada: Butterworth, 1981:105–25 (1981a). (Originally published in the *Journal of Criminal Justice,* 1979.)

Johnson, R. *Condemned to Die: Life Under Sentence of Death.* New York: Elsevier, 1981 (1981b).

Johnson, R. *Death Work: A Study of the Modern Execution Process.* Belmont, CA: Wadsworth, 1990.

Johnson, R., and S. Price. "The complete correctional officer: Human service and the human environment of prison." *Criminal Justice and Behavior* 8 (3) 1981:343–73.

Jurik, N. C. "Individual and organizational determinants of correctional officer attitudes toward inmates." *Criminology* 23 (3) 1985:523–39.

Jurik, N. C. "Striking a balance: Advancement strategies for women working as correctional officers in men's prisons." *Feminist Studies* 6 (1986) Chicago: Midwestern Sociological Association.

Jurik, N. C., and M. C. Musheno. "The internal crisis of corrections: Professionalization and the work environment." *Justice Quarterly* 3 (4) 1986:457–80.

Kissel, P. J., and P. L. Katsampes. "The impact of women corrections officers on the functioning of institutions housing male inmates." *Journal of Offender Counseling, Services and Rehabilitation* 4 (3) 1980:213–31.

Lasch, C. *The Minimal Self—Psychic Survival in Troubled Times.* New York: Norton, 1984.

Lasky, G. L., and B. C. Gordon."Occupational stressors among federal correctional officers working in different security levels." *Criminal Justice and Behavior* 13 (3) 1986:317–27.

Lockwood, D. *Prison Sexual Violence.* New York: Elsevier, 1980.

Lombardo, L. X. *Guards Imprisoned: Correctional Officers at Work.* New York: Elsevier, 1981.

Locy, T. "Jury finds harassment in D. C. agency: Corrections conduct leaves the district liable for damages." *The Washington Post* (Wednesday, April 5, 1995) A1 & A16.

Lombardo, L. X. "Mental health work in prisons and jails: Inmate adjustment and indigenous correctional personnel." *Criminal Justice and Behavior* 12 (1) 1985:17–28.

Lombardo, L. X. "Alleviating inmate stress: Contributions from correctional officers." In R. Johnson and H. Toch (eds.). *The Pains of Imprisonment.* Prospect Heights, IL: Waveland Press, 1988:285–97.

Lombardo, L. X. *Guards Imprisoned: Correctional Officers at Work.* Cincinnati, OH: Anderson Publishing, 1989.

Locy, T. "Jury Finds Harassment in D.C. Agency: Corrections Conduct Leaves the District Liable for Damages." *The Washington Post* (Wednesday, April 5, 1995): A1 & A16.

May, E., "Prison guards in America—The inside story." In R. R. Ross (ed.) *Prison Guard/Correctional Officer.* Canada: Butterworth, 1981:19–40. (Originally published in *Corrections Magazine,* 1976.)

Owen, B. A. "Race and gender relations among prison workers." *Crime & Delinquency* 31 (1) 1985:147–59.

Raymond, A. (director). *Doing Time: Life Inside the Big House.* New York: Video Verite, 1991. Videocassette.

Rodgers, B. R. "Inmate grievance procedure design and evaluation: The state of the art." *International Journal of Group Tensions* 1 (4) 1979:75–85.

Sennett, R. *Authority.* New York: Vintage Books, 1981.

Sheehan, S. *A Prison and A Prisoner.* Boston: Houghton Mifflin, 1978.

Showalter, D., and M. Hunsinger. "Social work within a maximum-security setting." In A. A. Roberts (ed.). *Social Work in Juvenile and Criminal Justice Settings.* Springfield, IL: Charles C. Thomas, 1983:257–74.

Stojkovic, S. "An examination of compliance structures in a prison organization: A study of the types of correctional power." Paper presented at Annual Meeting of The Academy of Criminal Justice Sciences, March 1984.

Szasz, T. *The Myth of Mental Illness: Foundations of a Theory of Personal Conduct.* New York: Dell, 1961.

Thomas, A. G. "The Carkhuff training program." In R. E. Hosford, and C. S. Moss. *The Crumbling Walls.* Champaign-Urbana: University of Illinois Press, 1975:35–44.

Toch, H. *Men in Crisis: Human Breakdowns in Prison.* Chicago: Aldine, 1975.

Toch, H. *Living in Prison: The Ecology of Survival.* New York: Free Press, 1977.

Toch, H. "Is a 'correctional officer' by any other name, a 'screw'?" In R. R. Ross (ed.). *Prison Guard/Correctional Officer.* Canada: Butterworth, 1981: 87–104. (Originally published in *Criminal Justice Review,* 1978.)

Toch, H. "Psychological treatment of imprisoned offenders." In J. R. Hays, T. K. Roberts, and K. S. Solway (eds.). *Violence and the Violent Individual.* New York: SP Medical & Scientific Books, 1981:325–42 (1981a).

Toch, H. "The disturbed disruptive inmate: Where does the bus stop?" *The Journal of Psychiatry and Law* (Fall 1982):327–49.

Toch, H., and J. D. Grant. *Reforming Human Services: Change Through Participation.* Beverly Hills, CA: Sage, 1982.

Toch, H., and J. Klofas. "Alienation and desire for job enrichment among correctional officers." *Federal Probation* 46 (1982):35–47.

Webb, G. L., and D. G. Morris. "Prison guard conceptions." In B. M. Crouch (ed.). *The Keepers: Prison Guards and Contemporary Corrections.* Springfield, IL: Charles C. Thomas, 1980:150–61.

Wiehn, P. J. "Mentally ill offenders: Prison's first casualties." In R. Johnson and H. Toch (eds.). *The Pains of Imprisonment.* Prospect Heights, IL: Waveland Press, 1988:221–37.

Wright, K. N. *Effective Prison Leadership.* Binghamton, NY: William Neil Publishing, 1994.

Zimmer, L. E. *Women Guarding Men.* Chicago: University of Chicago Press, 1986.

❖

PART III

Prison Reform

9

Corrections and Coping Competence

Stress, Adaptation, and Grassroots Prison Reform

At the turn of the twentieth century, a young writer named Hawthorne described his prison experience in a popular article entitled, "Our Barbarous Penal System" (Hawthorne, 1913). Hawthorne was writing about Atlanta Federal Penitentiary, but his point was that prisons, all prisons, were inherently corrupt and cruel. "Penal imprisonment," he observed,

> is an institution of old date, born of barbarism and ignorance, nurtured in filth and darkness, and cruelly administered. It began with the dominion of the strong over the weak, and when the former was recognized as the community, it was called the authority of good over evil. (Hawthorne, 1913:206)

For Hawthorne, prison reform was impossible, if not absurd. "No one talks of reforming the Black Death," he observed wryly (Hawthorne, 1913:206).

Many of today's prison critics share Hawthorne's cynical view. They would have us believe that penal institutions will never serve any constructive purpose. Rehabilitation, they assure us, is dead (see Alper, 1974; Martinson, 1974). We are urged to adapt Gertrude Stein's aphorism to our situation, acknowledge that "a prison is a prison is a prison," and make do with a notoriously unaccommodating institution. Since imprisonment is inevitably painful, the most we can do is lessen the pain. Prison reform amounts to rallying for, of all things, humane warehouses. The difficulty is that warehousing is, at best, a futile undertaking. People simply "are not commodities that can be stored, shelved and retrieved," even if they are permitted to develop an elaborate make-believe world to help them pass the time (Toch, 1985:59).

Public opinion on the matter of prison reform is less easily summarized than are the views of prison's scholarly critics. Most Americans seem to favor prisons that offer a combination of punishment and treatment; the view seems to be that criminals should take their medicine (punishment), get well (with the help of education and training) and then get on with their lives.[1] A vocal and these days influential minority, however, advocates long sentences idled away in grim prisons that offer, at best, the prospect of boring prisoners into submission or scaring them straight.

Politicians resonate to these repressive concerns. In a recent session of the Mississippi legislature, for example, "there was talk of restoring fear to prisons, of caning, of making prisoners 'smell like a prisoner,' of burning and frying, of returning executions to the county seat and of making Mississippi 'the capital of capital punishment'" (Nossiter, 1994:1). (The death penalty aspirations are those of the governor.) The difficulty with this line of reasoning, at least as it applies to the uses of prisons as distinct from the death penalty, is that inmates must cope maturely with imprisonment if they are to have any hope of going straight upon release. Warehouse prisons do not promote coping competence. Instead, such prisons further impair the coping skills of offenders; sooner or later, and always sooner than most of us would like, these embittered prisoners return to us—and to crime.

As we have seen over the last decade, we can build more prisons and confine more people in them but it hardly puts a dent in the crime problem. As James Bruton, Minnesota's deputy commissioner for penal institutions has cogently observed,

> "We cannot build ourselves out of the crime problem. Every state that's
> tried it has failed miserably. You'll never see a reduction in the crime rate
> by building more prisons. What you're going to find out is that you can't
> afford to operate what you've built." (quoted in Walsh, 1994:A3)

It is becoming increasingly apparent that the scope and cost of imprisonment in America are running out of control (Blumstein, 1994:405). "Between 1982 and 1992," Walsh (1994:A3) tells us, "state governments built 455 new prisons while total annual expenditures for corrections ballooned from $6 billion to more than $20 billion." During any given year, moreover, the "cost of operating the nation's penal institutions will increase more than $1 billion" (Walsh, 1994:A3). Nolan Jones, director of the justice and public safety program of the National Governors Association, reminds us that "the out-year costs" of running our growing penal archipelago will be nothing short of "astronomical" (Walsh, 1994:A3). The taxpaying public seems largely oblivious to the economic realities. Indeed, local communities these days compete in so-called prison derbies for the privilege of hosting new prisons, which bring to their communities new jobs and an expanded tax base (Walsh, 1994:A3). For society at large, however, substantial and growing investments in prison are a poor public policy choice.[2] Putting an expanding portion of budget dollars in prisons takes money away from a host of valuable enterprises such as schools and social services, investments that might well, in the long run, offer better defenses against criminality as well as a generally improved quality of life for the average citizen.

There is an apt saying in public policy, and in life generally, that goes like this: One can pay now or one can pay later, but either way you pay. In the matter of prison reform, this saying is only half right. One pays now *and* one pays later when large numbers of prisoners are allowed to languish in a growing colony of warehouse institutions, eventually to return to haunt us, and all the while draining resources from other key governmental functions. The point is not that we should reform prisons as a bribe to calm restive inmates, as if they were extorting better treatment from a frightened society (see Logan & Gaes, 1993:258–59). We should reform our prisons because *we as a society wish to make our penal institutions effective instruments of punishment.*

Prison reform has at least two connotations these days. On the one hand, reform can mean reducing the size of our prison behemoth. Corollary reforms would have to do with structuring sentencing decisions to assure that only the more serious offenders go to prison (see, for example, Forst, 1994:380), perhaps for longer terms than at present,[3] and with the development of intermediate and other sanctions to take up the slack of a smaller prison system (see, for example, Clear & Braga, 1994). A full and informed discussion of the proper size of America's penal system is beyond the scope of this book, which focuses on the prison experience and its import rather than on the scale of imprisonment and its significance for public policy (see Zimring & Hawkins, 1991). As a general matter, however, it is painfully apparent—no pun intended—that prisons are a prohibitively expensive public policy choice with limited demonstrated effectiveness in reducing crime (Blumstein, 1994).[4] As such, prisons should be treated as scarce commodities to be built and deployed only when necessary and certainly not, as is so often the case today, paraded to the public as general purpose cure-alls for criminality (see Irwin & Austin, 1994).

Our focus is on the second connotation of prison reform, that of improving individual prisons. However many prisons we seek to build and operate, this notion of reform makes it clear that individual prisons should be decent, humane enterprises (see Chapter One). Reformed prisons, following the line of argument developed in this book, must offer spartan but responsive conditions of confinement. The premise is that decent conditions of confinement, which include access to programs, will promote autonomy, security, and relatedness to others, and hence will allow offenders to shoulder responsibility for their conduct and embark on constructive lives. It stands to reason that, all things being equal, a system comprised of decent prisons, even a bloated system like our current one, is a vast improvement over a system populated with warehouse prisons.

At a minimum, then, prison reform means improving existing prisons, however many prisons there may be in existence, so that they reach or approximate our notion of decency and produce a reasonably effective penal enterprise. As a practical matter, this means that the pains experienced in any given prison must be kept to a minimum. Civilization demands as much, and our prisons are civilized insofar as correctional policy and practice are geared to minimizing the pain of incarceration. But since prisons will always produce pain, the pains of imprisonment must be coped with maturely. Prison reform thus demands that we acknowledge the pains of prison and, where possible, put them to constructive purposes. We must build our reform agenda, in other words, out of the deprivation and pain that are enduring ingredients of imprisonment. As I show in this chapter, we can make our civilized prisons also civilizing prisons, though to date we have only just begun to take up this challenge.

Historically, reformers have failed to come to grips with the pains of imprisonment; they have done little to adapt correctional ideals to prison realities (see Chapters One through Three). Some reformers have spoken of prison regimes in utopian terms as disciplined ways of living that would radically improve the characters of their subjects. This is perhaps most clear in the case of the penitentiary (see Beaumont & Tocqueville, 1833/1964:89), but utopian aspirations lingered in the Big House (see Jacobs, 1977:31) and the correctional institution (Irwin, 1980:47). More recently, prisons have been derided as inherently unnatural environments. In the extreme, they have been described as demeaning total institutions (Goffman, 1961) or brutalizing social jungles (Irwin, 1980). For a time, however, the programs offered in these admittedly bleak environments were praised in utopian terms. This contradiction reflected the logic behind the correctional institution. Programs were meant to transform custodial prisons into correctional institutions; when they did not, these programs were expected to be oases that somehow endured in the wasteland of the cell block and yard (Irwin, 1980). Neither reform agenda—utopian prisons or utopian programs—has borne fruit.

We now know that prisons too often have served as warehouses; warehouses do not reform offenders. Treatment programs could improve this situation, but programs do not often thrive in warehouses. Prison treatment programs, moreover, have been more illusory than real. It has been estimated, for instance, that in contemporary America less than $100 a year is spent on any given inmate for such basic social services as counseling, and that rehabilitation programs are extended to only 5 percent of the inmate population.[5] This is typical of the history of prisons. Never has anyone been able to "directly and effectively represent the 'silent majority' of problem inmates, the average man who suffers, the one who wastes away in shooting distance from potentially available resources" (Toch, 1981:9). Small wonder that we have inherited a legacy of frustration and failure, leavened with periodic violence and even brutality.

But legacies can be changed. Prisons can be seen for what they are, as settings in which the average inmate does indeed suffer. Rehabilitation can be defined as equipping offenders to cope with the pains of imprisonment in mature ways, not wasting away but rather growing through the adversity posed by imprisonment (see Chapter Four). This is a sober and workable correctional agenda. By their very nature, penal institutions produce psychological

pain; they provide plenty of stress. Our job is to translate those stresses into occasions for learning rather than invitations to immature and often destructive
behavior. In this chapter we will examine how the pains of imprisonment can
be harnessed in service of prison reform. The goal is not utopian prison environments or programs. We must simply make a pragmatic effort to meet the
concerns of the average prisoner for a livable prison, useful activities, and a
chance for a decent life upon release from confinement.

The ultimate goal of prison reform is to produce mature adults who can
live in society and cope with the daily problems of life without harming others. Ideally, mature adults also have the capacity to enter into constructive relationships with their fellows. Mature adults honor the minimal obligations of
citizenship by not preying upon others (Conrad, 1981a:17). They also strive to
be productive citizens, willing and able to work for their keep (Hawkins, 1976
& 1983) and to take some responsibility for the well-being of others in the
human community (Erikson, 1965). A prison that allows inmates to live within
its walls as citizens, and ideally as productive and even caring citizens, provides
a rehearsal for mature living in the free world.

Prisoners who are to live in the prison community as citizens must be afforded a safe and lawful existence, one in which it is possible to be neither
predator nor prey, criminal nor victim (Conrad, 1981b:56–62). Most inmates,
as we have seen, seek such an existence. They attempt to carve out niches in
which to shelter themselves from the violence and exploitation that thrives on
the prison yard and in other public areas of the prison (see Chapter Six). Correctional managers must take note of these trends. As Duffee has observed,
"managers in complex systems tend to be most effective when they take advantage of the self-direction of organizations rather than fight against it" (Duffee, 1980:16). At the same time, correctional managers must also be leaders;
they must have a commitment to excellence in the delivery of correctional
services, from basic security to living conditions and programs (see Wright,
1994). Accordingly, correctional policies can dovetail with and encourage the
development of constructive niches as pockets of ecological excellence, if you
will, building a robust reform agenda from the grass roots of daily life and adjustment in prison. The goal would be to permeate prisons with such niches,
so that these institutions are, in effect, communities that are honeycombed
with responsive neighborhoods. Terms like "the prison community," bandied
about in the sociological literature on prisons, would have real meaning in
such contexts.

Limited funds, custodial convenience, and concern for turf are major im-
pediments to changing day-to-day prison policy and practice (Hawkins,
1976:168).[6] Perversely, simply getting by in the way they always have becomes
a mark of competence and a badge of pride for many prison officials. Reforms
that fly in the face of these concerns by proposing novel and expensive activities are easily scuttled. In contrast, grassroots reforms that build upon existing
trends and stay within existing budgets have a chance of success. The reformer,
then, must show practitioners—correctional managers as well as line staff—
that "it is possible to rearrange the distribution of currently available resources

with the likely result that if we are not doing more with less, at least we are doing more for the same costs" (Levinson, 1988:241; see also England, 1990:63). The ecology of adjustment provides an ideal vehicle for reforms that exploit available prison resources.

PART ONE: PRISON ECOLOGY AND PRISON REFORM

The first order of business is to use prison environments, our most available reform resource, in the service of mature adjustment to the stresses of life in prison. One line of reform is to make prisons more "normal," which is to say, more like the free world. A second strategy is to use existing prison environments in a more rational and responsive way. Combinations of these approaches are of course possible.

As a general matter, the direction of prison reform, at least since the demise of the penitentiary, has been to make prisons more normal. For example, prison architecture has evolved over time to allow greater human contact and interaction (Atlas and Dunham, 1990:55). The same can be said for the arrangement of internal prison regimes, at least from the penitentiary through to contemporary prisons, as is made apparent in the historical chapters of this book.

From the point of view of mature coping, the benefits of increasingly normal prisons are evident. "The more closely the conditions of imprisonment can begin to approximate those normally seen on the outside," observe Zamble, Porporino & Kalotay (1984:140), "the better inmates can learn to survive without resort to criminal behavior." In making prisons more normal—more like the free world—we hope to offer lessons in mature coping that will readily generalize to the conditions of life outside prisons. Clues as to what is normal in a prison environment—other than relaxation of restrictions, as found most saliently in Dutch prisons—may be found in our analysis of recurring features of prison adjustment. In other words, in the human concerns that guide adjustment, prisoners tell us by their behavior what they feel they must "import" from the free world as they know it to make the prison "normal" for them.

Using our review of prisoner adjustment as a guide (Chapters Five and Six), we can conclude that a normal prison environment must offer, first and foremost, opportunities for the constructive expression of autonomy. A normal prison, then, must offer opportunities for each person to take responsibility for a progressively growing array of choices made within the confines of work, school, and play in the prison community. Such choices make it possible for prisoners to gain, from their own initiative, a sense of security in the world, because they have some control over their fate; and a sense of relatedness to others, because the social world in which they now operate is in some important measure shaped by their interpersonal choices.

Dutch prisons may well be the most normal prisons one can find today, and they appear to bear out these observations. Prisons in The Netherlands operate on a "principle of minimal restrictions" (Kalmthout and van der Landen, 1991:97). This means that "the prisoner has the same civil rights as any other citizen, unless the realization of these rights is impossible under the necessary conditions of detention" (Kalmthout and van der Landen, 1991:97). Dutch prisons feature relaxed internal regimes, with prisoners afforded considerable freedom of choice as to what they do, when they do it, and with whom they associate. It is fair to say that Dutch prisons are minimally intrusive, and hence that the pains of imprisonment are kept to a minimum (see Downes, 1988). The operating premise appears to be that prisons are inherently harmful; reform efforts focus on minimizing the harm by reducing the restrictive conditions of confinement. The ecology of adjustment in these regimes has not been researched, but anecdotal evidence suggests that prisoners do feel relatively autonomous, secure and related to others around them.[7]

To be sure, the prison community in most penal institutions reflects misguided efforts to secure autonomy, security and relatedness—through violence, primarily among the convicts, and through retreat into insular niches, primarily among the inmates (see Chapters Five and Six). This need not remain the case. The urge to be autonomous, secure, and related to others, present in adjustment efforts in prisons from the penitentiary to the contemporary penal institutions, can be guided to better ends. The continuing difficulty is that today's prisons, much like their various predecessors, have in place formal policies and informal practices that actively discourage constructive autonomy.

For example, all inmates currently receive the same goods and services regardless of differences in their behavior. One's meals or clothing or living conditions are the same whether one works or not. Yet it stands to reason that there should be "higher rewards for good behavior and lower benefits for freeloading" (Zamble, Porporino & Kalotay, 1984:141). To make matters worse, in today's prisons the convicts often live *better* than more compliant prisoners. By use or threat of violence, the convicts often secure a higher standard of living than their law-abiding inmate counterparts, including ready access to such valued commodities as sex and respect.[8]

It is also the case that "institutional privileges ought to be made at least partly contingent on behavior which is appropriate on the outside, rather than simply on the absence of institutional offenses" (Zamble, Porporino & Kalotay, 1984:141). In most prisons, inmates may gain privileges simply by avoiding trouble. This is not bad in itself, except that in many prisons, the absence of rule violations rather than the presence of prosocial behavior is the only route to a better prison life. One consequence of such a reward system is that at least some if not many prisoners, by dint of passivity or deception, are able to live as well as—or, indeed, better than—inmates who strive to improve themselves but occasionally break prison rules. Clearly, inmates who work to rehabilitate themselves should gain the lion's share of privileges, notably better housing and more flexible domestic schedules. These privileges, which amount to affording better neighborhoods and homes to high achievers, should be awarded on the basis of progress in areas that enhance one's capacity to cope with problems in mature ways, from social skills acquisition to education and vocational training.

Along the same lines, "if work assignments were made more meaningful, more realistic and more flexible, they would [reduce] the artificiality of the prison environment" by making one's lot more clearly reflect one's effort (Zamble, Porporino & Kalotay, 1984:141). Lompoc prison provides a case in point. Lompoc has been described as an "industrial penitentiary community" (Fleischer, 1989:27). Conformity and hard work pay off at Lompoc. Prisoners can and do live comparatively well at Lompoc; the prison is safe, in part, because prisoners feel they have a stake in the day-to-day quality of prison life and don't want to lose privileges or comforts as a result of misbehavior. For productive and conforming prisoners at Lompoc, behaving like a decent citizen of the prison community translates into "earning a reliable income, having a decent personal lifestyle, and enjoying the social freedom that comes in a peaceful prison community" (Fleischer, 1989:27). Reforms of the sort found at Lompoc alter the prison ecology, increasing the likelihood that prisoners will learn some specific lessons in living that are also of value in the free world.

A second type of reform capitalizes on the existing ecology of prison environments. This approach requires simply that we use existing prison environments, however they are constituted, in a rational and efficient manner. All prisons have an "ecology of survival"; this ecology can be measured, mapped, and deployed to promote better adjustment (Toch, 1977). Naturally, to the extent that prison environments are made more normal, ecological matches will be that much more likely to promote mature conduct with direct relevance to life and adjustment in the free world.

As things stand today, prison policy does not typically produce normal environments. Nor does it draw upon ecological resources in any systematic way. To be sure, officials sometimes make work or housing assignments or arrange recreation or program schedules with the aim of helping prisoners to adjust and perhaps even to pursue personal rehabilitation. But these are the exceptions rather than the rule. More often, assignments and schedules serve custodial needs rather than the adjustment needs of inmates (Toch, 1977; Fitzgerald & Sim, 1982:50). When the issue of adjustment influences these decisions, the goal is usually to reward conformity or punish infractions rather than to encourage a mature response to the demands of prison life. The result is a self-defeating reward system in which compliant inmates like Malinow are so comfortable they don't want to leave prison (see Chapter Six), and rebellious inmates like Abbott are so bitter and inured to violence they can't be trusted out of segregation (see Chapter Five).

Let me illustrate this point, since it highlights the need to use ecological resources to promote mature adjustment rather than to achieve custodial control. Every prison has some formally designated living environment that features a low-key approach to authority and a relaxed climate. There may also be a host of "perks," such as extra televisions for the block, extended phone privileges, and perhaps even refrigerators in the cells. These settings are generally called "honor blocks" or "privilege blocks," though San Quentin had the perspicacity to christen theirs "Citizens' Row," in recognition that the men there are treated more like citizens and less like prisoners. But hard-core convicts, whose violence is largely a product of authority problems and whose preeminent environmental demand is for freedom from circumscription of their autonomy, are never assigned to units even remotely similar to these. This is true, moreover, even though such settings could be stripped of the material rewards and special privileges that might be construed as incentives for misconduct.

Yet if prisoners who are prone to violence were assigned to settings that combined the ecological dimensions of freedom and support, it is probable they would live there with fewer incidents and explosions and more chances for learning to manage conflict maturely. Both the prisoners and the staff would be encouraged to resolve conflicts cooperatively instead of resorting to manipulation or force. Relationships, even friendships, would almost certainly develop, gradually undermining stereotypes and building community. Prisoner and staff alike might well come to think of themselves as fellow citizens of the prison community, each with a stake in the well-being of the other. Prison living in such environments might indeed promote a sense of individual responsibility that would hold up in the free world.

If this scenario sounds unrealistic, it is because only the model inmates of the prison, who can handle regular prison authority situations fairly well, are now permitted to make their home in these more congenial environments. The prevailing idea is that a compliant inmate like Malinow deserves something better than the normal round of prison life. A rebellious inmate like Abbott deserves more punishment. As a consequence, Abbott is assigned to the most repressive cell blocks, gets into trouble, and becomes a regular guest in segregation—where he continues to make trouble for himself and his keepers. Malinow finds what amounts to a luxurious niche but is encouraged simply to lie low and do his time there. Abbott does hard time, and is confirmed in his worst beliefs about prison and about himself. Neither is motivated to change or given any incentives or rewards for undertaking the difficult task of personal reform.

Environments that ameliorate stress and promote mature adjustment can become standard features of any prison regime and be made available to most if not all prisoners. The nub of the issue is classification that yields appropriate "man-environment matches" (Toch, 1977:284–85). The express purpose of classification is "to determine the personal requirements and assess the needs of individual inmates, and . . . to match requirements and needs with existing correctional resources" (Toch, 1977:286). The first step is to place people in appropriate environments. Then, constructive activities, from learning to cope with daily adjustment problems to participation in formal correctional programs, must be arranged.

Classification and the Development of Niches

It has been established both theoretically and empirically that classification that relates human and environmental variables can improve prisoner adjustment and prison management, sometimes substantially (see Wright, with Harris & Woika, 1985; Wright, 1991). There are a number of instruments that can be used in the classification process to provide individual and organizational data that make person-environment matches in ecological terms, and hence permit us to place inmates—especially the crisis-prone inmates—in niches.[9] These instruments provide "information on which inmates are in distress, what their needs are, what resources they see as available to satisfy needs, what settings best suit their needs, and how they fare in those settings" (Gibbs et al., 1983:561). They allow us to systematically exploit correctional environments, but can be expensive and time-consuming to use. Each requires an "ecological mapping" of a prison or prison system (Toch, 1977), and some correctional departments may be hard pressed to conduct such an inquiry. However, there are less ambitious options that are likely to produce similar results.

A promising alternative is the Quay (1984) classification system. With this approach, inmates are classified into three groups: "heavies" who prey on or manipulate others (they resemble the convicts discussed in Chapter Five and typified by Abbott); "moderates" who are competent to "do their own time" and willing to leave others in peace (they resemble the main group of inmates discussed in Chapter Six and typified by Malinow); and "lights" who are anxious, dependent, and readily victimized (much like the residual group of protection and high-risk inmates discussed in the closing pages of Chapter Six). The instruments developed by Quay for arriving at these classifications have the virtue of being based on official records and staff observations of prisoner behavior rather than inmate self-reports. (It stands to reason that the wolves of the prison world are not likely to identify themselves on a questionnaire. Some of the more susceptible prisoners may also be less than candid about their shortcomings.) These instruments, moreover, are inexpensive and easy to use. They can be completed by prison staff in the process of carrying out their normal duties (Quay, 1984:9–10).

Using the Quay system, inmates can be assigned to housing and perhaps even program units that segregate predator from prey (see Levinson, 1988). The middle or neutral group can be quartered separately, but also used to fill out bed- or program-space throughout the prison since they do not involve themselves in destructive prison games (Bohn, 1979 & 1980). Interestingly, the "heavies" settle down when the easy victims are removed from their midst; there is a cold war rather than a civil war in these units (Bohn, 1980). Most inmates are able to relax and go about the business of living in prison in a civilized manner. Within the comparatively stable prison worlds produced by this safety-oriented classification process, ecological variation will develop spontaneously to accommodate other kinds of needs. In particular, the natural development of niches and sanctuaries will proceed apace. Information about these ecological developments can be incorporated in subsequent classifications decisions. Thus prisoners can be assigned to living quarters, for example, that are suitable in terms of both their Quay level and their ecological profile. A "light" inmate with strong privacy and support concerns can be housed with other "light" inmates who have similar or compatible ecological concerns.

In the free world, people develop their own ecological matches (find their own niches) when they select the neighborhoods they live in, the people they associate with, and the activities they pursue. Their capacity to do this is always subject to practical limitations. Nowhere are these limitations more pronounced than in prison, where it is hard to know what different environments are available and often impossible to move from one setting to another. Classification can be used as an aid or even as a substitute for the self-selection process (Toch, 1981:7). Classification is particularly effective when it is undertaken by staff teams, who can pool their experiences to make better recommendations. Teamwork often breeds a sense of commitment among staff, and hence a greater willingness to take inmate concerns into account (Hepburn & Albonetti, 1978). When informed and responsive classification decisions are made, the natural diversity of prison environments can be better used to meet the diverse adjustment needs of inmates.

Classification can in fact do more than facilitate self-selection among existing prison environments. Classification permits staff to create special environments—formal enclaves or niches—and to manage them according to the needs and program objectives of their inhabitants. As Weiner (1988:304) has observed,

> we can attain a more flexible system by developing a variety of organizational structures and climates within the confines of a single institutional setting. . . . Different units can also be managed differently. Some institutional units may require tight organizational structure, with rigid rules and no input on the part of inmates regarding their living arrangements. Other living units may be more open and flexible, with fewer rules and more input by inmates regarding decisions affecting them. . . . [I]t seems both feasible and desirable to experiment on the degree to which such settings could be created and to examine the effects such environments might have on reducing stress among inmates and staff and, under certain conditions, providing viable contexts for treatment.

Experiences in the federal prison system, in over half the states (including some jail systems as well), and in such countries as Canada, Holland, Sweden, New Zealand, and Australia, bear out Weiner's remarks (see Levinson, 1991:44; Unit Management Guidelines, 1990). In these various systems, prisoners are routinely assigned to functional units that differ according to prisoner types, management styles, social norms, and program offerings.

Functional units, according to Levinson (1988:244–45), one of the originators of this key correctional innovation, share the following characteristics:

> (a) a relatively small number of offenders—75 to 125; (b) who are housed together—generally throughout the length of their institutional stay; (c) who work in a close, intensive relationship with a multidisciplinary, relatively permanently assigned team of staff members whose offices are located on the unit; (d) with these personnel having decision-making authority for all within-institution aspects of programming and disciplinary actions; and where (e) the placement of an offender in a particular living unit is contingent upon a need for the specific type of treatment program offered.

A prison with a thousand inmates, for example, would be subdivided into roughly ten functional units, with each unit functioning as a small prison with its own social climate and programmatic focus of operation. Prisons that use a unit management system are considerably better organized than other prisons; a high level of organization, in turn, permits responsiveness to the varying needs and concerns of prisons. As a general matter, prisons run on a functional unit model are safer, more humane, and more readily adapted to correctional programming than are traditional, undifferentiated prisons.

Functional unit management offers a flexible approach to the classification and management of different groups. With a functional unit management structure in place, special-risk or special-needs inmates can be readily offered a coherent routine that at once addresses their situation and also integrates them, in varying degrees, into the life of the larger prison. (Note that functional units are never isolation units; they are *in* and *of* the prisons within which they are housed.)

Prisoners with HIV/AIDS provide a case in point. In two states, Alabama and Mississippi, these inmates are segregated in what amount to isolation units, which are distinctly reminiscent of leper colonies (see Note 8, Chapter One). In other states and the federal system, prisoners with HIV/AIDS are mixed in with the general population, either presumptively—as a matter of course—or on a case-by-case basis (see Hammett et al., 1994:59–62). A functional unit approach allows correctional administrators to group such inmates together in constructive ways when this is appropriate. In a functional unit for inmates in the advanced stages of HIV infection, for example, unit activities could focus on the medical and psychological problems associated with the disease. Depending on the progression of the disease in individual cases, offenders could be integrated into regular prison program services and activities on a selective basis. For inmates with HIV/AIDS who are asymptomatic, placement in a particular functional unit would be determined by other variables, such as their work or program needs or their style of adjustment. (This is currently the case in most prison systems that use the functional unit model.) In such cases, the unit approach still gives correctional administrators the flexibility to offer some special services (such as unit-based support groups) that are tailored to the unique situation faced by these offenders.

When prisons are "unitized," as is said in correctional circles these days, the results are impressive. Social climate ratings improve; this proves true both "for tougher and for more vulnerable inmates" (Toch, 1981:7; see also Levinson, 1988 & 1991, and Smith & Fenton, 1978). Particularly worthy of note are reduced rates of violence. Data on violence rates from 1984 through 1989, a period of unitization in a number of systems, shows a startling 50 percent drop in violent deaths in our nation's prisons. This decrease in violence occurred, moreover, in the face of rapid prison population growth (Herrick, 1989). Violence decreases under a functional unit management system because these units, by their very nature, allow for the physical removal of predators from the environments populated by victims, and permit individualized management and treatment of aggressive inmates within the functional units to which they are assigned (see Levinson, 1991:48).

Specific success stories in which the use of unit management resulted in dramatic drops in violence and equally dramatic improvements in social climate include Rikers Island in New York, Folsom Prison in California and, perhaps most notably, Massachusetts's Walpole Prison (now known as Cedar Junction).[10] A report on Walpole in the late 1980s, after the introduction of unit management, concluded that a "10-year history of violence, cost overruns and general administrative turmoil" came to an end once functional unit management was introduced (Herrick, 1989:8).

> The hostile conditions at Walpole have been all but eliminated, and it is a much improved facility in which to live and work. . . . Although Walpole (MCI: Cedar Junction) is still overcrowded, there is much less violence and fear. (Herrick, 1989:8)

Unit management was subsequently adopted at other Massachusetts prisons (Herrick, 1989:8). It is worth noting that, at least as of 1991, "no system that has adopted unit management has subsequently abandoned it" (Levinson, 1991:44).

One reason for the longevity of unit management is that it receives strong staff support once it is in place. While staff may initially resist this innovation, just as people generally resist any profound change in the way things are done, staff quickly find that functional units are more appropriate to their personal and career needs than traditional prison management approaches. With functional unit management, it is easier for officers to get to know individual inmates and hence to evolve correctional rather than merely custodial roles (Levinson, 1988:245; Levinson, 1991). Conflicts between custody and treatment staffs are reduced, since functional units typically develop a healthy collegial climate (see Gerard, 1991:34; Pierson, 1991:30). Staff with functional units typically give their prisons high marks as working environments (Gerard, 1991). One reason is that staff are given more decision-making authority in functional unit systems. Each unit manager is, in effect, a warden; his or her staff are, in effect, high-level administrators of these miniature prison worlds. Since unit staff are more autonomous than their counterparts in regular prisons, they can become effective leaders; as one measure of such leadership, staff can offer more direct and indirect autonomy to the inmates in their care (see Levinson, 1988; Wright, 1994). Finally, there are indications that small but consistent drops in recidivism rates may be a consequence of this organizational reform, independent of the specific correctional programming offered to inmates (Levinson, 1988:242).[11]

Orientation, Monitoring, and Stress Reduction

Classification and placement in congenial settings is not enough to ensure effective adjustment. Prisoners must be carefully introduced to their new world and monitored in their reactions to it. Even the most accommodating prison environment can be a source of stress, particularly at the outset when the disjuncture between free world and prison world is apt to be great and, for some persons, traumatic.[12] For most prisoners, the initial stress of entering the prison produces social withdrawal and retreat within an emotional shell. This protective reaction, essentially a form of psychological shock, can be easily mistaken for callousness or hostility and used to justify neglectful or even repressive custodial measures. Yet "most stressed persons need and want assistance" (Toch, 1988:26). Ideally they should be given task-oriented support that provides reassurance, information, and reinforcement of problem-solving behavior as it applies in the new environment (Janis, 1969).

Toch has suggested an orientation program for incoming prisoners that would generate constructive anxiety about the prison situation. The newly arrived inmate should feel neither invulnerable ("prison is a snap") nor hopelessly demoralized ("nobody survives this joint"). Instead, common problems and feasible solutions are considered. For example, a prisoner is warned "you might be approached for sex," but advised, "guys who make friends are less likely to be bothered." Advice from selected prisoners may be valuable in this context.[13] Lifers, in particular, would seem able to draw on their personal experiences in prison to help newcomers frame individual adjustment strategies; wisely, they admonish newcomers to "do their own time" and to generally use their time in prison to improve themselves (see Zamble, 1992).[14] An overview of prison environments and programs that identifies options in problem-solving gambits is also appropriate. The idea is to apprise the newcomer of the problems at hand and the resources at his disposal, and then to encourage him to work out his own plans for reassuring and protecting himself. Two goals are thus achieved: (1) The individual's feelings of resourcelessness and vulnerability are reduced; and (2) Inmates as a group begin to see prison as a negotiable set of challenges, to which they might eventually learn to respond in mature and mutually supportive ways (Toch, 1988:26–27).

An effective orientation will help inmates get their feet on the ground and begin to use prison resources to address problems of adjustment, but there is no guarantee that all or even most problems will be handled constructively. Monitoring the placement of individual prisoners and revising assignments as required are essential to ensuring the viability of man-environment matches. Monitoring will also keep inmates and staff, especially the line officers who are in a position to observe adjustments over time, in continuing and supportive relationships with one another.

In an ideal prison system, no one would ever send inmates into an environment with which he (the classifier) was not intimately familiar, and where he couldn't personally monitor the consequences of his decisions. All classification would have to be tentative because people and settings change. There would also be routine opportunities for "trial classifications" in which inmates try settings out, and settings try out inmates, and for assignments that are strictly contingent on special conditions (such as peace and quiet, or personal involvement in therapy) in the absence of which they would be voided. . . . [G]uards and other staff would monitor classification. If the classifier is wrong, he must be told he is wrong. Since he may make mistakes, he must learn from them, to avoid endangering the next inmate on the assembly line. (Toch, 1981:6–7).

We know from research on pluralistic ignorance that many inmates act tougher than they really are, particularly when they first arrive at a prison. Monitoring will help identify those who were thus incorrectly classified.

As a practical matter, prison officers will be the primary agents of environmental monitoring. The more human service-oriented officers are well suited for this role; some of them will almost certainly expand it to include more ambitious functions. These officers already operate as a kind of indigenous cadre of "environmental engineers." Often they supplement advice and counseling, which make up the grist of human service work, with tangible assistance. In specific terms, they

> alter custodial routines, modulate surveillance and orchestrate assignments for the sole purpose of enhancing adjustment. They do so unsystematically, irregularly, and without a clear sense of the ecological factors being manipulated. The fact that they do so at all, however, suggests that . . . environmental variables can be manipulated naturally and effectively by those familiar with a setting. (Seymour, 1988:275)

Thus, officers need not be limited to a passive role as classification monitors. Nor need they be limited to a haphazard familiarity with the prison ecology. They can be trained to think in ecological terms and even to shape environments. Their task would be not only to monitor placements but, where possible, to improve man-environment matches. Ideally, in recognition of their expanded skills and responsibilities, the correctional officers' role would be invested with more autonomy. Their views on prison ecology and inmate adjustment would be formally taken into account and would influence official decisions pertaining to these matters (for instance, by way of staff classification and assignment teams).[15]

Special training is required to prepare officers for formal roles as environmental agents. Officers must be versed in the ecology of prison and alerted to the possible presence of niches in various locations within their particular facility (Johnson & Price, 1981:367). They must understand the various "ways in which ecological resources can be cultivated and deployed to reduce stress," ideally by examining their own human service activities and those of fellow staff (Johnson & Price, 1981:367). Moreover, training should help officers "to see their own experiences and characteristics, as well as those of their inmates, as environmental attributes" that can be used to solve problems (Johnson & Price, 1981:367).

The training process envisioned here is an active one. General ecological information must be assimilated and applied by officers to specific situations that matter to them. Training that is too general, even if it is otherwise quite thorough, merely frustrates and further alienates officers, who feel unprepared for the challenges they face in their particular prisons and job assignments (see Fitzgerald & Sim, 1982:128). The objective of ecological training, by contrast, is to "help staff to think through the implications of available options" and to evolve their own plans for maximizing their effectiveness (Toch, 1984:14). Like inmates, they must be introduced to the prison ecology. Hence, the training process parallels the prisoner orientation process, providing information, assurance, and reinforcement of problem-solving behavior. This training satisfies the often-stated desire of officers to develop skills that help them do their jobs right. The ultimate beneficiaries, however, are the inmates. For staff who are equipped to understand and use the prison ecology "can play active roles in providing sanctuaries for inmates in stress," and can serve as models of mature coping under pressure (Johnson & Price, 1981:367).

Participation, Support, and Community

A supportive prison culture emerges when staff and prisoners work together to make the prison a haven for citizens and not a lair for predator and prey. A supportive prison culture presupposes a classification and management process that, in effect, makes the typical prison environment a niche. It culminates when staff and inmates use these enclaves as arenas for autonomous action and constructive social learning. Niches, in other words, provide a bridge between personal adjustment and personal reform.

In constructive niches, staff and inmates evolve a problem-solving culture instead of merely a shelter from stress. These settings serve as prototypes of responsive or therapeutic prison communities (Toch, 1980:10); they also share some of the key attributes of other democratically run prison environments (see Fitzgerald & Sim, 1982:117).[16] Inmates and staff cooperate with one another in responsive or therapeutic communities because cooperation serves their individual needs; they quite naturally become altruistic egotists because they partake in a shared and reasonably stable future marked by frequent and durable interpersonal relations (see Chapter Four). An "adult principled moral perspective" can be a predictable product of the "intensive community life" that thrives in such milieus (Scharf, 1978:189; Scharf, 1980; Regens & Hobson, 1978, Toch, 1994:71). The reason is that inmates operate in these environments as responsible consumers of correctional services. The give and take of daily community life, in Toch's (1994:71) words, "involves adult-to-adult transactions between prisoners and staff. It requires prisoners to do something to get something." This is never easy, as Toch (1994a) reminds us, but the process can be profoundly rewarding.

In these environments, prisoners cope maturely; they meet the daily problems of prison life head on, without manipulation or deception, and with the cooperation and support of their fellows. Longer-term adjustment problems can also be broached. Inmates examine their adjustment styles and experiment with new ways of handling stress and resolving conflict (Jones, 1980; Grant, 1980). In such environments, Toch (1994:69) notes, "One learns to be prosocial by working with others and to govern oneself through involvement in governance. As one learns, one assists others to learn and is assisted by others in doing so." Prisoners in these environments can be transformed from impulsive adolescents who operate in a dangerous playground to self-governing adults who belong to a small and secure community within the larger prison.

Some level of direct participation in the governance process is an essential element of responsive communities in prison, and it is this feature that promotes a healthy adult autonomy among both staff and inmates. Participation can take many forms and can vary in degree (see Toch, 1994). Depending on skills, interest, and the overall stability of the institution, inmates can be involved, in collaboration with officials, in the governance of the entire institution or a segment of an institution (such as a functional unit). Inmates can be involved, again in conjunction with officials, in specific groups dealing with specific issues, such as orientation, programming, or food service. Or prisoners can "individually participate in their own management, sharing critical decisions along the way, and reviewing their progress at key junctures in their careers" with the appropriate officials (Toch, 1994:69). Participation brings with it a sense of involvement and commitment. Participants actively engage their environments. They have a stake in the community and a tangible reason to work to improve themselves.

(Inmates with HIV/AIDS are a much-maligned and often-marginalized group that might greatly benefit from involvement in responsive prison communities, ideally housed within functional units. These inmates face special challenges and stresses associated with their fateful diagnoses. One would suppose that if any group needed a constructive niche to help them in their adjustment to prison and indeed to life, it is this group. Their problems are many and the resources available to them in the larger prison, given the fear and loathing their illness may promote, are regrettably few. In a functional unit designed to support these prisoners, for example, community efforts could be focused on managing the disease. The internal regime could be built around efforts to humanize the sometimes painful delivery of medical care, experiment with coping techniques that help the prisoners to face and work through the implications of the illness, and develop self-help groups to foster a climate of relatedness to others. To the extent that these inmates can, as a community, come to grips with their shared problems, they may come to feel that they are living with AIDS rather than dying from it.)

Supportive communities, whatever the focus of group involvement, typically flower in relative isolation, in niches rather than in the public areas of the prison. They are intimate arrangements, on the order of neighborhoods rather than cities. To endure, they require support and leadership. "Even the most creative of us," Toch (1980:10) makes clear, "take wing from sure footing. The community catalyzer must provide an accepting, reliable, and supportive milieu (an oasis) before asking clients to take risks." At this juncture, one can engage "higher human needs" than mere survival at any price. "These higher needs include needs for companionship, for recognition, and for creative outlets"—needs that would seem to beg for expression in remedial programs that hold out the promise of enfranchising the emerging citizens of the prison community (Toch, 1980:11).

PART TWO: PRISON PROGRAMS

Prison programs were in recession during the 1970s and early 1980s, and though they have made something of a comeback over the last decade, the overall picture is still a discouraging one. The typical state prison, for example, offers few programs of substance. To make matters worse, existing programs are often of limited appeal to inmates. Most of them focus on an inmate's past life and future prospects; they seek to rectify yesterday's problems in order to build a better tomorrow. Too often, however, the struggle for personal survival *today*, in the here-and-now world of the prison, distracts the prisoner's attention from the few rehabilitation programs that do exist and might be of benefit to him. To make prison programs more relevant and useful, corrections must (1) operate prisons in which stress remains within manageable limits and is handled maturely, and (2) offer an adequate number of programs that enhance the prisoner's capacity to cope maturely with life stresses, both now in prison and later in the free world.

Reforming criminals is a formidable job. Persistent felons, who are the majority in any maximum-security prison population, are especially hard to reach. Yet they are desperately in need of help if they are to maintain hope for a constructive future. As Conrad (1981b:64) reminds us,

> a criminal career is a desperate career, a career in which hope must be satisfied by transient "scores," ultimately and inescapably terminated by the successive disasters of apprehension, prosecution, conviction, and incarceration. Anyone experiencing this sequence may well abandon hope of rejoining the conventional society, if he ever had any such aspiration. Most prisons do little to turn the convict from desperation to hope.

Hope is an especially rare commodity in today's prisons. The view that "nothing works" in corrections—a view now held by a sizable contingent of prison practitioners as well as by prison critics, not to mention politicians hard-pressed to cut prison budgets[17]—permits us to warehouse without pretense and to call it justice.

The view that "nothing works" originates with the observation by Robert Martinson (1974:25), based on a survey of studies of correctional programs, that "with few and isolated exceptions, the rehabilitative efforts that have been reported so far have had no appreciable effect on recidivism." A similar conclusion has been reached by the Panel on Research on Rehabilitative Techniques (Sechrest, White, & Brown, 1979) convened by the National Academy of Sciences. Why do most programs fail? Many fail (and here I am thinking of standard educational and vocational programs) because they offer too little too late to attract a prisoner's attention and motivate him to change his style of life. These programs often seem irrelevant in the prison context, where the quality of one's life normally is unaffected by performance in school or work. To the extent that a prisoner participates in such programs and learns something from them, these programs are unlikely, on their own, to remedy the deficits that account for his poor adjustment. He emerges from these programs not as a reformed citizen, but as a more literate mugger or as a robber who is also a handyman. Programs that seek to reform the person, rather than merely tinker with some aspect of his behavioral repertoire, fail for different reasons. They attempt too much. Rehabilitative goals are defined in utopian terms, with inmates forced to endure programs that do not address their real concerns.

Group therapy is perhaps the most common form of correctional intervention that aims to reform the person. Braly (1967:90–96), an ex-prisoner, has written a novel that touches on the core problem of this method; Manocchio and Dunn (1982:109–17), relating their experiences as therapist and patient, reinforce Braly's observations. In both accounts, the therapist is saddled with a group that has been assigned to him for no other reason than that its members must someday appear before a parole board and claim to be rehabilitated. Undaunted, each therapist asks the group to explore the dynamics of their criminality and, in the process, reveal and examine intimate details from the past. For each therapist, the aim is to elucidate and transform the characters of the reluctant clients; the goal is to produce some semblance of middle-class citizenry. Most of the inmates, however, want no part of the therapeutic agenda. The therapists' middle-class man, they know, will be eaten alive on the yard. So they mock the "hoosiers" who wallow in guilt and self-pity, and they generally subvert the therapeutic process through long silences, diversionary tactics, and caustic humor. Most resent being forced into therapy to please the parole board, and make little effort to hide this from the therapist. A cold war ensues. Little that can properly be called therapy takes place.

Note that there are some prisoners in these groups who are willing to explore their personal problems. The treatment climate is ruined, however, by the more numerous malcontents who correctly view the entire enterprise as an exercise in coercion that is patently irrelevant to their prison lives. When these groups do take up matters pertaining to prison life, the cynical inmates have nothing to say. Those who talk are seen as stupid (they don't know enough to shut up when officials pump them for information) or untrustworthy (they are "rats" who turn in their fellows to please the staff). The result is that the amenable therapy clients are, at a minimum, ridiculed by their peers. Some of these prisoners may nevertheless persevere and ultimately benefit from the treatment experience, but others may be psychologically harmed by it. The nonamenable prisoners are apt to view the treatment as a waste of time. They will be either untouched or embittered by the experience. It is hardly surprising that overall recidivism rates for the treatment groups would be unimproved, or even made worse, by such correctional programs.

But overall recidivism rates can be misleading. Some rehabilitation programs do indeed work for some offenders under some conditions. The problem is that differential effects are often masked by classification and assignment practices that mix amenable and nonamenable inmates in the same program. As we have just noted, such mixing of offenders contaminates the treatment climate and makes it less likely that the amenable prisoners will benefit from treatment. It also means that the predictable failures of the nonamenable prisoners will be counted as failures of the program, when in point of fact those inmates should not have been there in the first place (see Grant & Grant, 1959).

Differential treatment effects have not been considered systematically in correctional practice or research (Palmer, 1975, 1978, 1991 & 1994). This omission means that both the impact and the potential of correctional treatment are likely to be understated. Research that takes account of differential treatment effects—that examines the interplay of risk, need and responsiveness (Andrews et al., 1990)—reveals that programs can reduce recidivism substantially with a range of offenders in a range of settings. "At the very least," Gendreau and Ross conclude, following an extensive literature review, "the recent trends in the literature support a grudging acceptance of the renewed possibilities of a potent rehabilitation agenda" (1987:351).

Moreover, ecological factors relating to the inmate's general prison adjustment, which can make or break a treatment regime, have been largely ignored in the treatment area. When person-environment matches in living and working areas reinforce proper program placements, the result will be the development, on a large scale, of constructive niches. In these supportive milieus, trust is established. Prisoners feel secure enough to take the risks necessary to explore delicate matters of adjustment. Fellow participants serve as helpful colleagues rather than cagey adversaries. Mature coping becomes the norm. Under these propitious conditions, differential program effects should be substantially enhanced.

Martinson later repudiated the notion that "nothing works" (see Martinson, 1978), but this "despairing slogan . . . continues to dot the correctional landscape" (Levinson, 1988:242). One reason is the broad ideological appeal of the "nothing works" slogan.

> "Nothing works" seemed to satisfy conservative political reaction to the apparent disorder of the 1960s, liberal sorrow over perceived failures of the "great society," and the ideological and intellectual persuasions of those academics whose truly social visions of deviance asserted that only radical social change could impact on crime. (Andrews et al., 1990:370)

Yet "the 'nothing works' belief, reduced to its most elementary level," should satisfy no one, because it "suggests that delinquents are incapable of re-learning or acquiring new behaviors" in the contemporary prison context (Gendreau & Ross, 1980:5). This belief is as untenable as it is self-serving. It is indeed ironic, as Gendreau and Ross (1980:27) observe,

> that while we have often heard the clinical observation that many offenders today seem to avoid responsibility for their behaviors, the fact is that if we persist in the verdict that treatment is unsuccessful then the "nothing works" doctrine also encourages the correctional system to avoid responsibility. By labelling the offender as untreatable we make it apparent to one and all that we cannot be held responsible for his improvement or his deterioration.

A corollary view labels prisons as unregenerate institutions, incapable of anything other than dehumanizing those who enter its walls—a "nothing works" milieu offering "nothing works" programs. We are all off the hook, then, except the prisoners who suffer the consequences of our self-proclaimed impotence.

COLLABORATIVE TRAINING

Though the problems of prisons are serious, as we have seen, they are tractable. The same holds for the problems of prisoners. Robert B. Levinson (1988:247), a psychologist with years of experience researching rehabilitation programs in prisons, tells us that

> Offenders enter prisons with a variety of deficits. That is, some are socially or morally inept; others are intellectually or vocationally handicapped; some have emotional hang-ups that stem from internal psychological problems and/or have externally generated deficiencies as a consequence of environmental or family circumstances; and still others have a mixture composed of varying proportions of some or even all of these.

These deficits, which collectively express themselves in the immaturity we have examined at some length (see Chapter Four), can often be addressed and resolved by the inmates themselves—with guidance from the staff. "The role of staff," observes Levinson (1988:247), "is to help prisoners help themselves." It is not the staff's business to cure prisoners of psychological maladies or to overhaul their characters, but rather to "assist them in identifying where their deficits are and encourage them to participate in programs that are designed to help fill in the gaps" (Levinson, 1988:247). At issue is neither involuntary treatment (the hallmark of the rehabilitative ideal) nor calculated punishment (the hallmark of the warehouse prison). Instead, a voluntary collaborative training enterprise is sought. Here, inmates define themselves as amenable to help by seeking the program. They ally themselves with the staff, whose express function is to promote better coping by helping to "train inmates in the use of alternative ways of responding to the pressures of living" in both the prison and the free community (Levinson, 1988:247).

Staff engaged in collaborative training do not treat disorders or punish indiscretions. The focus of their activities "is not on seeking methods to eliminate 'wrong' behavior," but instead "becomes one of helping prisoners develop a more appropriate repertoire of responses" (Levinson, 1988:247). One of the more potent means of doing this is for staff to practice what they preach, that is, to be living examples of mature behavior under stress. This obligation may be too often honored in the breach. Yet constructive role modeling is quite consistent with how many line officers, the primary staff group with whom inmates come into regular contact, attempt to play their role (see Chapter Eight).

Staff can also draw upon a small but growing body of programs that promote mature behavior in prison. Such programs successfully "develop a more appropriate repertoire of responses" among a fairly wide range of prisoners, "either reducing anti-social behavior in the institution or . . . enhancing the offenders' academic achievement or industrial productivity" (Ross & McKay, 1980: 47–48). Of special interest are those interventions that promote mature responses in the face of interpersonal stress, helping many prisoners to relax under pressure (Abrams & Siegel, 1978; Ellis, 1979; Bleick & Abrams, 1984) and to relate to others, particularly figures of authority, in a more calm and rational way (Bornstein et al., 1979, Golden et al., 1980; see, generally, Bennett, Rosenbaum & McCullough, 1978).

The characteristics of these successful programs conform closely to the notion of collaborative training. They include the following, drawn from Ross and McKay (1980:49–50):

1. Successful programs were not imposed on the offenders in authoritarian fashion but involved the offenders in program planning.

2. Successful programs sought to strengthen prosocial behaviors rather than attempting directly to reduce the frequency of inappropriate or anti-social acts. They thus avoided the pitfall of strengthening anti-social behavior by giving it undue attention and avoided generating expectancies for anti-social behavior.[18]

3. Successful programs neutralized or mobilized the offender's peer group.

Increasingly, it has been recognized that successful programs must, in addition, offer "intensive services" to "high-risk clients" (Gendreau, 1989). Low-risk clients, it turns out, do not need services, and high-risk clients can only benefit from services if they are given in sufficient quantity to move them to alter their criminal lifestyles. The goal, broadly speaking, is to make conventional living a competitive alternative to a life of crime. Most often, this is done by reinforcing and modeling strategies of conventional living, and providing sufficient coping skills to allow inmates to adapt effectively in the conventional world. In particular, offenders must be helped to think clearly about problems and to exert self-control (see Andrews et al., 1990).

Broadly speaking, effective programs are characterized by what Gendreau has termed "integrity," meaning that they delivered, in a credible and caring way, on their promises (Gendreau, 1989). To maintain integrity, in turn, programs had to have the qualities of formal niches; they needed their own space, their own culture or climate, and a degree of independence from the larger prison (see, for example, Lipton, Falkin & Wexler, 1990:28). (Note that functional unit management provides a ready administrative vehicle for the provision of formal niches for correctional programs.) Offenders, voluntarily involved in meaningful programs that promoted a range of prosocial skills, tend to become more constructively autonomous and, as a result, less likely—and sometimes much less likely—to recidivate.

Levinson (1988) has described the implementation of Norval Morris's "model prison" at the federal prison in Butner, North Carolina. This program of voluntary, facilitated change, housed in functional units, is a prototype of collaborative training (Morris, 1974). Marked improvements in program participation and prison behavior came in the wake of this reform, beyond those associated with functional units and standard correctional programs elsewhere in the federal prison system. These inmates, with help from the staff, coped maturely with imprisonment. There was little violence; candid and constructive efforts at problem solving and relationship building were the norm

(Levinson, 1988:251). Some of these lessons in mature living may have carried over into the free world, resulting in a modest decrease in recidivism in comparison to a control group of prisoners exposed only to functional units and standard correctional programs in other federal prisons.[19] Additionally, the Butner graduates obtained and kept better jobs while on release, stayed out of prison longer than other releasees, and turned to crimes that were, on the whole, less serious than those of other former inmates (Witte et al., 1983). If personal reform is a matter of successive approximations of conventional lifestyles in the free world, then the Butner experiment is an important correctional intervention.

Toch has done seminal work on self-management as a means to self-control, particularly in the context of violence among police and criminal populations.[20] The core insight of this work—which is shared with all subsequently developed coping programs, including those with a cognitive focus, to be discussed below—is that people can learn to monitor and control themselves in social environments. They can become "social scientists" in the sense that they learn, with the support of peers in a group context, to objectively observe and then control their own conduct in a range of social situations. As Toch and Grant (1989:222–23) have observed,

> By sharing a review of one's patterned problems with one's peers and then sharing with such peers an accountability strategy for modifying one's pattern, a person can move through cognitive problem solving, to what Maxwell Jones called "emotional social learning."

The beneficiaries of such programs are transformed into autonomous actors, persons liberated by insight and constrained—or better, channeled—in their daily lives by emotional bonds to others.

An explicit focus on developing environments that support mature coping is advocated by Zamble and Porporino. They envision a prison "comprised of a set of modular units" that are, in effect, functional units. In these supportive living environments, programs on coping would predominate. Such programs would

> include training in problem recognition, problem analysis, and weighing and choosing coping alternatives. Because it is clear that inmates need to learn not only *when* to use certain types of actions but also *how* to use them, there should also be training in a variety of specific coping skills, such as negotiation, objectification of situations, and cognitive reevaluation. (Zamble & Porporino, 1990:69)

Inmates would also be helped to organize time more productively, and, as needed, offered "specific behavioral treatment for alcohol and drug abuse, using an approach consistent with the overall emphasis on coping" (Zamble & Porporino, 1990:69). Programs would begin at the start of a prisoner's term, when motivation for change is strongest; there would be a concentrated programming effort at the end of the prisoner's term and just after release, to facilitate reintegration into the free world (Zamble & Porporino, 1990:67). Ideally, the functional units, if not the larger prisons in which they are embedded, would reinforce mature coping, operating as "'total environments' that change coping behavior rather than ones that have no effect or that mostly maintain maladaptive patterns" (Zamble & Porporino, 1990:69–70).

A recent and promising innovation that systematically and comprehensively addresses general deficiencies in coping that are common among criminal populations has been undertaken in Canada under the rubric of Living Skills programming. Living Skills programs focus on autonomous self-management as an alternative to destructive criminal lifestyles. Living Skills programs, according to Canadian correctional officials, "were designed to be available throughout the incarceration period in order to meet the offender's most relevant needs in the process of preparing for reintegration" (Fabiano, Robinson & Porporino, 1991:1). Living Skills programs develop coping competence. The aim of Living Skills programs, quite explicitly, is to promote mature coping so that offenders can adapt constructively to life in prison and in the free community.

At the core of the Living Skills program is a module labeled "cognitive skills training." Subsequent programs tackle "living without violence," "family life/parenting skills," "anger/emotional management," "leisure education," and "community integration skills," which include skills relevant to finding and keeping a job and a place to live. It is considered axiomatic in this program that "cognitive inadequacies" are the main sources of criminal deviance (Fabiano, Robinson & Porporino, 1991:6). "Offenders with cognitive inadequacies," we learn, "are likely to evidence major difficulties in social adjustment" (Fabiano, Robinson & Porporino, 1991:6) They are impulsive, and tend to act before they think. When they do stop to think, they think poorly. They blame others, and fail to see their own impact on others. Their thought processes are variously described as "simplistic and illogical" and "exceptionally shallow, narrow and rigid" (Fabiano, Robinson & Porporino, 1991:5). They are egocentric, unable to see the world as others see it or indeed to see others as full-blooded human beings. Insensitive to others, they misread social situations. They fail to anticipate problems, and are unable to foresee solutions. They cannot, if you will, think their way through to a solution of a social problem.

This description of the general patterns of thinking and behavior among criminals is familiar to us from our review of the criminological literature in Chapter Four. The good news is that the Canadian program establishes that many if not most offenders can be *taught* to *think clearly* and *cope competently* across the range of life situations they will encounter in prison and in the free world (Fabiano, Robinson & Porporino, 1991:6). This is not, moreover, a one-way treatment process in which experts act on sick or defective inmates; while the curriculum is a standard one, implementation involves a two-way collaborative process in which staff both *train* offenders and serve as *role models* for clear thinking and mature coping. As noted by the Canadian authorities,

> the individuals chosen as trainers were those who had enough empathic ability to understand what the offender thinks and feels, those who were able to model the kind of effective reasoning and problem-solving that they hoped offenders would acquire, and those who were able to

communicate a substantial repertoire of socio-cognitive skills concretely and clearly. (Fabiano, Robinson & Porporino, 1991:8)

Offenders are given opportunities in group sessions to digest and relate program content to their own lives. Experiences in prison, with other inmates and especially with staff, are seen as opportunities to learn and rehearse various facets of mature coping. In point of fact, each staff member within the prison, and not just those directly involved in the program, "must be able to model effective reasoning and problem-solving" and hence "must model that which they hope the offender will acquire in the program" (Fabiano, Robinson & Porporino, 1991:10). To work, then, the prison is treated as a living environment that is staffed by correctional officers (as opposed to custodial officers) and in which mature coping is explicitly encouraged and rewarded.

It is significant to note that, as at Butner, the Living Skills program targeted high-risk and high-need offenders (Fabiano, Robinson & Porporino, 1991:15). The methods of education and training are diverse and interesting, including such media and activities as visual aides, puzzles, games, reasoning exercises, role playing, and group discussions (Fabiano, Robinson & Porporino, 1991). These activities resemble neither traditional treatment methods nor conventional educational approaches. Inmates may, as a result, feel safer and less threatened in these programs.[21] It is clear, in any case, that the offenders were much benefited by participation in the Life Skills program. Fabiano, Robinson and Porporino report that, based on a series of objective pre- and postprogram attitudinal and skill measurement tests, "there is substantial evidence that those offenders who participated in the program increased their levels of cognitive skills and became less criminally oriented in their attitudes" (1991:17) In particular, offenders "became more positive in their attitudes toward the law, courts and police, increased in their social perspective-taking abilities, improved in critical reasoning skills, and showed more capacity for [flexible] thinking" (Fabiano, Robinson & Porporino, 1991:21).

The participants in the Life Skills programs, moreover, perceived themselves to have made substantial strides. The program produced insight, in the sense that the offenders were able to apply the various curricula to their own lives in constructive ways. For example, fully nine out of ten perceived themselves to have improved in the following areas of personal adjustment:

Conversations with friends and others;

Controlling anger and other emotions;

Handling stress more effectively;

Thinking through problems;

Preventing jumping to conclusions;

Considering others' perspectives and why they react;

Patience and tolerance of self and others.

Eighty percent of the inmates felt they had improved in the daunting area of "setting goals and planning life more effectively" (Fabiano, Robinson & Porporino, 1991:19).

Follow-up research with Life Skills program graduates indicates a sizeable drop in recidivism, with a 20 percent rearrest rate for the program group and a 30 percent rate for the comparison group (Robinson, Grossman & Porporino, 1991:4). Focussing on high-risk offenders only, the figures are even more impressive: only 18 percent of the high-risk program group recidivated, compared with a 42 percent rate for the high-risk inmates among the comparison group (Robinson, Grossman & Porporino, 1991:8). Clearly, this comprehensive program, particularly when targeted at high-risk and high-need offenders, offers great promise as a correctional intervention. It is encouraging that Life Skills programs have been adopted in a number of states.

Other promising cognitive and behavioral programs exist as well, each with varying approaches to collaborative programming, and each sharing the goal that offenders become more autonomous. Favorable results have been reported for the Cognitive Self-Change Program, developed jointly by the National Institute of Justice and the U.S. Navy (Bush & Bilodeau, 1993), and for the Criminal Violence Program (Bush, 1988; see also Hunter 1993), which is modeled on the Cognitive Self-Change Program. Of related interest are programs that deal with drug abuse (discussed below), which could be readily offered in conjunction with, or in addition to, Living Skills programs.

As noted earlier, important advances have been made in helping offenders control anger and aggression. Effective programs are also available for drug and alcohol abusers, who can be helped to manage their lives without resort to these addictive substances. As we noted in Chapter One, drug offenders make up almost one-third of a typical prison population. Moreover, roughly two of every three criminals uses drugs regularly in the free world; fully one third of this group uses hard drugs like cocaine or heroin on a daily basis. By the time these offenders enter prisons, whether confined for drug offenses or for other felonies, they are "entrenched in a lifestyle that includes drugs and crime" (NIJ, 1989:1). Often, the drugs serve as an anesthetic for the pain and anger that characterize the dead-end lives of so many felons (see Chapter Four). It is of considerable import, then, that there are now "large-scale evaluations" of collaborative drug treatment programs, notably Stay'n Out and the Cornerstone program, that "provide solid evidence that prison-based therapeutic community treatment can produce significant reductions in recidivism rates among chronic drug abusing felons" (Lipton, Falkin & Wexler, 1990:23; see also Wexler & Williams, 1986). Given long-term treatment—nine to twelve months in duration—success rates with this "highly predatory" group are impressive; fully three of every four offenders treated "reenter the community and lead a socially acceptable lifestyle" (Lipton, Falkin & Wexler, 1990:24). Note that many of these offenders mix alcohol and drugs indiscriminately. Effective programs are available for offenders whose predominant problem is alcohol (see Gendreau & Ross, 1987:384).

To work effectively, collaborative treatment programs must in effect become responsive (and hence therapeutic) communities. This is true independent of the specific content of these programs. The ethos in all such communities is one of self-help through helping others. Relations occur between and among inmates and staff, who function as equals in the program process; destructive stereotypes are shattered by continuing interpersonal contacts. The medium of helping sends an almost tangible message that each and every member of the community is a person of value. This message is profoundly anticriminogenic. As Staub (1989:277) has observed, "We devalue those we harm and value those we help. As we come to value more highly the people we help and experience the satisfaction inherent in helping, we also come to see ourselves as more caring and helpful." This new sense of oneself as a caring person, once it is firmly in place, readily generalizes to other situations and circumstances. One's self-image as a person who cares, in turn, can provide the basis for a prosocial identity, and can serve as a keen source of motivation to cope maturely in the course of one's life.

It is something of a paradox that these supportive environments, to retain their integrity, must become formal niches that are set apart from the mainline prison. Helping is, of course, an inclusive activity; a formal niche is, by definition, an exclusive undertaking. Yet "it is vital," observe Lipton, Falkin & Wexler (1990:28), "for a therapeutic community in a prison to have living space and therapeutic areas isolated from the general prison population." In the absence of such isolation, overcrowding or other pressures on the larger prison impinge on the program, destroying its social climate and with it, the ethos of helping. Note that functional unit management, which readily provides responsive communities with the sheltered context they need to carry out their correctional missions, provides a possible resolution to our paradox. In a prison run entirely on a functional unit model, it is at least possible to envision the institution as a collection of responsive communities. In such a prison, no one is arbitrarily placed beyond the reach of help.

Contractual Programs

A collaborative training model of corrections is quite adaptable. It lends itself most readily to programming under determinate sentencing schemes. Here, prisoners are released on a given date whether or not they participate in programs. They would collaborate with the staff in a purely voluntary manner, with nothing to gain but the benefits of the programs themselves. In this context, the programs—and the inmates—would speak for themselves. A collaborative training model can also be adapted to indeterminate sentencing schemes. Here, the prospect of a favorable parole decision, and hence early release, would be an incentive to complete a program plan. While prisoners serving an indeterminate sentence might well feel forced to participate in some type of program in order to impress the parole board, they would be able to collaborate freely with staff in the development of the particular program or sequence of programs they chose. This is not an ideal arrangement; some resentments about being coerced into treatment may well linger on among indeterminate-sentence prisoners. But it is better than making inmates enter programs chosen for them unilaterally by the staff. Finally, a collaborative training approach can also be used with program contracts. Prisoners, in collaboration with the staff,

would formulate their own correctional programs. By the terms of their particular contracts, they would be promised an early release date or given some
other incentive to complete the programs.

Program contracts, sometimes called release or parole contracts, take many
forms. Cullen and Gilbert (1982:273) propose that "participation by each inmate and the state in the formulation of parole contracts be made *universally
mandatory*" (emphasis added). There is no other way, in their view, to "reaffirm
rehabilitation" as a vital correctional policy. If correctional programs are not
mandatory, Cullen and Gilbert fear, they will be the first items cut when budgets come under scrutiny.

Yet involuntary programs, whether in the context of indeterminate sentences or mandatory program contracts, may create more problems than they
solve. As Irwin (1977:296–97) has observed, "the necessary therapeutic relationship between the helper and the helped" may well be

> *irrevocably damaged* if the person to be helped is forced into the relation-
> ship. Psychiatrists have argued that in order for psychotherapy to be effec-
> tive, the client must enter the relationship voluntarily. When he is coerced
> into the relationship, resentment, suspicion of the motives of the therapist,
> and lack of commitment to the therapeutic goals destroy any chances of
> success. (emphasis added)

And many prison administrators doubt that programs would ever be cut on a
massive scale, under any conditions. The reason: programs provide an important part of the daily life of any institution, offering outlets for energy and cu-
riosity and providing incentives for good behavior (see DiIulio, 1991). After
all, without programs, inmates would in effect be relegated to their cells for
the greater part of each day.

Fortunately, there is a middle ground on the matter of programming: offenders can be forced to undergo testing (to assess program needs) and to complete an orientation to the prison's programs (to familiarize themselves with
program offerings), but then be free to elect or reject programs of their own
volition. Spread before them would be a cafeteria of options, together with
some guidance as to which programs might serve them best. Should they elect
to take programs, contract terms can then be fashioned. Obligating the authorities to honor these contracts would circumvent the problems caused by
coerced change. It would also ensure that programs are provided to interested
prisoners by a prison system that was willing to hold itself accountable for de-
livering on its promises.

Contracts would normally include incentives such as "program time," time
taken off one's sentence for completion of programs. Incentives of any kind
reserved exclusively for those who take programs may encourage some inmates to take programs for the wrong reasons: to obtain the rewards and not
to learn from the programs, with the very real risk that they may ruin the programs for the sincere inmates. Some prisoners may feel compelled to "serve
time" in programs, particularly if the incentive is early release. This can be construed to be implicitly coercive (Morris, 1974). However, unless incentives are

excessive and arguably irresistible, so that inmates with no interest in self-improvement flock to programs, they should be viewed as proper uses of rewards. It is reasonable for us to encourage inmates to help themselves and unreasonable to expect them to embark on a major life change without at least some tangible benefits in the offing. Choice in this context may not be entirely free, but some choice is better than no choice at all.[22]

Contracts with program time incentives, when combined with progressive eligibility for placement in less security-oriented institutions, hold open the prospect of major reforms in the allocation of prison populations and resources. Program contracts of this sort would make it possible to (1) shorten sentences and thus reduce overcrowding through the early release of the more motivated and hence more deserving prisoners; and (2) develop comparatively inexpensive "low" or even "no-security" confinement facilities for the bulk of offenders (van den Haag, 1980), the vast majority of whom are now classified "at too high a risk level and could instead be managed safely in minimum-security institutions" as they go about the business of pursuing their program plans (Austin, 1983:575). Of critical importance is the fact that these reforms can be achieved without increasing the risk to the public of increased recidivism.[23]

Contracts that are voluntarily entered into by inmates but binding upon staff offer a rational and fair way to ease prison crowding. They seem, moreover, to be the ideal arrangement in a rehabilitative scheme in which the objective is to promote mature coping. The process of negotiating the contract would itself be an exercise in adult conflict resolution. Here the offender is a bona fide consumer of services rather than a dependent and incompetent recipient of therapeutic or correctional largesse. The prison is transformed from a repository of nonnegotiable treatments or other coercive solutions to problems to a source of services that can be accepted or rejected on their merits. In this context, mature coping means using the services at one's disposal and demanding services when they are absent. Doing the best one can with what is available—while not resorting to violence, deception, or disregard of others—presupposes having done one's best to get what one has coming.

Part of the correctional task, then, is to "produce active, even militant, citizens who can survive and grow because they can successfully demand accountability from the agencies and institutions ostensibly in existence to serve them" (Johnson & Price, 1981:356). A contract for programs, freely entered into and fulfilled by both parties, can build a sense of indebtedness to the society that provides these services, and perhaps even a willingness to serve others in turn. Such reciprocity would be a tangible sign of concern for one's fellows, and as such would be a measure of maturity. One negotiates as a mature adult, and becomes more mature and more adult in the process.

Inmates should have the right to negotiate release contracts that the state is required to honor. Failure of correctional officials to negotiate in good faith or to uphold contracts should result in either monetary damages or early release. Breaches of contracts by inmates would presumably result in the failure to gain whatever skills or knowledge the programs were meant to impart, as well as the forfeiture of any sentence reductions or other tangible benefits associated with the completion of the contract. It is fair to say that "in the long run *the very existence* of a contract system will exert pressure on correctional officials to improve treatment services" (Cullen & Gilbert, 1982:271) (emphasis added). It will also reinforce the core notions of mature coping, particularly that violence is a primitive and inappropriate way to solve problems. As Fogel (1975:206) has observed, "Men who negotiate their fates do not have to turn to violence as a method of achieving change." Nor need they use deception or assume a pose of indifference to hide hurt feelings. Instead, a constructive relationship with the correctional authorities provides a vehicle for personal reform.

Prisons in Scotland are currently implementing many of the innovations we have reviewed relating to the treatment of prisoners as consumers of correctional environments and correctional service. Scottish prisoners are accorded considerable autonomy as a matter of policy (see Scottish Prison Service, 1990). The logic, as explained by John Pearce, Regional Director of the Scottish Prison Service, is that

> if he [the prisoner] is not treated as a Responsible Person whilst in custody, and if he is not given opportunity whilst in prison to exercise some choice over his daily life, then it would be difficult to see how he was being assisted to exercise responsible choice on discharge (Pearce, 1994:8).

The Scottish penal system regularly surveys the quality of life and work in its institutions, and uses this ecological information to inform a management system whose guiding premise is that the *"actual delivery of service [is] the most important part of the organisation"* (Pearce, 1994:12; emphasis in original; see also Toch, 1994:68).

Consumer surveys uncover preferences among prisoners that may differ substantially from those held by bureaucrats removed from the daily ebb and flow of life in the prison. Officials are apt to focus on readily visible features of the prison such as how well it is maintained, how many staff it employs and inmates it holds, the number of programs offered, and so on. In England, this has recently taken the form of a major investment in plumbing, to put toilets in individual cells. (As recently as 1990, most English prisoners "slopped out" each morning because their cells lacked toilets. This had become something of an embarrassment for officials, since it gave their prisons a third-world appearance in international correctional circles.) Inmates, in contrast, are apt to focus on the experience of life inside prisons. Though many Scottish prisoners, like their English counterparts of a few years ago, live in cells without toilets, when they were surveyed the installation of in-cell toilets ranked a mere fourth on their priority list. Concerns relating to a productive human environment were paramount. "Overwhelmingly from prisoners was the desire for more and deeper contact with families, for better and more varied opportunities to develop skills and indeed for better relationships and even improved training for staff" (Pearce, 1994:14). It seems entirely likely that similar results would have obtained among the English prisoners, had they been surveyed as to their consumer preferences.

Scottish inmates, moreover, participate actively in sentence planning, where they in essence contract for services. They have a role in selecting the prison in which they will do time and the manner in which their prison time will be spent. They are assisted in this process by a "Personal Officer," which is to say, a line correctional officer whose job is to help them "work through a series of discussion and assisting papers in order to decide what should be the process and nature of the prisoner's activities through the sentence—that is, to create a Sentence Plan" (Pearce, 1994:10).

Given the aim of treating prisoners as autonomous consumers of correctional services, prison staff are seen as "facilitators in the process of change and personal development" (Pearce, 1994:8). Prison officers, in particular, play a key human service role in the change process. It is, states Pearce, "the ambition shared by Social Work Departments and the Prison Service that prison officers should deliver basic welfare services to prisoners and be supported in this by the professional, trained social worker who can then focus on the chronic and more specialist problems of prisoners" (Pearce, 1994:1) Experience in Scotland bears out these ambitions. With training and support, line officers have been "a vital pivot in addressing issues with prisoners ranging from the deeply personal through to the really practical" (Pearce, 1994:8–9) The deeply personal issues referred to by Pearce have included working in a supportive way with inmates suffering from HIV/AIDS or struggling to end their addiction to drugs. More practical issues have related to running decent units on a daily basis.

The key features of the Scottish Prison Service have been summarized by Pearce (1994:17) in the following five points.

1. That a Prison *Service* is just that—a service—and prisoners are properly a very important part of the customer base.

2. That the prison officer is *the* key worker and with proper support and training is able to deal extremely professionally with the most personal and sensitive areas of a prisoner's life as well as the good order and control tasks.

3. That regimes should reflect the needs of the prisoners to facilitate their better coping at and following release.

4. That bottom up strategic planning [as exemplified in consumer surveys] produces exciting innovation, flexibility and responsiveness and turns the place upside down like no centralised organisation could ever achieve.

5. That glossy, centrally produced programmes usually fall flat on their face.

The first point on the list is crucial. Pearce stresses that "Service Delivery is what is now driving our prisons. We are about not just clean underwear and nice food. We are about the manner in which our inmates interact with each other, interact with us and interact with their families" (Pearce, 1994:20). This focus on service delivery gives great latitude to decision makers in the field, who tailor general management directives to fit the specifics of the ecology of the prisons under consideration. Prison regimes in Scotland and elsewhere, Pearce concludes, can promote better coping through the kinds of collaborative efforts we have reviewed. "I personally believe, after many years experience, that there is much we *can* do with prisoners, *there always was*, the difference these days is that no longer are we doing it *at* them, we are doing it *with* them" (Pearce, 1994:20). It is significant to note that in Scotland, the collaborative, consumer-oriented approach is used across the board, with all types of prisoners and all types of prisons. Even Scotland's version of the super-max prison, reserved for Scotland's most violent and disruptive prisoners, is no exception. Scotland's super-max units offer an instructive contrast to the purely repressive and largely unproductive model of the super-max prison found in America.[24]

Program Contracts

Program contracts are a useful means to both express and reinforce the collaborative efforts of prisoners-as-consumers and concerned prison staff, wherever and whenever such efforts occur. To be sure, the notion that prisons should offer program contracts to inmates as consumers of services naturally raises the question, do prisoners want correctional programs? If so, what kinds of programs should make up the substance of this enterprise?

The answer to the first question is clearly "yes." There is a strong and persistent demand for programs in prisons and even in local jails (see Toch, 1977; Smith, 1984). In prison, this observation holds true whether inmates are serving determinate or indeterminate sentences; in either sentencing context, it is the desire for self-improvement that motivates inmates to participate in programs (Goodstein and Lutze, 1989; see, generally, Goodstein & Wright, 1989). Programs are "particularly welcomed" by minority group members and others "who see themselves as handicapped in the past by deficiencies in skill or knowledge" (Toch, 1977:71; Smith, 1984). As noted above, Scottish prisoners clearly preferred that correctional investments be made in programs that might improve their lives rather than investments that might make them more comfortable behind bars. Prisoners want a chance at a decent life. In the Scottish prison surveys, this materialized as a desire for stable relations with others and jobs with some substance. Our job, if you will, is to help them reach these goals.

Little is known, however, about what specific programs prisoners want or need to reach their general goals. This presents a practical difficulty. As Pearce has noted in the Scottish context, difficulties linking inmate needs with specific programs can be substantial. We cannot negotiate program contracts open-endedly (due to scarce resources), but neither can we offer so narrow a range of options as to discount the needs and preferences of the prisoners. Descriptions of programs are often general. Indeed, some program descriptions, emanating from distant central offices, resemble glossy brochures and feature a misleadingly broad message of appeal to would-be consumers (see Pearce, 1994:10). The difficulty here is that the typical prisoner's aspirations for change tend to be fragile; programs that do not relate in some obvious way to an inmate's life are apt to frustrate and discourage him. Moreover, it is common for "the impetus for change," which is often salient at the outset of a prison term, to "crumble under the niggling pressure of routine and habit" (Zamble, Porporino & Kalotay, 1984:75). We must do what we can to encourage change by appreciating each individual prisoner's predicament and taking his specific concerns seriously.

The program preferences of any given prisoner may prove hard to identify, however, in part because they are apt to be broad and even vague, and may shift over time. This is especially true during the middle years of a prison term, when the inmate's status in life is much like that of the teenager who experiments widely (one is tempted to say, wildly) with lifestyles and career possibilities. Moreover, while the average prisoner is in his twenties, he retains many adolescent character traits. At this juncture of his life and for the greater part of his prison experience, notes Irwin (1970:102),

> the convict, like the teenager, is suspended in a temporary status and is barred from participation in the status toward which he is moving, the free adult-civilian status. He may engage in artificial and/or preparatory activities which bear a similarity to future activities of the free adult-civilian status—e.g., some prison jobs and prison training assignments. However, he is acutely aware that these are very different from the actual activities on the outside.
>
> Furthermore, like the teenager, he is free from many of the responsibilities of the free adult-civilian. His necessities are taken care of. His routine within certain limits is planned for him. With these responsibilities and the opportunity to engage in adult-civilian activities removed, he has unusual freedom to speculate and vacillate on his future plans.

The prisoner also has "unusual freedom" to experiment. Typically, this experimentation involves unlikely lifestyles and prospects, and smacks of fantasy in search of escape from the boredom of prison life. But program options could be arranged to encourage a flexible yet realistic inquiry into one's life prospects, much on the order of the prisoner who observed, "I look at [education in prison] as trying to get myself ready for the unknown" (Toch, 1977:72–73). The unknown approaches as men prepare for release, and they "tend to decrease speculating on various styles and to focus on one specific life style. At this stage, with release approaching and the possibility of rearrest drawing near, there is a shift toward conventional styles" (Irwin, 1970:104). If realistic conventional options have been pursued in program offerings and our prisoner-as-consumer has sampled them with some care, this shift of focus would be less a matter of giving up dreams and more a matter of making final preparations for an important and potentially liberating life transition.

To treat inmates as consumers of program services does not mean to cater to their every whim. But prisoners' preferences matter, since they in effect "purchase" programs with their participation and "boycott" programs through non-participation. Consumers in prison, like their counterparts in the free world, should be periodically surveyed to determine their perceptions of both their needs and the means to meet those needs. This, we have noted, is being done in Scottish prisons. Such surveys, again like their counterparts in the free world and in Scottish prisons, should be seen as a guide to program development.

Survey results indicate problem areas that should be considered and types of approaches that might most fruitfully address those problems. Guidance should also be obtained from patterns of program selection. On the premise that one cannot make horses, even thirsty horses, drink water on command, programs that prisoners don't want or use should be modified or discarded, while those sought and completed should be retained and used as models for future program development.

The virtual absence of specific information on prisoner program preferences is itself a telling indication that inmates have not been taken seriously as consumers of correctional services. Still, there are indications of the general direction programs should take, from prior research and from the Scottish prisoner surveys. Broadly speaking, we know that many prisoners feel they need educational and vocational services (Coffey & Louis, 1979), and admit to problems in relationships and deficiencies in self-control (Toch, 1977; Pearce, 1994). When exposed to programs that deal with cognitive deficiencies, inmates respond with considerable enthusiasm and a dogged willingness to consider new ways of thinking about themselves and the world—the old ways, they know, breed pain and failure. (Note the highly positive subjective appraisals of the Living Skills program, discussed above.)

Prisoners often dream of playboy jobs and upon release sometimes turn to improbable crimes (the proverbial "big score") in search of that dream. As a practical matter, however, many have been chastened by their recurring failures in life and indeed, in prison, and are ready to settle down to a home and family, supported by a legitimate job. There is even a willingness to consider "slave" jobs, which entail "laborious, unskilled, menial, dirty, monotonous and subservient work" (Irwin, 1970:93). In the words of one inmate, speaking of an ex-prisoner who appears to have settled down,

> Yeah, man, did ya hear about _____ ? He's making that slave everyday, got himself an old lady, a couple of rug rats and is staying home. You know, I hear he digs it. I think it's beautiful. This is the first time he stayed out over six months in the last twelve years. Maybe he's gonna make it this time. I'm all for him. (Irwin, 1970:95)

It is not clear from this excerpt whether the ex-prisoner in question developed a realistic perception of his options and hence prepared himself to make the most of a limited life, or simply became discouraged by years of confinement and came to accept what was for him, on balance, a less noxious existence. Probably each of these factors operated to suspend (and perhaps terminate) a criminal career of some standing. It is clear, in any case, that prison programs can provide the basic educational and job skills needed to land semiskilled and even some skilled working-class jobs (Hawkins, 1976), which presumably are even more rewarding than "slave" jobs. Programs can also provide training in the cognitive and social skills needed to keep those jobs and establish a decent domestic life (compare The Living Skills program, discussed above; see also Priestly et al., 1984).

Correctional work cannot operate in a vacuum, however. When prisoners ask for programs, even broad-based programs such as the Life Skills program, they are not just seeking technical assistance. Educational or vocational or social adjustment programs alone will never be enough to reform prisoners. They also need support (Toch, 1977:70–80). To provide relevant and useful support, one must meet men "where they're at" developmentally, and then gradually move them toward a proficient level of useful skills (Toch, 1977:78). There must also be a system of incentives, such as time reduced from sentences or adequate wages (Conrad, 1981b:65–66).

The most basic element of the support enterprise is caring. This is true both in prison and out, and independent of the particular program at issue. "To be supported," Toch makes clear, "means to be met halfway. This means being provided not only with the tools to success" in the form of credible programs offered in decent environments, "but also with an expression of human interest" (Toch, 1977:76).[25] Claude Brown sees the same need among today's "manchildren" of the ghetto, who are working their way toward prison with distressing regularity. "Most of them," he tells us, "possess a hunger for guidance and advice so profound it would be too humiliating to express even if they could" (Brown, 1984:78). One young boy told Brown that "he lost interest in school when the teachers had no obvious interest in instructing him. 'It's all about knowing somebody cares,' he said. 'That's what makes you care.'" (Brown, 1984:78)

In the prison, caring is expressed by staff "who grease the wheels or who smooth the road when the going gets rocky. It means persons who understand the difficulties of what one is trying to achieve. It means gentle coaxing or firm urging if one's motivation temporarily flags" (Toch, 1977:77). It also means insulation from destructive peers and, better yet, exposure to "peers who are strongly inclined toward achievement, who can provide mutual assistance and who can help strengthen one's resolves" (Toch, 1977:77). Program environments, like living and working environments, must become constructive niches—sanctuaries with a purpose—if they are to provide genuine learning experiences. The alternative is to offer programs that do little more than raise expectations but not capabilities, setting prisoners up for failure (Glaser, 1975).[26]

The transition from free world to prison can be difficult. For this reason, corrections cannot stop with prison programs, even programs that have an explicit focus on community reintegration (such as the Living Skills program, for example, which includes a sequence on community reintegration skills). Transition-related problems must be directly addressed, and prisoners must be tangibly assisted in their efforts to make the transition back to civilian life. One option is to include within prison programs any of a host of "transfer training techniques" that reinforce the link between mature coping in the prison and mature coping in the community (Gendreau, 1989). More ambitiously, programs can come equipped with a "relapse prevention" sequence featuring supportive supervision in the community (Gendreau, 1989). (The original design of the Butner program included such a plan, but it was not implemented for administrative reasons. See Note 8.) Support of this type will reduce the chances that prisoners, upon release, will be unable to get their careers started or will be lured away from the comparatively humdrum existence of conventional life (Toch, 1977:79–80).[27] The actual aspirations of prisoners, as distinct from their dreams, may well be for a "modest conventional life" (Irwin & Austin, 1994:143); still, the change from a disorganized life of crime to a life restrained by the recurring obligations of work and home is a substantial one. By any reckoning, this is a tall order, even for inmates who have made great improvements in coping competence during their confinement.

Securing a good job, or at least a job one can live with, is one of the key challenges facing prisoners upon release. A number of work programs have emerged over the last decade to address this problem. In these various programs, prisons once again become, in the words of former Supreme Court Chief Justice Warren Burger, "factories with fences." In sharp contrast to their predecessors in the penitentiary, however, today's prisoner-workers are not reduced to human chattel, but are typically well fed, well trained, well paid and, ideally, provided decent jobs upon release from prison (Hawkins, 1976 & 1983). Such programs are either modeled on private industry—for example, LEAA's Free Venture program or the Federal Bureau of Prison's Federal Prison Industries (FPI) program—or, as with the Prison Industries Enhancement Program (PIE), "require the actual involvement of private business in correctional industries" (Hawkins, 1983:107).

PIE is in many respects a model of free-world work and responsibility in a prison context. "The PIE program requires that the prisoner-workers receive wages in connection with the work they do at the prevailing local wage rate, minus up to 80 percent of gross wages for taxes, room and board, family support, and victim compensation funds" (Hawkins, 1983:111). A mechanism for post-release job placements is typically included in these programs. These programs continue to grow, providing jobs to inmates, earnings to companies, tax dollars to state and federal governments, and payments to defray the costs of the prisoner-worker's confinement and to support their families. "It's a win-win situation," PIE's director, Robert Verdeyen, recently claimed in an interview with journalist Chuck Thompson. Continuing, Verdeyen noted that "Inmates earn self-respect and, in some case, a considerable wage. Taxpayers win because inmates pay taxes from their incomes and make other contributions to the system" (Thompson, 1994:45).[28] As a caveat, however, it should be noted that PIE and related programs employ only a fraction of any given prison population. And it is hard for even the best of these programs to provide the long-term support needed to help offenders establish themselves in conventional careers and go on to become self-supporting citizens.[29]

The Federal Prison Industries program, marketed and best known under the trade name UNICOR, has met with consistent and continuing success. (As noted earlier, the success of this program is at the heart of the decent living conditions found at such federal prisons as Lompoc.) FPI's UNICOR program is a "wholly owned, nonappropriated Government corporation" and is run much like a regular business, except that the goal is not to maximize profits (though the operation is profitable); the goal is to maximize the employment and training of prisoners (Seiter, 1994:529). UNICOR "was created to provide work for inmates, instill a work ethic for individuals with little past work experience or training, and teach inmates skills so that they will be better prepared to return to the community" (Seiter, 1994:528). A recent controlled study of the impact of participation in this industrial work program indicated that, in comparison with a control group, participants in UNICOR were less likely to violate prison rules (and when they did, to commit less serious rule violations than other inmates), and more likely to be rated as autonomous and responsible by officials. On release, UNICOR workers made better adjustments than other inmates. They were more likely to land jobs in the community, and to get better-paying jobs than other inmates. Their rates of recidivism were lower than that of controls, and this important finding was described as "both statistically significant and substantively meaningful" (Saylor & Gaes, 1994:538). Their enhanced autonomy in prison, it would appear, carried over to the free world, promoting more mature adjustment there as well.

Regrettably, many prisoners leave prison having had little or no correctional treatment of any kind, dealing with work or any other aspect of adjustment to life in the free world. Others are exposed to programs so inadequate and perfunctory as to leave them utterly unprepared to reenter the free community. Thus, many inmates suffer diminished autonomy as a result of their experiences in confinement. They are, as a consequence, deeply apprehensive on leaving the prison, as fearful of entering our world, the free world, as we are of entering theirs, the prison world. As these inmates see it, they are leaving prison unprepared for a world that is unreceptive to them and is, moreover, filled with "opportunities for relapse" that threaten to undermine their best coping efforts (see Besozzi, 1993). (Interestingly, the word recidivism means, literally, to "fall back" or relapse. See Nouwens, Motiuk & Boe, 1993:23.) To compound matters, recent research indicates that inmates today, even with the advent of pre-release programming in many prisons, often have done poor planning or no planning at all for their upcoming release (Besozzi, 1993). In the face of mounting anxiety about their impending failure in the free world, the prison begins to look better all the time, now masquerading in their eyes as a curious "mother who provides and protects" (Besozzi, 1993:38; see also, Duncan, 1988). Thus prison, for some, offers an almost comfortable alternative to the struggle to adjust in rejecting free-world communities.

The fears of prisoners facing release cannot be assuaged with a few kind words; nor will harsh admonitions help them go straight. The truth is, for many prisoners, their feelings of inadequacy and their fears of the free world are justified. They find, on release, that they have not improved their coping competence and there is, indeed, no place for them; continued poor coping in the free world lands them back in prison. As Zamble's research has revealed, poor coping habits retained in prison—or at least, not ameliorated by imprisonment—are replayed in the free world, yielding emotional turmoil that in turn promotes destructive behaviors such as alcohol and drug abuse, undertaken mainly as an escape from the pains of readjustment to life in the free world. This cycle feeds on itself, until it culminates—sometimes quite soon after release—in impulsive acts of crime, followed by arrest and return to prison (see Zamble, 1993). Others succeed, but on the most pathetic terms. They may, for example, live for a time with support of relatives or some form of state or federal support, drifting along on the fringes of society, perhaps in and out of crime but never, in any case, a part of the conventional society, and all too often destined for homelessness and an early death on the streets of our cities (Irwin & Austin, 1994:131–39).

Today, and no doubt for the foreseeable future, effective correctional programs will be available to only a minority of prisoners. Programs that extend their reach into the community will be even more rare. It is therefore urgent to note that with or without programming during the course of their confinement, offenders must be given assurances that, on release, they will not be abandoned. They must be assured that they will receive not only supervision, but also some support services relative to finding and keeping a job, securing an education, and dealing with emotional and other problems likely to surface during the period of readjustment that awaits them. Supportive follow-up services are essential; even intensive supervision, on its own, has only a minimal effect on recidivism (see NIJ, 1993). When support services are routinely provided, and especially when they are provided by volunteers in the community—whose very presence is a source of hope for apprehensive releasees—recidivism rates drop, sometimes substantially (see NIJ, 1993).

Broadly speaking, the objective of rehabilitation programs is to create constructive niches where none exist and to enrich those already in existence. Ideally, all inmates should be exposed to niches in which they and their keepers solve the daily problems of prison adjustment in a mature manner, and in which these elementary but vital coping skills are augmented in formal programs. All prisoners, in other words, should both be supported in their prison adjustment efforts and offered the opportunity to acquire the social, educational, and vocational skills needed to live a peaceful and ultimately self-sufficient life upon release from confinement. As we have seen, programs exist that promote mature coping—that is, clear thinking about the nature of problems and legitimate solutions to those programs (for example, the Living Skills program), coping without resort to violence or to drug or alcohol addiction (for example, various self-management programs), and living effectively in human communities (for example, various prison therapeutic community programs, whether the focus of such communal living programs is clear thinking, nonviolence, or desistance from drugs or alcohol). Transitional services would extend the reach of programs and support into the community. If prisoners are to maintain hope for a conventional life in the free world, nothing less than a combination of program resources and human support will suffice.

NURTURING HOPE AND
REFORMING CRIMINALS

Some prisons operate exclusively as barren human warehouses, and virtually all contemporary prisons lapse into this condition from time to time in at least some of their internal environments. When prisons assume a warehousing function, even one in which pain is minimized, they tax the human spirit and undermine hope. They are vestigial manifestations of the worst features of the historical prison, where storage marked by idleness and isolation comprised the whole of the prison experience. Such prisons may mete out civilized punishments, but they are utterly incapable of civilizing their inhabitants.

When prisons become overcrowded, moreover, the temptation to warehouse inmates as a *matter of policy*—rather than as a failure of policy—is strong. This situation faces all too many of today's penal institutions, where there is a critical absence of commitment among prison leaders to a constructive vision of the prison.[30] For the administrator who must run a prison that is bulging with excess bodies and threatening chaos, custodial concerns are apt to take on an uncommon salience. The administrative agenda will typically be formulated in terms of unit space and musical beds instead of ecology and niches; it will seek containment and control rather than coexistence and coping; it will settle for cell time and surface tranquility rather than program time and the "improvement mess"[31] that often accompanies personal reform.

These compromise goals will serve only to further compromise an environment already in decline. For crowding exaggerates the more primitive side of prison life (Smith, 1988; Fitzgerald & Sim, 1982). Physical conditions are apt to deteriorate; garbage, stench, and noise may become standard features of the daily routine. Even such basic commodities as food and clothing may be in short supply (Smith, 1988; Cobb, 1985). Social life becomes especially precarious. The simple density of bodies in crowded prisons means that inmates, including state-raised convicts, come into more abrasive public contact with one another. At the same time, the private culture of the prison shrinks as bodies take up the space formerly deployed more flexibly, forcing more and more guards and inmates out of niches and personal roles and into places and roles that are unfamiliar to them. Tension and the potential for violence, including collective violence, become tangible facts of crowded prison life (Smith, 1988; Lombardo, 1988). The need for classification and management strategies that preserve environmental sanctuaries, and for programs that provide constructive activities, becomes urgent (Toch, 1984). Crowded prisons must be explicitly managed as human ecologies—as places where people spend constructive time rather than where they merely serve time—or they will degenerate, slowly but inexorably, into inhumane warehouses. And it is entirely feasible to preserve a decent human ecology, even in a crowded prison. For "even in times of severely crowded correctional institutions," research and practice reveals that functional unit management "has achieved a high degree of success" and can serve to reduce the ill effects of high population density (Webster, 1991:420).[32]

Warehouse prisons may snuff out hope with disheartening regularity, but hope does not necessarily live in more congenial penal environments. It takes more than a secure and responsive prison with decent programs to promote hope. For hope is ultimately the belief that one has "an accepted place in the community" (Conrad, 1981b:66), that one has not been abandoned and forgotten but has a chance, however remote, to live once again as a citizen in the free society. As a practical matter, "the reality of this acceptance has to be expressed in the interest and sustained involvement of the community" in the life of the offender and the prison (Conrad, 1981b:66).

If hope is to be preserved, then, the experience of reintegration into the free community must be "an ongoing process rather than an event reserved for those inmates who are about to be released" (Weiner, 1988:306). Constructive relations with one's keepers, whether line staff or treatment staff, are one important source of human bonds that contribute to reintegration; staff members are living embodiments within the prison of the larger community to which most inmates will return (Glaser, 1969). Some peer associations, particularly those that develop in the context of responsive communities or other constructive prison activities, may also promote reintegration; these relations build bridges between adaptation in the prison world and subsequent adaptation in the free community (Toch, 1980). Community volunteers, too, can do much to promote prosocial attitudes and relationships among prisoners, particularly during the transition to the free world (Andrews et al., 1973 & 1977; Parker & La Cour, 1983). The critical element in the reintegration process, however, is almost certainly the prisoner's relationship with his family and friends, his significant others in the free community (Cobean & Power, 1978). A number of studies have found "a significant difference in the recidivism rate of prisoners who have had regular, continuing visits from family members as compared to those who did not have visits or had only sporadic visits" (Homer, 1979:47). This finding, moreover, has stood up over some fifty years of research covering diverse prison populations (see Schafer, 1978; Burstein, 1977).

Our relations with others, and particularly our family and friends, are the ties that build our self-esteem and bind us to the larger human community. These are "the animating relations with others that sustain us, enrich our lives with meaning, and make life worth living" (Conrad, 1981b:66). Human relationships make it possible for men to persist in dead-end jobs and to endure lives of quiet desperation, lives that in objective material terms offer meager rewards.[33] Relations with others make the work of mature coping—at home, at work, in the neighborhood, even in the prison—a labor of love rather than a test of endurance. These human connections make real for each individual the core notion that they, as autonomous persons, secure in themselves and in their ties with others, have the power to change themselves and, in both small and large ways, the world around them.

Jesse Jackson artfully explored the theme of personal change in his 1994 Christmas Day message to the prisoners of Chicago's Cook County Jail. Though his remarks were tailored to a black audience, it is clear that the message is a universal one:

The key to change is in your mind, in your heart. Malcolm turned a jail cell into a classroom. Racism didn't change for him; the job situation didn't change for him; the police didn't change. Nothing changed but him. (Quoted in Raspberry, 1994:A23)

Change must occur within individuals, as Jackson makes clear, but the capacity for change—the will to change—draws on hope, which in turn is rooted in supportive ties to others in the human community. If these ties are absent—if they fail under pressure or never materialize at all—community becomes an empty abstraction, the self an impoverished shell, the future an exercise in narcissism and self-aggrandizement. Life becomes not so much a matter of coping well or badly as maintaining the will to cope at all. At this juncture, conventional life seems pointless and onerous beyond human endurance; crime becomes at once an irresistible temptation to self-indulgence and a poignant expression of anger and despair.[34] It is as if the violence of crime summarizes the violence done to the criminal's life, initiating yet again a sequence of crimes and punishments that reflect and extend that violence and constrict even further the community we all wish to share. Violent crime, increasingly the refuge of hopeless, brutalized children, mirrors the hopelessness and brutality in their lives. It follows, in the wise logic of William Raspberry, Pulitzer-prize-winning columnist for the *Washington Post*, that "Our communities won't be safe *from* our children until we first make them safe, decent and nurturing places *for* our children" (1994:A19).

By the same token, our prisons can't be decent and nurturing places unless they are run properly and reserved for those who clearly and unambiguously deserve this fateful sanction. Prisoners can feel abandoned and forgotten by the larger society if they conclude that their very confinement is an injustice. It is wise to recall the admonition of Albert Camus, the distinguished French existentialist, that injustice is a form of violence.[35] For the unjustly confined, even a congenial and responsive prison can be experienced as a human warehouse and as a profound violation of human dignity. Such troubling perceptions may be more common—and more valid—than we in the larger society would care to admit. We noted in Chapter One that our prisons are full to overflowing, bloated with offenders at a rate unparalled elsewhere in the world. A sizable and growing segment of that population is made up of drug offenders and minorities. Many of these offenders feel themselves to be unjustly confined, and a case can be made for the legitimacy of those perceptions.

It is, of course, entirely conceivable that our crowded prisons are filled with people who deserve to be confined and that such a deployment of our limited penal resources is wise. In other words, our crowded prisons could be the result of society's efforts to cope maturely with a difficult crime problem. This is true in principle, but as a practical matter, one has to be skeptical, at the very least. There is, for example, no evidence suggesting that our massive use of imprisonment over the last two decades has reduced the crime rate in any consistent or substantial way (see Blumstein, 1994:416). Moreover, our long-standing tendency to use prison sentences, and sometimes lengthy prison sentences, for lesser property crimes seems patently unwise and out of step with penal trends in other nations in the West (see Lynch, 1994:37). The recent and considerable growth of drug offenders in our prison population, many serving long sentences for what amounts to possession or small-time trafficking, suggests a hysterical response to the social problems that shape patterns of drug use and abuse in our society. The phenomenal growth of the black male prison population over the last decade, partly a product of our misguided war on drugs, suggests racist crime control practices (see Tonry, 1995). To the extent that we are using prisons as instruments of repression to deal with problems and populations that make us uncomfortable, the case can be made that our penal policy is, indeed, a form of violence. In my terms, such a state of affairs is a classic instance of immature coping in the face of the social stresses produced by crime in modern America.

It is easy to reject this line of argument out of hand. One might readily contend that blacks experience high rates of confinement because they commit crimes at high rates. Young African-American men are, after all, frisked daily on ghetto streets because they appear to police to be behaving suspiciously, and they are arrested and locked up at high rates for criminal behavior, not simply for being black. Yet many of the contacts between the justice system and the inner-city blacks who disproportionately fill our prisons occur on slum streets, where police have easy access to ghetto residents, and these encounters involve actual or suspected drug-related behavior. As we have noted in Chapter One, the astronomical growth of our prisons over the last decade or so has been fueled by incarceration of persons—disproportionately young black men—convicted of drug-related offenses. It is society's choice to wage an aggressive drug war that in effect targets those who inhabit inner-city streets in contrast to, say, suburban homes or Wall Street offices, two settings that feature deceptively widespread patterns of drug use. Penalties in existing laws, especially federal laws, are such that the drugs of choice in inner cities come in for harsher penalties than the drugs of choice in the surrounding—largely white—communities (see, generally, Reiman, 1995; Tonry, 1995; Lusane, 1991).

The point is that patterns of police deployment and our ever-growing prison populations are not random events, but rather "are very much a function of policy choices" (Mauer; 1992:27). As Tonry (1995:4) has made clear,

> the rising levels of black incarceration did not just happen; they were the foreseeable effects of deliberate policies. . . . Anyone with knowledge of drug-trafficking patterns and of police arrest policies and incentives could have foreseen that the enemy troops in the War on Drugs would consist largely of young, inner-city minority males.

Different policies would target different groups, resulting in different rates of police contact and, ultimately, in confinement of different groups of offenders. A focus on white-collar crime, for example, would produce a very different prison population. Even a difference in drug enforcement practices as seemingly minor as focusing on powdered cocaine (sniffed in offices and at parties of the professional classes) rather than rock cocaine (that is, crack, smoked on street corners or in abandoned houses in the inner city) would produce different patterns of enforcement, which in turn would yield different patterns of confinement—in this instance, relatively fewer black offenders and more white offenders than is the case today.[36] It should be apparent that political considerations shape policy in this area, making inner-city blacks an easy target of opportunity in what amounts to a selective assault on the drug problem (Tonry, 1995:39).

And while it is true, as I have argued throughout this book, that prisons can be arranged to help reform offenders, in many cases that help could be more effectively, more cheaply, and more humanely rendered in community settings rather than in prisons (see Zamble, 1992; Clear & Braga, 1994). People who deserve prison deserve to be helped while they are there; for them, we must strive to make hard time into constructive time. Prisoners are sent to prison for punishment that, when properly arranged, can prove helpful. Offenders who don't deserve the punishment of prison should not be sent there for punishment or treatment. Those offenders can certainly be offered help, but that help should be provided in the community, not in confinement.

Prisoners spend their sentences apart from the community, but the notion that we can forget prisoners—put them out of sight and out of mind—is an illusion. In a subtle but important sense, prisoners are always with us, and we with them. Society penetrates prison walls, shaping many aspects of prison life and adjustment; virtually all offenders return to the community, bringing a little bit of prison life with them in the process. Even those offenders slated to live out their days behind bars remain members of the larger human community, which encompasses both the free society and the society of captives. Prison reformers, then, must strive to build the human bonds that at once sustain decency in the prison and serve to link the prison to the larger social world of which it is a part.

Debts must be paid, to be sure, and prisoners, through their suffering, pay dearly for their crimes. But so too must new lives commence, both in prison and, on release, in the free world. Historically, the prison has failed to play a constructive role in the crucial process of reintegration; it has offered punishment, but that punishment, more often than not, has been neither civilized nor civilizing. Too often, the prison has isolated offenders from one another and from the free world. As a result, destructive stereotypes—fostering fear and loathing rather than care and compassion—have flourished in and out of prison. To be sure, the limits of prison as an instrument of reform are substantial, but they are not insurmountable. As we have seen in this book, prison can be a constructive punishment, one that promotes community and citizenship within its walls even as it maintains ties with the community of citizens outside its walls. The knowledge is there; we know how to run decent prisons. What has been lacking is the will to act, to translate humane intentions into humane prisons.

Today's prisons can, in principle, address the noble goal of the penitentiary—which was meant to fashion its wards into citizens—while categorically rejecting the empty custodial quarantines that have been both the heritage and the legacy of that penal institution. That we might build citizens as we punish offenders has been an enduring aspiration, and one worthy of our best efforts. Each and every one of us, as responsible citizens, has a stake in this endeavor. We may properly dedicate ourselves to the task of prison reform, working to improve ourselves and expand our ranks.

NOTES

1. See, for example, Hawkins & Alpert, 1989. Tonry (1995:9) has summarized the evidence from public opinion surveys on this point:

Although National Opinion Research Center surveys for many years have shown that large majorities of respondents say they believe that sentences are insufficiently harsh, large majorities of Americans also want prisons to rehabilitate offenders. When [a Gallup survey] asked respondents to choose between punishment and rehabilitation as the primary goal of imprisonment, by 48 percent to 38 percent they chose rehabilitation.

A 1991 survey of U. S. legal codes indicates that rehabilitation was the most common formal goal of prisons, affecting forty-one states. Most states sought multiple goals, however, and punishment is becoming an increasingly popular formal goal, especially in the South (see Burton, Dunaway & Kopache, 1993).

2. To be sure, prison budgets eat up only a small share of overall state and federal budgets, where big-ticket items like education and medicaid predominate. "But in terms of growth, prisons are where the action is" (Walsh, 1994:A3).

There are those who maintain that prisons, though indeed expensive, are a bargain because they pay for themselves. The logic is this: A high rate of incarceration keeps many offenders behind bars—this prevents confined criminals from victimizing the public (incapacitation), and it discourages other would-be criminals from committing crimes as well (deterrence). Crime reduction due to incapacitation and deterrence therefore saves vast amounts of money, since crime is believed to exact a heavy economic and social price on individual victims and on the larger society

(see, for example, Piehl & DiIulio, 1995). This is, in my view, an area of analysis that requires a series of heroic assumptions, namely, that prisons have sufficient deterrent and incapacitative effects to substantially reduce crime rates, and that such reductions in crime rates will generate real savings for the society that can be said to offset the direct outlays of money undertaken by governmental bodies to build and operate prisons. The work of Blumstein, Forst, and others casts doubt on the value of this line of analysis, at least, as it applies to the growth in prisons over the last two decades. In general, it would appear that demographic and socioeconomic forces influence crime rates to a much greater extent than do sentencing policies.

3. At present, as Wilson (1994:499) reminds us, most serious offenders serve less time in prison than they did as recently as the 1940s. One reform strategy would be to send serious offenders to prison for longer terms while sending other offenders, notably low-level drug offenders and lesser property offenders, to community supervision.

4. More broadly, Tonry (1995:17) reminds us that "For at least twenty-five years, researchers have shown and honest politicians have known that manipulations of penalties have relatively little or no effect on crime rates." The problem is the general weakness of deterrence with respect to run-of-the-mill street criminals, who as we have noted in Chapter Three are quite immature and whose "crimes are as impulsive as the rest of their feckless, sad, or pathetic lives" (this quote is drawn from a 1990 White Paper prepared for the English Parliament; see Tonry, 1995:18). It should come as no surprise, then, that "The clear weight of the evidence in

every Western country indicates that tough penalties have little effect on crime rates" (Tonry, 1995:19).

5. This estimate is based on the work of Gendreau & Ross (1980:25). I am aware of no more current estimate. It is my impression that, in constant dollars, we may well spend less on rehabilitative services these days.

6. Good theory often fails to get implemented because of practical obstacles to reform. This is a general problem in criminal justice reform, and indeed one that is encountered in efforts to change a range of organizations in society. (See Wright, 1994 and Bennett & Bennett, 1982.)

7. The anecdotal evidence is comprised of observations drawn from site visits made to penal institutions in Holland in the summers of 1992 and 1994 in my role as director of the Comparative Corrections Institute of The American University.

8. This was quite apparent in Blecker's account of life in Lorton's dorms, and is a theme that runs through much of the ethnographic descriptions of prison life. (See, for example, Blecker, 1990 and Fleisher, 1989.)

9. These instruments include the following: (1) To measure stress: SCL 90 (Derogatis, Rickels, & Rock, 1976:280) or the well-known MMPI (which, as Derogatis et al. indicate, correlates highly with SCL-90 on stress-related items). Gibbs et al. (1983:38) found the SCL-90 easy to modify for use with a jail population. (2) To assess environmental needs as reflected in individual inmate perceptions: Prison Preference Inventory (Toch, 1977); the Jail Preference Inventory (Gibbs et al., 1983); and the Smith jail Preference Inventory (Smith, 1984). (3) To pinpoint environmental resources and "organizational climates [that] arise from members' shared experiences in the environment" (Wright, 1991:225): such instruments as the Environmental Quality Scale (Gibbs et al., 1983), any of a variety of the Moos correctional climate scales (for example, Moos, 1974), and Wright's Prison Environment Inventory (Wright 1985). Most recently, an eight-dimension quality of prison life instrument has been developed and implemented by Logan and applied to

a study of three women's prisons (Logan, 1992). This instrument could be readily adapted for use with prisons for men.

10. Silberman (1995) reports that the use of functional units in conjunction with the Quay classification system (also known as AIMS—Adult Inmate Management System) reduced violence effectively in "Central Prison," a pseudonym for what appears to be a high-security prison in Pennsylvania.

11. These findings reflect a paradox of planned change within penal institutions, namely that "to make a unit completely different from the prison yard may be easier to accomplish than . . . to introduce selective, piecemeal reform" (Toch, 1984:16–17). (Incidentally, Toch points out that this observation applies to "culture building" in other contexts as well.) The reason is that guards and inmates can start fresh in a new unit, as a group with shared goals and an open horizon, in effect leaving old resistances and rivalries behind.

12. At entry, inmates are markedly depressed and anxious. "The incidence of severe depression . . . was about 8 times that in the general population, and that for moderate depression was about 5 times the normal rate . . . a substantial number of our subjects had elevated anxiety scores; in fact, 41% had scores above the mean level for the anxiety reaction patients" (Zamble, Porporino & Kalotay, 1984:72).

13. Periodically, prisoners or ex-prisoners write books on prison etiquette that are meant to orient newcomers to the culture of confinement. The most recent entry in this small field is designed for persons soon-to-be-imprisoned (see Tayoun, 1995).

14. First-termers, in particular, may be reassured by the presence of inmates in the orientation process (see Hirschorn & Burck, 1977). However, the involvement of inmates must be carefully monitored by staff, who are ultimately responsible for the contents and consequences of the orientation process. If staff do not exercise this monitoring obligation in a visible way, novice prisoners may gain the wrong impression as to who runs the prison. Inmates have considerable subcultural clout, but it is misleading to imply that

they run the formal institution as well.

15. Here my aim is to anticipate "organizational-level barriers" to these individual-oriented reforms (see Jurik & Musheno, 1986:19). Simply having good officers who are committed to the notion of human service and responsive to ecological concerns may not be enough to ensure the effective uses of correctional authority. Unless officers are offered training and support for expanded roles and responsibilities, some and perhaps even many of them are apt to get discouraged, becoming pessimistic about helping prisoners and dissatisfied with their jobs (see Jurik & Musheno, 1986:29).

16. Most constructive niches were routinely subsumed under the heading "therapeutic community" when the term had rather broad and positive connotations in the prison context. The label remains apt and is still in use, but for my purposes the connotation of therapy is often too narrow. The therapy offered in some therapeutic communities, for example, takes a very heavy-handed approach to help; essentially bogus treatments are more or less forced on offenders, who may come to feel violated in the process (see, for example, Silberman's discussion of coercion in some therapeutic communities; Silberman, 1995). Even when helping arrangements in therapeutic communities are benign, they often still occur at the behest of experts, and this downplays our growing concern with facilitating rather than imposing personal change, so that offenders might better take responsibility for their own conduct. The term "responsive community" is meant to capture both the notion of helpfulness at the root of therapy and the notion of responsibility at the root of personal accountability for one's actions. These terms will be used interchangeably in this discussion, since the literature embraces communities that offer therapy as an adjunct to social learning in the community (for example, therapeutic communities for drug or alcohol offenders), as well as communities that offer no formal treatment or therapy but are explicitly organized as staging grounds for social learning (for example, units that involve varying degrees of participatory management, including democratization).

17. The budget-cutting strategies of Virginia Governor George Allen provide a case in point. Allen has called for the cessation of all treatment programs for sex offenders in Virginia's prisons on the grounds that such programs don't work. In point of fact, there are a number of program approaches that reduce recidivism among sex offenders, notes Miller (1995:A17), who aptly calls Allen's proposal "the worst kind of folly."

18. Behavior that is both severely punished (for example, by parents) and highly rewarded (for example, by peers) is most resistant to change. The behavior gains strength from what is called "punishment training," which, as explained by Newman (1978:253), has clear implications for the management of prisoners. A juvenile gang member's misbehavior may bring him immediate rewards, such as status or "rep" with other gang members. If his parents find out, he may be severely physically chastised. Thus he is punished and rewarded, the net result being the strengthening of his mischievous gang behavior. According to punishment research, subsequent punishment will merely facilitate this undesirable behavior.

19. The original plan included a phased transition into the community, with graduates of the program supervised and supported in the community by the staff who had manned the program in the prison. This part of the plan proved unworkable, for a host of administrative reasons, and was not carried out. It is probable that had this part of the plan been retained, the reintegration of the prisoners would have occurred with more success.

20. See, for example, Toch, Grant & Galvin (1975), Toch (1980), Toch & Adams with Grant (1989), among others.

21. I am indebted to David Blansky, a former student assistant, for this point.

22. Toch makes this point succinctly. "One established way of promoting inmate participation" in programs, he notes,

is to offer to negotiate contracts in which persons agree to behavior goals whose attainment will be rewarded. It is true that one can point to power imbalances in such contracts between staff and clients who sign them. Limited choice, however, is better than no choice, and volition that is exercised in the absence of constraints or incentives is rarely encountered anywhere. (Toch, 1988:46)

23. This point is backed by controlled empirical research. One study, conducted in California prisons, involving both violent and nonviolent offenders, has been summarized as follows:

experimental and control groups . . . differed only on the lengths of their prison terms. The experimentals served six months less time in prison than they would have been expected to serve [x = 31.3 months], while the prison term for the controls was not changed [x = 37.9 months]. . . . Within the first and second years following release to parole, the experimentals and controls did not differ on the likelihood of their being returned to prison either by a court conviction for a new felony or as a result of a parole violation. . . . [Hence,] prison terms can be reduced without affecting recidivism to a significant and practical degree. (Berecochea & Jaman, 1981; summarized in Criminal Justice Abstracts, S 30484, 1982:370–71)

A similar study was conducted by the Wisconsin Department of Health and Social Services (1983), though here the experimental group was composed entirely of nonviolent offenders who were afforded intensive parole supervision upon release from prison. (Given the findings of the California research, the selection and supervision process used in Wisconsin may have been superfluous). Most recently, the expansion of "good time" in Illinois and Oklahoma has resulted in substantial savings accrued from early release without compromising public safety (Austin & Bolyard, 1993; Irwin & Austin, 1994:172–73).

24. Super-max prisons are run in a number of states (for example, California's Pelican Bay prison) and in the Federal Bureau of Prison (Marion Penitentiary, after the closure of Alcatraz in 1962, and now its successor, the Administrative Maximum Facility in Florence, Colorado, opened in 1994). American super-max prisons are in operation in twenty-five states; six more states plan to open such facilities (Cline, 1994:B1). Still, super-max prisons are few in number compared to regular maximum-security prisons, and house less than 1 percent of the American

prison population. These institutions, relying on the long-term segregation of prisoners and often featuring continuous camera surveillance, would appear to be high-tech throwbacks to the days of the Big House or even, in some key respects, the solitary version of the earliest penitentiaries. (The Administrative Maximum Facility, for example, in keeping with its maximally sterile name, has been described as offering "hermetic cells" and "a super-controlled environment that enforces a hard-edged solitude to contain the risk of social mixing and violence" among offenders. What is this if not a twentieth-century version of Eastern Penitentiary, reserved exclusively for the clientele of a classic, tough Big House like Alcatraz? See Cline, 1994:B1). Unsurprisingly, administrators of these settings view them as exemplary versions of hard time for hard-core predators, while the prisoners view these institutions as profoundly inhumane (see Haney, 1993; Immarigeon, 1992).

The best known of Scotland's units is Barlinnie Special Unit (see McKinlay, 1992). This unit was for many years a model of special programming with violent offenders but in recent years had lost its community focus and is being closed down (Toch, personal communication). Whatever Barlinnie's failings were, the prison did not degenerate into violence. In contrast, violence seems to lurk just beneath the surface of life in America's super-max prisons. California's Pelican Bay is a case in point. Recently Thelton Henderson, chief federal district judge in San Francisco, ruled that Pelican Bay violated "the Eight Amendment's restraint on using excessive force" (quoted in Hentoff, 1995:A17). At Pelican Bay, Henderson concluded, force was often "gratuitous, intended maliciously to inflict injury rather than to restore order" (quoted in Hentoff, 1995:A17). The institution has been placed under the supervision of a special master, with the aim of making the prison more humane (Hentoff, 1995:A17).

25. Support-oriented inmates appear to be of the opinion that like-minded peers are rare in prison. Most demands for support are probably directed to staff, who are presumed to possess competencies not

shared by fellow prisoners. These suppositions are borne out by Smith's (1984:75) jail inmate survey, in which prisoners made it clear that they wanted to be left alone by peers, but cared for, protected, and helped by staff and the facility in general, particularly "via program opportunities."

26. Wormith (1984:611) notes that "minimal or inadequate training may . . . be antirehabilitative." It raises hopes that can be easily dashed and gives the offender a false sense of efficacy that "can be readily extinguished by disconfirming experiences" (Bandura, 1977:198).

27. Linden and Perry (1982) apply these observations to prison education programs, noting that successful programs are intensive, establish an alternative community within the prison, and offer postrelease services.

28. A 1991 government report on PIE programs revealed that "At the end of fiscal year 1990, BJA [Bureau of Justice Assistance] had 20 certified programs fully in effect involving 59 projects and 857 employed inmates. By end of January 1991, BJA had granted two additional state certifications to South Dakota and Tennessee" (Report, 1991:8). Seven more applications were pending. These programs have produced substantial earnings—$16,714,581—from the manufacture of products ranging from "wooden tool boxes to children's clothing to limousines" (Report, 1991:4). Some $1,700,000 in state and federal taxes have been paid out; roughly $2,600,000 in prison costs (room and board) have been paid out as well. Finally, "family support payments total more than $2,000,000 and contributions to victims' compensation and assistance programs exceed $900,000" (Report, 1991:4).

29. See Piliavin & Gartner (1981) and Jacobs, McGahey, & Minion (1984). The small but growing interest in private industry in prison reflects changes in the larger economic picture that make prison industry less threatening to American businesses or workers. As Hawkins (1983:109) has observed, "the small private manufacturers who feared prison competition have been largely replaced by larger manufacturers and industrial conglomerates which have no reason to fear the very limited competition of the typically small production unit in a prison setting in one state." Moreover, the "new" factories with fences typically produce the kinds of labor-intensive goods that are increasingly manufactured not in the United States but in foreign countries, primarily in the Third World. Hence, American workers' resistance to prison labor is reduced because "prison manufacturing operations will pose a greater threat to Hong Kong and Seoul than they do to Detroit or Pittsburgh" (Schaller & Sexton, 1979:4). These industrial programs are promising (Cullen & Travis, 1984), but they remain the exception rather than the rule.

30. As Toch (1985:59) has observed, "two disasters" beset corrections in the 1980s: "The advent of (1) unprecedented overcrowding . . . [and] (2) the loss of faith in correctional rehabilitation." These problems have only worsened in the intervening years. It would seem that some variant on a warehousing stance is the only option that many administrators see as open to them, although a number of scholars have identified ways to enrich correctional environments, and hence to avoid warehousing—or at least to minimize its harmful effects (see, for example, Toch, 1985). Innovative, policy-relevant ways to measure crowding and its variation over time are also under development (see Klofas, Stojkovic & Kalinich, 1992). The need for constructive prison leadership to set an agenda for coping with these and other programs is insightfully identified by Wright (1994).

31. As Redl (1980) tells us, people experiencing personal growth often get worse before they get better. They are dealing with problems—at first clumsily and emotionally, later with more poise and self-control—rather than denying problems, suppressing feelings, and doing time. They must be permitted, indeed encouraged, to take risks, fail, and start again.

32. A more modest but also useful organizational reform involves the use of cubicles in dormitories, shops, and classrooms. With proper supervision, these cubicles can serve as a poor man's cell; a group of such cubi-

cles can form the core of a rudimentary functional unit. The point is that functional units and related arrangements provide privacy, which ameliorates the impact of crowding and is "very desirable for the physical and psychological welfare of the inmates as well as from a prison management perspective" (Cox, Paulus & McCain, 1984:1156; see also, Johnson, 1992)

33. As Irwin and Austin (1994:162–63) have reminded us, "job stability and marriage sharply mitigate one's criminal activities."

34. Renzema's (1988:160–61) research with parolees makes it clear that "more important than either the stressors in the environment or the discomfort they generated was the respondent's ability to maintain hope. When hope of achieving a satisfactory life through legitimate means failed, trouble followed."

35. See, for example, Camus's profound essay, "Reflections on the Guillotine" (1969).

36. An editorial in *The Washington Post* (August 4, 1993, A:16), entitled "Same Drug, Different Penalties," underscores the injustice of this situation.

Possession of five grams of crack cocaine carries a federal mandatory minimum sentence of five years without parole for a first offender. But possession of cocaine in the form of powder carries no mandatory minimum sentence at all; offenders could get off with probation. This sentence disparity, mandated by Congress in 1988, is even more egregious than it appears. Crack is the preferred form of the drug in black communities, while powder is more widely used by whites. . . . A representative sample of 1992 federal drug cases prepared by the U.S. Sentencing Commission revealed that all defendants convicted of simple possession of crack during the time studied were black.

REFERENCES

Abrams, A. I., and L. M. Siegel. L. "The transcendental meditation program and rehabilitation at Folsom State Prison." *Criminal Justice and Behavior* 5 (1) 1978:3–20.

Alper, B. S. *Prisons Inside-Out: Alternatives in Correctional Reform.* Cambridge: Ballinger, 1974.

Andrews, D. A., J. G. Young, J. S. Wormith, C. A. Searle and M. Kouri. "The attitudinal effects of group discussions between young criminal offenders and community volunteers." *Journal of Community Psychology* 1 (October 1973):417–22.

Andrews, D. A., J. S. Wormith, D. J. Kennedy, and W. Daigler-Zinn. "The attitudinal effects of structured discussions versus recreation association between young criminal offenders and undergraduate volunteers." *Journal of Community Psychology* 5 (January 1977):63–71.

Andrews, D. A., I. Zinger, R. D. Hoge, J. Bonta, J. Gendreau and F. T. Cullen. "Does correctional treatment work? A psychologically informed meta-analysis." *Criminology* 28 (1990):369–404.

Atlas, R. I., and R. G. Dunham. "Changes in prison facilities as a function of correctional philosophy." In J. W. Murphy and J. E. Dison (eds.). *Are Prisons Any Better? Twenty Years of Correctional Reform.* Beverly Hills: Sage, 1990:43–59.

Austin, J. "Assessing the new generation of prison classification models." *Crime & Delinquency* 29 (4) 1983:561–76.

Austin, J, and M. Bolyard. *The Effectiveness of Shorter Prison Terms.* San Francisco: National Council on Crime and Delinquency, March 1993.

Bandura, A. "Self-efficacy: Toward a unifying theory of behavioral change." *Psychological Review* 84 (2) 1977:191–215.

Beaumont, G. D., and A. D. Tocqueville. *On the Penitentiary System in the United States and Its Application in France.* Carbondale: Southern Illinois University Press, 1833/1964.

Bennett, L. A., T. S. Rosenbaum and W. R. McCullough. *Counseling in Correctional Environments.* New York: Human Services Press, 1978.

Bennett, R. R., and S. B. Bennett. "Translating criminological theory into action programs: Theoretical and political considerations." *Criminal Justice Review* 7 (2) 1982:1–8.

Berecochea, J. E., and D. R. Jaman. "Time served in prison and parole outcome: An experimental study." California Department of Corrections, 1981.

Besozzi, C. "Recidivism: How inmates see it." *Forum on Corrections Research* 5 (3) 1993:35–38.

Blecker, R. "Haven or Hell? Inside Lorton Central Prison: Experiences of Punishment Justified." *Stanford University Law Review* 42 (May 1990):1149–249.

Bleick, C. R., and A. I. Abrams. "The transcendental mediation program and criminal recidivism in California." Unpublished paper, 1984.

Blumstein, A. "Prisons." In J. Q. Wilson and J. Petersilia (eds.). *Crime.* San Francisco: ICS Press, 1994:387–420.

Bohn, M. J. "Classification of offenders in an institution for young adults." *FCI Research Reports* 10 (1) 1979:1–31.

Bohn, M. J. "Inmate classification and the reduction of institution violence." *Corrections Today* (July/August 1980):48–55.

Bornstein, P. H. et al. "Interpersonal skills training: evaluation of a program with adult male offenders." *Criminal Justice and Behavior* 6 (2) 1979:119–31.

Braly, M. *On the Yard.* New York: Penguin Books, 1967.

Brown, C. "Manchild in Harlem." *New York Times Magazine* (September 16, 1984):36–41, 44, 54, 76, 78.

Burstein, J. Q. *Conjugal Visits in Prisons: Psychological and Social Consequences.* Lexington:Lexington Books, 1977.

Burton, V. S., R. G. Dunaway, and R. Kopache. "To punish or rehabilitate? A research note assessing the purposes of state correctional departments as defined by state legal codes." *Journal of Crime and Justice* 16 (1) 1993:177–88.

Bush, J. M. "Violent Offender Program: Review of the First Year." St. Albans, VT: Northwest State Correctional Facility, December 1988.

Bush, J. M. and B. Bilodeau. *Options: A Cognitive Change Program.* NIJ: U.S. Department of Justice, June 1993.

Camus, A. "Reflections on the guillotine." In *Resistance, Rebellion and Death.* New York: Knopf, 1969.

Clear, T. R. and A. A. Braga. "Community corrections." In J. Q. Wilson and J. Petersilia (eds.). *Crime.* San Francisco: ICS Press, 1994:421–44.

Cline, F. X. "A futuristic prison awaits the hard-core 400." *New York Times* (October 7, 1994):B1 & B10.

Cobb, A. "Home truths about prison overcrowding." *The Annals of the American Academy of Political and Social Science* 478 (March 1985):73–85.

Cobean, S. C., and P. W. Power. "The role of the family in the rehabilitation of the offender." *International Journal of Offender Therapy and Comparative Criminology* 22 (1) 1978:29–38.

Coffey, O., and C. N. Louis. "Unemployment, crime, and the local jail." *Corrections Today* 41 (2) 1979:36–39.

Conrad, J. P. "Where there's hope there's life." In D. Fogel and J. Hudson (eds.). *Justice As Fairness.* Cincinnati, OH: Anderson, 1981:3–21 (1981a).

Conrad, J. P. "The state's strongest medicine." In J. P. Conrad. *Justice and Consequences.* Lexington: Lexington Books, 1981:51–70 (1981b).

Cox, V. C., P. B. Paulus, and G. McCain. "Prison crowding research: The relevance for prison housing standards and a general approach regarding crowding phenomena." *American Psychologist* 39 (10) 1984:1148–60.

Cullen, F. T., and K. E. Gilbert. *Reaffirming Rehabilitation.* Cincinnati, OH: Anderson, 1982.

Cullen, F. T., and L. F. Travis. "Work as an avenue of prison reform." *New England Journal of Criminal and Civil Confinement* 10 (1) 1984:45–64.

Derogatis, B. R., K. Rickels, and A. F. Rock. "SCI-90 and the MMPI: A step in the validation of a new self-report scale." *British Journal of Psychiatry* 128 (March 1976):280–89.

DiIulio, J. J. *No Escape: The Future of American Corrections.* New York: Basic Books, 1991.

Downes, D. *Contrasts in Tolerance: Post-War Penal Policy in the Netherlands and England and Wales.* Oxford: Clarendon Press, 1988.

Duffee, D. *Correctional Management.* Englewood Cliffs, NJ: Prentice-Hall, 1980.

Duncan, M. G. "Cradled on the sea: Positive images of prison and theories of punishment." *California Law Review* 76 (6) 1988:1202–47.

Ellis, G. A. *Inside Folsom Prison: Transcendental Meditation and TM-Sidhi Program.* Palm Springs, CA: ETC Publications, 1979.

England, D. "Developments in Prison Administration." In J. W. Murphy and J. E. Dison *Are Prisons Any Better? Twenty Years of Correctional Reform.* Beverly Hills, CA: Sage, 1990:61–75.

Erikson, E. "Youth: Fidelity and diversity." In E. Erickson (ed.). *The Challenge of Youth.* New York: Doubleday, 1965:1–28.

Fabiano, E. A., F. J. Porporino, and D. Robinson. "Canada's cognitive skills program corrects offenders' faulty thinking." *Corrections Today* (August 1991):102–108.

Fabiano, E. A., D. Robinson, and F. Porporino. *A Preliminary Assessment of the Cognitive Skills Training Program: A Component of Living Skills Programming.* Correctional Service of Canada, 1991.

Fitzgerald, M., and J. Sim. *British Prisons.* London: Basil Blackwell, 1982.

Fleischer, M. S. *Warehousing Violence.* Beverly Hills, CA: Sage, 1989.

Fogel, D. *"We Are the Living Proof": The Justice Model for Corrections.* Cincinnati, OH: Anderson, 1975.

Forst, B. "Prosecution and sentencing." In J. Q. Wilson and J. Petersilia (eds.). *Crime.* San Francisco: ICS Press, 1994: 363–86.

Gendreau, P. "Principles of effective intervention." Unpublished paper, November 1989.

Gendreau, P., and R. R. Ross. "Effective correctional treatment: Bibliotherapy for cynics." In R. R. Ross, and P. Gendreau. (eds.). *Effective Correctional Treatment.* Toronto: Butterworth, 1980:3–36.

Gendreau, P. and R. R. Ross. "Revivification of rehabilitation: Evidence from the 1980s." *Justice Quarterly* 4 (3) 1987:349–407.

Gerard, R. E. "The ten commandments of unit management." *Corrections Today* (April 1991):34–36.

Gibbs J. J., L. A. Maiello, K. S. Kolb, J. Garofalo, F. Adler, and S. R. Costello. *Stress, Setting, and Satisfaction: The Final Report of the Man-Jail Transactions Project.* Rutgers University School of Criminal Justice, 1983.

Glaser, D. *The Effectiveness of a Prison and Parole System.* Indianapolis: Bobbs-Merrill, 1969.

Glaser, D. "Achieving better questions: A half century's progress in correctional research." *Federal Probation* 39 (September 1975):3–9.

Goffman, E. *Asylums.* New York: Anchor Books, 1961.

Golden, D., C. P. Twentyman, M. Jensen, J. Karan, and J. D. Kloff. "Coping with authority: Social skills training for the complex offender." *Criminal Justice and Behavior* 7 (2) 1980:147–59.

Goodstein, L., and F. E. Lutze. "Prisoner program involvement and the determinate sentence: An exploration of perceived motivations." Paper presented at the Academy of Criminal Justice Sciences meeting, Washington, D.C., March 1989.

Goodstein, L., and K. N. Wright. "Inmate adjustment to prison." In L. Goodsteinand D. L. MacKenzie (eds.). *The American Prison: Issues in Research and Policy*. New York: Plenum Press, 1989:229–51.

Grant, J. D. "From 'living learning' to 'learning to live': An extension of social therapy." In H. Toch (ed.). *Therapeutic Communities in Corrections*. New York: Praeger, 1980:41–49.

Grant, J. D., and M. Q. Grant. "A group dynamics approach to the treatment of nonconformists in the Navy." *Annals of the American Academy of Political and Social Science* 322 (1959:126–35.

Hammett, T. M., L. Harrold, M. Gross, and J. Epstein. *1992 Update: HIV/AIDS in Correctional Facilities: Issues and Options*. National Institute of Justice, January 1994.

Haney, C. "Infamous punishment: The psychological consequences of isolation." *National Prison Project Journal* 8 (2) 1993:3–7.

Hawkins, G. *The Prison: Policy and Practice*. Chicago: University of Chicago Press, 1976.

Hawkins, G. "Prison labor and prison industries." In M. Tonry and N. Morris (eds.). *Crime and Justice Annual*. Chicago: University of Chicago Press, 1983:85–181.

Hawkins, R. and G. P. Alpert. *American Prison Systems: Punishment and Justice*. Englewood Cliffs, NJ: Prentice Hall, 1989

Hawthorne, J. "Our barbarous penal system." *Hearst's Magazine* (1913):205–12.

Hentoff, N. "Supermaximum Pelican Bay." *The Washington Post* (February 25, 1995):A17.

Hepburn, J. R., and C. A. Albonetti. "Team classification in state correctional institutions: Its association with

inmate and staff attitudes." *Criminal Justice and Behavior* 5 (1) 1978:63–73.

Herrick, E. "The surprising direction of violence in prison." *Corrections Conpendium* 14 (6) 1989:1 and 4–17.

Hirschorn, S. I., and H. D. Burck. "Utilizing inmates as group leaders in the admissions phase of incarceration." *Offender Rehabilitation* 2 (1) 1977:45–52.

Homer, E. L. "Inmate-family ties: Desirable but difficult." *Federal Probation* (March 1979):47–52.

Hunter, D. "Anger management in the prison: An evaluation." *Forum on Corrections Research* 5 (1) 1993:3–5.

Immarigeon, R. "Marionization of American Prisons." *National Prison Project Journal* 7 (4) 1992:1–5.

Irwin, J. *The Felon*. Englewood Cliffs, NJ: Prentice-Hall, 1970.

Irwin, J. *Prisons in Turmoil*. Boston: Little, Brown, 1980.

Irwin, J. "Adaptation to being corrected: Corrections from the convict's perspective." In R. G. Leger and J. R. Stratton (eds.). *The Sociology of Corrections*. New York: John Wiley, 1977:276–300.

Irwin, J., and J. Austin. *It's About Time: America's Imprisonment Binge*. Belmont, CA: Wadsworth, 1994.

Jacobs, J. B. *Stateville: The Penitentiary in Mass Society*. Chicago: University of Chicago Press, 1977.

Jacobs, J. B., R. McGahey, and R. Minion. "Ex-offender employment, recidivism, and manpower policy: CETA, TJTC, and future initiatives" *Crime & Delinquency* 30 (4) 1984:486–506.

Janis, I. L. *Stress and Frustration*. New York: Harcourt Brace Jovanovich, 1969.

Johnson, R. "Crowding and the Quality of Prison Life." In C. Hartjen (ed.). *Correctional Theory and Practice*. Chicago: Nelson-Hall, 1992:139–45.

Johnson, R., and S. Price. "The complete correctional officer: Human service and the human environment of prison." *Criminal Justice and Behavior* 8 (3) 1981:343–73.

Jones, M. "Desirable features of a therapeutic community in a prison." In H. Toch (ed.). *Therapeutic Communities in Corrections.* New York: Praeger, 1980:34–40.

Jurik, N. C., and M. C. Musheno. "The internal crises of corrections: Professionalization and the work environment." *Justice Quarterly* 3 (4) 1986:457–80.

Kalmthout, A. M. V., and D. Van Der Landen. "Breda Prison, Holland: From water cell to container cell—the state of the Dutch prison." In D. Whitfield (ed.). *The State of the Prisons—200 years on.* London & New York: Routledge, 1991:88–118.

Klofas, J. M., S. Stojkovic, and D. A. Kalinich. "The meaning of correctional crowding: Steps toward an index of severity." *Crime and Delinquency* 38 (2) 1992:171–88.

Levinson, R. B. "Developments in the classification process: Quay's aims approach." *Criminal Justice and Behavior* 15 (1) 1988:24–38.

Levinson, R. B. "The future of unit management." *Corrections Today* (April 1991):44–48.

Levinson, R. B. "Try softer." In R. Johnson and H. Toch (eds.). *The Pains of Imprisonment.* Prospect Heights, IL: Waveland Press, 1988:241–56.

Linden, R., and L. Perry. "The effectiveness of prison education programs." *Journal of Offender Counseling, Service, & Rehabilitation* 6 (4) 1982:43–57.

Lipton, D. S., G. P. Falkin, and H. K. Wexler. "Correctional drug abuse treatment in the United States: An overview." Paper presented at NIDA Technical Review, Rockville, MD, May 24, 1990.

Logan, C. H. "Well kept: Comparing quality of confinement in private and public prisons." *The Journal of Criminal Law and Criminology* 83 (3) 1992:577–613.

Logan, C. H. and G. G. Gaes. "Meta-Analysis and the rehabilitation of

punishment." *Justice Quarterly* 10 (2) 1993:245–63.

Lombardo, L. X. "Stress, change, and collective violence in prison." In R. Johnson and H. Toch (eds.). *The Pains of Imprisonment.* Prospect Heights, IL: Waveland Press. 1988:77–93.

Lusane, C. *Pipe Dream Blues: Racism and the War on Drugs.* Boston: South End Press, 1991.

Lynch, J. P. "Crime in international perspective." In J. Q. Wilson and J. Petersilia (eds.). *Crime.* San Francisco: ICS Press, 1994:11–38.

Manocchio, A. J., and J. Dunn. *The Time Game: Two Views of a Prison.* Beverly Hills, CA: Sage, 1982.

Martinson, R. "What works? Questions and answers about prison reform." *The Public Interest* (Spring 1974):22–55.

Martinson, R. "Martinson revisited." *Criminal Justice Newsletter* (December 4, 1978):4.

Mauer, M. "Americans behind bars—A comparison of international rates of incarceration." In Wall, Churchill and J.J. Vander (eds.). *Cages of Steel: The Politics of Imprisonment in the United States.* Washington, D.C.: Maisonneuve Press, 1992.

McKinlay, P. "Good staff-prisoner relations key to success of Scotland's supermax." *National Prison Project Journal* 7 (4) 1992:22–25.

Miller, J. G. "The folly of not treating sex offenders." *The Washington Post* (January 10, 1995):A17.

Moos, R. H. *Evaluating Treatment Environments: A Social Ecological Approach.* New York: John Wiley, 1974.

Morris, N. *The Future of Imprisonment.* Chicago: University of Chicago Press, 1974.

Newman, G. *The Punishment Response.* Philadelphia: Lippincott, 1978.

NIJ—National Institute of Justice. "Research in action: Prison programs for drug involved offenders." October 1989.

NIJ—National Institute of Justice. "What works? A review of the correctional literature on program effectiveness." April 1993.

Nossiter A., "Making hard time harder: States cut jail TV and sports." *The New York Times* (September 17, 1994):1 and 11.

Nouwens, T., L. Motiuk, and R. Boe. "So you want to know the recidivism rate." *Forum on Corrections Research* 5 (3) 1993:22–26.

Palmer, T. "Martinson revisited." *Journal of Research in Crime and Delinquency* 12 (2) 1975:133–52.

Palmer, T. *Correctional Intervention and Research*. Lexington: Lexington Books, 1978.

Palmer, T. "The effectiveness of intervention: Recent trends and current issues." *Crime & Delinquency* 37 (3) 1991:330–46.

Palmer, T. *A Profile of Correctional Effectiveness and New Directions for Research*. Albany: State University of New York Press. 1994.

Parker, J. G., and J. A. La Cour. "Common sense in correctional volunteerism in the institution." In A. A. Roberts (ed.). *Social Work in Juvenile and Criminal Justice Settings*. Springfield, IL: Charles C. Thomas, 1983:275–84.

Pearce, J. (Regional Director of the Scottish Prison Service). Untitled speech to Middle Atlantic States Correctional Association, Killington, VT, May 25, 1994.

Petersilia, J., and S. Turner. "Comparing intensive and regular supervision for high-risk probationers: Early results from an experiment in California." *Crime & Delinquency* 36 (1) 1990:87–111.

Piehl, A. M. , and J. J. DiIulio. "'Does prison pay?' Revisited: Returning to the scene of the crime." *The Brookings Review* 13 (1) 1995:21–25.

Pierson, T. A. "The Missouri experience: One state's success with unit management." *Corrections Today* (April 1991):24–30.

Piliavin, I., and R. Gartner. *The Impact of Supported Work on Ex-offenders*. New York: Manpower Demonstration Research Corporation, 1981.

Potter, J. "Can ex-offender job programs survive Reaganomics?" *Corrections Magazine* 8 (3) 1982:15–17, 20–22.

Priestly, P., J. McGuire, D. Flegg, V. Hensley, D. Welhem, and R. Barnitt. *Social Skills in Prison and the Community-Problem Solving for Offenders*. Boston: Routledge and Kegan Paul, 1984.

Quay, H. C. *Managing Adult Inmates: Classification for Housing and Program Assignments*. American Correctional Association, 1984.

Raspberry W. "Beyond Gun Control." *The Washington Post* (August 10, 1994):A19.

Raspberry, W. "Power in the prisons." *The Washington Post* (December 28, 1994):A23.

Redl, F. "The concept of 'therapeutic milieu'." In H. Toch (ed.). *Therapeutic Communities in Corrections*. New York: Praeger, 1980:21–33.

Regens, J. L., and W. G. Hobson. "Inmate self-government and attitude toward change: An assessment of participation effects." *Evaluation Quarterly* 2 1978:455–79.

Reiman, J. *The Rich Get Richer and the Poor Get Prison*. New York: Allyn and Bacon, 1995.

Renzema, M. "The stress comes later." In R. Johnson and H. Toch (eds.). *The Pains of Imprisonment*. Prospect Heights, IL: Waveland Press, 1988:147–62.

Report of the Secretary of Labor to the U.S. Congress on compliance by State Prison Industry Enhancement Projects with section 1761 (c) of Title 18 of the U.S. Code as required by Section 2908 of the Crime Control Act of 1990, March 1991.

Robinson, D., M. Grossman and F. Porporino. "Effectiveness of the Cognitive Skills Training Program: From pilot to national implementation." Research and Statistics Branch, Correctional Service of Canada: *Research Brief No. B-07,* 1991.

Ross, R. R., and H. B. McKay. "Behavioral approaches to treatment in corrections: Requiem for a panacea." In R. R. Ross, & Gendreau, P. (eds.). *Effective Correctional Treatment.* Toronto: Butterworth, 1980:37–53.

Saylor, W. G., and G. G. Gaes. "The post-release employment project: Prison work has measurable effects on post-release success." In P. C. Kratcoski (ed.), *Correctional Counseling and Treatment,* Third Edition. Prospect Heights, IL: Waveland Press, 1994:535–42.

Schafer, N. E. "Prison visiting: A background for change." *Federal Probation* 42 (3) 1978:47–50.

Schaller, J., and G. E. Sexton. "The free venture program: An overview." In *A Guide to Effective Prison Industries* vol. 1. Philadelphia: American Foundation, 1979.

Scharf, P. "Democratic education and the prevention of delinquency." In *U. S. Department of Health, Education and Welfare, National Institute of Education, School Crime and Disruption: Prevention Models.* Washington, D.C.: Government Printing Office, 1978.

Scharf, P. "Democracy and justice in a prison therapeutic community." In H. Toch (ed.). *Therapeutic Communities in Corrections.* New York: Praeger, 1980:94–102.

Scottish Prison Service. *Opportunity and Responsibility: Developing New Approaches to the Management of the Long Term Prison System in Scotland.* Crown copyright, May 1990.

Sechrest, L., S. O. White, and E. D. Brown. *The Rehabilitation of Criminal Offenders: Problems and Prospects.* Washington, D.C.: National Academy of Sciences, 1979.

Seiter, R. P. "Federal prison industries: Meeting the challenge of growth." In P. C. Kratcoski (ed.). *Correctional Counseling and Treatment,* Third Edition. Prospect Heights, IL: Waveland Press, 1994:528–34.

Seymour, J. "Environmental sanctuaries for susceptible prisoners." In R. Johnson and H. Toch (eds.). *The Pains of Imprisonment.* Prospect Heights, IL: Waveland Press, 1988:267–84.

Silberman, M. *A World of Violence: Corrections in America.* Belmont, CA: Wadsworth, 1995.

Smith, D. E. "Local corrections: A profile of inmate concerns." *Criminal Justice and Behavior* 11 (1) 1984:75–99.

Smith, D. E. "Crowding and confinement." In R. Johnson and H. Toch (eds.), *The Pains of Imprisonment.* Prospect Heights, IL: Waveland Press, 1988:45–62.

Smith, W. A., and C. E. Fenton. "Unit management in a penitentiary: A practical experience." *Federal Probation* 42 (3) 1978:40–46.

Staub, E. *The Roots of Evil: The Origins of Genocide and Other Group Violence.* New York: Cambridge University Press, 1989.

Tayoun, J. *Going to Prison?* Biddle, 1995.

Thompson, C. "Luke Gets a Job." *American Way* 27 (4) 1994:44–46.

Toch, H. *Living in Prison: The Ecology of Survival.* New York: Free Press, 1977.

Toch, H. "The therapeutic community as community." In H. Toch (ed.). *Therapeutic Communities in Corrections.* New York: Praeger, 1980:3–20.

Toch, H., "A revisionist view of prison reform." *Federal Probation* (1981):3–9.

Toch, H., "Enhancing the quality of survival in prison." Paper delivered at the Symposium on Institutions and Dependent Populations, in the Nelson A. Rockefeller Institute of Government, Albany, N. Y., April 1984.

Toch, H. "Warehouses for people?" *Annals of the American Academy of Political and Social Science* 478 (March 1985):58–72.

Toch, H. "Rewarding convicted offenders." *Federal Probation* (June 1988):42–48.

Toch, H. "Studying and reducing stress." In R. Johnson and H. Toch (eds.).

The Pains of Imprisonment. Prospect Heights, IL: Waveland Press, 1988:25–44.

Toch, H. "Democratizing Prisons." *The Prison Journal* 73 (1) 1994:62–72.

Toch, H., "Inmate involvement in prison governance." Paper presented at the 12th Annual Conference of the New Jersey Chapter of the American Correctional Association, October 24, 1994(a).

Toch, H., J. D. Grant, and R. Galvin. *Agents of Change: A Study in Police Reform.* Cambridge, MA: Schenkman, 1975.

Toch, H., J. D. Grant. "Noncoping and maladaptation in confinement." In L. Goodstein and D. L. MacKenzie. (eds.). *The American Prison: Issues in Research and Policy.* New York: Plenum Press, 1989:209–27.

Toch, H., and K. Adams with J. D. Grant.*Coping: Maladaptation in Prisons.* New Brunswick, NJ: Transaction Publishers, 1989.

Tonry, M. *Malign Neglect: Race, Crime, and Punishment in America.* New York: Oxford University Press, 1995.

Unit Management Guidelines. *Achieving Leadership Excellence in Victorian Prisons.* Office of Corrections, Victoria, 1990.

Van Den Haag, E. "Prisons cost too much because they are too secure." *Corrections Magazine* 6 (2) 1980:39–43.

Walsh, E. "Strapped small towns try to lock up prisons: Building boom is seen as economic salvation." *The Washington Post* (December 24, 1994):A3.

Webster, J. H. "Architectural Implications: Designing Facilities for Effective Unit Management." *Corrections Today* (April 1991):38–42.

Weiner, R. I. "Management strategies to reduce stress in prison: Humanizing correctional environments." In R. Johnson and H. Toch (eds.). *The Pains of Imprisonment.* Prospect Heights, IL: Waveland Press, 1988:299–309.

Wexler H. K., and R. Williams. "The stay 'n out therapeutic community: Prison treatment for substance abusers." *Journal of Psychoactive Drugs* 18 (3) 1986:221–30.

Wilson, J. Q. "Crime and public policy." In J. Q. Wilson and J. Petersilia (eds.). *Crime.* San Francisco: ICS Press, 1994:489–507.

Wisconsin Department of Health and Social Services, Division of Policy and Budget, Bureau of Evaluation, "Evaluation of special action release." Madison, 1983.

Witte, A. D., D. F. Woodbury, S. H. Smith, H. Barreto, and R. Beaton. "The effects of a less coercive prison environment and gradual reintegration on postrelease performance: An evaluation of Morris' model of imprisonment as implemented at the Federal Correctional Institution at Butner, N.C." (Mimeo) Federal Bureau of Prisons, June 1983.

Wormith, J. S. "Attitude and behavior change of correctional clientele." *Criminology* 22 (4) 1984:595–618.

Wright, K. N. "Developing the Prison Environment Inventory," *Journal of Research in Crime and Delinquency* 22 (1985):257–77.

Wright, K. N. "A study of individual, environmental, and interactive effects in explaining adjustment to prison." *Justice Quarterly* 8 (2) 1991:217–42.

Wright, K. N. *Effective Prison Leadership.* Binghamton, NY: William Neil Publishing, 1994.

Wright, K. N., with J. M. Harris and N. Woika. *Improving Correctional Classification Through a Study of the Placement of Inmates in Environmental Settings.* Final Report, NIJ Grant 83-lJ-CX-00 1 1, 1985.

Zamble, E. "Behavior and adaptation in long-term prison inmates: Descriptive longitudinal results." *Criminal Justice and Behavior* 19 (4) 1992:409–25.

Zamble, E. "Expanding the recidivism inquiry: A look at dynamic factors."

Forum on Corrections Research 5 (3) 1993:27–30).

Zamble, E., and F. Porporino. "Coping, imprisonment, and rehabilitation: Some data and their implications." *Criminal Justice and Behavior* 17 1990:53–70.

Zamble, E., F. Porporino, and J. Kalotay. *An Analysis of Coping Behavior in Prison Inmates.* Ministry of the Solicitor General of Canada: Programs Branch User Report, 1984.

Zimring, F. E., and G. Hawkins. *The Scale of Imprisonment.* Chicago: University of Chicago Press, 1991.

Credits

21, 35, 80, scattered quotations from *Discipline and Punishment: The Birth of the Prison* by Michel Foucault. Copyright © 1975 by Editions Gallimard. Reprinted by permission of Georges Borchardt, Inc.

27, 28, 35, 36, 57, excerpts from A. J. Hirsch, *Michigan Law Review, 80,* 1179, 1982. Reprinted by permission of the author.

33–34, 38, 41, 51–54, from *The Discovery of the Asylum: Social Order and Disorder in the New Republic* by David J. Rothman. Copyright © 1970, 1991 by David J. Rothman. Used by permission of Little, Brown and Company.

43–44, excerpt from *The Prison and the Factory: Origins of the Penitentiary System* by D. Melossi and M. Pavarini. (Translated by G. Cousin.) Copyright © 1981 by Barnes & Noble. Reprinted by permission.

65, excerpt from *Stateville: The Penitentiary in Mass Society,* by J. B. Jacobs. Copyright © 1977 by The University of Chicago Press. Reprinted by permission.

82, 86, 87, 136–37, excerpts from *The Society of Captives: A Study of Maximum Security Prisons* by Gresham M. Sykes; Atheneum, 1966. Copyright ©1958, renewed 1986 by Princeton University Press. Reprinted by permission of Princeton University Press.

83–84, 154, 185–86, 191, poems from *The Light from Another Country: Poetry from American Prisons,* Joseph Bruchac, ed.; Greenfield Review Press, 1984. Reprinted by permission of the publisher.

Index